Everything You Ever Wanted to Know about Trans
(But Were Afraid to Ask)

of related interest

Trans Teen Survival Guide
Owl and Fox Fisher
ISBN 978 1 78592 341 8
eISBN 978 1 78450 662 9

Yes, You Are Trans Enough
My Transition from Self-Loathing to Self-Love
Mia Violet
ISBN 978 1 78592 315 9
eISBN 978 1 78450 628 5

Queer Sex
A Trans and Non-Binary Guide to Intimacy, Pleasure and Relationships
Juno Roche
ISBN 978 1 78592 406 4
eISBN 978 1 78450 770 1

To My Trans Sisters
Edited by Charlie Craggs
ISBN 978 1 78592 343 2
eISBN 978 1 78450 668 1

How to Understand Your Gender
A Practical Guide for Exploring Who You Are
Alex Iantaffi and Meg-John Barker
Foreword by S. Bear Bergman
ISBN 978 1 78592 746 1
eISBN 978 1 78450 517 2

The Trans Partner Handbook
A Guide for When Your Partner Transitions
Jo Green
ISBN 978 1 78592 227 5
eISBN 978 1 78450 503 5

EVERYTHING YOU EVER WANTED TO KNOW ABOUT TRANS

(BUT WERE AFRAID TO ASK)

Brynn Tannehill

Jessica Kingsley *Publishers*
London and Philadelphia

First published in 2019
by Jessica Kingsley Publishers
73 Collier Street
London N1 9BE, UK
and
400 Market Street, Suite 400
Philadelphia, PA 19106, USA

www.jkp.com

Library of Congress Cataloging in Publication Data
A CIP catalog record for this book is available from the Library of Congress

British Library Cataloguing in Publication Data
A CIP catalogue record for this book is available from the British Library

ISBN 978 1 78592 826 0
eISBN 978 1 78450 956 9

Printed and bound in the United States

CONTENTS

ACKNOWLEDGEMENTS

This book could not have been written without the help of many people. First and foremost, I would like to thank my wife, Janis, for putting up with the endless hours of writing, research, conferences, and speaking engagements that have vied for my attention over the past half-decade. I'd also like to thank her for her patience; she's let me bounce ideas and information off of her without complaint, even when I might as well be speaking Swahili.

I'd also like to thank the people who worked with me to edit the chapters in this book on their own time, out of the goodness of their own hearts and a belief in this project. Drea Leed has been my "first pass" editor on everything I have written in the past three years, and helped immensely getting this book into a form where I could submit a draft. Kryss Shane put in a seemingly endless amount of time and energy building the references list and editing the document in a second pass to help make sure that the content is digestible by someone not already intimately familiar with LGBT issues. There's no way this book would have happened without both of them.

I've also had the benefit of editors who have nurtured and encouraged me to write, and to become a better writer. They gave me my first opportunities and bore with me as I learned and grew into it. Again, thank you to John Becker, Bil Browning, Diane Anderson-Minshall, Neal Broverman, David Badash, Sunnivie Brydum, David Small, and Noah Michelson for metaphorically teaching me to fish.

Other people have contributed bits and pieces of writing in this book in places where they said it far better than I could. Some of their work and concepts are used here with their kind permission. Natalie Reed helped explore myths about transgender women before I started writing, and was one of my early inspirations as a writer. Mitch Kellaway wrote myths about surgery from a trans-masculine perspective. Jillian Weiss provided the material that evolved into the discussion of the US court system and constitutional law. Thank you all.

Lastly, there are the other subject matter experts who volunteered their time to ensure that the material presented in this book is accurate. Thank you to Sarah McBride for helping me with Chapters 1–3. Thanks to Dr. Jo Olson-Kennedy, Arlene Istar Lev, and Dr. Dan Karasic for their work on reviewing the health and medicine chapters. Thanks to Tony Varona, Alexandra Sydon, Baili Volluz, and Mark Joseph Stern for their efforts with the chapter on law. Zack Ford and Harper Jean Tobin, thanks for bearing with me on the politics chapter. Thank you to Kathy Baldock and Ross Murray for reviewing the section on religion, and to Nick Adams for taking a look at the section on transgender people in popular media. Last in this list (but certainly not least), thank you to Julia Serano for her work on the chapter on gender and feminism.

And Sue Fulton, you're in a league of your own as an ally. I cannot thank you enough not just for your input into this book, but everything you've done in our six years of working together.

Finally, to Jenny Boylan. You didn't know it at the time, but when we first met you said exactly the right thing at exactly the right time to motivate me to become an author. Thank you, in all sincerity and gratitude, for your mentorship in this endeavor.

INTRODUCTION

When I started writing for print and online publications, I had no idea where it would lead. I certainly didn't imagine I would be good at it or enjoy it enough to do it on a regular basis. Four years and over 250 articles later, people started telling me, "You should write a book!"

The problem was, I had no idea what the book should be about. My articles tackled a multitude of different topics; despite having written hundreds of thousands of words, there wasn't enough material on any one topic to write a full-sized book. The articles themselves tended to be about issues that were either hot topics in popular culture about transgender people, or issues that I thought needed greater exposure and education. Other articles were dedicated to busting the myths about transgender people that I saw cropping up repeatedly.

In the summer of 2016, it finally dawned on me that there was a unifying thread between most of what I had written: almost all of it represented things people should know about the transgender community. Some of them were things people should know because the public was asking about it. Sometimes the material was stuff people needed to know because of deliberately deceptive information about transgender people being put out there. Sometimes the articles covered things the public really should know, but that no one was talking about.

Thus, when I looked at what I had written over the past five years, there were articles that covered Trans 101 and Trans 201 topics, as well as articles covering the relationship between transgender people and politics, law, medicine, mental health, religion, feminism, gender studies, sex, sexuality, and even the military.

In short, what my articles had in common was that they addressed almost all of the most important issues facing the transgender community, and I had more than enough material available to tell people what they needed to know. It was, in effect, Everything You Ever Wanted to Know about Trans.

When I looked to see if any other book did something similar, I didn't find any. There are some that are excellent in their specific areas, such as *Transgender 101* by Nicholas Teich, *Whipping Girl* by Julia Serano, and *Trans Bodies, Trans Selves* by Laura Erickson-Schroth. However, these were all comparatively narrow in their focus. Other books, particularly those on religion and politics, were often written by people hostile to the transgender community. These books presented poor science, while groundlessly advocating for legal and social marginalization of transgender people.

Thus, there are books that address individual topics, and many that have bad information, but none that present a holistic and integrated view of how all these pieces fit together to illuminate the reality of life in America today as a transgender person. I mean to address this now.

The goal of this book is to walk the reader through transgender issues, starting with Trans 101-level information ("What does transgender mean?"), Trans 201 discussions ("What is it like being transgender in America today?"), and then through the other areas where transgender people and issues are in the news. At the end of this book, it is my hope that someone who reads this cover to cover would be highly conversant on most of the critical public conversations around transgender people, and, I hope, a better ally as a result.

This book provides citations and peer-reviewed evidence. It also relies heavily on the consensus of mainstream subject matter experts and organizations, such as the American Medical Association, American Psychological Association, American Psychiatric Association, and the World Professional Association of Transgender Health (WPATH).

In a few areas where there isn't a body of research on a particular point, I refer to my own experiences. Generally, these are not critical ones, but anecdotes added to help the reader understand how the topic affects transgender people.

I also hope that this book will serve as a professional reference book and as a useful tool for transgender people and allies to better understand the myriad of pieces in play. The information within this book is fact based and rooted in medical and peer-reviewed research, hopefully ensuring a well-rounded experience for all readers.

Understanding transgender people and the challenges we face is crucial to making progress. More than anything else, I hope this book contributes in some way to that better future for us all.

> There is an appendix of Case Law available to download at www.jkp.com/voucher using the code SOONEHE

Chapter 1

TRANS 101

Answering the basic questions

For people who are reading this because they're curious and want to know more, great, thank you, and welcome aboard! For those of you who already have a background in transgender issues, this chapter may help you explain to other people the basics on what transgender means, what it is, isn't, and even put together your own Trans 101 presentations. Few people have close friends or family who are transgender, so many of us end up as ambassadors for the community whether we want to be or not.

So, let's get started.

Q: What is the difference between sex and gender?
A: In very simplistic terms, sex is what's between your legs, and gender is what's between your ears. Sex refers to physical characteristics and gender relates to behavioral and psychological ones. This includes not just genitalia, but a whole host of physical factors such as chromosomes, genetics, and epigenetics. Gender is how we see ourselves, whether man, woman, neither, or somewhere in between. Transgender people are those whose sex and gender do not match.

Q: What is the difference between gender identity and gender expression?
A: Gender identity is how a person would describe their gender. Gender expression is an individual's characteristics and behaviors (such as

appearance, dress, mannerisms, speech patterns, and social interactions) that may be perceived as masculine or feminine.[1] Gender identity and expression don't always match and that's just a normal part of human diversity. For instance, there are people who identify as women who were born female (cisgender women) and who also prefer to have short hair and play contact sports, which are behaviors typically assumed to be something men do (referred to as "masculine leaning gender expression").

Q: Is gender purely a social construct, or is it biological?
A: It's a bit of both. Pink and blue do not intrinsically have a gender, and are thus very much a social construct. However, research also shows that people have a biologically determined gender identity,[2] and that even very young children can have gendered preferences in toys.[3] Researchers are still exploring the interaction between the two, though it can be said that culture has a great deal to do with how we express our gender.

Q: Are sexual orientation and gender identity the same thing? Are they related?
A: They are not the same thing, though in some cases they are correlated. They are almost perfectly uncorrelated when describing transgender women. The National Center for Transgender Equality's (NCTE) landmark study of over 6000 transgender people in the US found that transgender women are about equally likely to be attracted to men, women, or both. Transgender men are somewhat more likely to be oriented towards women.

Q: What does it mean to be transgender?
A: The term transgender describes individuals whose inherent sense of their own gender doesn't match the sex they were assigned at birth. Many transgender individuals have experienced some degree of gender dysphoria, which is an intense and persistent sense of distress or discomfort with their birth sex.

Q: How is the term transgender used?
A: The word "transgender" is an adjective umbrella term that covers a wide spectrum of people. Transgender also includes persons who are

gender non-conforming. Gender non-conforming people may not consider themselves transgender, but have an appearance or gender expression that does not conform to gender stereotypes.[4] In contrast to the term "transgender," *transsexual* is not an umbrella term, and many people who identify as transgender do not identify as transsexual. While transsexual refers to people who have or desire to medically transition, it is usually considered an outdated or clinical term.

Q: Are transgender people pretending to be someone they know they're not?

A: No. Transgender people are who they say they are. They are fully aware of their biology, but due to gender dysphoria do not relate to their sex assigned at birth. For example, if you woke up tomorrow and your body was that of the opposite sex, you would still be you and you would still consider yourself the gender you were yesterday, even though your sex and gender identity didn't match.

Q: What about drag performers (drag queens and drag kings)?

A: Drag is a form of performance art. The performers may or may not identify as their birth sex, but occasionally express themselves in a way that is different from the gender aligned with their birth sex. Drag is a matter of expression, rather than identity.

Q: What about cross-dressers?

A: The key component differentiating cross-dressers is gender identity. These individuals wear clothing stereotypically associated with members of the opposite gender without identifying as that sex or gender. According to the GLAAD Media Guide: "...the term cross-dresser is typically used to refer to men who occasionally wear clothes, makeup, and accessories culturally associated with women. Those men typically identify as heterosexual. This activity is a form of gender expression and not done for entertainment purposes. Cross-dressers do not wish to permanently change their sex or live full-time as women."[5]

Cross-dressers have also been called transvestites in the past, but this term is considered dated and pejorative now.

Q: What is gender dysphoria?

A: The *Diagnostic and Statistical Manual of Mental Disorders* (*DSM*) is the handbook used by health care professionals in the United States and much of the world as the authoritative guide to the diagnosis of mental disorders. *DSM* contains descriptions, symptoms, and other criteria for diagnosing mental disorders. Gender dysphoria is the diagnostic term used in the *DSM-5* to describe "a marked difference between the individual's expressed/experienced gender and the gender others would assign him or her, and it must continue for at least six months."[6]

Q: Does this mean that people who identify as transgender should be considered mentally ill?

A: No. According to the American Psychiatric Association, "It is important to note that gender nonconformity is not in itself a mental disorder. The critical element of gender dysphoria is the presence of clinically significant distress associated with the condition."[7] In other words, if a transgender person is happy where they are, there's no issue.

Q: What causes an individual to be transgender?

A: The precise causes are unknown, though some of the mechanisms are partially understood. Sexual differentiation of the brain happens later in pregnancy than differentiation of sex organs, and is controlled by testosterone. If testosterone levels are too high or too low, the surge is mistimed, or the fetus does not process the testosterone correctly (due to androgen insensitivity or endocrine-affecting chemicals), it has been shown to affect gender identification, role behavior, and sexual orientation.[8] [9] [10] Epigenetics also seem to play a role (more on this in Chapter 4).

Q: What does "transgender man" mean? How about "transgender woman"?

A: A transgender man is a person who was seen as female when they were born, but identifies and lives as a man. A transgender woman is someone who was seen as male when they were born, but identifies and lives as a woman. In short, a transgender man is a man, and a transgender woman is a woman in the here and now.

Q: Are "transgendered," "transgenders," or "transgenderism" words?

A: Transgender is an adjective, and thus the variants above are not grammatically correct. When they are used, it is often by people unfamiliar with the community, or hostile to it. "Transgender people" is preferable in most cases. While "transgenderism" is used in a few academic journals, it is most often used by people hostile to transgender people.

Q: What is intersex?

A: Intersex and transgender are often conflated. Intersex individuals are born with physical characteristics of both sexes. Some of these are obvious at birth when genital abnormalities are noted. Others can go undetected until adulthood (such as chimeras or women with XY chromosomes and androgen insensitivity), and some individuals never have it diagnosed. A more clinical term also used to describe intersex conditions is disorders of sexual development (DSD).

Q: Is hermaphrodite the same as intersex?

A: Hermaphrodite is an archaic and disused term that is now generally considered offensive when applied to people. Intersex is now the preferred term.

Q: Is intersex the same as transgender, part of it, or different altogether?

A: Medically they are separate conditions. Legally there is some overlap. Many intersex individuals face biases, discrimination, and legal hurdles similar to transgender people, particularly those who were misclassified at birth. Medical teams often assign a gender at birth (i.e. perform genital corrective surgeries) on intersex babies based on whether they think the genitals more closely resemble a penis or a vagina. Intersex advocates are fighting against such practices today. This surgery may result in gender dysphoria for the intersex individual, since as we now know (and discuss later) genitals, and chromosomes, do not always predict gender identity.

Q: What is gender transition (or, transition)?

A: This is the process of changing one's gender presentation and expression from the one assigned at birth. Some people have changed, or are in the process of changing, their physical bodies to conform to their internal sense of gender identity. For others, this is purely a social process without medical intervention. The types of medical treatment a person receives (including none at all) do not determine whether or not a person is transgender. This collective process is known as *gender transition* or *transitioning*. The World Professional Association of Transgender Health (WPATH, pronounced double-u path), an international organization devoted to the study and treatment of gender-identity issues, publishes WPATH Standards of Care, which provide clinical guidance to health care professionals on safe and effective treatment of gender-identity issues.

As explained by the WPATH Standards of Care, gender transition *may* proceed in the following order. First, the transgender person will meet with a mental health care provider to ascertain what steps are appropriate in addressing the incongruity between the person's gender identity and the sex that the person was assigned at birth. This could include social transition, without any medical intervention. After appropriate counseling, the person may begin hormone therapy, under the supervision of mental and health care professionals. This step will begin the process of changing the person's secondary sex characteristics (such as breast size and shape or facial hair) to those associated with the gender with which the person identifies. After a period of time on hormone therapy, many transgender people transition to "real-life experience" by living full-time—both at home and in the workplace—in the gender role consistent with their gender identity. Last, some transgender people may undergo surgical procedures to change their appearance to conform with their identified gender.

Q: Do all transgender people who transition follow the same process, or even transition medically?

A: Not all transitioning people go through the same process. Some may not undergo medical treatment for various personal, financial, or medical reasons, but may modify their gender expression—their dress, mannerisms, and so forth—to be consistent with their gender identity. Regardless of these factors, all transgender people are entitled to undertake the transition steps that are appropriate for them, and must be treated with dignity and respect as they do so.[11] Others may have hormone replacement therapy (HRT), breast augmentation or reduction (top surgery), hair removal, facial surgery, or gender confirmation surgery.

Q: How is transsexual different from transgender?

A: Every transsexual is transgender, but not every transgender person is transsexual. A transsexual is a person who experiences dysphoria (mental discomfort) with their societal role and their appearance as it relates to gender and sex, and attempt to change it medically. Other transgender sub-sets do not necessarily experience this type of dysphoria, such as gender non-binary, genderqueer, or gender fluid people.[12]

Transsexual is something of an archaic, clinical term, much the same as homosexual is. Most of the issues discussed in this book directly pertain to individuals who do not identify with their gender assigned at birth and attempt to change this medically and legally. While other segments of the transgender community are important, the vast majority of the current public debate centers on the segment of the transgender community that would have been called "transsexual" 20 years ago.

Q: What does cisgender mean?

A: Just like heterosexual is the antonym of homosexual, cisgender is the opposite of transgender. "Cis" is a Latin prefix meaning same, and "trans" means across or opposite. The term is not inherently pejorative, though it is intensely disliked by some people. Cisgender has primarily been used only in academia until recently; it is increasingly being used in less formal settings, similar to the way "straight" refers to heterosexual people. Many transgender people believe there is a need for this word, as it helps prevent the inference that "transgender" and "normal" are antonyms, which would imply that transgender people are somehow unnatural or "wrong."

Q: Are transgender people a new phenomenon?

A: Individuals who are gender non-conforming, live as members of the opposite sex, or take steps to align their bodies with their gender identities have existed throughout human history. In earliest civilizations, throughout Europe,[13] Asia, the Middle East,[14] [15] and Northern Africa, tribes of different types venerated what they often identified as "The Great Mother."[16] In many of these traditions, priestesses who had been assigned male at birth presided over religious ceremonies.[17] Often, these individuals have been voluntarily made eunuchs.[18] Indeed, the Bible makes reference to eunuchs 21 times, and includes a reference to those "who have made themselves eunuchs."[19]

The hijra of India have a special place in Hinduism as a third gender, and are mentioned in the Kama Sutra, meaning they have been a part of Indian culture since at least 200 BC. In the south Pacific, the fa'afafine are considered all genders and none, and have been around since the first missionaries arrived in the 1700s.[20] In 2011, in the Czech Republic, archaeologists found the 5000-year-old skeleton of a male buried in a manner consistent with the funerary rights generally provided for females in the Copper Age culture of the area.[21]

Q: How many transgender people are there in the US?

A: There are approximately 1.4 million transgender people in the US.[22] This translates into about 0.7 percent of the US identifying as transgender.

Q: Are there laws protecting transgender people?

A: There is no overarching federal law explicitly protecting transgender people from discrimination in employment or most other areas of life. The only federal laws specifically enumerating transgender people are the Violence Against Women Act and the Matthew Shepard and James Byrd Hate Crimes Prevention Act. Most states do not include transgender people in their own hate crimes or non-discrimination laws.

Many courts have held that the definition of sex under Title VII of the 1964 Civil Rights Act and Title IX of the Education Amendments of 1972 includes transgender people because transgender people do not adhere to sex stereotypes. Neither has been ruled on yet by the Supreme Court and the matter is the subject of an intense and ongoing legal fight.

Twenty-two states and 225 jurisdictions include protections for transgender people in housing, employment, and sometimes in public accommodations.[23] As a result, transgender people in most parts of the country have very limited legal protections against discrimination.

Any recourse for people in places with no explicit legal protections at state or local level must be sought through federal-level lawsuits, which are complicated, time consuming, and expensive.

Q: Are transgender people discriminated against?

A: Yes. In 2011, the (then) largest survey of transgender people ever conducted sampled more than 6600 transgender people in the United States. It found that transgender people experienced discrimination in housing, employment, education, health care, public accommodations, and other areas of life far higher than the general US population.[24] A follow-up survey in 2015 of almost 28,000 transgender people in the United States returned similar results.[25] For example, 90 percent had experienced harassment or mistreatment at work, 47 percent of transgender individuals had lost a job or been denied promotion for being transgender, transgender people were twice as likely to be unemployed, and they were four times as likely to live on less than $10,000 a year of income.

Additionally, transgender people struggle to obtain accurate government identification (ID). Often getting a gender marker changed on a state document (for example, where it says "M" or "F" on your driver's license) requires surgery that the individual cannot have, cannot afford, or does not want. In Ohio, Tennessee, and Idaho, it is impossible to change your gender marker on your birth certificate even if you have had surgery, and many states will not issue a driver's license with the correct gender marker unless you have had gender confirmation surgery (GCS). As a result, getting correct ID requires navigating a jumble of state and federal laws which often conflict with one another, making obtaining correct ID complicated, difficult, and expensive.[26]

Dos and don'ts of transgender etiquette

The transgender community has something of its own sub-culture within the United States. Just like interacting with any other minority group with their own distinct culture, there are unwritten rules of etiquette.

This section is meant as a set of very basic "dos" and "don'ts" with regards to daily interactions with transgender people. These are not hard and fast, but represent norms that tend to be true more often than not in my experience.

Do:

- *Listen to and believe transgender people:* when transgender people talk about their experiences, it's not your job to filter them through your own. Transgender people have had different experiences, and are telling you the truth from their perspective. You are not the expert on their lived experiences—they are.
- *Ask what pronouns people prefer:* there will be times when you don't know whether a transgender or gender non-conforming person identifies as male, female, or neither. The simplest way to be respectful of their identities is to ask, "What pronouns do you prefer?" If I were asked this, I would reply with "she, her, hers," or "feminine pronouns, please." This is the standard in most circles now.
- *Respect how people identify:* if someone tells you how they identify, make every effort to respect that identity by using the name and pronouns they prefer. Deliberately using the wrong names and pronouns intentionally isn't just rude, it constitutes a hostile work environment.[27]
- *Let transgender people discuss their lives at their own pace:* there's a lot of stigma in being transgender. There's also a lot of trauma that tends to go with it as well. Asking probing questions about someone's divorce or recent hysterectomy is in bad taste, especially if you weren't very close friends to begin with. It's fine to ask how people are doing or if they need anything. If they want to fill you in on the details, they will. Otherwise, they're likely to still be processing their experiences and emotions about what they have gone through.
- *Use people's chosen names:* a person's chosen name is how they prefer to be addressed, and is often the same as their legal name. This should be an easy one. If someone tells you their name is

Bill, you don't turn around and say, "Nah, you look more like a Steve. I'll call you Steve instead." Using someone's chosen (and frequently legal) name is a matter of common courtesy. Like pronouns, though, deliberate abuse constitutes a form of verbal harassment.

- *Quickly apologize and move on if you make a mistake:* most transgender people know it is hard to break old habits. If you've known us for decades but our name and pronouns just changed, there will be slips of the tongue. It's okay. We get that, especially from people we have had long relationships with. The best way to deal with these is to immediately apologize, correct yourself, and move on. Pretending like it didn't happen leaves doubt as to whether it was intentional, or if you regretted the error. Example: "When Bryan was young... Sorry. When Brynn was young, she played soccer."
- *Keep the pronouns consistent:* this is a hard one, especially for parents and siblings who have known a transgender person since childhood. When referring to a transgender person in the past (pre-transition) tense it is even easier to make mistakes with pronouns and names. Again, quickly apologize, and move on.
- *Challenge transphobic remarks:* this is probably the hardest one of all for allies—when you see or hear something you know is transphobic you need to stand up against it. While sometimes things are said out of ignorance, outright malice is readily understood. This is particularly true in the workplace and in schools where cultures of bullying and "ganging up" on someone can take place. Much like racism, it only takes a few people willing to stand up to casual transphobia to put a stop to it, and label it as unacceptable.

Don't:

- *Ask things you wouldn't of a cisgender person:* stop for a moment and ask yourself if you would ask this same question of a cisgender person. If the answer is "probably not," then you can avoid many of the "don'ts" in this section. An easy example of this is if you would ask a person you have just met if they've been circumcised?

The answer is obviously no, of course not. Thus, don't ask transgender people what sorts of genital surgery they have had either.

- *Out a person as transgender:* being transgender is often stigmatizing in our society. Someone's status as a transgender person is personal information that is theirs to keep or share. Outing someone can result in intense embarrassment and shame. For most of us, we simply wish to be seen as men or women, and putting an asterisk next to that is usually harmful. In other circumstances, the risk is much higher, including exposure to ridicule, discrimination, and even violence.
- *Use slang terms for transgender people:* referring to transgender people as he-shes, its, shemales, trannies, transvestites, or other slang terms is considered highly offensive and demeaning. Transgender woman, transgender man, transgender people, or transgender person are the preferred terms when referring to the community collectively.
- *Give backhanded compliments:* many transgender people have been exposed to "compliments" such as "I'd never know you weren't a real woman!" or "Wow, you don't look transgender!" This implies a biased belief that transgender people look or sound a particular way, and usually that expectation of appearance and presentation is something along the lines of "linebacker in a house dress."
- *Do or say things that heighten their dysphoria:* most transgender people are keenly aware of what their body looks like via dysphoria, down to the smallest detail. Calling attention to someone's appearance in negative ways can result in additional dysphoria and stress. For example, asking "Your hands are so big for a woman. I don't think there's anything you can do about that though, is there?" would be a huge no-no. The transgender person subjected to this is already very much aware of the size of her hands compared with other women, as well as the fact that she cannot do anything to change this.
- *Offer unsolicited advice:* we know you're trying to be helpful, but offering us tips on how to do makeup, clothes, shoes, movements, and so on in order to "be more masculine/feminine" generally only makes people feel more insecure or neurotic in their identities.

There are ways to broach the topic, but often these attempts can be counter-productive. Like any other person, transgender people have to find their own style through trial and error. Even if you love makeup, fashion, and so on, this can come across as an unwanted critique on a person's gender expression or simply their competence to dress themselves.

- *Ask if a person has had "the surgery":* don't ask about their breasts, either. This one is simple: asking another person about their genitals is only okay if you're their doctor or their lover. If you're neither, then what their bits look like, and their history, is none of your business. If I were to ask you point blank if you were circumcised, or if you had a clitoral hood piercing, or how many people you have had sex with, it would be completely out of bounds (especially in a workplace environment). Asking a transgender person about their genitals is no different. Additionally, gender confirmation surgery is somewhat rare. Many choose not to get it based on marital status, health reasons, or that their dysphoria is not focused on their genitals. Most others cannot afford it, or the recovery time it requires. The current Standards of Care make it clear that the mental well-being of the patient determines the course of treatment.
- *Ask "how it works in bed":* would you ask a near stranger, a co-worker, or even a friend outside of work in casual conversation if they like anal play? Or if they do it doggie-style? How about if they've tried reverse-cowboy? Cisgender people generally don't have to field these awkward questions and neither do transgender people. They can have sex the same ways everyone else has sex. How they prefer to have sex is no one's business but theirs and their partners'.
- *Ask what a transgender person's "real" or original name was:* unless you're doing a background check for the human resources department or are their tax attorney, a person's previous legal name is irrelevant. If we wanted people to call us by our original names, we would have kept them. Again, this is a piece of information that we can understand the curiosity about, but is generally something we will talk about only if we're comfortable.

- *Ask to see "before" pictures:* you know that picture of yourself from eighth grade with the puffy-sleeved satin vintage dress from the 1980s, braces, and big round glasses? Or the vintage senior prom picture from the 1970s in the powder blue rented tux and an acne marred complexion worthy of a Domino's meat-lover's special? Do you really want to show those pictures off to every random person? Neither do transgender people, for the exact same reasons. They're embarrassing, it's not who we are now, and it often comes from a tawdry sort of interest.
- *Assume you can spot a transgender person:* even transgender people can't reliably pick out other transgender people, especially when they transitioned early in life. I've erred both directions before (assumed a cisgender person was transgender, and vice versa), and learned to keep my mouth shut.
- *Refer to "real" men or women:* this implies that transgender people are "fake" or "faking it." It's hurtful and puts us on a lower rung on the social ladder than cisgender people.
- *Make assumptions about a transgender person's sexual orientation:* we've already touched on the fact that sexual orientation and gender identity are separate. In the case of transgender women, the two are almost perfectly uncorrelated.[28] This happens a lot to lesbian, gay, or bisexual (LGB) people as well, and all of us often have to gently correct someone when they ask us about our significant others.
- *Ask, "Are you a boy or a girl?":* this is social custom thing as much as anything else. Asking about preferred pronouns is generally the safest way to go if you're not sure which way someone identifies. However, transgender people often get this one from children below an age where they are aware that this may not be polite, and we simply answer it based on how we identify.

Maybe:

- *Ask questions:* this is one of the more difficult ones, and whether it is a "do" or a "don't" depends on the situation. Often there is a lot of stigma, shame, and trauma associated with the lives of transgender people. How much or little a person talks about their experiences should be up to them. In situations where a person is clearly making themselves and their experiences available, asking open-ended questions that give room for as much or as little detail as the transgender person feels comfortable with is okay. For example, "How are things with your family?" might be a good follow-up to someone talking about their brother in a social context. Highly specific, personal questions are inadvisable regardless (e.g. "Do you have a penis and, if so, what does it look like?" remains off-limits).

Being transgender isn't a choice

One of the most frequent (and unfair) criticisms of people who transition is that they did not take the effects of their transition on others into account. Implicit in these criticisms is that being transgender is somehow a choice and that transitioning was a bad one because of how it affected other people. This is untrue on several levels. Most transgender people agonize and delay transition for years precisely because of how hard it will be. When they do transition, it is because, of all options available, transitioning is the least devastating.

When a lesbian or gay person chooses a life of celibacy and isolation for religious reasons, many people condemn that choice because they see it as both harmful to the person making the choice and damaging to society as a whole because it accepts the religious opprobrium given to homosexuality. Another related situation is when lesbian and gay people find themselves in heterosexual marriages with children because they felt pressured to conform. We generally see such demands on lesbians and gays as unacceptable. When similarly draconian ones are imposed on transgender people, it creates a double standard.

However, I have seen cases where the same people who would advise lesbians and gays to come out and be themselves instead counsel transgender people to stay in the closet because being transgender is so socially stigmatized. Other times they suggest transgender people should remain closeted for the sake of everyone else in their life. In some of the cases where people have questioned my own transition, I suspect that they would have not held LGB people to a similar standard.

I don't believe this seemingly inconsistent viewpoint comes from a place of malice. Instead, I believe it comes from the mistaken perception that being transgender is a choice, or that transition is more of a choice than whom you love. Not only are both perspectives harmful to transgender people, but they hurt the LGB community's ability to push back on narratives that we should all just be in the closet for the good of society.

There's little evidence to suggest that gender identity is any more of a choice than sexual orientation is. The medical and psychiatric establishments tried for decades to change both, without success. More recent studies have suggested that gender dysphoria is deeply hard-wired neurologically.[29] However, when people who are otherwise sympathetic to the LGB community seem to agree with leaders at anti-LGBT hate groups, it actually diminishes their ability to argue that being gay isn't a choice either.[30]

The assertion that transition is a choice worthy of legalized discrimination is more common, and even more damaging. Maggie Gallagher of the anti-LGBT National Organization for Marriage (NOM) publicly states that she believes that orientation isn't a choice but that acting on it is, and that that's worthy of moral and legal disapproval.[31] When similar arguments are applied to transgender people and transition, it makes me wince, because the parallels seem so clear.

For me, there have been times when it feels as though the message I'm hearing is that I'm free to be anyone I want to be as long as that person fits within some stereotype of masculinity, or that I can express myself as much as I want as long as I keep it discreet. I imagine this feels as patronizing to me as it did to LGB people when Orson Scott Card of NOM wrote:

> In the first place, no law in any state in the United States now or ever has forbidden homosexuals to marry… Any homosexual man who can persuade a woman to take him as her husband can avail himself of all the rights of husbandhood under the law.[32]

It feels just as patronizing when the message is, "You can be anyone you want, as long as they're male." I suspect most lesbians and gays would also chafe at the suggestion that "you can be gay, as long as you don't act gay." All of these ideas are linked, in that they seek to deny people their essential identities and circumscribe their life, liberty, and pursuit of happiness.

Another misconception surrounding choice and transition is medical care and surgery. It is true that different transgender people have different medical needs. The medical Standards of Care for treating transgender people set forth by WPATH make this clear.[33] However, it's hard to say that something is a choice when the American Psychological Association, American Psychiatric Association, American Medical Association, and even the Internal Revenue Service recognize this as medically necessary for many individuals.[34]

In short, for many transgender people, transition is a choice only inasmuch as choosing between leading a full life and a sharply limited and unpleasant one is a "choice." As one 14-year-old transgender youth in a recent study said, "It isn't a choice, even though a lot of people think that. Well, actually it is a choice: living a happy life or living an unhappy life."[35]

The goal of living authentically is central to the identities of most lesbian, gay, bisexual, and transgender people. When people place moral disapproval on expressing sexual orientation *or* gender identity, LGBT people are more likely to stay in the closet and live a lie. The closet is a very dark place. The longer LGBT people live that lie, the harder it becomes to extricate ourselves from it. The only way to end this vicious catch-22 is to stop stigmatizing LGBT people.

LGB is getting there.

Trans has a long way to go.

Chapter 2
TRANS 201

Okay, so you get that gender identity is different from gender expression, which is different from sexual orientation. You know the difference between transsexual, transgender, genderqueer, and gender fluid. You know that not everyone wants "the surgery," and not to ask if they do. You're good with the idea transgender didn't choose to be transgender. You want to be an ally.

Great!

However, there's a lot more to life as a transgender person than just the basics. The sections in this chapter address many of the difficult realities transgender people face every day. There are challenges in finding and keeping a job, and most states have no state-level legal protections for transgender people to prevent employment discrimination. It can be very difficult to get government ID, especially in states that have hefty surgical or legal requirements. There are a lot of myths and misconceptions about transgender people that make life more difficult. There's outright danger of violence, and how transgender people are treated by the police and the legal system.

The deck is stacked against transgender people, and potential allies need to understand the effects of a frequently hostile culture and legal system. When you know about these effects, it allows you to see them when they happen, and recognize where positive change can be made.

Two Americas for trans people

One inescapable fact that transgender Americans have to live with every day is that without specific legal protections, our lives are very much affected by the winds of politics. After the 2014 and 2016 elections, leaders in the LGBT movement knew we would be losing ground for a couple of years.[36] The crop of incoming conservatives in 2014 featured many legislators with an anti-LGBT history.[37] The 2016 election ushered in cabinet members, judicial nominees, and political appointees with long histories of anti-LGBT animus, and there came the concern that it could take a decade or more to recover.[38] [39] [40] [41]

We were right to be worried.

The new Secretary of the Department of Education almost immediately revoked Obama-era protections for transgender students in 2017.[42] The Department of Justice has taken the position that workplace discrimination against gay and transgender people is entirely legal, and that religious freedom laws exempt people from following non-discrimination ordinances at the state and local level.[43] [44] [45] The Trump Administration went so far as to attempt to unilaterally ban transgender people from the military.[46]

At the state level, though, the legislative threats to transgender people are even more pronounced. So far, several states have nullified all local non-discrimination ordinances protecting LGBT people.[47] Other bills grant special religious exemptions to people wishing to discriminate, one of which passed under (then) Indiana Governor Mike Pence, and another in Mississippi.[48] [49] None of them has been found unconstitutional.

States have frequently been attempting bills that would make it nearly impossible for transgender students and citizens to use a public bathroom, and North Carolina became the first to do so in 2016. In some of these bills, business owners who let transgender people do so would face fines and lawsuits. One bill in Texas proposed putting a $2000 bounty on finding transgender students in bathrooms.[50]

Pause there for a second.

State legislators are introducing bills putting bounties on transgender children.

Let that sink in a little more.

Bounties.

On children.

On the flip-side though, there are deep blue states like California, where LGBT rights organizations are working to solve issues that no other state has addressed yet. This includes specifically prohibiting abuse of LGBT elders and ensuring that transgender people's identities are respected on their death certificates.[51]

However, all of these bills (good and bad) are just the continuation of a process. LGBT Americans, like most of the country, live in one of two distinct political environments, with very little in between. LGBT people are either full citizens, or are left completely to the whims of the multitudes who would do them harm. This trend is even more pronounced for transgender people.

States either offer a host of protections, or they offer very few. A quick study of transgender rights looked at state-level conditions for transgender people in the US.[52] It clearly showed the gap between the two Americas. There is a cluster of states with high (good) scores where transgender people enjoy protections in almost every facet of life.

Attitudes towards transgender people in the US are more divided than just about anywhere else in the world. The US leads the world in the percentages of people who believe being transgender is a sin and that society has gone too far in accepting them. At the same time, 73 percent of the public in the US believe that transgender people should be protected from discrimination by the government.[53]

There is an even bigger cluster of states with very low (bad) scores where transgender people have virtually no legal protections. Access to any sort of redress requires a federal lawsuit. The same pattern holds true for LGBT protections as a whole.

Again, there are two groups, and the distance between these clusters is only going to increase as more and more bills pass that are designed to nullify protections and provide religion as a legal excuse to discriminate. The Movement Advancement Project looked at legal rights for transgender people by state, and found that 35 fit in either the very highest level of protection or the very lowest, while only 15 fell somewhere in the two middle categories.[54] There are almost certainly

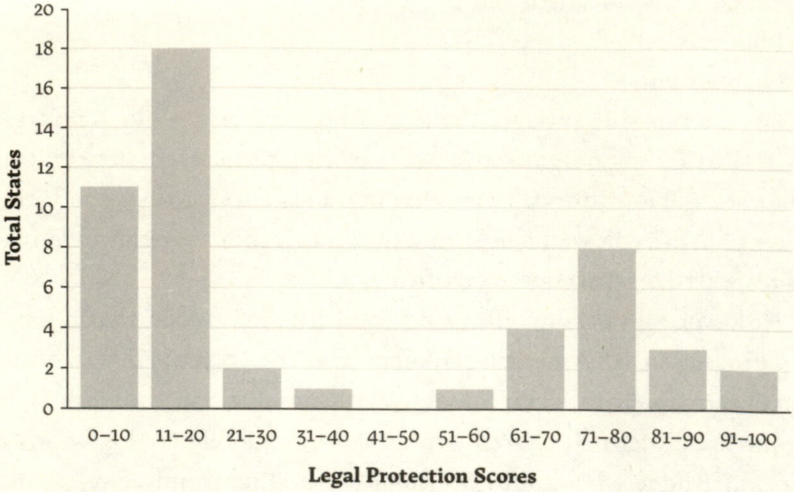

Figure 2.1: Transgender protections

(Data compiled by Andrea Wood of Equality Ohio in 2013. Histogram generated by author.)

Figure 2.2: State-level LGBT protections

(Data compiled by Andrea Wood of Equality Ohio in 2013. Histogram generated by author.)

going to be more bills aimed at transgender people, and the attacks have become both more frequent and intense since the Supreme Court enacted marriage equality. Just as conservatives rolled back women's rights with Targeted Restrictions on Abortion Providers (TRAP) laws, they will try to peel back any protections LGBT people have. Until functionally, there are none.

Additionally, two other factors are working against the LGBT community legislatively. One is gerrymandering (the manipulation of political boundaries to favor one party or class), which helps keep red states red.[55] It also means that comprehensive federal legislation protecting LGBT people won't happen in the foreseeable future.[56]

The other is the fact that most Americans generally don't care about their candidates' views on LGBT people, no matter how outside the mainstream of society they are. Case in point: the election of former Colorado State Representative Gordon Klingenschmitt, who attributed transgender identity to possession by "demons of rape."[57] He had a long history of making outrageous statements about LGBT people, yet was elected anyway by a wide margin.

The result of this widening gap is an America where people can marry the person they love, but also be fired, denied housing, refused health care, denied service, and refused public accommodations because of it.

Culturally, though, it is already far too easy for people living in states where there is acceptance and legal protections to forget that this is the exception rather than the rule. When singer Kelly Clarkson was asked about her lesbian and gay fan base, she remarked, "I think it's silly that we're still talking about gay rights. I just live in this world where people are accepted, so it's very hard for me to even realize that that still exists. It's hard for me to wrap my brain around it."[58]

It isn't just Clarkson who lives in something of a bubble of acceptance and legal protections. In a "let them eat cake" moment, one transgender celebrity, Our Lady J, remarked that the secret to dating as a queer person is to simply date other queer people. She seemed oblivious to how queer people in most states are being actively legislated against, or are isolated in rural, red areas of the US.

And that's the whole point of these kinds of anti-LGBT bills, especially those focusing on transgender people.

Transgender people are seen as a social evil by some conservatives in government and the judiciary. Their leadership denies transgender people exist and says that they should be put in reparative therapy (presumably whether they want to be or not), and their religious leaders claim transgender people are a threat to humanity equal to nuclear weapons.[59] [60] [61]

Whether transgender people self-deport, detransition, or never transition, social conservatives want them to disappear. They're working to make sure we cannot access the health care needed to transition.[62] They've passed bills making it impossible to participate in school activities.[63] They've passed bills making it impossible to get correct government identification documentation.[64]

Finally, bathroom bills like the ones proposed in Texas, Florida, and Kentucky are designed to legally drive transgender people out of the state or back into the closet.[65] This is in stark contrast to blue states, where such legislation is unthinkable, and even a Republican governor in Massachusetts signed a bill granting public accommodations protections for transgender people.[66]

Transgender people have to pay more attention to politics than we would like, because we can be so immediately adversely affected by it. Transgender people, like almost everyone else in the US, tend to live in red or blue bubbles. For transgender people, however, the effect of living in them is even more pronounced.

Myths and misconceptions about transgender people

One of the biggest challenges about being transgender is the endless stream of bad ideas and general hostility we have to deal with. Many of these come from social conservatives who wouldn't mind it if transgender people simply disappeared, but sometimes they come from concern trolls.[67] At other times, these comments and questions are well meant, but uninformed or insensitive.

There are also some enduring myths and misconceptions about transgender people, and transgender women in particular. The facts presented in Chapter 1 address some of these myths, but explicitly debunking them is still valuable given their persistence. Part of this chapter is an adaptation of a mythbusting piece written by Natalie Reed (who was one of my inspirations when I first started writing), and of a related article I wrote as a follow-up in 2013.[68] Unfortunately, many of these myths and misconceptions are still an issue now, a half-decade later.

Myth 1. Trans women are just *very* gay men

Except for the fact that only a third of transgender women are exclusively attracted to men.[69] Plus, gay men don't identify as women, and transgender women don't identify as gay men. The origins of this myth date back to the 1970s and 1980s when gatekeeping mental health professionals wouldn't let people transition unless they swore they were going to be straight. This is discussed in more detail in Chapter 4.

Myth 2. So you're going to get your penis cut off?

That's not how it works. There are plenty of videos and diagrams online of how gender confirmation surgeries work, but almost all of the tissue in a vaginoplasty is re-purposed to form labia and a vaginal canal. The penis is still there, just in different places.

Myth 3. So you've chosen to get a sex change operation?

As described in the previous chapter, transition isn't much of a choice for a lot of transgender people. Similarly, as Chapter 4 describes in detail, transition-related care is considered medically necessary by every major professional medical organization in the US.[70]

Myth 4. "It's a trap." Trans women are just gay guys trying to attract straight dudes

See number 1 first: transgender women aren't gay men.

Second: about a third of transgender women are exclusively attracted to women, making them lesbians. We can be pretty sure they're not "stealing" men.

Also, given everything we know about how difficult dating while transgender is, it takes some heroic assumptions to conclude that anyone would transition in order to have sex, when finding partners is so much easier as a cisgender person.

Finally, transgender women are women. Being attracted to women doesn't make you gay.

Myth 5. Aren't you sort of reinforcing stereotypical gender roles? Aren't you just going along with the idea that having a feminine personality means you must be female? Doesn't that perpetuate the idea that there are certain ways women and men are "supposed" to be like?

There are butch transgender women and femme transgender men. There are gender fluid, gender non-binary, and genderqueer transgender people as well. Asserting that transgender people reinforce stereotypical gender roles ignores all of these people, while conflating gender identity and expression.

Fundamentally, though, transgender people break the stereotypes, by illustrating that sex, gender identity, and gender expression can all be decoupled, and that we should be free to identify and express ourselves without the constraint of gender norms.

Simultaneously, cisgender people are not punished for adhering to gender norms, yet transgender women are somehow guilty of... something...if they choose to express themselves in a normative way at any time. This is a double standard demonstrating an implicit bias.

Myth 6. You're so brave!

Being transgender wasn't a choice, and the thought of *not* transitioning is often as terrifying as the idea of transition itself. It's not brave; it's just making the best of a bad situation. The world can still be a scary place after transition as well, and the person calling us "brave" instinctively knows it. Transgender people would much rather hear someone tell us how they're going to make the world less scary than be called "brave."

Myth 7. You're appropriating the female body

Natalie Reed wrote in 2011, "Appropriation is about co-opting someone else's identity. We're not doing that. We're expressing *our* identity."[71] While she acknowledges this is something of a simplification, and that gender is an inevitable outcome of biological differences in a complex society, in the final analysis gender expression is ultimately about how we see ourselves regardless of sex.

Myth 8. Why can't you just accept yourself? Why not just learn to be comfortable with who you are?

No one has ever demonstrated a successful treatment for gender dysphoria to make transgender people cisgender, any more than they have demonstrated a treatment to make gay people straight. This is discussed in more detail in Chapters 4 and 5.

Myth 9. Transsexuality is just an invention of the modern medical establishment, a symptom of Western culture

As discussed in Chapter 1, there is a wealth of historical, archaeological, and anthropological proof that transgender people have existed across different cultures (including non-Western ones) for millennia.

Myth 10. Transgender people are infiltrating women's spaces and making them unsafe

Chapter 7 discusses in detail why bills banning transgender people from bathrooms were never about safety, but rather were about targeting transgender people as a solution to a problem that didn't exist. Politifact concluded that there has never been an instance in the US of transgender people, or people pretending to be transgender, exploiting public accommodations laws to commit crimes.[72] Simply being uncomfortable around a class of people is not sufficient grounds for discrimination; otherwise we'd still have "whites only" drinking fountains.

Myth 11. "If you can identify as a woman, I can identify as an attack helicopter"

This meme was going around in alt-right websites for a while. Chapter 4 discusses how people have an innate gender identity. People do not naturally have an innate identity as an inanimate object. This sort of argument is just the anti-transgender version of "If guys can marry a man, I can marry my lawnmower." (Someone did try to marry their lawnmower, and of course failed.)[73]

So yes, transgender people can have a gender identity, just like everyone else. And no, people do not naturally identify as objects. The two are not comparable, just as marriage to a person v. marriage to an object are not comparable.

Myth 12. You shouldn't change your body when what you really need is therapy to accept how you were born

Great idea! It would have saved me $50,000 and a 35 percent pay cut. So, where do I sign up for a cure that's accredited by the American Psychological Association or the American Psychiatric Association? Because the programs you guys recommend mostly look like a lot of praying away the trans[74] (I'm an atheist), or people screaming and beating the crap out of pillows.[75]

Oh, wait, there isn't one.

Next.

Myth 13. "If you chose to be an outsider, you'd better be prepared to be an outsider"[76]

We've been over this already. It's not much of a choice. That's why every major medical and mental health organization agrees on the medical necessity of transitioning for many transgender people. (The "medical organizations" that disagree are anti-LGBT hate groups masquerading as medical organizations; more on this later.)

Second, way to go blaming the victims! Thought that you guys had decided that was a bad idea after Richard Mourdock and Todd Akin made comments about "legitimate rape." Or Donald Trump tweeted that if women didn't want to get raped in the military they shouldn't have joined.

Apparently, the classics never go out of style.

Myth 14. Girls have XX chromosomes, boys have XY chromosomes—period

Unless you have Complete Androgen Insensitivity Syndrome (CAIS). Or an XO karyotype. Or XXY. Or XYY. Or 5-alpha-reductase deficiency. Or Swyer syndrome. Or genetic mosaicism. Or 17-β-Hydroxysteroid dehydrogenase III deficiency. Or Progestin-induced virilization...and so on...

Myth 15. God made you this way, and the only way to make God happy is to just endure it[77]

So let me get this straight. God intentionally made me in a way that causes suffering? In order to make your God happy, I have to forgo treatment that alleviates this suffering? And did you give this same advice to people with cleft palates?

Maybe you didn't pick who you thought you did with this whole good and evil thing.

Myth 16. Transgender people are mentally ill

The American Psychological Association, American Medical Association, American Psychiatric Association, WPATH, and the Department of Defense (DOD) folks who issue security clearances would beg to differ. The American Psychiatric Association flat out says gender non-conformity (being transgender) isn't in and of itself a mental illness.[78]

Myth 17. Psychologists and psychiatrists are just a bunch of godless liberals who tell people what they want to hear and push diagnoses

Yes, because figuring out I am transgender didn't complicate my life at all. Because therapists get paid to tell people what they want to hear. Because it in no way shape or form violates their professional ethics to tell people things which are highly likely to result in divorce, mental trauma, and unemployment.

Oh, and my therapist? She was a practicing Catholic and a Republican.

Myth 18. Have you tried enjoying "guy" stuff?[79]

Besides boxing, wrestling, judo, four years at a military academy, ten years on active duty, three deployments to combat zones, getting a master's in applied mathematics, getting married, designing systems to train fighter pilots, playing fantasy basketball, and flying attack helicopters?

No.

I'll take suggestions, but I'm over 40 years old, five foot four, and 138 pounds, so professional MMA fighting or special forces is sort of a long shot at this point.

Myth 19. "I'm saying this with love..."

People who start conversations with this one remind me of that not-so-bright kid in boot camp who heard from some guy you could say anything you wanted to the drill instructor if you started the sentence, "With all due respect..." You can guess how well that goes over.

Usually, this phrase is followed with an opinion about how much God hates what I am doing, my existence is an anathema, I need to repent now and accept Jesus, and so on... Trans people really aren't feeling the love when they're told that they're going to burn in hell for something they can't change.

Myth 20. You'll never be a "real" woman/man (or other deliberate mis-gendering)

Beyond the philosophical and medical argument of what makes a "real" man or woman (which is discussed in detail in Chapter 11 on gender and feminism), there is the simple level of civility. When you deliberately attack someone's core identity, you have foregone the basic rules of decency.

Let's start with a simple example. We meet, and you introduce yourself as Dave. I take one look at you, and declare, "You don't look like a Dave. You look more like a Steve, so I'll call you Steve. Nice to meet you Steve." It doesn't matter if I think you look like a Steve. You identify as Dave, and someone who deliberately calls you the wrong name is being uncivil. When someone uses the wrong name or pronouns with a transgender person, this is deliberately offensive, and would be treated as such.

Indeed, the Employment Equal Opportunity Commission has found that deliberately using the wrong names and pronouns for a transgender person is a form of harassment and creates a hostile workplace environment.[80]

Additionally, no single variable unequivocally and universally defines someone as male or female. Not chromosomes (see 14, above), not hormones, not secondary sex characteristics. What differentiates us as people is the gray matter between our ears that confers on us consciousness and identity, and not our individual cells, DNA, chromosomes, or genitals. The latter are not what gives us our sense of self and awareness.

Myths and misconceptions about the lived experience

Some conversations I have had have revealed prevalent myths and misconceptions about transgender people that we need to move beyond. Simple definitions aren't enough: we need to be talking about lived realities.

Myth 1: Getting a job as a transgender person is just like getting a job as a gay person

No. Virtually every transgender person is outed during the vetting process. Whether it is because the person is not "passable" in some way, or because the background check reveals their previous name, or there is a DD214 (military discharge) they couldn't update until recently, or a Google search. If you're transgender, you *will* be outed eventually during the hiring process, and it will likely (negatively) affect whether or not you are interviewed, much less extended, a job offer.

Several studies have shown the effects of bias against transgender people in employment, even in places with non-discrimination ordinances. An undercover study by the Washington DC Office of Human Rights showed that almost half of employers preferred less qualified cisgender applicants to transgender ones.[81] Another study showed that when transgender women transition, their pay drops by about a third.[82]

Anecdotally, one of my closest friends also works in government as a high-level cyber-security analyst. We transitioned at the same time, and both of us are pretty visible as transgender people in industry. Before we transitioned, getting interviews—and doing very well in them—was easy.

I never interviewed for a job I didn't get before I transitioned.

My friend bounced from job to job, moving up the ladder, while pursuing whatever career seemed most interesting at the time, because getting interviews and offers was always so easy for her.

Since we have transitioned, the job-seeking process has become much harder. Between 2013 and 2014 I put out dozens of resumes for jobs I was qualified for, got one interview, and no offers. That one interview only happened because they still thought I was my "dead name." My friend has had similar experiences.

In short, if you're transgender, finding a job is far, *far* harder than it is for others.

Myth 2: Dating for transgender people is just like LGB dating

Dating for transgender people is a unique experience. For starters, there is the question of what to tell about your history, and when. This can be extremely dangerous, and frequently goes very poorly. Violence is often a result.

Even when there isn't violence, it can still be humiliating. A friend recently told me the story of her date responding loudly with "Oh, just what I fucking needed!" when she told him she was transgender. He then stormed out of the restaurant and stuck her with the bill for both their dinners.

Another issue is that transgender women frequently don't fit inside traditional notions of beauty. Men who do find transgender women attractive are often acting on a fetish rather than interest in them as individuals. Transgender women who are attracted to women often have an even more difficult time finding romantic partners than those attracted to men.

As such, it's often the case that only a transgender person can love another transgender person. However, in the hinterlands of America—where there often isn't another transgender person for an hour in any direction—this isn't an option.

This is part of why loving a transgender person is a revolutionary act, and dating is a minefield, both of which are discussed in greater detail later in Chapter 3.

Myth 3: "Don't pay attention to what others say." "Just love yourself." "Words only have power if you give them power"

If all of this was true, then anti-bullying programs would be so easy! Just give kids a quick lesson in pop-psychology buzz phrases and boom! Bully-proof kids.

Except the human mind doesn't work that way.[83] And this is wrong from a moral perspective as well. People can't maintain a positive sense of self when there is literally *nothing* in their day-to-day life that they can touch/see/hear/feel that affirms their identity. For a transgender kid in Nowhere, USA, who is being treated like an abomination every day by virtually everyone, it does them next to zero good hearing that someone they will never meet who lives in a place they have never been "supports" them, in a non-specific "I've-never-met-you-and-never-will-but-I-value-people-like-you" sort of way.

Support, and love, needs to be tangible to resist tangible hate.

Beyond this, telling the victims of bullying that it is their fault if they can't fight off the omnipresent messages of hate and loathing is victim-blaming. Telling people "Words only have power if you give them power" is blame-shifting in the same way programs that teach women to avoid getting raped do.

They both move the burden of guilt to the innocent. It implies that it's your own fault if you are victimized or suffer emotionally. Thus, telling someone to simply not let it get to them is both unhelpful, and blaming the victim.

Myth 4: Geography doesn't matter

As described earlier, living as a transgender person in London is different from California, is different from Ohio, is different from the Deep South. You go from being a person in a protected class with full government recognition at all levels (and access to transgender-specific health care) at one end (the UK), to a person who has human rights in name only on the other. It's the difference between full legal equality, and living as a member of an untouchable caste.

This was never more evident than when I spoke at the Transgender

Leadership Summit in 2014, when people who mostly live in the Los Angeles, California, area were stunned and appalled by stories being told by visitors from out of state.

Just because transgender people in your area seem to be doing okay doesn't mean it's true for those of us elsewhere.

Myth 5: Career field doesn't matter

Transgender people working in career fields that are traditionally LGB-friendly have a far different experience from those working in industries that are not friendly to women or the LGB community. In those industries, if you want to keep your job, you try to blend in, especially when finding a new job can be next to impossible.

For many transgender professionals, including myself and some of my closest friends, being transgender is that elephant in the break room that no one acknowledges. It may be an open secret in the office, but the fact that I have pictures of my wife and children in my cubicle is already considered "edgy."

Myth 6: Everyone knows the difference between drag and transgender

No. The religious right capitalizes on the conflation of drag and transgender and uses it to claim that transgender people will show up to the office dressed like it's Saturday night at The Masque. If people didn't conflate the two, then the religious right wouldn't be nearly so successful at fighting against workplace and employment protections for transgender individuals.

The difference between drag and transgender is pretty obvious to people who have been around either (or both) communities for any length of time. However, given that only approximately 16 percent of Americans know someone who is transgender, this nuance escapes many people.[84] This is especially true in areas where transgender people are widely scattered and often trying to blend into the woodwork.

Myth 7: Race doesn't matter in these discussions

This is absolutely a myth. Most of the LGBT people murdered in hate crimes are transgender women. Of those transgender women, the vast majority are women of color.

When you have any conversation about the transgender community, you have to include transgender women of color. They're dying at a rate about 22 times higher than gay men in hate crimes.[85]

Transgender women of color need veto power in any discussions involving policy. They are the ones who will bear the consequences of whatever decisions are made.

Myth 8: Cisgender people get to decide what is hurtful or offensive to transgender people

When a non-transgender person is doing something that many transgender people find painful and offensive, the only appropriate response is, "I'm sorry. I won't do that again." When someone continues to do something deliberately offensive simply because they don't see it as offensive and hurtful, it exposes a lack of empathy.

If you're really a friend to the transgender community—and a lot of us are telling you that you're damaging us with your actions—you should listen (and probably modify your behavior) regardless of the circumstances. You may have good intentions, but there's a saying about that sort of thing...

Myth 9: "Transgender" only means transsexual

There is considerable debate over who fits under the umbrella term "transgender." Some people reject the label, but most accept it.

Ultimately, it is a matter of self-identification: if someone identifies as transgender, that's their identity and you should respect it. There's also genderqueer, gender fluid, agender, and so on... Generally, though, all of these fit within transgender.

Myth 10: One voice can speak for all of us

The lived experiences of transgender people are as diverse as the American experience itself. There is no such thing as *the* "transgender experience." No one voice can speak for the entirety of the community. The amount of intersectionality is staggering, and can't be ignored. We all speak from our own lived experiences, and our own truths. Denying them is a rejection of our identities that we have worked so hard to claim.

Chapter 3

DATING AND SEX

Talking about sex and dating involves some of the most taboo conversations about transgender lives. What is it like trying to find love and companionship as a transgender person? When should a transgender person reveal that they are transgender to a partner or potential partner? What does it mean to love a transgender person in the greater scheme of things? What does having sex with a transgender person say about a person's sexual orientation? Is the English language even suited to discuss these questions?

All of these are addressed in this chapter.

The ethics of dating while trans

There isn't a lot of research on transgender people and dating, but the data that exists isn't particularly encouraging. Forty-seven percent of LGB people would consider dating a transgender person, and 44 percent would not.[86] Transgender women are the members of the LGBT community most likely to try dating online, in part because they almost always need to search a larger geographical area than any other segment of the LGBT population to find someone willing to date a transgender woman. This effect is magnified for transgender women in rural areas with a lower population density, where they might have to drive for hours to meet another queer, single person.

For transgender and queer people in the rural areas, online dating applications have become the primary way of meeting other people, and the number of queer spaces and "gay bars" is falling accordingly.[87] Putting that you are transgender right up front in your profile might cut down on the number of responses, but it also reduces the chances of "jerks and surprises."

Or at least jerks and surprises on dates. Online is another matter.

When transgender women choose to disclose online, they are often fetishized on dating sites, being treated like "just an item to check off someone's sexual bucket list."[88] "Chasers" present something of a dilemma too: sometimes they represent the only potential attention a transgender woman might receive in a rural area. Transgender men seem to be less subject to prurient interest on gay dating sites, but often feel misunderstood or unwanted. They frequently are subjected to ignorant, insensitive, or hostile comments on sites like Grindr.[89]

There is often a more blanket level of acceptance of transgender people within the kink and BDSM (bondage and discipline, dominance and submission, sadism and masochism) scenes and sites such as FetLife. These are groups of people who have already opened themselves up to a greater range of romantic and erotic possibilities, and transgender often just adds to the smorgasbord. However, the risk of being just another fetish is even higher than with a standard dating site.

The news is even worse for transgender people who identify as heterosexual. Only 12 percent of straight people in one survey said they would be open to dating a transgender person, while 65 percent would never consider it.[90] There is a great deal of stigma attached to being a man who dates a transgender woman, even when that transgender woman is someone beautiful and successful like Janet Mock.[91] The horror of accidentally dating a transgender woman continues to be a source of humor for a public still generally uncomfortable with the idea.[92]

Despite the very strong incentive against putting your "transness" out front as part of your profile, an analysis of Match.com surveys revealed that 61 percent of transgender people tell potential partners they are transgender before they ever go out on a first date.

But what of that remaining 39 percent?

Like so many other things, the answer to when and if a transgender person discloses their history is "it depends."

The risk v. reward calculation for a stealth, post-operative transgender woman in her 50s who has lived as a woman for 35+ years, whom no one in her circle of friends has ever known as anything but a woman, is very low. She is not "cheating someone out of a family," as a woman of her age isn't expected to be able to bear children.

Others wait until after a few dates to find out if there is any chemistry before disclosing their history. This is particularly true if they believe that finding such chemistry may make people who weren't open to the possibility more receptive to the idea, once they realize transgender people aren't the boogeymen they imagined (or boogey women. Or boogey persons).

Waiting until intimacy occurs to disclose is at the very high end of the risk spectrum, particularly for pre-operative or non-operative individuals. The potential for violence at this point is exceedingly high.[93] There are numerous incidents of trans women being murdered by people they were romantically involved with for this reason.[94]

This brings us to the ethics of disclosure, which is an entirely separate question from when to disclose in order to get the best probability at a good outcome in the risk-reward matrix.

Transgender people are treated differently both culturally and legally when it comes to disclosing genetic and sexual history. Right-wing websites accuse transgender women who do not disclose their history of being rapists.[95] Law in the UK has been interpreted this way, with a 25-year-old transgender man in Scotland being sentenced to eight years in prison for not telling his partner he was transgender before they had sex.[96] There is often a resulting assumption that when transgender women, like Gwen Araujo,[97] are beaten to death by their intimate partners, these murders were actually a form of self-defense.[98] This sort of logic is applied to transgender people whether they are pre- or post-operative.

This is regarded differently from any other sort of genetic or sexual history issue where consent and violence are concerned. For example, suppose a woman had a Jewish grandmother. She failed to disclose her ancestry prior to sex, and was beaten to death by her anti-Semitic partner afterwards because he found out. It would be difficult to find a judge or jury willing to consider what she did rape, much less a mitigating circumstance for her murderer. Similarly, failing to disclose that you have black, white, Latino, or any other sort of heritage does not constitute rape or justification for violence.

There is generally no requirement for an individual to fully disclose sexual history to partners unless there is a known health risk. Nor does an individual have to provide a complete list of whom they have slept with, when, and what acts they have performed. Nor is there a legal requirement to list surgeries you have had. It would be exceptionally hard to convince a jury, much less the police or a prosecutor, that you were raped by fraud because your partner did not disclose that they had breast augmentation, rhinoplasty, or labial reduction.

The simplest explanation for these logical and legal inconsistencies is a toxic mix of homophobia and transphobia. Men are afraid of being labeled gay, or doubting their own masculinity, if they have sex with a transgender person. People in general have a visceral "ick" reaction to a stereotype of transgender people, *whether or not they were able to tell the person was transgender.* This is the definition of bias.

As such, transgender people, and particularly transgender women, are facing an array of difficult double standards. The odds aren't great with dating within the LGB community, but scarcity is its own problem. Many transgender people live isolated from community by the vast distances of middle America.

Ethically, transgender people should not be expected to disclose intimate details of their lives and histories earlier than any other group, particularly when it doesn't actively harm others. Treating an already marginalized population as a special case further adds to the perception of transgender people being part of an "untouchable" caste. Indeed, the acceptance of the violence visited on transgender women based on non-disclosure has a chilling parallel with "honor killings" of women.

Thus, the real question being asked isn't whether transgender people are ethically obligated to tell partners. It is about double standards, and about why people who find transgender individuals threatening to their self-image seek justification for violence.

The experience of dating while trans

As illustrated by the previous section, both statistically and practically, dating while trans is a difficult and potentially dangerous experience. In some parts of the country there are fewer stigmas than others, but even some people in the transgender community don't realize how difficult it is to find romantic love as a transgender person, and particularly as someone who doesn't fit inside a binary box. This section is focused on providing a "ground level" view of what it's like trying to form and maintain relationships as a transgender person, with an emphasis on being a transgender woman. While the observations in this section are anecdotal, they give insight into the statistics and analysis provided in the previous section.

During an episode of the TV show *True Trans*, Against Me!'s Laura Jane Grace addressed how being transgender affects relationships. Laura Jane's description of how it impacted her relationship with her wife in the first half of the episode was a very accurate portrayal of my own observations about the challenges of holding a pre-existing marriage together post-transition.[99]

However, the second half of the episode—which dealt with dating—presented an incomplete or potentially misleading picture of what dating (or attempting to find a date) is like for transgender women. Almost everyone interviewed about the topic was younger and lived in large metropolitan areas with significant LGBTQ communities (Los Angeles, San Francisco, and Chicago).

The reality of trying to date while transgender is far more difficult and complicated than simply "dating other queer people," however. This also focuses primarily on the experiences of transgender women, who are the most likely to be subject to stigma and violence. The only upside to some of their experiences is that cisgender women also have to deal with jerks who send dick pics.

So, at least there's some equality. Yay?

Or not.

1. Marriages that do survive are irrevocably changed

The *True Trans* episode quoted a statistic that only 7 percent of marriages survive transition. However, even if a marriage doesn't end, the statistic doesn't tell the whole story.

For most marriages that I am aware of, transition is the end of sex. How individual couples deal with it varies. Some choose celibacy, others open the marriage up, others choose some version of polyamory. This lack of intimacy is usually a source of friction, and contributes to the sense of loss felt by both partners.

However, as some responses to an online query I posted indicate, this friction can sometimes lead to self-discovery by both partners:

> During the first year of my transition I did discover that I have a growing attraction to men, something I never had before. I had by then been in a wonderful 11-year relationship with a woman who is still my partner today. Being newly minted with the label of pansexual and beginning to identify as polyamorous (legitimizing in a way years of consensual and healthy non-monogamy), I entered the dating pool primarily through online dating. *C, a 34-year-old pansexual transgender woman in the Los Angeles area*

> I don't love her because she's trans, or despite the fact that she's trans. It's not something I ignore or something that I focus on; it's a part of her. But she is trans. I've learned a lot just by being with her.
>
> I've learned to be grateful for things I'd previously taken for granted: my safety walking down the street; the fact that I can be reasonably confident of finding a job if I look for one; my

assumption that others see me as I see myself with no need for me to constantly evaluate my behavior and others' reactions to it. *D, a 42-year-old cisgender partner of a transgender woman*

2. Queer culture is an urban phenomenon

In the *True Trans* video, Our Lady J states, "I found that it's easier to date people who don't really identify—period. There's just a fluidity that has to be there. And I think if you have a rigid definition of your sexuality you're going to have a hard time being open to someone who breaks that definition."

This is a fair definition of a queer orientation. Dating such individuals is indeed probably easiest; however, people with such attitudes are rare, and those who do possess them are nearly non-existent outside urban centers with queer communities. As such, transgender women outside such areas struggle to find dates, much less partners.

> On OKC [OkCupid] some days I get upward of 30 messages. And some men just do not take no for an answer. *E, a 40-year-old queer transgender woman in New York City*

> I've had a fully filled out OKC profile for 18 months, and updated it regularly. I've listed myself as both bi and lesbian, but don't hide the fact that I'm trans. I haven't had a single unsolicited message in that time regardless. *J, a 38-year-old queer trans woman in rural Ohio*

> I turned to online dating (OKC), but in over a year now I've never actually gone on a date with anyone from the site. Overall, I don't get messages. Occasionally, I get a few responses when I contact someone, and then they disappear. It's a huge source of frustration. *N, a 31-year-old queer transgender woman in rural Wisconsin*

As a result, living outside a queer-friendly urban area can lead to nearly impossible odds for many transgender women.

3. Dating in conservative areas is almost not worth it

For trans women in the South, dating is both rare and dangerous for everyone, including would-be suitors.

> I live in Tennessee and had to wade through legions of creepy mouth breathers before I got to meet someone who treated me like a human, much less a woman... The biggest problems I've had dating revolve around location and culture. Southern culture shames the f**k out of anyone queer. Folks on the West coast might get to act like it ain't no thing, but around here not passing could actually get you seriously hurt. Naturally this extends to cis people with trans attractions, especially cis men. You have to really expand your scope, lower your standards, and have zero f***s to give in order to date as a trans woman in the rural South. *J, a 38-year-old straight transgender woman in Tennessee*

> I've dated around, but I have very few options, and with each person I date I feel like I am running out of opportunities for finding anyone, since I am not in a big city and the idea of dating a trans woman is kind of new and scary for a lot of women, I think. I mean, the dates were good, at least I thought, but they ghosted and disappeared. *K, a 26-year-old lesbian transgender woman in eastern Tennessee*

4. Dating men has specific challenges

Transgender women are often fetishized by straight men, resulting in a very skeezy-feeling experience.

> I find a lot of men fetishize trans women in a way that they don't other women. I often hear statements that no man would ever say to a ciswoman. For example: "I've always been curious about sex with a transsexual. Can you tell me what your penis is like?" *E, a 40-year-old queer transgender woman in New York City*

After reassignment surgery, it seems that the chaser pool dried up and I haven't had much luck with dating. The one time where I almost had a date post-surgery, after I disclosed to him he of course had an existential crisis and cancelled. *J, a 30-year-old straight transgender woman in East Lansing, Michigan*

5. Dating women has its own challenges as well

Transgender women often have trouble finding safe spaces or acceptance in both gay and lesbian circles.

I met two educated, professional women through OKC who identified as lesbian. I got immediate responses after coming out as trans to them: 1.) "Ann, I'm no longer able to communicate with you," and 2.) "Sorry I have to cancel our call tonight, something's just come up." *Ann, a 64-year-old lesbian transgender woman in Palm Springs, California*

I've been comfortable going to gay bars since my early 20s, but now feel ignored and out of place, and in more lesbian spaces, it feels like I'm seen with great suspicion. *G, a pansexual/queer transgender woman in her late 40s, living in rural Maine*

I identify as a lesbian, yet I have no idea how I would be received in a lesbian-only space. The hate-filled messages from trans-exclusionary radical feminists (TERFs) make me question how I would be received in a lesbian space, and even more so as a potential dating partner. I have zero confidence I would be welcome. *G, a 45-year-old lesbian transgender woman in San Francisco*

6. Younger people are more accepting, but age is still a barrier

Older transgender women—particularly those attracted to women—find a lot more acceptance among Millennials. However, age differences are still challenging.

What I have found is that I see more interest from 20-something ladies. *Much* more interest, where my past seems to be greeted

> with acceptance. That being said, I do find it difficult to accept a relationship with a 23-, 24-, or 25-year-old. Life experience and station in life mean something. Age is *not* just a number. *M, a 43-year-old lesbian transgender woman in Orlando, Florida*

> The few, the very few, experiences I've had in the past four years have been with much younger cis women (20–25 years younger). One identified as queer and the other as bisexual. They both know me very well and know I'm trans. *G, a pansexual/queer transgender woman in her late 40s, living in rural Maine*

7. Transgender people often end up dating other transgender people

For many transgender people, it is easiest to find acceptance with other transgender people. This can make it even more difficult for people living in areas without a substantial queer community, and long-distance relationships are common as a result of the internet.

> Thankfully, the love of my life is a trans man with who I would trust with my life. *Anonymous*

> In learning to love who I am through transition, I learned that I could be attracted to and love other women who are like I am. I suspect that my last statement may be true for many other trans women. We share a history with and understand each other in ways that few others can. *J, a 58-year-old lesbian in Seattle*

> My girlfriend is also trans. We live 2000 miles away from each other. Fortunately, we are sufficiently well-off that we can visit each other every four to six weeks, with phone and Skype filling in the gaps between. Dating a trans woman eliminates the doubt that I will be rejected because I was assigned male at birth, and ensures that we have a common experience. *G, a 45-year-old lesbian transgender woman in San Francisco*

8. Dating other transgender people also poses significant challenges

Getting through transition—and losing friends, family, and relationships as a result—leaves a mark. So does dysphoria. Sharing the same hurts isn't always a good thing.

> Looking into our lover's eyes is like peering into a looking glass, but a distorted one. Because we see all the signs of what our society has taught us is "imperfect" and wrong with us. There is almost no way to look into that mirror and not project our own fears and desires of what we would like our body to look like...
>
> It takes a strength that on many days can be too great for us. Days when we've been mispronouned, misgendered, harassed, ridiculed for our appearance, it can be hard to come home and see those same things in your partner. Some days though, coming home to someone who knows what it is like to go through those things can be a source of strength...
>
> In this way, loving another transgender or gender-variant person is a double-edged sword, and it is unpredictable which side we may find ourselves on depending on the day. *K, a 29-year-old queer transgender woman in Washington, DC*

9. Race/education/religion can make a difficult situation nearly impossible

When you add racial, religious, and educational barriers to transgender ones, it can greatly narrow the available dating pool even further.

> It's very difficult to find friends, much less someone to regularly date, being a trans woman of color. I've found that the same class and race bias that people have before they transition are what they keep when they start living as their target gender.
>
> I live in complete isolation today. Not by choice. The support groups for trans here are almost entirely white and middle class. We have almost nothing in common. The black trans people I've met can't relate to another black with education and [who] comes from a successful career. *A, a 57-year-old queer transwoman in Mesa, Arizona*

Since I am Christian, not a lot of guys in church are ready to date a trans woman. Nothing in the last five years. *M, a 40-year-old straight transgender woman outside Chicago, Illinois*

I'm 70 and Jewish too. Think some mumser gonna look at me? *S, a 70-year-old straight transgender woman in Florida*

10. The kink and BDSM communities are often accepting

Some transgender women find an accepting environment within the kink/BDSM communities. While these are more common in urban settings, they also exist in places with much smaller queer communities.

People in the kink communities are almost by definition open to experimenting sexually. Transgender people are just another variation in the realm of possibilities. From a transgender person's perspective, though, it can be disconcerting and dehumanizing to be treated more like a rare Pokemon that needs to be caught to complete someone's collection.

I find the BDSM/kink community to be extremely open-minded and welcoming in every way; it is a place of sexual liberation. This includes of alternative genders running the whole gamut from part-time cross-dressers to full-time trans girls and trans men to gender-fluid types, as well as alternative religious beliefs and alternative relationship structures.

For what it's worth, I have found acceptance from both lesbians and straight men. But in all cases they've been specifically "trans-interested" rather than generally looking for a woman and agreeing to date me because they see me the same as a woman.

I would like to be seen as no different from a ciswoman. But I find more advantage and companionship through embracing that I am a creature apart. In life, we all do better when we own our uniqueness, and while for a transwoman this can be difficult because it may feel like a failure of transition, it may be better in the end. *E, a 40-year-old queer transgender woman in New York City*

11. Despair is a common theme

Many transgender women who transitioned later, and lost marriages in the process, despair of having a relationship again. They see the odds and circumstances as being so stacked against them that they no longer try.

> So, really if you are older than 30 let's say, and your current relationship fails when you come out as trans, your prospects are dim at best. You also seem to have diminishing returns the older you get. A life of dysphoria, then rejection, then loneliness...great. *A, a 39-year-old lesbian transgender woman in Southwick, Massachusetts*

> At this rate, I do not hold out much hope for finding my love. I've tried all the dating sites with not much success. I do actually feel at this point that it is highly likely I will live out my remaining days alone despite being "amazing" as my friends describe me. What I feel is amazingly lonely. *M, a 43-year-old lesbian transgender woman in Florida*

12. Loving a transgender person is a revolutionary act

Studies on suicide, and my own personal experiences, testify to the power that love and connection have in the lives of transgender people. Loving a transgender person openly is still radical and edgy in our culture. It even carries a lot of risk of the stigma bleeding over onto the partner of the transgender person.

In 2014, the Williams Institute at UCLA released a study which analyzed data on suicide attempts by transgender people. It found that bullying, homelessness, familial rejection, and even rejection by health care providers significantly increased the odds of a suicide attempt.[100]

It isn't being transgender that's killing us, though. It is the culture we live in, discriminating against us and instilling in us a deeply rooted self-hatred.

How can we value our own lives, when we are constantly bombarded with messages that we have less than zero worth as a person because we are transgender? How can we love ourselves enough to live, when our environment tells us that nothing in creation could love a transgender person?

We are told repeatedly that, at best, our bodies are the subject of prurient interest, from the tawdry Maury Povich[101] to the respectable Katie Couric.[102] At worst, our bodies are objects worthy of only disgust and revulsion.[103] When we fail to accede to demands that we make our bodies public knowledge, we are told that the violence against us which follows is justified. We are called liars, deceivers, and traps for failing to announce our transgender status to the world. We are then beaten and murdered when we give the information demanded of us.

Being transgender is seen as so vile that our partners, parents, and children often reject us. We learn that love isn't unconditional, that in fact we cannot be loved by the people who mean the most to us. We are sent the message over and over again, that no one could love us as romantic partners. Life holds only a promise of loneliness and abandonment, and that we deserve solitude for refusing to remain in the closet.

This extends even to the supposedly unconditional love of God. The dominant message from Christianity towards transgender people is "return to living in your birth gender, or burn in hell."[104] We are not welcome. God only loves us if we aren't transgender.

We are told our core identities are a delusion that needs fixing.[105] The ignorant believe we should be put in camps, or thrown in mental hospitals.[106] Pockets of supposed professionals whom we are not allowed to gainsay push their pet theories that gender identity doesn't exist: That all transgender individuals are either self-hating homosexuals or heterosexuals with a fetish.[107] Either way, we are told our identities are wrong, and that in being wrong, we are worthy only of pity and disgust.

We are told that when we are mistreated, bullied, fired, denied housing, or refused service, it is exactly what we deserve[108] for being freaks.[109]

In a post-*Lawrence v. Texas* America, where lesbians and gays have had the right to be with whom they love for over a decade, transgender people are having their basic bodily functions criminalized.[110] We are told that we are rapists and violators of women[111] and children.[112] We are told the only difference between a transgender person and a convicted pedophile is the conviction. We are ordered to accept the fact that other people's irrational fears supersede our actual need for physical safety, because we are too alien and loathsome to ever hope for empathy.

When we do try to set boundaries, the reaction is swift.[113] We are told it's all in good fun, we should expect the kind of language we endure, that people have a right to know about our bodies, and to stop being so sensitive. When we try to preserve ourselves from actual physical harm, we go to prison.[114] When we die at the hands of our attackers, they try to mitigate the crime with the worthlessness of all transgender people.[115]

All the while, most of the LGBT people murdered in hate crimes are transgender women.

In the face of such unremitting and remorseless pressure to despair, we dream of simply being loved by anyone, even if it is only in the internal security of believing a higher power does so. Yet, even that simple hope is often asking too much. In response, we do not dry up, fester, sag, crust over, or explode.

We implode.

Whether with a bang or a whimper, a gun or a bottle full of pills, transgender people often see suicide as an escape from the omnipresent message that our lives lose all value the instant we come out. We cannot resist when everything around us tells us so; to do otherwise requires us to assume, against conventional wisdom and external evidence, that we are right and everyone else is wrong; that there is a person worth loving beneath the label.

Even in death, though, we are often not granted the dignity of the identity we gave everything to claim. The families, who shunned us in life, then bury us in clothes and names we eschewed.[116]

Being loved requires friends, partners, and family to embrace a belief that runs against our cultural dogma, to act despite the stigma of being seen with "those people," and embrace an unpopular people that are not their own.

This is why loving a transgender person is a truly revolutionary act.[117]

13. Sex

Almost everyone wants to know how transgender people have sex. This is the big one everyone secretly wants to ask, but usually (thankfully) don't.

The problem is the answer isn't very satisfying because, in this case, the answer to a question can best be answered with another question: how does anyone have sex? Transgender people aren't some alien species that copulates through means never seen by human eyes. They have the same urges, kinks, fetishes, orientations, hang-ups, taboos, and so on...

Transgender people can be gay, straight, bi, pansexual, demisexual, queer, asexual, or any other label ascribed to cisgender people. We can have solo sex, sex with lots of people (sometimes all at once), sex with cisgender people, sex with other transgender people, gay sex, straight sex, you name it.

The only real difference is that some transgender people have primary (i.e. genital) sexual characteristics that are phenotypically different from their secondary sexual characteristics (e.g. breasts, hair patterns, fat distribution, etc.). Some transgender people are uncomfortable with certain parts of their bodies, especially during sex. However, there are plenty of straight people who also have body issues when it comes to sex.

In the end, transgender people have the same sorts of body parts as everyone else, and can use them in pretty much the same ways as the rest of humanity. If you ask "Do transgender people do X in bed?" my answer would be, "Can cisgender people do X in bed?" If the answer to the second question is yes, then I am almost certain that some transgender people out there somewhere also do X in bed.

Where the whole thing breaks down is in how we talk about sex, and sexual orientation, when transgender people are involved. The English language, and cultural understandings of sexuality, simply can't handle the nuances of transgender people and the act of sex and sexual attraction.

One of the classic thought exercises in quantum mechanics is Schrödinger's cat. The imaginary cat is sealed inside a lead-lined box along with a radioactively unstable atom, some poison, and a sensor that releases the poison and kills the cat if that atom decays. The decay of the atom is completely random and unpredictable. Thus, the cat is simultaneously alive and dead to the outside universe in terms of its quantum state as long as it remains unobserved.

Oddly enough, no one bothered to ask the cat whether it had joined the choir invisible.

This seems a great metaphor for defining sexuality as a transgender person. Labels, and orientation, are primarily based on the gender(s) and sex(es) of the people involved in an intimate relationship. Thus, depending on whoever is looking at me and my relationships, I can fall anywhere on the spectrum.

For example, my father, a strict Mormon, believes that you are whatever sex and gender you were assigned at birth. I married a woman, therefore I am straight.

Period. End of sentence.

Because having a simultaneously transgender and lesbian child would probably make his head explode.

Then there are other people who would take me at my word when I say I identify as female, and am attracted to women. Fine. That makes me a lesbian, right? But...then there's surgical status. Can you be a lesbian with a penis? A gay man with a vagina? I would say yes, but many others (mostly non-transgender people) would say no.

Just to make it even more complicated, how do you label relationships between two transgender people? Does identity supersede sex at birth? Does surgical status trump identity when assigning labels? If a man has been only with male-identified individuals, but some of them are transgender, do they count as bi or gay? Do you get to keep your gold star gay (or straight) award if you've slept with a transgender person? I, and many others, would argue that gender identity matters most.

Saying that only you get to define your own orientation may seem like the simple way to solve this Gordian Knot. But, as we all know from the marriage debates, the opinions of others on our sexuality affect our daily lives. While the overwhelming consensus of the transgender community is that a person is whatever they identify as, others (including sometimes the government) base it on other things. The problem is, it's done completely inconsistently.

In a marriage case from 1999, one lawyer wrote about a transgender person's marriage rights then:

> Taking this situation to its logical conclusion, Mrs. Littleton, while in San Antonio, Tex., is a male and has a void marriage; as she travels to Houston, Tex., and enters federal property, she is female and a widow; upon traveling to Kentucky she is female and a widow; but, upon entering Ohio, she is once again male and prohibited from marriage; entering Connecticut, she is again female and may marry; if her travel takes her north to Vermont, she is male and may marry a female; if instead she travels south to New Jersey, she may marry a male.[118]

If being gay means being a second-class citizen in the US, transgender is at least one class below that. In 2012, I was female in Ohio for the purposes of a driver's license, male for the purposes of a birth certificate. Back then, the DOD wouldn't change my gender markers to female because they didn't feel like dedicating the legal resources required to figure out if transgender nuptials performed in states without marriage equality are valid. The Pentagon took one look at our cat-keeping transgender lead box and said, "Hell no, we're not going there. That's a big bowl of nope."

However, other parts of the federal government see just the opposite. The Department of State, Veterans Administration, and Social Security Administration will now recognize me as female, and recognized me being in (legal) a same-sex marriage even before *Obergefell*. My employer recorded me as female, but until 2014 my insurance company had me as a male so that my marriage would be "straight" for the purposes of partner benefits.

In a world that requires gender for labels, I have torn mine up, doused them in gasoline, lit a match, and feverishly danced around the resulting bonfire like it is Burning Man. All the while, it feels as if the world has watched aghast because they just don't know what to say; the English language just can't cope with this. I am many shades and none simultaneously, each completely defined by the observer.

I am Schrödinger's trans.

Chapter 4

MEDICINE/ MENTAL HEALTH

For much of the 20th century, homosexuality was considered a mental disorder, or categorized as such in the *Diagnostic and Statistical Manual* (*DSM*) of the American Psychiatric Association (APA). Much of the animus towards lesbians and gays was couched in patronizing language by medical and mental health professionals, exemplified by a quote by Edmund Bergler in 1956: "I have no bias against homosexuals; for me they are sick people requiring medical help..."[119] It was not removed from the *DSM-II* until 1973, when an APA subcommittee "reviewed the characteristics of the various mental disorders and concluded that, with the exception of homosexuality and perhaps some of the other 'sexual deviations,' they all regularly caused subjective distress or were associated with generalized impairment in social effectiveness of functioning."[120]

Diagnoses which treated distress about being lesbian, gay, or bisexual remained in the *DSM* for another 14 years. However, these were eventually removed because distress over just about anything could then be considered a mental disorder.[121] There are some parallels to how the psychiatric community has evolved on transgender issues as well in recent years, from a disease model, to one based on distress, and there are strong indications that it will eventually be depathologized altogether.[122]

The diagnosis of "gender identity disorder" (GID) was first introduced in the *DSM-III* in 1980 under the category of "transsexualism." The *DSM-IV*, released in 1994, replaced "transsexualism" with "gender identity disorder in adolescents and adults." At the time, transgender individuals were concurrently classified based on their sexual orientation. In theory, treatment was supposed to be agnostic to orientation. In practice, transgender women who were attracted to men were more likely to be approved for treatment by gatekeepers.

Another issue with the *DSM-IV* was that the criteria for diagnosing transgender youth did not require that a child experience dysphoria or have a cross-gender identity, merely that they exhibited stereotypically cross-gender behaviors. For example, a boy who plays with dolls, dresses up, prefers female friends, but does not identify as a girl could have been (and often was) diagnosed with gender identity disorder (juvenile).[123] This created problems later on, as some therapists were claiming to "cure" children who were never transgender to begin with. This conflation of gender identity and gender expression also led to problematic results in research.[124]

The *DSM-5* was a radical departure from earlier versions. Being transgender (or having a transgender identity) isn't in and of itself a mental disorder according to the *DSM-5*, but the distress caused by being transgender still is under the name of "gender dysphoria." The *DSM-5* also rectified labeling children who do not have a cross-gender identity as transgender. Much like the *DSM-II*, the *DSM-5* was something of a compromise. But, as scientific understanding of transgender people is increasing, the way transgender people are regarded is following a similar arc to the depathologizing of homosexuality.[125] The World Health Organization is almost certain to entirely de-list being transgender as a mental disease from the *International Classification of Diseases* guide in the forthcoming *ICD-11*.[126]

Unlike being lesbian, gay, or bisexual, however, there is often a significant medical component to being transgender. Non-surgical interventions may include hormone replacement therapy, intramuscular injections, or transdermal patches or gels.[127] Other non-surgical and non-hormonal cosmetic procedures include laser hair removal, electrolysis, and hair transplants. Surgical treatments to change primary and/or secondary sex characteristics can include procedures to change breasts/chest, external and/or internal genitalia, vocal surgery, or facial features.[128] A transgender person may need any, or none, of these in order to alleviate their gender dysphoria.

This chapter goes through some of the most common questions, myths, and misconceptions about the mental health and medical care of transgender people.

Bottom line up front, however: *if you take away nothing else from this chapter*, know that every major medical and mental health care professional organization in the US (including the American Medical Association, the American Psychological Association, and the American Psychiatric Association) officially supports access to affirming care for transgender people, and the necessity of treatment both legally and for insurance purposes.[129] As such, the positions presented here are not simply my own, they are those of the vast majority of the medical profession.

Myths about gender confirmation surgery

People have a visceral negative reaction to the idea of genital surgery. In many ways, the reaction to the idea of gender confirmation surgery (GCS) resembles the reaction some people have to the thought of two men having sex. At the same time, this allows for a lot of false information and misconceptions about health for transgender people to be perpetuated.

The problem is that the lack of understanding about GCS for transgender people is the biggest impediment to actually receiving medically necessary care. This section addresses some of the most common that I have observed over the years.

Myth 1: All transgender people want specific treatments

Treatment of gender dysphoria does not include any specific treatment. Indicated treatment is whatever allows relief from the distress caused by the incongruence between someone's identity and their lived experience.

As such, some people only undergo a social transition. Others may have HRT, breast augmentation or reduction (top surgery), hair removal, facial surgery, or GCS. However, for those people who need GCS, access to care is a serious issue.

Myth 2: It's not life or death

For individuals with severe dysphoria, the inability to obtain GCS can negatively affect sexual functioning, self-esteem, body image, socio-economic adjustment, family life, relationships, psychological status, and general life satisfaction. This is supported by the numerous studies, which also consistently show that access to GCS reduces suicidality by a factor of three to six (between 67 percent and 84 percent).[130] [131] [132] [133] [134] Eighty percent of transgender people contemplate suicide, and 41 percent of transgender people attempt it.[135] Lack of access to care is in fact likely to kill many transgender people. If this was a type of cancer that had the potential to kill 41 percent of the people who developed it, and it was possible to reduce the mortality rate by similar percentages, there wouldn't be any argument happening.

It doesn't even have to be life or death to be medically necessary, though. A herniated disk won't kill you, but it will wreck your quality of life. Similarly, this is why every major medical, psychological, psychiatric, and therapist organization in the US has issued statements supporting the medical necessity of GCS.[136] The court system is increasingly acknowledging this, with five circuit courts having ruled that withholding transgender-specific health care from prisoners is a violation of the 8th Amendment, because it is medically necessary.

Myth 3: These people need therapy, not surgery

Medical and mental health care professionals have known for over 50 years that efforts to change a person's gender identity are ineffective. Dr. Harry Benjamin deduced as much in 1966:

> Psychotherapy with the aim of curing transsexualism, so that the patient will accept himself as a man, it must be repeated here, is a useless undertaking with present available methods. The mind of the transsexual cannot be changed in its gender orientation.[137]

Given that aligning mind with body had proven wildly unsuccessful, Dr. Benjamin concluded:

> Since it is evident, therefore, that the mind of the transsexual cannot be adjusted to the body, it is logical and justifiable to attempt the opposite, to adjust the body to the mind. If such a thought is rejected, we would be faced with a therapeutic nihilism to which I could never subscribe in view of the experiences I have had with patients who have undoubtedly been salvaged or at least distinctly helped by their conversion.

In the 50 years since Dr. Benjamin wrote this, no one has ever demonstrated a way to change a person's gender identity under controlled, clinical conditions. Not that they didn't try.

The mental health community tried for decades to change people's gender identities, the same way they tried to change sexual orientation. Drugs. Talk therapy. Physical abuse. Aversion behavioral modification.[138] Electroshock therapy.[139] Lobotomies. Chemical castration. Institutionalization. It doesn't work.[140] Dr. Benjamin described some of the torturous methods applied to transgender people in the 1950s and 60s:

> The transvestitic patient is given an emetic drug (such as apomorphine). As soon as nausea develops, he has to view slides of himself dressed as a woman, prepared beforehand, and at the same time he has to listen to tape recordings describing in detail the mode and technique of "dressing." This form of treatment continues until vomiting occurs or acute illness prevents continuation.[141]

Fifty years later, Dr. Jack Drescher, one of the authors of the *DSM-5* section on gender dysphoria, addressed the issue of changing people's gender identity: "...I don't know of anybody who's discovered a way to actually talk a transgender person out of their gender dysphoria."[142]

This is why California, Illinois, New Jersey, Washington DC, and others have banned reparative therapy in minors to change sexual orientation *or* gender identity. Those bans are holding up in court, because the overwhelming scientific consensus is that you can't change a person's gender identity, and you can't just make their dysphoria go away with anti-depressant drugs or talk therapy. If you could, then that would be the preferred treatment, not expensive and invasive surgery.

Support for the necessity of GCS is based on scientifically based national medical research, professional medical specialty organizations, and widely and generally accepted medical standards, and is supported by prevailing peer-reviewed medical literature.

The opposition to the notion of necessity comes from religious objections to transgender people, well, mostly just existing, and from people who generally aren't qualified to be making medical decisions anyway.

Myth 4: It's cosmetic

Again, every major medical, psychological, psychiatric, and therapist organization agrees GCS isn't cosmetic. AMA Resolution 122 states:

> An established body of medical research demonstrates the effectiveness and medical necessity of mental health care, hormone therapy and sex reassignment surgery as forms of therapeutic treatment for many people diagnosed with GID... Health experts in GID, including WPATH, have rejected the myth that such treatments are "cosmetic" or "experimental" and have recognized that these treatments can provide safe and effective treatment for a serious health condition.[143]

Indeed, GCS improves functionality in socio-economic status, family life, sexuality, and mental health.

The irony surrounding the first three myths on this list is that they are generally perpetuated by people who would be outraged if bureaucrats were making medical decisions for them instead of their doctors. These same people, however, are perfectly fine with the public making health care decisions for transgender people instead of actual doctors, psychiatrists, and psychologists.

This should be a giant red flag. Consider that the last few times we ignored medical ethics on the treatment of unpopular minorities, we ended up with the Tuskegee Experiment and the AIDS (acquired immune deficiency syndrome) epidemic.

Myth 5: Transgender people are just wimps because they can't handle the mental strain

Existing halfway between genders is stressful. Imagine for a moment if you woke up one morning with the wrong factory equipment. Most people can't. However, Chloë Sevigny, who played a transgender assassin on the TV series *Hit & Miss*, found wearing a prosthetic penis unbearable. "I cried every day when they put it on," she said in an interview. This, for a prosthetic that she knows isn't real, and comes off when the day is over.

When lesbian journalist Norah Vincent tried to live as a man as a social experiment, it took less than a year before the strain caused her to have herself voluntarily committed.[144]

When straight, healthy, cisgender people try and pull off what transgender people do on a daily basis (live in the wrong gender), the strain is enough to cause a deterioration in mental health.

Myth 6: It's not like being born with one arm

Actually, it's similar neurologically. There's significant evidence by Ramachandran that transgender people are hard-wired with their brains expecting one set of physical characteristics, but physically having another.[145] Ramachandran found similar phenomena in people with phantom limb sensations.

This is potentially the reason why GCS has been successful where other treatments have failed. It is far easier to align the body with the mind than the other way around when body image is so deeply hard-wired.

Myth 7: Mental health has nothing to do with your physical body

If something was physically wrong with your genitals, how desperate would you be to have it fixed? How would you feel if the problem couldn't be fixed? Think you'd be depressed because you potentially face a lifetime of solitude and celibacy? Of feeling like a freak every time you looked in a mirror, went in a bathroom, took a shower...?

It is very difficult for transgender people to have romantic relationships, because many cisgender people's sexuality isn't able to handle mismatched primary and secondary sexual characteristics. The incongruence between the brain's internal body map and the physical body is also very distressing.

Myth 8: Treat the depression, not the gender dysphoria

It's better to treat the underlying problem than the symptoms. Some people with gender dysphoria have depression, and it needs to be addressed. However, it is unlikely that the depression will be resolved without treating the gender dysphoria. Doing so would be sort of like treating a herniated disk with opioids instead of surgery.

Myth 9: I don't want to pay for that

Study after study shows that including medical benefits for transgender people costs close to nothing in the aggregate.[146] The Transgender Law Center put it in perspective when it noted that if a health care plan costs you $4000 in a year, then adding transgender coverage would add 17 cents per year to the cost of the policy. For comparison's sake, the DOD spends at least ten times as much on erectile dysfunction drugs as it does on transgender health care.[147]

In short, the cost of covering transgender health care is so small that people would not even notice if it was added.

Myth 10: It's mutilation of healthy tissue

GCS is not mutilation. It is reconstructive.

Professionals generally agree that "genital surgery" cannot be considered purely cosmetic but, rather, an intervention to end lifelong suffering, and therefore "*reconstructive*."[148] Given Ramachandran's findings, GCS is much more accurately described as reconstructive surgery. The overwhelming body of evidence showing an improved quality of life (including sexual function) for people who have had GCS also supports this description. As WPATH explains, "medical procedures attendant to sex reassignment are not 'cosmetic' or 'elective' or for the mere convenience of the patient. These reconstructive procedures are not optional in any meaningful sense, but are understood to be medically necessary for the treatment of the diagnosed condition."[149] The AMA has also stated that these procedures are not cosmetic:[150] "It is important to stress that surgery is not a cosmetic intervention, but one that attempts to reconcile an individual's core identity and physical characteristics."[151]

When objective arbiters have looked at this question, they have come to the same conclusion: that GCS is reconstructive, and not cosmetic. An appellate court found: "We do not believe, by the wildest stretch of the imagination, that [genital reassignment] surgery can reasonably and logically be characterized as cosmetic."[152] Treating GCS as "cosmetic" ignores the wide variety of consequences associated with lack of access to care. The same court stated, "It is clearly impossible to conclude that transsexual surgery is cosmetic surgery."[153] Similarly, in *Davidson v. Aetna Life & Casualty Insurance Company*, the insurance company argued that "there is nothing physically wrong" with the body and that the problem is purely mental.[154] The court disagreed and found that:

> The papers submitted herein on behalf of the plaintiff indicate that in order for the plaintiff to live a normal life, sex-reassignment surgery is imperative and necessary. Cosmetic surgery is surgery which is deemed optional or elective. The surgery, which is lengthy, requires extensive modification and realignment of the human body. It is requested rarely, and done even more infrequently. It is performed to correct a psychological defect, and not to improve muscle tone or physical appearance. While many seem appalled at such surgery, it nevertheless has demonstrated proven benefits for its recipients, although psychological in nature. From all of the above the court concludes that the treatment and surgery involved in the sex change operation of the plaintiff is of a medical nature and is feasible and required for the health and well-being of the plaintiff. The same cannot be considered to be of a strictly cosmetic nature.[155]

Myth 11: I'm actually a feline trapped in a human's body. Can I get surgery to make me a cat?

When people use this argument, they assume that transgender people are mentally ill (they're not), assume it's a delusion that can be cured via reparative therapy or lots of praying and self-flagellation (wrong), and ignore one key fact. People can naturally be mentally hard-wired to identify as male or female. We have 40-plus years of neuroscience research basically telling us that gender identity and body image are written early on in development, and sometimes they don't match. People naturally identify as one gender, or another, or neither.

People, however, do not naturally identify as a cat, or as an attack helicopter for that matter.

Myth 12: I don't like the term gender confirmation surgery

The other two most common medical terms used are sex reassignment surgery (SRS), and gender reassignment surgery (GRS). However, given the growing evidence that gender dysphoria stems from incongruence between the brain's internal body map and the physical body, gender confirmation surgery is probably the most accepted term currently.

Myth 13: Eww. Ick

All surgery is inherently icky. That doesn't mean it isn't necessary or beneficial. If someone's mind isn't aligning with their body and surgery is the best option to fix this issue, then this is the appropriate action, regardless of whether it squicks people out. Eye surgery gives me the heebie-jeebies, and I'm not waging a war on ophthalmologists.

Myth 14: They should pay for it themselves

Fundamentally, we live in a culture where insurance, which spreads costs around, pays for our medical expenses. Most people cannot afford medical care in the US without insurance. Who has $25,000 lying around, a corporate short-term disability policy, a supportive supervisor, and/or the means to fight an 18-month legal battle against an insurance company? Unless you're one of the lucky few transgender people who work at a big company with very pro-LGBT policies, these are the hurdles you face. Simultaneously, transgender people face massive discrimination in the workplace, suffer twice the national average unemployment rate, and live in extreme poverty four times more often than the general public (despite being twice as likely to hold advanced degrees).[156]

For most transgender people, this isn't even an option.

Myth 15: It doesn't change your DNA

While true in a technical sense, this is irrelevant as to whether this is an appropriate treatment. While GCS does not change one's DNA, it changes one's physical body in a way that relieves distress and improves functioning by making the mind and body more congruent.

Additionally, there are intersex people whose identities vary from their chromosomes as well. The relevant part of the discussion is whether GCS is medically necessary (it is, in the opinion of everyone who matters), and if it significantly improves quality of life (it does).[157] In the end, it does not matter if it makes you a "real" man or woman by some definition, only that it produces healthier, more functional individuals. Which it does, hence the support of medical necessity by medical and mental health organizations.

Eight myths about transgender men's genital reconstructions

Note: I did not write this section. It was written by Mitch Kellaway, an award-winning journalist and transgender man in response to the section I wrote about GCS myths. I am including it here not just because I think a transgender man should write about medical care for transgender men, but because it's better than anything I would have written. It is presented here with Mr. Kellaway's permission.

Recently, writer Brynn Tannehill produced a list of misconceptions that plague people's understanding of gender confirmation surgeries (in particular, those of the genital variety). Perusing her inventory, I nodded in recognition at every barb; like her, I've heard all these and more hurled at me, my loved ones, or my comrades online. "It's not life or death," "It's cosmetic," "You need therapy, not surgery," and "It will burden taxpayers" are among the many toxic myths in need of exploding.

Inspired, I decided to build on this conversation by considering the specific fictions concerning trans male procedures and embodiments.

So—with the caveats that this list is not exhaustive and I am no medical expert—it's time to bust some myths!

Myth 1: Without genital reconstruction, transgender men aren't "real" men

I look forward to a day where this goes without saying: Being a man is so much more before and beyond what's in one's pants.

Rather, being a man is first and foremost about knowing oneself as a man, working toward being the kind of man one wants to be, and being acknowledged publicly and intimately as a man if that's necessary to one's self-actualization.[158] The individual—not the system—knows best.

Cisgender and transgender men share these needs, and we also share feelings of hurt (and possibly threats) when our manhood goes unacknowledged or denied, particularly based on external factors like perceptions of our anatomy. This is the case whether one's genitals are exposed (which is irrelevant to 95 percent of interactions) or not.

Myth 2: There's only one kind of genital reconstruction

Media portrays transgender people as seeking *the* surgery—you know, that one, single "sex-change" operation?

The reality, however, is that transgender people seek many gender confirming surgeries, and the most popular among men—chest reconstruction—does not even have to do with the genitals.[159] Concerning genital reconstruction, the go-to image is of a surgery that creates a penis (or whatever a man may refer to this organ as). For this goal, there are actually two different procedures men seek.

A metoidioplasty is the removal of the ligaments surrounding a testosterone-enlarged phallus/clitoris, allowing it to protrude further from the body.[160]

A phalloplasty is a construction of a penis from tissue harvested from either the forearm, the side of the chest, the pubic area, or the thigh.[161] Men sometimes first undergo a metoidioplasty and then later undergo a phalloplasty.

In addition, there is a host of other reconstructive surgeries that take existing tissues to construct or enhance parts: urethraplasty/urethral lengthening, scrotoplasty (constructing the scrotum),[162] and glansoplasty (constructing the head of the penis).[163]

Furthermore, there are surgeries that pertain to the removal of internal sex organs: hysterectomy (removal of the uterus), oophorectomy (removal of the ovaries), and vaginectomy/colpectomy (removal of the vagina). A mons resection removes external pubic fat so that the genitals protrude further.

All of these are among what transgender men informally refer to as "bottom surgeries." Knowing a man is seeking bottom reconstruction doesn't necessarily clue a listener in to what surgery he seeks—nor should it. A person's body parts are private knowledge, unless they choose to share that knowledge with others. Nobody has a right to know simply by virtue of being curious.

Myth 3: All transgender men want genital reconstruction

This misconception emerges in part from a cultural logic that says that no man would consider himself whole without genitals that most closely resemble those of the average cis male.

In reality, however, transgender men vary in their need for specific embodiments (and cis men vary in their genital shapes!). Just as we should trust the individual to know their own gender, we should trust that they know their own body's needs best.

Two mitigating factors should also be acknowledged here: (a) economic constraints, and (b) identity shifting over time. Many men who need genital reconstruction simply cannot afford it. This adds to the perception that very few transgender men are seeking surgery and is one of the reasons that health-insurance reform is so crucial.[164]

Furthermore, men may live happily for many years without genital reconstruction and then come to know that they need it as part of their self-actualization journey. Shifts in self-perception should be respected even if they seem to contradict what one "knows" about an individual's history.

Myth 4: No transgender men want genital reconstruction

For decades, a type of logic has circulated within and outside transgender communities that male genital surgeries simply aren't "worth it." This could refer to the expense, the pain of recovery, the time investment, or satisfaction with results.

It's important to note that such assumptions aren't merely rooted in practicality. There is a tendency among trans men to dismiss their need for a penis (should they feel this way) because they know they are already men before taking physical measures to manifest this socially, and they are perhaps acutely aware of how damaging gender stereotypes like "size matters" can be.

Furthermore, as Shannon Minter points out in the introduction to *Hung Jury: Testimonies of Genital Surgery by Transsexual Men* (Transgress Press, 2012), many trans men have internalized and perpetuate negative "blanket pronouncements" about surgeries as a coping mechanism for being unable to access them:

> When faced with financial and other barriers that seem to place genital surgeries out of reach, we [trans men] may seek to protect ourselves by devaluing what we cannot have. In addition, because many transgender men have been conditioned to deny our deepest needs, we may believe that we do not deserve genital surgery, or even unconsciously fear that we will be punished if we dare seek it out.[165]

In reality, many transgender men *do* need genital reconstruction to feel somatically whole, so it's important to discuss, openly and without shame or dismissal, the desire and realities of becoming men with penises. Awareness that satisfying surgical options are available is essential to transgender men's well-being.

Myth 5: Genital reconstructions are excessively risky

Every surgery involves risk, and genital procedures are no exceptions. Risks vary for common procedures like metoidioplasty, phalloplasty, hysterectomy, and scrotoplasty. Certain procedures also have multiple steps and techniques that affect risk.[166] A final mitigating factor is an individual's body and health history.

But philosophically speaking, what makes one consider risk excessive or prohibitive? As long as a doctor feels safe performing a procedure, perception of risk largely lies with the patient. And this perception often does not emerge from weighing statistics.

The idea that transgender men's genital reconstructions are too risky is intimately tied up with that previous question of whether surgery is worth it, and with the following question: "Can he do **** with his body afterwards?" And the responses are as varied as the bodies being considered.

If we forego the expectation that any particular appearance constitutes a *real* penis, or that possessing certain functions is all that makes a penis valuable, the question of risk becomes too complex to boil down to "it's too much," and it becomes clearer how risk assessments partly emerge from limiting gender norms—which is often not a great place from which to make self-affirming decisions anyway.

Myth 6: If you can't ** afterwards, there's no point in having genital reconstruction**

It's undeniable: penises hold a reverential place in patriarchal societies. Being born with or without a specific kind of penis (i.e. one of classifiable appearance and functions) is an automatic shorthand for "male" or "non-male" in Western societies. Because of this, having a medico-legally official penis doesn't simply confer a biological sex, it also confers social status and privilege.

So in response to this misconception, I'd first have to ask: Why should "penis = man"? That one-shot deal doesn't leave enough room for the beautiful diversity of lived gender. No one, transgender or cisgender, should have to "prove" that they have any specific body parts to have their gender respected. And indeed, a transgender man can understand himself as having a penis without any surgical intervention.

Still, if we try to fill in the blank, it's easy enough to come up with preconceived answers: "urinate while standing," "no longer be able to become pregnant," "have an X-inch-long penis," "have penetrative sex," "have testicles," "ejaculate sperm," "non-manually produce an erection," "no longer have a vagina," "have a certain genital shape," "feel certain sensations," "be able to impregnate someone," and so on.[167]

But the realities of why men seek surgery are again more complex than normative expectations. Every individual certainly does not desire all these things. Furthermore, if there are desires men have for their genitals that are not quite achievable through surgery, this does not mean that the reconstructions they do receive are a wholly unnecessary step on their journey. In fact, the "ideal" male genitalia these ideas evoke aren't achievable for many cisgender men either.

Myth 7: Little progress has been/will be made in available procedures

Genital reconstructions, like most surgeries, continue improving as surgeons practice them. As scholar Dr. Trystan Cotten points out in *Hung Jury*:

> New developments and breakthroughs in medical knowledge, surgical techniques, and technology are occurring every year. Surgical outcomes depend on a variety of factors...[that] combine in ways that are unique and specific to each person, affecting everyone's healing and surgical outcomes differently. Thus it is difficult (and perhaps impossible) to make objective generalizations...[168]

Misconceptions about a lack of progress emerge mostly around phalloplasty. However, it's clear from the array of techniques available that this procedure has improved greatly over the past several decades and will continue to do so. There are multiple options for skin donor sites, length and appearance, achieving and maintaining rigidity, and the construction of the scrotum (if needed).

Considering surgeons' websites and portfolios, consulting with them directly, talking with former patients, and reading research are some of the quickest ways to bust this myth.

Myth 8: Transgender men cannot obtain correct legal gender documentation without genital reconstruction

My answer to this myth is admittedly US-centric, as that's where my personal experience lies, but I imagine and hope its applicability ranges to many countries.

Historically, proof of "sex-change" surgery was required for a transgender person to be able to change their gender on legal documents in the US. However, according to the National Center for Transgender Equality, about half of US states have nixed that requirement, and more are expected to do so.[169] A major policy change in 2013 saw the Social Security Administration implicitly acknowledge that not all transgender people need surgery, nor are they all able to access it if needed.[170]

There are many identifying documents whose use varies from situation to situation: state IDs, passports, birth certificates, marriage certificates, death certificates, Social Security cards, and more. Policies on these shift across state lines or over time, making it impossible to say whether surgery will be required (and what *kind* of surgery, since chest reconstruction can often count).

One thing is for certain, however: a transgender man is a *man* whether he has a legal "M" on all his documents or on none of them, or has a mix of gender markers; whether or not he needs or obtains surgery; and, finally, whether or not he has enough socio-economic privilege to access health care.

Again, my thanks to Mitch Kellaway for allowing me to include his material on GCS for transgender men in this book.

Myths about transition regret

One of the most common attacks on access for medical care for transgender people are concern trolls who ask the leading question, "What if they end up regretting it?" Their usual goal is to lead people down a rhetorical path towards supporting "reparative therapy" on transgender people, which is basically "pray away the gay" with a different label. They leave this detail out, of course, along with the fact that no one has ever demonstrated an effective way to change someone's gender identity. Also left out is that the overwhelming majority of peer-reviewed studies on regret rates show them to be low by any objective standard.

Unfortunately, socially conservative people with media platforms who have no actual psychological, psychiatric, or medical training[171] are frequently given the opportunity to expound in conservative media on why they believe transgender people aren't real, shouldn't be allowed to transition, or just need some old-school "reparative therapy" complete with screaming, pillow whacking, and cuddling with a "therapist."[172]

Recently there have been some blog posts raising the specter of transgender people regretting transitioning.[173] Social conservatives have seized on these anecdotes to allege that no one should transition, without actually looking more deeply into the root causes of regret, how such a ban would affect most transgender people, or even if these people wanted their stories to be used this way.[174]

These people with no credentials usually cite their two favorite studies, without actually looking at what the studies say. In short, they try to muddy the waters in the same way that climate-change deniers or creationists do: by throwing up a cloud of chaff and hoping no one will look any closer. And then there's the fact that the authors of these blog posts also thought that same-sex marriage would abolish all marriage (which clearly didn't happen).[175]

Let's deconstruct the arguments being trotted out one by one.

Myth 1: Regret is common

Surgical regret is actually very uncommon. Virtually every modern study puts it below 4 percent, and most estimates put it between 1 and 2 percent.[176] [177] [178] [179] [180] In some other recent longitudinal studies, none of the subjects expressed regret over medically transitioning.[181] [182]

These findings make sense given the consistent findings that access to medical care improves quality of life along many axes, including sexual functioning, self-esteem, body image, socio-economic adjustment, family life, relationships, psychological status, and general life satisfaction. Indeed, one of the most recent studies found that:

> In both samples we found high levels of satisfaction in all the areas explored (including sexual life after surgery), and levels of psychological and social well-being comparable to those of the general population... Our results support previous studies suggesting that SRS not only alleviates gender dysphoria but also improves quality of life and psychosocial functioning in transsexual persons.[183]

Regret rates have also declined significantly over the past four decades as societal stigma has declined and surgical technique has improved. Dr. Cecilia Dhejne noted that, over the period of 1973–2010, regret rates in Sweden dropped from 2.4 percent. The rates dropped to 0.3 percent (three tenths of 1 percent, or 3 out of a thousand) in the 2001–2010 time period. This is despite the number of GCS surgeries increasing threefold over that period.[184]

Regrets were always rare, and are becoming ever more so as care for transgender people improves and they live in more accepting societies. Restricting access to a medical procedure that benefits 98–99 percent of people receiving it is not supported by the evidence.

Myth 2: A Swedish study shows post-operative people are more much more likely to commit suicide[185]

This statement grossly misrepresents the findings of the study and suggests that the study argues against transition-related care—quite the opposite. The study states outright that medical transition is supported by the other research, and the study is not intended as an argument against the availability of such treatment. Dr. Cecilia Dehjne wrote in her 2011 study:

> For the purpose of evaluating whether sex reassignment is an effective treatment for gender dysphoria, it is reasonable to compare reported gender dysphoria pre- and post-treatment. Such studies have been conducted either prospectively or retrospectively, and suggest that sex reassignment of transsexual persons improves quality of life and gender dysphoria.

In a 2017 interview, when Dr. Dhejne was asked how her study cannot and should not be used, she wrote, "I have said many times that the study is not designed to evaluate the outcome of medical transition. It *does not* say that medical transition causes people to commit suicide."[186]

Dhejne's study has been consistently misrepresented by right-wing pundits to try and prove that medical care for transgender people is ineffective. They deliberately leave out Dr. Dhejne's own caveats, as well as the fact that her study did not compare treated and untreated transgender people. Indeed, another study in 2009 found that 95 percent of individuals who transitioned reported positive life outcomes as a result.[187]

Additionally, the higher mortality rates are in comparison with the general populace rather than other transgender people who have not received treatment, and only apply to people who transitioned before 1989:

> In accordance, the overall mortality rate was only significantly increased for the group operated on before 1989. However, the latter might also be explained by improved health care for transsexual persons during the 1990s, along with altered societal attitudes towards persons with different gender expressions.[188]

It should come as no shock that as society accepts transgender people, they suffer fewer side effects of minority stress, which is exemplified by the chronically high levels of stress faced by members of stigmatized minority groups and is discussed in detail later in this chapter. This conclusion is supported by other recent studies that found that individuals who receive treatment are not only better off than those who didn't, but not significantly different in daily functioning from the general population:

> Male-to-female and FM individuals had the same psychological functioning level as measured by the Symptom Checklist inventory (SCL-90), which was also similar to the psychological functioning level of the normal population and better than that of untreated individuals with GID...[189]

> The mental health quality of life of trans women without surgical intervention was significantly lower compared to the general population, while those transwomen who received FFS, GRS, or both had mental health quality of life scores not significantly different from the general female population.[190]

Myth 3: But there's the 2004 British study that says gender confirmation surgery (GCS) isn't effective[191]

This statement is another gross misrepresentation of the research. The study in question was an update of a 1997 study and concluded that, between 1998 and 2004, only two studies on the effectiveness of GCS had partially met the criteria of being peer reviewed and having both a control group and a dropout rate of less than 50 percent. Of those two studies, both showed that patients benefited from the treatment. But the small sample size of the studies prohibited the update from drawing any conclusions on the effectiveness of GCS.

The problem is that meeting the requirement of double-blind studies with control groups using transgender individuals is both impractical and ethically unacceptable. You cannot refuse treatment to a group of people who are at high risk without it, and there's no placebo for gender confirmation surgery or hormone treatment.

But this does not mean there hasn't been research: there are almost 80 peer-reviewed journal articles showing the effectiveness of transition-related medical care, most of which were conducted after 2004.[192] In 2014, another study by Dr. Cecilia Dhejne, the lead author of the first Swedish study described above, addressed the dropout-rate issue in a study of all Swedish applicants for GCS between 1970 and 2010. She found a 2.2 percent regret rate for both sexes, and a significant decline in regrets over the time period.[193]

In short, this meta study is over a decade old, leaves out scores of new peer-reviewed studies and the conclusions drawn by every major medical and mental health professional organization in the US, and ignores the reality that conducting "gold standard" studies is nearly impossible when there is a strong reason to believe you could kill the patient by ignoring the established standards of care.

Myth 4: But what about the people who had regrets?

Any surgery comes with a risk of regret. It just happens that the risk of regret for GCS is actually much lower than for many other surgeries. Indeed, the regret rate for GCS compares favorably with gastric banding.[194]

When asked about GCS regrets, only 2 percent of respondents in a survey of transgender people in the UK had major regrets regarding the physical changes they had made,[195] compared with 65 percent of non-transgender people in the UK who have had plastic surgery.[196]

Risk factors for negative outcomes often mentioned in studies are lack of support from the patient's family, poor social support, late-life transitions, severe psychopathology, unfavorable physical appearance, and poor surgical results.[197] [198] [199] [200] Another study concluded that results of surgery may be more important for global outcome than preoperative factors.[201] As techniques have been perfected, the risk of long-term complications has fallen to less than 1 percent in male-to-female surgeries.[202] [203] [204] This follows the pattern of falling regret rates as well.

People who regret physically transitioning are outliers, not the norm.

Myth 5: The transgender community is intolerant of people who regret surgery

No, transgender people just really don't like it when people try to get between us and our doctors.

Given the level of harm involved when medical care is denied, and given how unusual regret is, denying medical care to everyone based on the outliers makes no logical or ethical sense. In other words, you would do more harm to more people by denying everyone access than by keeping the system we have in place or even expanding access. Every major medical organization supports access to transition-related care and deems it medically necessary for a reason: The actual peer-reviewed evidence supports it.[205]

The standards set in place by the World Professional Organization of Transgender Health Professionals, Standards of Care (SOC) v7, are designed to ensure that regret rates are kept low.[206] Many of the anecdotal cases of regret would have been avoided if the SOC had been followed.

The push shouldn't be for less access to care, but for better availability of mental health care and better educated care providers.

Dispelling myths, misconceptions, and lies about gender non-conforming children

One of the transgender issues that seems to draw the most visceral responses is transgender children and youth. It's also an area where the misinformation and myths run the most rampant, often perpetrated by individuals using the "Oh, won't somebody please think of the children!" strategy. As a result, the same bits of misinformation about transgender youth keep coming up over and over again.

Many of these myths are similar to those perpetrated about transgender adults, but others are particular to transgender children.

It's time to put these misconceptions to bed.

Myth 1: Children are too young to know these things or make these decisions

The overwhelming consensus of the psychological community is that gender identity is formed by the age of 2 or 3.[207] The consensus of the medical community is that sexual dimorphism of the brain occurs *in utero* as a result of exposure, or lack thereof, to androgens. In other words, gender identity and expression are often determined before a child is even born.[208] It is only at 2 or 3 that they can express it.

As for making decisions, at early ages the only potential action taken *may* be social transition, which is completely reversible.

Myth 2: You are whatever your bits say you are

This is an evolving area of neuroscience, and there is an emerging body of evidence of the effect of sex hormones on brain development. In utero, the reproductive organs develop and differentiate earlier than the brain does. When the brain later develops in ways that typically differentiate between male and female, it seems to be based on whether or not the androgens are present and received.[209] Usually, because the gonads are already in place and producing minute amounts of hormones, this differentiation allows the brain development to match the typical pattern. When something (such as endocrine-disrupting chemicals) interferes with this process, you can get a mismatch between phenotypes.[210]

A person's sense of self and their gender identity and expression are based on what's between their ears. Who you are as a person is defined by gray matter, not by genitalia.

Myth 3: Gender non-conforming behavior and identities are a result of something the parents did

Usually this line of attack is meant to imply that the children grew up in a broken home, or that somehow the parents were gender non-conforming, ultra-liberal, or somehow encouraged it. This does not account for the many transgender kids who live in conservative, religious, two-parent military families with both parents filling stereotypical gender roles. Wayne Maines became an advocate for his transgender daughter, and transgender children nationwide, despite previously having very conservative philosophies and values. He did not believe transgender children existed until he had one of his own. Watching his child grow, however, he could not deny the fact that she was indeed a girl, not a boy.[211]

But these stories are all anecdotal. Let's see what research has to say about the matter:

> There is no proof that postnatal social environment has any crucial effect on gender identity or sexual orientation.[212]

Myth 4: If you just made them behave like a proper boy/girl, it would fix the "problem"

Let's look at two of the most famous case studies of trying to "fix" gender non-conforming children. There was George Reker's case study of "Kirk," an effeminate boy whom he put through reparative therapy as a child in the 1970s by having his parents punish him every time he did anything that wasn't stereotypically male. This "therapy" destroyed Kirk, and he committed suicide at the age of 38.[213]

Then there was the case of David Reimer, who was raised as a girl after a botched circumcision.[214] [215] After the failed circumcision, a behaviorist psychologist named John Money convinced David's parents to have a vaginoplasty (GCS) performed on him, and to raise him as a girl based on the theory that gender was entirely a social construct and entirely a learned behavior and identity.[216] Despite growing up with every social and outward biological factor telling him he was female, Reimer never identified as such, and began living as a male as a teen. He ended up killing himself as well.

In both cases, trying to cram these children into a box they didn't fit in ended up killing them.

Nearly every parent of a transgender child I have met has told me that they reached a point of acceptance when they realized that they had a choice: either accept their child, or lose them altogether.

Myth 5: My kid said he is an elephant. Does that mean I should put him on an all-peanut diet? No! These parents are just being indulgent of a child's fantasy

This book has already discussed that this isn't a fantasy; there are biological origins, and simply identifying as male or female is not abnormal. However, this reminds me of nothing so much as the same sort of ill-considered opinions that people have about raising other special needs children, such as the view that autism can be cured by parents simply disciplining their children more.

It also bears repeating that many of the parents who have children who socially transitioned reached a point where they feared for their child's life. Suicidal ideation can be seen even in very young transgender children.[217] These parents legitimately feared for their children's lives.

Myth 6: When I was young I was a tomboy, and I didn't turn out to be transgender

Individuals saying this sort of thing may have demonstrated some cross-gender behaviors but not a persistent cross-gender identity. The differences between gender expression, gender identity, and gender non-conformity are described in detail in Chapter 1. In general, gender identity is how you see your own gender, and gender expression is how you express yourself overlaid with societal stereotypes of gender.

Thus, there are key differences between them, and such comparisons represent a false analogy.

Myth 7: If you let them socially transition, you're just setting them up to be bullied

This is another form of blaming the victim. Shouldn't we focus on preventing bullying rather than making the victim conform? We do not accept that forcing kids to act "less gay" is right; subjecting an innocent child to coercive behavioral modification is unacceptable. Most people reject the notion that a woman is responsible when she is raped, or that it is her responsibility to avoid being raped rather than it being the responsibility of people not to commit rape.

The parents of transgender and gender non-conforming children aren't to blame if their children are bullied. More often than not, they are already doing everything they can to keep their child alive and happy. If blame is to fall anywhere, it more rightly belongs on those doing the bullying, school administrators who allow it to happen, and the adults in the community encouraging it.

Myth 8: They're giving 10-year-old children hormones!

No. Doctors are prescribing drugs which block the onset of puberty in order to give the child's brain time to mature, and to see how their gender identity solidifies. Generally these drugs are not prescribed until they are 12 or 13.[218] One of the most commonly used drugs to block puberty in transgender children is leuprolide, and has been used on children who aren't transgender to prevent precocious (early onset) puberty.[219] It has been approved for this purpose by the US Food and Drug Administration (FDA) since 1993.[220] The reason that doctors block puberty in transgender children is that forcing a transgender child to go through the wrong puberty is more or less irreversible, does permanent harm in terms of ongoing dysphoria, and results in greater difficulty living in their identified gender when they do transition later. Undoing the effects of going through the wrong puberty with surgery or hormones can be difficult, expensive, or impossible.

Unlike puberty, however, leuprolide is reversible. If a youth on leuprolide decides not to transition, the drug is discontinued and puberty proceeds as normal. Indeed, the Endocrine Society describes this treatment as "fully reversible."[221] The Endocrine Society Guidelines describe why puberty suppression is desirable in terms of physical and psychological outcomes as well:

> Another reason to start blocking pubertal hormones early in puberty is that the physical outcome is improved compared with initiating physical transition after puberty has been completed (60, 62). Looking like a man or woman when living as the opposite sex creates difficult barriers with enormous life-long disadvantages. We therefore advise starting suppression in early puberty to prevent the irreversible development of undesirable secondary sex characteristics.[222]

Myth 9: We don't know what the long-term effects are!

This is usually a form of concern trolling. Leuprolide has been approved by the FDA for blocking puberty in cisgender children since 1993. The people demanding this burden of proof are essentially asking for a clinical trial period of more than 25 years. This is clearly ridiculous, and wouldn't be applied to any other drug or condition. There is much that we don't know about every drug on the market. Clinical trials simply don't last 50+ years; if they did we'd be waiting on Ibuprofen until 2022. The studies we do have on the safety of blockers as a treatment for transgender youth indicate a low clinical risk.[223]

Myth 10: What if these kids change their minds?

Children who haven't undergone any sort of medical treatment would transition back socially.[224] However, after age 11 or 12, this becomes very uncommon. If they are older (12–16) and on leuprolide, they stop taking it, and puberty proceeds typically, just as it would for a child who had been given it to stop precocious puberty.

According to Dr. Norman Spack, a pediatric endocrinologist who specializes in this field:

> [A]t the time that puberty begins—that means between about age 10 to 12 in girls, 12 to 14 in boys, with breast budding or

> two- to three-times increase in the gonads in the case of genetic males—by that particular point, the child who says they are in the absolute wrong body is almost certain to be transgender and is extremely unlikely to change those feelings, no matter how anybody tries reparative therapy or any other noxious things.[225]

Even the most ardent opponent of letting youth socially transition, and proponent of the "80 percent desistance myth" (more on this later), admits that it is very unusual for teens with gender dysphoria to change, and recommends leuprolide for such patients, stating: "...in adolescence the most likely outcome is the persistence of gender dysphoria... The treatment would be social transition and biomedical treatment."[226]

At the age of 16, if the child is still asserting a cross-gender identity, there is almost zero chance that this will change.[227] Very few transgender youth whose dysphoria persists past 13 or so decide they wish to stop treatment. In one Dutch study, 70 transgender youth were offered puberty suppression. None of them decided to stop the treatment over the course of the multi-year study.[228] Only after reaching 16 are cross-gender hormones administered.

In short, the medical and mental health protocols are designed to only take permanent medical steps after everything possible has been done to ensure that this is the correct course of treatment. Until that point, everything is reversible. Along the way, however, steps are being taken to minimize potential harm to the patient whether or not they are transgender. As a recent study concluded, "most of the risks that children who socially transition and their families may experience are based on minority stress in response to unsupportive environments."[229]

Myth 11: These kids should have to wait until they're 18 before doing anything medically (including puberty-blocking drugs). What if they regret it later?

By that time, it is too late to prevent permanent physical changes which will cause lasting psychological harm, and result in increased difficulties functioning in a society which punishes individuals who are visibly gender non-conforming. Puberty has already given them a body that can't be easily fixed. Medical science can attempt to mitigate the harm, but at that point it is expensive and painful, and the results only partially compensate for the effects of going through the wrong puberty. In short, forcing them to wait can (and often does) cause massive, irreparable harm. We see evidence of this in the poor mental health outcomes associated with non-treatment and unsupportive environments, and conversely the excellent mental health outcomes associated with early, affirming treatment.[230]

For example, a March 2018 study of young transgender men who underwent chest reconstruction found that the surgery was effective in relieving their dysphoria. Their mental health was significantly better than the control cohort who were denied the surgery. Surgical complications were rare, and only 1 out of 68 participants expressed even mild regret, which was unrelated to his gender identity.[231]

None detransitioned.

Myth 12: You transgender activists want to force all these children down a medical track

No. No. And a thousand times no. Many of these kids may express themselves differently but do not have a cross-gender identification (e.g. they are a boy who identifies as a boy but likes things that are gender-stereotyped as more feminine). No one wants children who are simply gender non-conforming going down a medical track. Nor do other advocates, nor do mental and medical professionals. This line of argument is a straw-man, since no authoritative figure actually holds this view.

This is also a complete misrepresentation of what affirming therapy actually is. Dr. Colt Keo-Meier, the lead author of Division 44 (LGBT issues) of the American Psychological Association's guidance for treating transgender children, refutes this fear-mongering claim:

> The gender affirmative model supports identity exploration and development without an a priori goal of any particular gender identity or expression. Practitioners of the gender affirmative model do not push children in any direction, rather, they listen to children and, with the help of parents, translate what the child is communicating about their gender identity and expression. They

> work toward improving gender health, where a child is able to live in the gender that feels most authentic to the child and can express gender without fear of rejection.[232]

What parents of transgender and gender non-conforming children want is the same thing that every other parent wants: for their children to be happy, safe, loved, and protected. If medical care will help their children go out into the world with every chance of achieving their potential and having a happy life, then they will fight tooth and nail for it.

It's what any good parent would do.

The desistance myth

Over the past few years, an endless parade of "concerned" people (trolls) have trotted out the same (misrepresented) statistic over and over again: approximately 80 percent of transgender kids supposedly stop being transgender on their own. They have used this to justify everything from reparative therapy on youth, to denying medical care to transgender teens,[233] to suggesting that reparative therapy on adults will work,[234] to justifying legal arguments that transgender people should not have any legal protections from discrimination.[235]

The problem is that the desistance narrative is built on bad statistics, bad science, homophobia, and transphobia.

For starters, the most cited study, which alleges an 84 percent desistance rate, did not actually differentiate between children with consistent, persistent, and insistent gender dysphoria, and kids who just acted more masculine or feminine than their birth sex and culture allowed for.[236] (This is because under the older *DSM-IV-TR* definition of gender identity disorder, distress wasn't a necessary criterion: simply being gender non-conforming was sufficient. Under the *DSM-5*, the criterion was more specified and now there must be distress and a cross-gender identity present for a diagnosis of gender dysphoria.) It also did not take into account the intensity of the feelings of dysphoria, which were already known to be predictive of persistence.[237]

The Steensma study also could not locate 45.3 percent of the children for follow-up, and made the assumption that all of them were desisters. Other studies used to support the desistance narrative also suffered from similar methodological flaws.[238] The conflation of gender identity and gender expression in such studies leads to problematic and flawed interpretations of the results.[239]

As a result, the 84 percent desistance figure is meaningless, since both the numerator and denominator are unknown, because you have no idea how many of the kids ended up transitioning (numerator), and no idea how many of them were actually gender dysphoric to begin with (denominator). When Dr. Steensma went back in 2013 and looked at the intensity of dysphoria these children felt as a factor in persistence, it turned out that it was actually a very good predictor of which children would transition.[240]

Thus, the children who actually met the clinical guidelines for gender dysphoria as children were much more likely to be transgender adults. Further research has shown that children who meet the clinical guidelines for gender dysphoria are as consistent in their gender identity as the general population.[241]

For the past several decades, the biggest promoter of the desistance myth was Dr. Kenneth Zucker at the Centre for Addiction and Mental Health (CAMH) in Canada. Zucker's long and problematic history with the transgender community is discussed in greater detail in Chapter 5. It finally caught up with him in 2015, when an independent investigation[242] led to Dr. Zucker's firing[243] and his clinic being closed.[244]

Perhaps the most eye-opening piece of information coming out of the CAMH investigation was a refutation of Dr. Zucker's claims that gender dysphoria desisted in 80 percent of cases. When questioned by investigators, Dr. Zucker admitted that 70 percent of the kids he saw were "sub-threshold," i.e. did not meet the clinical definition of having gender dysphoria.[245] This means that almost 90 percent of the kids he claimed to have "cured" were never transgender in the first place under the *DSM-5* definition. He built his reputation convincing homophobic and transphobic parents that he could fix their kids. When someone actually got around to listening to the transgender community and pulled back the curtain, they found the wizard was a humbug.

Dr. Kristina Olson is another researcher who works primarily with transgender youth and similarly noted that much of the desistance narrative came from the *DSM-IV-TR* labeling all gender non-conforming children as transgender. She points to Zucker's own observation from 1993 that when asked what their gender was, more than 90 percent of children with gender identity disorder (under the *DSM-IV*) reported an answer that aligned with their natal sex.[246]

Perhaps the most damaging data to the desistance narrative so far comes from Australia. In late 2017, the Australian Family Court examined the desistance narrative using the largest sample of transgender youth ever. The Royal Children's Hospital Gender Service in Victoria began treating transgender youth in 2003, and has taken in 701 patients for assessment. The court found that 96 percent of all youth who received a diagnosis of gender dysphoria from 2003 to 2017 continued to identify as transgender or gender diverse into late adolescence. No patient who had commenced (blockers) had sought to transition back to their birth assigned sex.[247]

The desistance myth is promoted by reparative therapists, religiously motivated anti-LGBT hate groups, concern trolls, and charlatans. It's also no better than a percentage pulled out of a hat to begin with. It's time for the 80 percent desistance figure to be relegated to the same junk science bin as the utterly discredited link between vaccines and autism.

And maybe people should start listening to the transgender community when we say something is going horribly, horribly wrong inside some of the medical institutions with power over us.

The truth about transgender suicide statistics

Sixteen-year-old transgender teen Leelah Alcorn committed suicide in December 2014 by stepping onto an Ohio interstate highway and in front of a tractor trailer. Before she did, she also left behind a note on Tumblr that was a wake-up call to the world regarding what it means to be a transgender youth in a conservative Christian family. She finished her final post with the plea: "Fix society. Please."[248]

Her family rejected her gender identity and made it clear that being loved and accepted was conditional. They put her in Christian "reparative therapy." They systematically cut her off from her social support networks. They denied her the medical care she begged for. In fact, they did everything their Christian leaders command parents of transgender children to do.[249]

Statistically, though, her parents did just about everything possible to maximize Leelah's risk of self-harm, according to the research on risks for transgender youth.[250]

Sadly, Leelah's death was used to intensify attacks on the transgender community and spread misinformation about what causes the high suicide rate. One of the most prevalent attacks on transgender people is that they, as a population, suffer from high levels of suicidality. The anti-transgender argument nested in this is that transgender people are innately mentally unhealthy, and the best way to address this is to make them "not-transgender" by forcing them to spend their lives in the closet or to detransition. Usually this involves some implication of reparative therapy of some sort.

However, when examining the actual factors associated with suicidality, it is not being transgender that is the cause. It is the society they live in which stigmatizes them that results in such high numbers.

It is known that transgender people are at a higher risk of suicide, but why this risk is higher is often not understood by the public, or is misused by people who wish us further harm. The statistic that 40 percent of transgender people have attempted suicide is used all the time to justify all sorts of things that have absolutely zero basis in science.

The reasons why transgender people are at risk is a form of minority stress: something that has actually been studied in great detail by psychologists and sociologists. They have found many of the same factors increase risk across multiple peer-reviewed studies.

Cause 1: Rejection by friends and family increases suicide risk

Transgender people who are rejected by their families or lack social support are much more likely both to consider suicide, and to attempt it.[251] Rejection is not just limited to kicking them out of the house, but can include subjecting them to reparative therapy, using religion to label them as "wrong," and rejecting their identity by refusing to use their preferred name and pronouns.

Conversely, those with strong support were 82 percent less likely to attempt suicide than those without support, according to one recent study.[252] Numerous recent peer-reviewed studies show that transgender youth who are supported in their gender identity by parents, schools, and their peers have significantly better mental health outcomes than those whose identities are rejected or stigmatized.[253] [254] [255] A 2018 study found that simply by using a transgender youth's preferred name reduced suicide risk by 56 percent, and significantly improved their mental health.[256]

Cause 2: Discrimination increases suicide risk

Transgender people in states without LGBT legal protections are at higher risk of suicide. Other studies have found that transgender people who have been discriminated against are at a higher risk of suicide.[257] What makes this worse is that discrimination against transgender people in health care, employment, accommodations, and housing is very common.[258] Even in places with legal protections for transgender people, like Washington DC, cultural bias and discrimination remain.[259]

Cause 3: Physical abuse increases suicide risk

Transgender people who have been physically or sexually abused because they are transgender are at a higher risk of suicide.[260] Additionally, abuse seems to have a multiplicative effect on suicidality with other factors in transgender people.[261] As the number of abusive incidents increases, the more likely the person is to have attempted suicide. The amount of abuse is also associated with the number of times suicide has been attempted. Again, studies on how often transgender people are assaulted show shockingly high levels of violence.[262]

Cause 4: Being seen as transgender or gender non-conforming increases suicide risk

People who are seen as transgender or gender non-conforming are more likely to have attempted suicide.[263] Also, people who have had access to surgery which allows them to "pass," such as facial feminization surgery, report qualities of life not significantly different from the general population.[264] This is significant evidence for the case that minority stress is the primary cause of transgender suicide rates, since it strongly suggests that when transgender people are treated the same as cisgender people, the risk of suicide becomes no different from that for anyone else.

Cause 5: Internalized transphobia increases suicide risk

Internalized transphobia is when a transgender individual applies negative messages about transgender people in general to themselves. Conservatives have run multi-million dollar campaigns smearing transgender people as dangerous sexual deviants in places like Houston and Anchorage as part of efforts to roll back civil rights for LGBT people. These sorts of messages take a toll on the psychological well-being of the transgender people hearing them.[265] When transgender people start applying such messages to themselves, the suicide attempt rate skyrockets.[266]

Cause 6: Intersecting minority identities increases suicide risk

Multiple studies[267] have found that transgender people of color are at higher risk of suicide than white transgender people.[268] This is a result of the combined effects of racial and gender identity discrimination.

Notice a pattern here? None of these risks for suicide are about being transgender. They're about what is being done to transgender people. And therein lies the rub.

There's nothing inherently wrong with being transgender.

There is something horribly, horribly wrong with the way we as a culture treat transgender people.

The US Department of Health and Human Services has addressed the issue of suicide in LGBT populations, and reached the same conclusions on the actual causes of suicide in the transgender community:

> Suicidal behaviors in LGBT populations appear to be related to "minority stress," which stems from the cultural and social prejudice attached to minority sexual orientation and gender identity. This stress includes individual experiences of prejudice or discrimination, such as family rejection, harassment, bullying, violence, and victimization. Increasingly recognized as an aspect of minority stress is "institutional discrimination" resulting from laws and public policies that create inequities or omit LGBT people from benefits and protections afforded others. Individual and institutional discrimination have been found to be associated with social isolation, low self-esteem, negative sexual/gender identity, and depression, anxiety, and other mental disorders. *These negative outcomes, rather than minority sexual orientation or gender identity per se, appear to be the key risk factors for* LGBT *suicidal ideation and behavior.*[269]

This doesn't change the fact that people who push for discrimination against transgender misuse studies,[270] cite "experts" who are proponents of religious-based reparative therapy for all LGBT people,[271] and have no relevant experience working with transgender people. Their so-called logic is that if people weren't transgender and didn't transition, they wouldn't commit suicide. This is the intellectual equivalent of suggesting we should prevent rape by making women wear burqas and chastity belts, and never letting them leave the house.

Their pray-away-the-trans "solutions" to bringing down the suicide rate in the transgender community are almost a guarantee of more suicides. Studies show religious counseling increases the suicide rate in LGB people.[272] Reparative therapy has never been demonstrated to be successful on transgender people, isn't approved by any psychological organization, has no guidelines on how to conduct it, and has no standard metrics of success.

In other words, any attempt to suggest that the solution to the problem of suicide in the transgender community is to stop being transgender is nothing more than chaff. These individuals are more interested in enforcing their brand of Biblical morality on society than the actual well-being of transgender people.

The research on how to best serve transgender youth is unambiguous. Transgender youth who have families that support their transitions and affirm their identities have far better mental and physical health outcomes than those who are not supported.[273] [274] [275] [276] Rejecting the identities of transgender youth does not help them; it only makes life worse for them. It's not a form of "tough love" or "hating the sin and loving the sinner." It's causing direct harm to a child, and the research backs it up.

They're hoping that no one will read this though. They're hoping that no one will think the problem through. What happens when you rape, beat, fire, evict, reject, isolate, demonize, and humiliate a class of people on a daily basis? Would you expect a group of people experiencing this to thrive?

Or would you expect 40 percent of them to try to find escape in oblivion?

Leelah was right. If we want to end the scourge of suicide, it's time we stop trying to fix transgender people.

It's time to fix society.

It's time to ban reparative therapy

In the wake of Leelah Alcorn's death there were renewed calls to legally end the practice of using so-called "reparative therapy" to change children's sexual orientation or gender identity or expression. A Change.org petition to end the practice garnered more than 350,000 signatures.[277] Laws in California, Illinois, New Jersey, Oregon, Vermont, and the District of Columbia have banned the practice.[278] These laws have stood up in court,[279] and no further serious challenges appear to be on the horizon.[280] The jury in a New Jersey case found reparative therapy to be a fraudulent practice, and as a result the National Center for Lesbian Rights, Human Rights Campaign, and Southern Poverty Law Center filed a complaint with the Federal Trade Commission to declare the practice fraudulent at a federal level.[281]

But that hasn't stopped the right from pushing hard on talking points claiming that transgender teens need to be pushed into (religious) "therapy" that no reputable, licensed mental health professional would provide. Their rationales are riddled with half-truths, logical fallacies, and outright lies. As a result, the Williams Institute at the UCLA School of Law estimates that 20,000 LGBT youth currently between the ages of 13 and 17 will be subjected to conversion therapy by a licensed health care professional before they reach the age of 18 in the 41 states that do not ban the practice. Another 57,000 LGBT youth will be subjected to religious-based conversion therapy.[282]

Given the immense harm being done by these practices, here are the facts about conversion (reparative) therapy on LGBT youth.

Fact 1: Transgender and gender non-conforming youth do better in homes that are accepting and supportive of their gender identity

What proponents of reparative therapy always leave out of their talking points is that research by the Trans Pulse Project,[283] the Family Acceptance Project,[284] and the Williams Institute[285] repeatedly shows that the best indicator of positive mental health outcomes in LGBT youth is familial support.

Just so we're clear here: putting a child in reparative therapy, telling them God will send them to hell if they don't stop being transgender, accusing them of being delusional, punishing them for stepping outside gender norms, and denying medically necessary care doesn't fall in the "supportive" category.

Fact 2: By the time a transgender youth reaches adolescence (like Leelah), it is very unlikely that their gender identity will change

Even studies quoted by opponents of transgender equality acknowledge that children with cross-gender identification after puberty rarely change their minds. According to one such study, "One reason for the differing attitudes has to do with the pervasive nature of gender dysphoria in older adolescents and adults: it rarely desists..."[286]

The data coming from the Royal Children's Hospital Gender Service in Victoria supports this observation, in that none of the youth who went on puberty blockers changed in their gender identity.[287]

Fact 3: There is no widely accepted evidence that upbringing can make someone gay or transgender

According to neurobiologists Dick Swaab and Ai-Min Bao, writing in the 2013 textbook *Neuroscience in the 21st Century: From Basic to Clinical*:

> Gender identity (the conviction of belonging to the male or female gender) [and] sexual orientation (hetero-, homo-, or bisexuality)... are programmed into our brain during early development. There is no proof that postnatal social environment has any crucial effect on gender identity or sexual orientation.[288]

Michele Angello, a clinical psychologist who specializes in gender-variant youth, offered her experience in working with transgender youth:

> It's completely inaccurate to assume that someone "becomes" transgender because they have an unstable home environment, experience or witness domestic violence or have been abused.[289]

In other words, upbringing does not affect sexual orientation or gender identity.

Fact 4: According to a recent study, religious counseling makes sexual minorities more likely to attempt suicide

The Williams Institute also found that lesbian and gay people who underwent religious counseling were more likely than those receiving no therapy at all to attempt suicide.[290]

Fact 5: The American Psychological Association and other major clinical organizations consider reparative therapy or coercive behavior modification on transgender adolescents to be harmful

According to the APA's *Gender Diversity and Transgender Identity in Adolescents* fact sheet: "Attempts to force gender diverse and transgender youth to change their behavior to fit into social norms may traumatize the youth and stifle their development into healthy adults."[291]

The World Professional Association of Transgender Health concurs, stating:

> Treatment aimed at trying to change a person's gender identity and expression to become more congruent with sex assigned at birth has been attempted in the past without success,[292] [293] particularly in the long term.[294] [295] Such treatment is no longer considered ethical.[296]

Dr. Angello has experience with these types of therapies. She observes:

> This form of so-called therapy succeeds in shaming the individual and often can appear successful for a finite period of time because the person receives such significant levels of positive reinforcement for returning to their sex assigned at birth. Eventually one of two things typically happens, in my experience: they end up in therapy, with a great deal of shame and guilt, and have to wade through the exhausting battle of self-forgiveness as they begin to acknowledge their authentic gender identity, or they attempt suicide.

Fact 6: Attempts to change transgender people's gender identities won't bring down the suicide-attempt rate

The religious right already tried telling lesbian and gay people they'd be so much happier if they just stopped being gay, since they assume people can simply choose not to be gay at any time. We all know how well that works out.

According to Dr. Angello, "The answer is not attempting to convince an individual that they're not transgender; that's not only ridiculous but impossible long-term."

Transgender people can't choose not to be transgender either. Using coercive behavioral modification on a youth who cannot change who they are is futile and abusive regardless of whether you are trying to change sexual orientation or gender identity.

Fact 7: Depression is a result of gender dysphoria and discrimination, not the cause

Does saying we should try to "cure" homosexuality with anti-depressants because gay people are more likely to be depressed sound stupid? It should, because it is.

While it is true that transgender people do suffer high rates of depression, this is primarily a result of minority stress, discrimination, and lack of access to supportive medical care.

Research bears out the notion of first treating the dysphoria as the underlying cause of the depression. Murad[297] and Ainsworth[298] both found that individuals who receive affirming treatment not only are better off than those who didn't but are not significantly different in mental health functioning than the general population. The oft-cited 2011 study by Dr. Dhejne actually found that health outcomes for transgender people improved over time, suggesting that societal discrimination is a key component of depression in transgender individuals.[299]

In fact, the relationship between minority stress and health is well understood. If you could cure gender dysphoria with Wellbutrin, Zoloft, Prozac, or any other sort of anti-depressant, it would be the preferred method of treatment. However, it is telling that no major medical or mental health organization supports treating gender dysphoria primarily as a symptom rather than a cause.

Fact 8: There is a large volume of peer-reviewed evidence supporting potential biological origins of gender identity

There is a sizeable body of evidence that biological factors seem to influence gender identity, particularly *in utero* hormone exposure and timing. There have been over 100 studies examining biological origins of gender identity and sexual orientation.[300] Recent studies have found brain differences, and hints at combinations of genes that may be the cause.[301] [302]

Just because two studies show that gender dysphoria isn't caused by certain types of chromosome abnormalities[303] or particular kinds of gene mutations[304] doesn't mean that there is no biological basis for being transgender, or that transgender people don't exist. It simply means that those two hypotheses didn't pan out. Given the size and complexity of

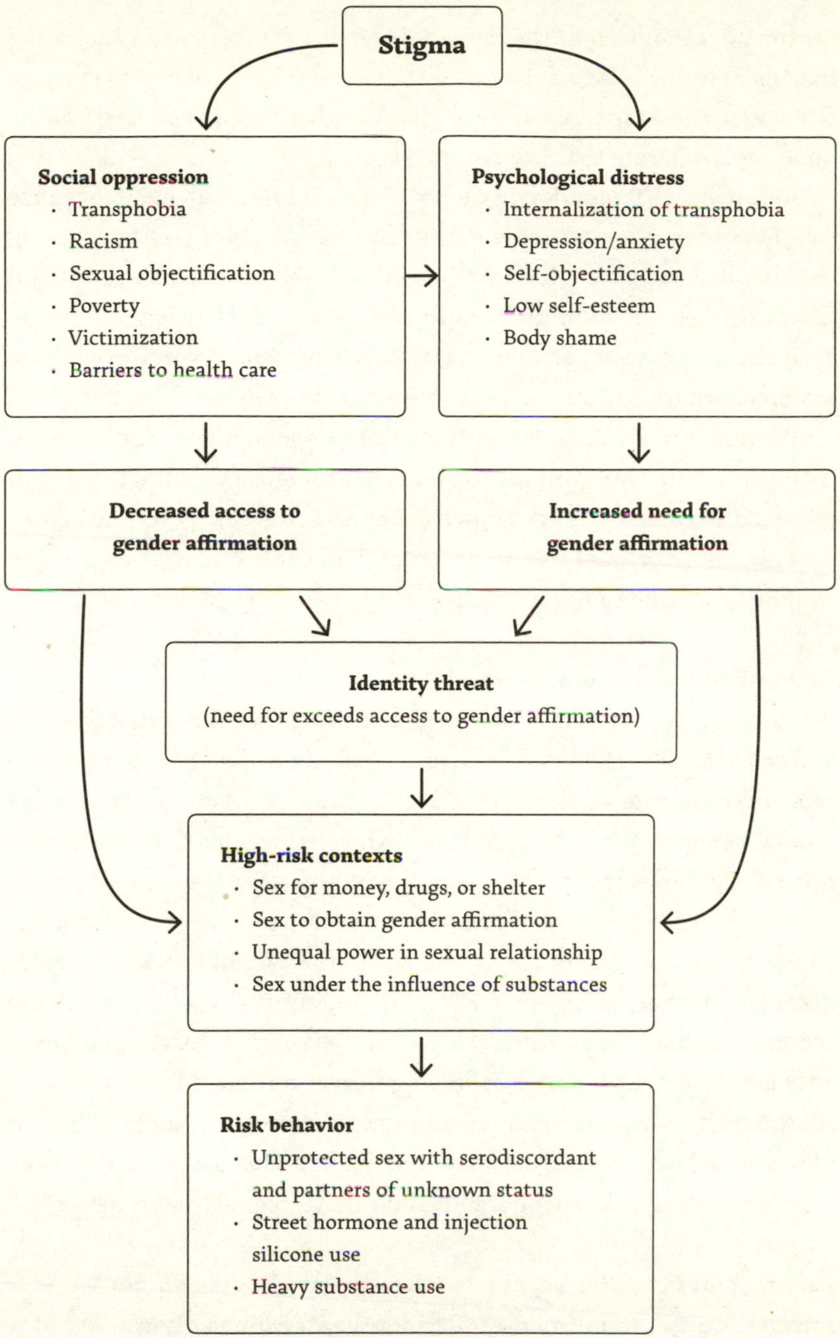

Figure 4.1: Gender affirmation framework for conceptualizing risk behavior among trans women of color[1388]

the human genome, plus the burgeoning field of epigenetics, concluding that there is no biological basis for transgender identities based on two failed hypotheses is a bit like checking your back yard for bears, finding none, and declaring that bears don't exist.

Asserting that gender identity has no biological basis because two hypotheses were disproved is the logical equivalent of saying that because research didn't find a link between vaccines and autism (seriously, there is no link—the original study was falsified), there's no such thing as autism, or that because we can't find a specific gene for sexual orientation, there's no such thing as gay people.

We do not fully understand the origins of gender identity. However, this is not sufficient grounds to state that there is no biological origin, particularly when there is so much evidence to suggest potential causes.

Chapter 5 discusses this evidence, and how it is consistently ignored by groups seeking to harm transgender people, in greater detail.

Fact 9: Transition regret is rare

While covered elsewhere, it is worth reiterating that the actual research and statistics show just how unusual transition regret is. Virtually every modern study puts it below 4 percent, and most estimates put it between 1 and 2 percent.[305] [306] [307] [308] [309] In some other recent longitudinal studies, none of the subjects expressed regret over medically transitioning.[310] [311]

Compare a regret rate of 1–4 percent with regret rates for other surgeries, which runs as high as 65 percent in the case of cosmetic surgery, according to one survey.[312] In short, if you simply went by verifiable regret rates, you'd have to disallow gastric bypass, rhinoplasty, and breast augmentation long before disallowing transition-related care.

Anecdotal evidence cannot take away from the simple fact that affirming related to transition greatly benefits the vast majority of the people receiving it. Denying it harms far more people than it helps.

Fact 10: Laws banning reparative therapy on minors will not force therapists to railroad gender non-conforming children into transitioning

This falls squarely in the category of "pants on fire." The bible of transgender health, the WPATH Standards of Care 7, makes it clear that treatment of the individual is dependent on their specific needs, and that care does not follow a "checklist." The SOC states:

> The overall goal of the SOC is to provide clinical guidance for health professionals to assist transsexual, transgender, and gender-nonconforming people with safe and effective pathways to achieving lasting personal comfort with their gendered selves, in order to maximize their overall health, psychological well-being, and self-fulfillment... [T]his version of the SOC recognizes and validates various expressions of gender that may not necessitate psychological, hormonal, or surgical treatments.[313]

The New Jersey law banning efforts to change sexual orientation and gender identity in minors states:

> b. As used in this section, "sexual orientation change efforts" means the practice of seeking to change a person's sexual orientation, including, but not limited to, efforts to change behaviors, gender identity, or gender expressions, or to reduce or eliminate sexual or romantic attractions or feelings toward a person of the same gender; except that sexual orientation change efforts shall not include counseling for a person seeking to transition from one gender to another, or counseling that:
>
> (1) provides acceptance, support, and understanding of a person or facilitates a person's coping, social support, and identity exploration and development, including sexual orientation-neutral interventions to prevent or address unlawful conduct or unsafe sexual practices; and
>
> (2) does not seek to change sexual orientation.[314]

In other words, if therapists follow both the law and the WPATH Standards of Care 7, they still have a great deal of latitude in treatment options. What they cannot do is work to change the individual's gender identity, whether male, female, or any non-binary possibility.

According to Dr. Angello, "The responsible and ethical therapeutic answer is supporting people's exploration without heaping unnecessary condemnation on them."

That's it. There's no mention of going down any particular medical path.

Fact 11: Laws banning reparative therapy on minors have no effect on clergy or religious counseling

California's law banning reparative therapy on minors defines those affected thus:

> "Mental health provider" means a physician and surgeon specializing in the practice of psychiatry, a psychologist, a psychological assistant, intern, or trainee, a licensed marriage and family therapist, a registered marriage and family therapist, intern, or trainee, a licensed educational psychologist, a credentialed school psychologist, a licensed clinical social worker, an associate clinical social worker, a licensed professional clinical counselor, a registered clinical counselor, intern, or trainee, or any other person designated as a mental health professional under California law or regulation.[315]

Clergy aren't licensed by the state as mental health care providers and are therefore exempt.

Proponents of reparative therapy are essentially concern trolling. It's not that they want to help gender non-conforming children be healthier. It's that they want them back in the closet, and not going to hell, regardless of how it affects them emotionally and physically.

To most of them, this is about religion, and not clinical research into health care outcomes.

Transgender athletes don't have an unfair advantage

Perhaps no transgender issue brings out more anger than the idea of transgender women competing in athletics.[316] This was evident again when a female transgender CrossFit athlete was told, in writing, by the CrossFit governing body that she could not compete as a woman. She in turn filed a suit. However, the most disturbing part of this incident was the offensive and ignorant language used by CrossFit in its letter of explanation:

> We have simply ruled that based upon [Chloie] being born as a male, she will need to compete in the Men's Division... The fundamental, ineluctable fact is that a male competitor who has a sex reassignment procedure still has a genetic makeup that confers a physical and physiological advantage over women... Our decision has nothing to do with "ignorance" or being bigots—it has to do with a very real understanding of the human genome, of fundamental biology, that you are either intentionally ignoring or missed in high school.[317]

They were kind enough to note that transgender women are welcome to compete, so long as they do it in a division in which they have no hope of being competitive. "Transgendered [sic] athletes will be welcomed with open arms in this community, but what we will not waver from is our commitment to ensure the fairness of the competition."[318]

The first, most glaring, problem with these statements is that they are not based in any sort of modern evidence about transgender people in sports. Additionally, saying such things as a representative of a corporate entity has legal implications. The case was filed in California, where transgender employment protections are embedded into state law, and the Ninth Circuit long ago applied heightened scrutiny to sex discrimination claims filed by transgender plaintiffs.

Fundamentally, though, it shows a lack of awareness of the current medical thought on the issue of transgender athletes. The overwhelming consensus is that after some period of time on hormone replacement therapy, transgender individuals should be allowed to compete in accordance with their legal gender.

The International Olympic Committee (IOC) settled the issue of transgender athletes in 2004, when it released the rules for them to compete.[319] These were updated in 2016 by removing surgical requirements and bringing the period of HRT in line with existing National Collegiate Athletic Association (NCAA) rules. The current IOC rules boil down to four basic points:

- They do not need to have had gender reassignment surgery.
- They must have legal recognition of their assigned gender.
- They must have been on HRT for at least one year.
- Their (transgender women) testosterone levels must fall within the range of female norms.[320]

At the 2016 Rio Olympics, as far as is known, no transgender athlete competed at the games themselves (although some participated in qualifiers). None has ever medaled. Caster Semenya (who is intersex, not transgender) did.[321] As such, arguing that letting transgender athletes compete will destroy sports is ridiculous on its face, given that in the 12 years and eight Olympic Games (summer and winter) where transgender people have been allowed to compete, it has had no effect on the outcomes.

Given these conditions, the IOC does not consider being transgender an unfair advantage. The IOC did, however, consider drinking too much coffee an unfair competitive advantage for nearly 20 years.[322] The IOC still considers baking soda a potential doping agent.[323] Many common cough syrups, lozenges, eye drops, cold medications, diet products, nasal sprays, and allergy medications will also result in a medical disqualification for being at an unfair advantage.[324] Clearly, the IOC does not approach matters of unfair advantage with an under-abundance of caution.

The NCAA instituted guidelines in 2011 that were less stringent than the IOC at the time.[325] (The two policies are now nearly identical.) They do not require surgery, and they require only one year on testosterone suppression for male-to-female transgender athletes. The conclusions of the consulting medical experts on the NCAA policy were unambiguous:

> It is also important to know that any strength and endurance advantages a transgender woman arguably may have as a result

> of her prior testosterone levels dissipate after about one year of estrogen or testosterone-suppression therapy. According to medical experts on this issue, the assumption that a transgender woman competing on a women's team would have a competitive advantage outside the range of performance and competitive advantage or disadvantage that already exists among female athletes is not supported by evidence.[326]

In an interview regarding transgender mixed martial arts fighter Fallon Fox, Dr. Marci Bowers explains why there is no effective competitive advantage in being a transgender woman:

> Most measures of physical strength minimize, muscle mass decreases, bone density decreases, and they become fairly comparable to women in their musculature. After as much time as has passed in her case, if tested, she would probably end up in the same muscle mass category as her biologically born female counterpart.[327]

Current research into the performance of transgender athletes backs up this observation.[328] The study looked at the performance of transgender runners before and after transition. They found that if a runner was (for example) in the 90th percentile before, they were in approximately the 90th percentile after transition. The study concluded: "Collectively, the age graded scores for these eight runners were essentially the same in both genders."

Indeed, given that women get 25 percent of their circulating testosterone from their ovaries, post-operative transgender women typically have less testosterone than their cisgender female counterparts.[329] Fox noted, "Any of the women I'm competing against, my testosterone levels are drastically lower than theirs; it's almost nothing."[330]

Dr. Bowers agreed: "When you test her, she's going to come out with low testosterone levels and muscle mass that is remarkably similar to her counterparts." These observations were borne out in Fallon Fox's first defeat at the hands of Ashlee Evans-Smith, where Fox's muscle fatigue in later rounds gave Smith an advantage. "She put up a fight, but I could feel her really getting tired," Evans-Smith said afterwards.[331] Smith also observed, "I won because I hit harder, grappled better, had better ground techniques, cardio and leg strength."[332]

The only dissenting medical professional I could find has no actual experience with transgender medicine, couldn't define transgender, and based his objections on claims that "all the evidence isn't in yet."[333] This rationale simply isn't true, given we have over a decade of Olympic and NCAA competition in which transgender people have been allowed to compete, but have not dominated by any definition.

So yes, there is empirical evidence out there. If being a female transgender athlete is such an unfair competitive advantage, why aren't transgender women dominant at the highest levels? Why aren't there more of them? The fact that we see none of these things suggests that there really isn't a significant competitive advantage.

In professional sports, any tiny advantage translates into the difference between a win and a loss. If being a transgender woman translates into a substantial competitive advantage, one would expect to see them consistently dominating at the top levels of their sports. In fact, we see exactly the opposite: professional female transgender athletes are exceedingly rare and have never dominated a sport.

For anyone left on the fence, though, I have a question: would you prefer to base your opinions on what all the top medical experts, and empirical evidence, says? Or would you rather side with people who speak from a position of complete ignorance on the subject?

Chapter 5

(BAD) SCIENCE

Transgender people face a lot of challenges in life. Perhaps the most devastating, however, is the history of bad science as it has been used against the community. For the purposes of this book, "bad science" refers to obviously biased research, poor research, or good research that is misused by very biased people. The ways bad science is used are legion.

Before reading this chapter, the reader should bear always in mind what was presented in the previous chapter: the overwhelming consensus of medical and mental health care providers who are experts on transgender issues support affirming care and the medical necessity of it. They do not support reparative (e.g. conversion or change) therapy designed to change someone's gender identity or expression.

It is also worth stating up front that the people and organizations opposing the positions above all fit into at least one of the following categories:

1. Religiously motivated anti-LGBT hate groups posing as professional organizations (e.g. American College of Pediatrics).
2. Religiously motivated doctors on the fringes of their profession (e.g. Paul McHugh).
3. Vanishing 70s and 80s medical old guard who see their job as doing everything they can to prevent transgender people from transitioning, and who have a history of denigrating transgender people, and are also increasingly on the fringe (e.g. Blanchard, Zucker, Bailey).

4. People who are religiously motivated, have no medical or scientific background, and misuse existing research to support their anti-transgender positions (e.g. Walt Heyer).

"Bad science" frequently pops up in court cases where defendants who have discriminated against transgender people wish to provide justification. These forms of discrimination include firing transgender employees, denying health care benefits, denying medical care to prisoners, and defending discriminatory laws like House Bill 2 (HB2, The Bathroom Bill) in North Carolina.[334] It has also been used by legislators in South Dakota to justify discrimination against transgender students, in the hope that living in adversity will help convince them to stop being transgender. (Hint: it doesn't. Ask Leelah Alcorn.)

At other times, the misuse of science is meant to hurt transgender people on an individual level. Bad science is used in popular media like *The Wall Street Journal*[335] or on *Fox News* to make people feel justified in their prejudices. It is also used to make transgender people unfairly doubt their own memory, perception, and sanity. This is a form of psychological abuse known as gaslighting.

This chapter is designed to help the reader identify bad science, understand how it is used and by whom, debunk it, and see the devastating effects it has on transgender people legally, legislatively, and socially.

Do your homework, Dr. Ablow

One of the most common attacks on transgender people as a group is pundits stating that there is no evidence that there is a biological cause for being transgender. While the exact causes aren't known, there are over 100 peer-reviewed studies which point toward a series of biological causes for our own sense of gender. Saying that there is no evidence is simply untrue.

It doesn't stop anti-transgender people from trying, however.

In 2014 Dr. Keith Ablow, formerly of the Fox News Medical A-Team, dismissed any biological origins of gender dysphoria, stating:

> I don't believe we have definitive data (although many psychiatrists with very impressive credentials, who seem to mean well, assert that we do) that any male or female soul has ever in the history of the world been born into the wrong anatomic gender.
>
> Let me put that more clearly: I am not convinced by any science I can find that people with definitively male DNA and definitively male anatomy can actually be locked in a cruel joke of nature because they are actually female.[336]

One might ask, "So what sort of evidence is there that being transgender has some sort of biological origin, that indeed someone can be wired to be one gender, and physically another?"

Short answer: lots. Here are excerpts from 15 studies, out of the hundred-plus out there, showing likely biological origins of gender dysphoria. The excerpts from studies listed below are just a sample of the material out there, and picked based on the unambiguous statements they make which can be understood by the general public.

> 1. There is also evidence, albeit clinical, for a role of testosterone in the sexual differentiation of the human brain, in particular in inducing male gender role behavior and heterosexual orientation. *Bakker, Focus on Sexuality Research, 2014*[337]
>
> 2. We conclude that there is sufficient evidence that EDCs [Endocrine Disrupting Chemicals] modify behavioral sexual dimorphism in children, presumably by interacting with the hypothalamic-pituitary-gonadal (HPG) axis. *Winneke et al., Environmental Health Perspectives, 2013*[338]
>
> 3. Gender-dependent differentiation of the brain has been detected at every level of organization—morphological, neurochemical, and functional—and has been shown to be primarily controlled by sex differences in gonadal steroid hormone levels during perinatal development. *Chung & Auger, European Journal of Physiology, 2013*[339]

4. Gender identity (the conviction of belonging to the male or female gender), sexual orientation (hetero-, homo-, or bisexuality), pedophilia, and the risks for neuropsychiatric disorders are programmed into our brain during early development. There is no proof that postnatal social environment has any crucial effect on gender identity or sexual orientation. *Swaab & Bao, Neuroscience in the 21st Century, 2013*[340]

5. Testosterone, estrogen and dihydrotestosterone are the main steroid hormones responsible for the organization and sexual differentiation of brain structures during early development. *Karaismailoğlu & Erdem, Journal of the Turkish-German Gynecological Association, 2013*[341]

6. In human males, we show that variation in fetal testosterone (FT) predicts later local gray matter volume of specific brain regions in a direction that is congruent with sexual dimorphism observed in a large independent sample of age-matched males and females from the NIH Pediatric MRI Data Repository. *Lombardo et al., The Journal of Neuroscience, 2012*[342]

7. Testosterone measured in infancy predicts subsequent sex-typed behavior in boys and in girls. *Lamminmäki et al., Hormones and Behavior, 2012*[343]

8. The finger length ratio between the second and fourth digits in transgender men was significantly lower than in female controls in the right hand in this study. 2D:4D showed a positive correlation with GIS score. Because 2D:4D influences are assumed to be established in early life and to reflect testosterone exposure, our results suggest a relationship between GID-FtM and perinatal testosterone. *Hisasue et al., The Journal of Sexual Medicine, 2012*[344]

9. ...growing evidence shows that testosterone exposure contributes similarly to the development of other human behaviors that show sex differences, including sexual orientation, core gender identity,

and some, though not all, sex-related cognitive and personality characteristics. *Hines, Annual Review of Neuroscience, 2011*[345]

10. There is strong evidence that high concentrations of androgens lead to more male-typical behavior and that this also influences gender identity. *Jürgensen et al., Journal of Pediatric Endocrinology and Metabolism, 2010*[346]

11. However, when the process of genital development and of brain sexual development does not match the same sex, females with a male brain and vice versa can arise. These transsexual people have problems with their gender identity and have the conviction of being born in the wrong body. *Worrell, master's thesis, Faculty of Medicine, Universiteit Utrecht, 2010*[347]

12. In this study, more than 150 individuals with confirmed or suspected prenatal diethylstilbestrol (DES) exposure reported moderate to severe feelings of gender dysphoria across the lifespan. *Kerlin, paper prepared for the International Behavioral Development Symposium, 2005*[348]

13. Secondly, as predicted twin girls where one displayed gender dysphoria had a more masculine pattern of cerebral lateralization, than non-transgender girls. These findings support the notion of an influence of prenatal T on early brain organization in girls. *Cohen-Bendahan et al., Psychoneuroendocrinology, 2004*[349]

14. It thus appears conceivable that due to local hormone dependent changes during development at least some areas of the brain may follow a different course than the genitals during the process of sexual differentiation. A partial or even complete brain-body sex reversal may eventually be the result. *Kruijver, dissertation, Faculty of Medicine, University of Amsterdam, 2004*[350]

15. Results support the notion that the gender identity is related to the sex steroid-driven sexual differentiation of the brain, and that

certain genetic variants of three of the genes critically involved in this process, may enhance the susceptibility for transsexualism.
Landén, doctoral thesis, University of Gothenburg, 1999[351]

The current body of peer-reviewed, scientific evidence indicates that the origins of gender identity, and particularly transgender identities, likely have biological origins. The most recent study of transgender identities was a meta-study of the body of literature on the subject that concluded transgender identities have a biologic origin.[352]

The researchers at Boston University included research on disorders of sexual development, such as penile agenesis, neuroanatomical differences, such as gray and white matter studies, and steroid hormone genetics, such as genes associated with sex hormone receptors. They conclude that current data suggests a biological etiology for transgender identity, *but that the exact mechanisms that cause people to be transgender are unknown at this time.*[353]

Over the past 25 years, over a hundred peer-reviewed journal articles and studies have looked at the role of genetics, epigenetics, hormones, and other influences on gender identity and sexual orientation in humans.[354] It has been understood for decades that prenatal exposure to androgens affects both sexual orientation and gender identity.[355] Other studies since then have continued to show that a variety of genetic, epigenetic, and other prenatal factors seem to influence gender identity in children and adults as well.[356] Differences in gray matter structures have been observed, even in transgender women who have not undergone HRT treatment.[357]

While some studies have suggested there is a link between autism and transgender identities, the most recent peer-reviewed meta-analysis of the data suggests that this conclusion is not statistically supported, and any connection between the two remains speculative.[358]

Neither is there credible evidence to support the idea that parenting has any influence on a child's gender identity. For decades, male homosexuality was blamed on weak fathers and domineering mothers. The same Freudian nonsense was also applied to transgender people as well, assuming they were just some sub-type of homosexuals.

David Reimer (mentioned earlier, in Chapter 4) provides a case study in how parenting seems to have no effect on gender identity. David was born male in 1965, but his penis was destroyed in a botched circumcision at seven months. His parents were convinced by a behaviorist psychologist, Dr. John Money, that it would be best if he were instead raised as a girl since he could not function as a male. Money believed that gender was completely a social construct, and that how a child was raised would determine how they identified with their gender. David was raised thereafter as Brenda, and vaginoplasty performed at 22 months. However, Reimer failed to identify as female from the age of 9 onward, and lived as a man from age 15 on.[359]

Money hid this failure of his theory from the world, which led to behaviorist theories about sexual orientation and gender identity continuing to dominate psychological theories about sexual orientation and gender identity for another two decades, well into the 1980s and 1990s. It wasn't until 1997 that Money's perfidy was revealed.

There have been some studies that looked at very specific potential causes of gender dysphoria, such as selected gene sequences involved in hormone receptors, and some gene sequences involved in sexual differentiation.[360] [361] [362] They did not find a genetic difference between transgender individuals and the control population when looking at these specific genes. However, drawing a broader conclusion on the origins of transsexualism and gender identity on the basis of these studies would be a mistake, particularly as a more recent genetics study has come back with positive results.[363]

Using a single study to conclude that there is no biological basis is logically flawed. For example, concluding that gay people decide to be gay based on not having found a "gay gene" is a mistake, since other factors such as epigenetics seem to be a potential cause.[364] Another real-life analogy would be the studies that have shown vaccines do not cause autism. Based on ruling out vaccines as a cause, one should not therefore determine that autism, or a biologic cause for autism, doesn't exist.

Currently, the preponderance of studies indicates that gender identity (and transsexualism) has biologic origins, rendering it an immutable trait in much the same way as sexual orientation. While the exact causes of gender identity are uncertain, it does seem to be a deeply rooted part of our human biological condition. This is why attempts to change a person's gender identity have proven futile and actively harmful.

It seems unlikely that any amount of evidence would convince Dr. Ablow and others like him. It's very unlikely someone will develop a "soul-o-meter" that measures the gender of a person's inner essence. However, there is essentially a consensus within the medical community that different sexual orientations and gender identities are part of natural human variance.

Thus, while the exact biological mechanisms are not fully understood, there is a general consensus that gender identity and sexual orientation have a biological basis, and are not somehow caused by overbearing mothers and distant fathers, as was promoted by the Freudian researchers of the 60s and 70s such as Robert Stoller.

Bad science at Johns Hopkins University

The name Johns Hopkins University (JHU) connotes an institute of higher learning in medicine to most people. It also has a long, and very ugly, history with the transgender community. JHU professors have headlined conferences on reparative therapy, cozied up with many Southern Poverty Law Center (SPLC)-certified hate groups, and taken money from the government to argue in court that transgender people don't need medical care.

The administration has also allowed staff members at JHU to ignore standards of care, reject evidence-based medicine, and skip over the guidelines of their professional organizations as long as the transgender community is at the receiving end of such malpractice.

Just prior to an October 2015 gathering of the World Congress of Families (which is an SPLC-certified hate group), a radio station in Utah held a pre-conference event called STAND4TRUTH 2015,[365] sponsored by the Family Research Council (another hate group), American Family Association (another hate group), and MassResistance (yet another

SPLC-designated hate group).[366] Their speakers included some of the most radical anti-LGBT leaders from these groups, such as Peter Sprigg, Peter LaBarbera, Michael Brown, Dave Welch, Matt Staver, and Brian Camenker.

And then there was Dr. Paul McHugh of JHU, prominently displaying his JHU credentials in support of reparative therapy and anti-LGBT animus.

When I contacted JHU regarding Dr. McHugh's participation in this conference, the university informed me he had "declined the invitation" and that "Johns Hopkins Medicine lives by its mission and its vision and embraces diversity and inclusion."

However, when I spoke with the STAND4TRUTH 2015 organizers, they informed me that McHugh was in town for the event but missed his panel because he set his alarm to the wrong time. They also claimed he came to the conference after his panel. STAND4TRUTH organizers deny that McHugh declined their invitation. Wherever the actual truth lies, however, the conference's brochure suggests he had said yes at some point.

Dr. McHugh has a lot in common with these hate groups. McHugh is a self-described orthodox Catholic whose radical views are well documented.[367] In his role as part of the United States Conference of Catholic Bishops' review board, he pushed the idea that the Catholic sex-abuse scandal was not about pedophilia but about "homosexual predation on American Catholic youth."[368] He filed an amicus brief arguing in favor of Proposition 8 on the basis that homosexuality is a "choice." Additionally, McHugh was in favor of forcing a pregnant 10-year-old girl to carry to term even though she had been raped by an adult relative, and was part of the campaign that led to the murder of abortion provider Dr. George Tiller in 2009.[369]

His words and actions toward the transgender community are the most egregious, however. He has compared medical care for transgender people to "the practice of frontal lobotomy."[370] McHugh's disdain for his own patients is evident, calling them "caricatures of women"[371] and pushing the demeaning narrative that all transgender women are either self-hating gay men or perverted heterosexuals.[372] Worse, the damage McHugh has done to transgender health care is incalculable. McHugh shut down one of the few gender clinics in the US in 1979,[373] and his lobbying in 1981 was instrumental in getting a national coverage decision forbidding the government from covering gender-affirming care. As a result, all but one gender clinic in the US was shut down by 1982, leaving most transgender Americans without access to reliable health care. It wasn't reversed until 2014. Due to his outspoken desire to see transgender people in the closet, Dr. McHugh has become the go-to "expert" for right-wing organizations.[374]

McHugh also signed on to a position statement[375] from the American College of Pediatricians (ACPeds) opposing all affirming care for transgender youth. The ACPeds is not a real professional organization. It is a hate group pretending to be one, which exists as hardly more than a website.[376] The ACPeds is a group of less than 200 ultra-conservative people (most of whom aren't even pediatricians)[377] who oppose letting gay people be parents, the HPV (human papillomavirus) vaccine, marriage equality, birth control, and medical care for transgender people for religious reasons. They are in favor of reparative therapy and abstinence-only education, though.[378]

The ACPeds was full of easily debunked falsehoods and distortions that have already been covered in this book.[379] The position statement encouraged rejecting the identities of transgender youth, denying them medical care, and subjecting them to some sort of reparative therapy. It was effectively encouraging parental behaviors that would significantly increase the chances that their children would kill themselves. This constitutes a reckless disregard for innocent life.

While Johns Hopkins claims "respect for patients' backgrounds and beliefs" is vital in its Diversity and Inclusion Mission Statement, the actions of staff members and the administration should make it clear that these are just words where transgender patients are concerned.[380] When other JHU staff members have made controversial and public anti-LGB statements, the organization has been quick to put space between it and the positions of its staff. Dr. Ben Carson (also of JHU, also holding bizarre and offensive beliefs about lesbians and gays)[381] went a step too far by comparing same-sex marriage to bestiality and the North American Man/Boy Love Association.[382] Johns Hopkins University publicly distanced itself from him as a result.[383]

"Controversial social issues are debated in the media on a regular basis, and yet it is rare that leaders of an academic medical center will join that type of public debate," said Dr. Paul Rothman, CEO of Johns Hopkins Medicine, in an April 2015 statement. "However, we recognize that tension now exists in our community because hurtful, offensive language was used by our colleague, Dr. Ben Carson, when conveying a personal opinion. Dr. Carson's comments are inconsistent with the culture of our institution."

Rothman's statement highlighted JHU's non-discrimination policy as being inclusive of sexual orientation and gender identity, noting that Carson's statements mean "the fundamental principle of freedom of expression has been placed in conflict with our core values of diversity, inclusion and respect."

But then there's McHugh, who has also very publicly gone against the World Professional Association of Transgender Health Standards of Care[384] for transgender people and the positions of his own professional organization, the American Psychiatric Association,[385] in his 2014 *Wall Street Journal* article.[386] McHugh suggests in the article that he speaks for Johns Hopkins when he states, "And so at Hopkins we stopped doing sex reassignment surgery, since producing a 'satisfied' but still troubled patient seemed an inadequate reason for surgically amputating normal organs... It now appears that our long-ago decision was a wise one."

This biased and dangerous misrepresentation of evidence on transgender people was called out by prominent members of the American Psychiatric Association in a rebuttal letter to the *Journal*,[387] as was his flagrant misuse of a 2011 study on outcomes for post-operative transgender people by Dr. Celia Dhejne. His deliberate misinterpretation of the 2011 study led Dr. Dhejne to publicly denounce McHugh's actions as "unethical."[388]

Even some of his colleagues at Johns Hopkins have taken the unusual step of calling him out publicly for his shoddy, biased, and harmful work. In an open letter to the *Baltimore Sun* newspaper, the faculty at the JHU Bloomberg School of Public Health stated:

> ...we believe [his work] mischaracterizes the current state of the science on sexuality and gender... Science, and particularly the fields of psychiatry and psychology, has made major advances in our understanding of the complex issues of sexual orientation and gender identity. For instance, accumulating data support the concept that gender identity is not strictly a binary phenomenon. And scientific evidence clearly documents that sexual and romantic attractions to people of the same and/or different sexes are normal variations of the diversity of human sexuality.
>
> As faculty at Johns Hopkins, we are committed to serving the health needs of the LGBTQ community in a manner that is informed by the best available science... That is why the recent report, released by one current and one former member of our faculty on the topic of LGBTQ health, is so troubling. The report, "Sexuality and Gender: Findings from the Biological and Psychological and Social Sciences," was not published in the scientific literature, where it would have been subject to rigorous peer review prior to publication. It purports to detail the science of this area, but it falls short of being a comprehensive review.[389]

When McHugh and Mayer published an article in the non-peer-reviewed journal *The New Atlantis*, it misrepresented the current consensus on LGBT people so extensively that hundreds of his contemporaries signed an open letter denouncing his work, stating that the "conclusions do not reflect current scientific or medical consensus about sexual orientation or gender identity research findings or clinical care recommendations."[390] JHU faculty also wrote an op-ed in the *Baltimore Sun* denouncing *The New Atlantis* article.[391]

McHugh has a history of engaging in behavior that endangers people he disagrees with for religious reasons. Kansas Attorney General Paul

Morrison issued a cease and desist legal order in 2007 against McHugh for appearing in an inflammatory video that railed against Dr. George Tiller and which was arranged by anti-abortion activists.[392] It ended up on Bill O'Reilly's show, and right-wing outrage spread in response to the *Fox News* segment. Then Dr. Tiller was assassinated in 2009.[393]

If it were just McHugh, though, it wouldn't be a pattern. However, other members of JHU's staff who were acolytes of McHugh have become the "go-to" people whenever a defendant needs to justify denying transgender people health care.[394] JHU's Dr. Cynthia Osborne has been a witness in at least three cases in which transgender people were seeking health care. She says prisoners should never receive gender confirmation surgery. As a result of her testimony, all three inmates lost their cases, and two of them resorted to self-castration out of desperation.[395]

The university's Dr. Chester Schmidt has also been a star witness for defendants who wish to ignore standards of care. Schmidt testified that he has never recommended transgender surgery out of the 300 transgender patients he's had. During his testimony, Schmidt stated (against WPATH standards of care) that the correct course of treatment for gender dysphoria is, in his opinion, "psychotherapy and medication."[396] Schmidt has availed himself of right-wing news outlets to make a case that transgender people should not be given affirming care.[397]

For both Osborne and Schmidt, their positions at Johns Hopkins lent credence to their opinions in court, despite violating both the WPATH Standards of Care and the positions of their own professional organizations. A First Circuit Court of Appeals decision cites their positions at JHU as authoritative in its decision against providing health care to transgender inmates.[398] Schmidt was also brought in by government as a defense witness in an employment discrimination case, where he testified that transgender people should not be legally protected under Title VII of the US Civil Rights Act of 1964, since he viewed being transgender as a matter of sexual deviance rather than one of gender.[399]

Anti-transgender bias at JHU has a long and sordid history. The study McHugh ran in the late 1970s was deeply flawed, having been designed to get a particular answer. As a result, the psychiatric community no longer considers this study persuasive or credible.[400] Fellow psychiatry staff member Dr. Thomas Wise has also espoused similarly outdated, offensive views on transgender people, including a belief that transgender people need reparative therapy, and not affirming medical care. In 1979, Dr. Wise wrote the following Freudian gobbledygook:

> The genesis of this perversion appears to be identification with a phallic maternal figure... Identification of important losses in this patient's recent life allowed proper diagnosis and appropriate ongoing therapy to prevent the patient from irreversible surgery for a condition that was a symptom not an ingrained belief of gender dysphoria.[401]

McHugh, Schmidt, and Wise have made it clear that their opinions on medical care for transgender people have not wavered in the last 40 years, despite the rest of the medical and psychiatric community moving on.

These biases and adherence to discredited hypotheses have had a direct effect on the quality of patient care. Transgender patients have described humiliating, abusive, and demeaning treatment by JHU staff for years.[402] Jennifer McCandless, a transgender woman, described to me in an email how she was treated by Dr. Schmidt and JHU staff:

> I was sent to JHU by a sympathetic doctor who just didn't know what dosages of hormones to give me. JHU charged me $900 out of pocket for the appointment. During intake, they asked lots of sexually leading questions on their background questionnaire. They kept trying to want to find some kind of underwear fetish in my past. Chester Schmidt came in and chewed me out for being nothing more than a closet transvestite, then ranted about how my therapist must have filled my mind with these crazy ideas. I was grilled for an hour. I was constantly challenged about my identity by a bunch of white-coat underlings...just grueling. Schmidt also called my therapist and chewed her out; she (my

therapist) said he (Schmidt) was really arrogant and obnoxious during the call.

She never went back, and sought medical and therapeutic help elsewhere.

Some might note that the Johns Hopkins Bloomberg School of Public Health published a study supporting insurance coverage of transgender-specific health care. However, this study was ten years behind the research done by other organizations,[403] and half a decade behind the American Medical Association, American Psychological Association, and the American Psychiatric Association.[404] This is the public health policy equivalent of a physics department confirming Newtonian theory.

The abysmal treatment of transgender people and failure to follow evidence-based medicine have been noticed by younger staff members at JHU. They are also upset at how McHugh, Schmidt, Wise, and other members of the psychiatric staff are protected by the administration. One younger doctor at JHU spoke with me on the condition of anonymity. He stated flatly that the institution's mistreatment of transgender people directly affected his decision to leave.

A number of disturbing facts emerge from all of this. Staff members at JHU appear free to participate in hate groups, ignore standards of care, disregard the positions of their professional organizations, deliberately misuse and misrepresent research, advocate for and practice medicine that isn't evidence-based, and let their biases affect the quality of care that patients receive.

This raises the question: are the staff always allowed to do this, or only where transgender people are concerned? If the former, it speaks very poorly of the organization as a whole. If the latter, it means the organization is actively supporting discrimination against, and mistreatment of, a community that is already extremely vulnerable.

Either way, there is a lot of explaining to do.

UPDATE: Johns Hopkins reopened a medical practice for transgender patients in 2017. However, as of the writing of this book, the psychiatric Gender Clinic associated with McHugh, Wise, Osborne, and Schmidt remains open, and treating transgender patients.

"Rapid onset gender dysphoria" is biased junk science

In 2017, a new anti-transgender narrative emerged. The narrative states that teens, particularly those assigned female at birth, are going on the internet and convincing themselves that they are transgender because being transgender is "trendy." It treats transgender identities as a form of social contagion. This theory has been picked up on by numerous hate groups and conservative news outlets, including LifeSite, Barbara Kay, the Catholic Institute for Marital Healing, the Minnesota Family Council, MercatorNet, the Illinois Family Institute, the Family Research Council, the Heritage Foundation's Daily Signal, and an advocacy group for anti-LGBT therapists.[405]

The entire theory is based on a single poster abstract in 2017 by Dr. Lisa Littman.[406] Poster abstracts are often published when the material is too weak to be a journal article and of insufficient quality to even be accepted for oral presentation at a conference. As such, the academic bar for a poster abstract getting accepted is very low.

Littman's abstract suffers from so many methodological flaws, logical errors, and unacknowledged biases that it fits firmly in the category of junk science. Given how glaring these issues were, it is surprising that the *Journal of Adolescent Health* published it regardless of how low the bar was set.

Here's why this abstract by Littman is poor science, and should be retracted.

1. The sample group has a heavy and unacknowledged bias that affects the results

Littman posted a survey on three websites asking parents about their transgender teens.[407] What she failed to mention in her abstract is that all three websites (4thwavenow.com, Transgendertrend.com, and YouthTransCriticalProfessionals.org) are dedicated to parents who do not recognize the gender identities of their children, and do not support their transitions. Littman did not post her survey to sites where parents of transgender adolescents support their children.

This creates an obvious bias, one she fails to acknowledge anywhere in her poster abstract. Based on the obvious viewpoints of the websites, it gives the appearance that she is deliberately trying to hide the bias in her results. Other issues with her abstract support this perception of deliberate academic malfeasance.

2. One of her survey questions appears to be a deliberate attempt to hide her bias

One of the survey questions asked respondents whether they believe "transgender people deserve the same rights and protections as other people." The abstract notes that 87.7 percent answered yes, and this is presented in such a way as to suggest that the respondents did not harbor anti-transgender animus. However, this question, and statistic, appears to be deliberately misleading.

This phrasing suggests a deliberate attempt to hide bias in the study, because even people who are vehemently against transgender people are likely to answer yes. For over a decade, anti-LGBT hate groups have framed protections for LGBT people, and even marriage equality, as "special rights."[408]

A quick perusal of the websites where Littman drew her surveys from shows that the people posting there are often ideologically aligned with these anti-LGBT hate groups.[409] There are frequent posts stating that transgender people are sexual deviants. They quote Paul McHugh, cite Michelle Cretella of the anti-LGBT hate group (and fake medical organization) ACPeds, oppose legal protections for transgender people, and call for legislation to prevent people from transitioning until they are in their late 20s.

Thus, at best, this 87.7 percent statistic provides no useful information about how the respondents feel about transgender people. Given how the author failed to mention any of the ideological skew of the places where she asked for respondents, it appears more likely to be a deliberate attempt to hide the bias within her sample.

3. The unacknowledged bias in Littman's sample leads her to ignore plausible explanations for her data supported by extant literature

Littman asks "before and after" coming out questions in her survey. This includes things such as whether the parent–child relationship improved or got worse after they came out, and whether the mental well-being of the child improved or declined. Based on parents' perceptions, both declined according to her survey. She notes that this observation contradicts the existing body of research, which shows improvement when trans youth come out.

She also notes in the data that parents perceived transgender youth as having a more LGBT-centric circle of friends, and as getting their information from transgender-friendly sources on the internet.

However, Littman fails to note that this was a survey of parents who do not support their children. Viewing Littman's results through the lens of trans youth in unsupportive homes, her results do not contradict the current body of research. There is a large body of evidence showing that transgender youth in unsupportive homes have worse mental health outcomes than those in supportive ones.

Accounting for the bias in her sample, a picture consistent with the existing body of evidence emerges.

Transgender youth in unsupportive homes are much more likely to share their thoughts and feelings with LGBT friends at school and peers online than with family. Questioning youth are unlikely to go to hostile sources of information online which label them as deluded, mentally ill, or sexually perverted. Given the social stigma and moral opprobrium associated with being transgender, they stick to "safe" LGBT social groups.[410]

After coming to grips with their gender identity, the transgender youth then delay telling hostile parents until they cannot bear not to, which makes it appear to the parents that this came out of nowhere. After they come out, and their parents do not support them, the parent–child relationship deteriorates, and the mental health of the youth declines. An interview I conducted with the (now adult) child of one of the parents who participated in this survey confirms this narrative as true for him.

Littman does not in any way pursue this plausible hypothesis, which conforms with current findings. Instead, Littman appears to be deliberately ignoring the bias in her sample to claim that she has found a new phenomenon.

4. The conclusions reached by this abstract rely on poor logic and what appears to be a deliberately biased sample

The abstract concludes that "rapid onset gender dysphoria" is dangerous, real, and is caused by interactions with friends and people on the internet. This conclusion is based on some rather heroic leaps of logic.

The most grievous logical error is the conclusion that this is a new phenomenon, when current literature in the context of youth living in unsupportive homes would explain the observations. The abstract conclusion also seems to imply that sources of information which encourage parents to reject the identities of transgender youth are mainstream voices.

Instead, with a biased sample (which she makes no attempt to account for), biased questions, no context, and with no attempt to understand her data within the context of existing research, she ignores Occam's Razor and leaps to a conclusion that what we are observing is sinister and new, rather than simply what we already expect from transgender youth in unsupportive environments.

Additionally, "rapid onset gender dysphoria" was first proposed as a diagnosis on anti-transgender websites in 2016, and this study appears to be a post-hoc attempt to legitimize anti-transgender animus with a veneer of academic respectability.[411] In the process, however, Littman's work shreds all standards of academic integrity.

The abstract is an egregious example of biased junk science. Given that it encourages behaviors which endanger an at-risk group of children, this article should be retracted not only for its poor scholarship, but for what appears to be the deliberate attempts made to hide the bias within it.

Meet the last "respectable" reparative therapist

At this stage in the debate, you would think that reparative therapy would be dead as disco.

Reparative therapy (also known as conversion therapy) has been denounced by all the major psychological, psychiatric, and medical organizations in the US. California, New Jersey, and Washington DC have passed laws forbidding its use on minors, and they have held up in court. Exodus International has folded, and the "ex-gay" movement is generally an apathetic and little-noticed side show.[412 413] Exodus was part of the industry that tried to convince gay men that they could change their sexual orientation by doing "manly" things, and punishing themselves for non-heterosexual thoughts. Its principles, like most "ex-gay" organizations, were based on conservative Christian theology.

However, there's one PhD-level psychologist out there pushing a brand of reparative therapy that skirts the ethical guidelines of all the professional organizations that have come out against it. He is still cited as an "expert" in the media, and especially by those with an anti-LGBT ideology.[414] In 2017, he was given an hour-long TV show on the BBC to expound on why transgender youth should undergo reparative therapy.[415]

It would be easy to dismiss this person if he were somebody no one listened to, or if he was a poorly regarded crackpot. Unfortunately, he isn't. In fact, until recently he was one of the most influential psychologists in the field.

Meet Dr. Kenneth Zucker. He's a professor at the University of Toronto, editor-in-chief of *Archives of Sexual Behavior* for the last 12 years, former member of the American Psychological Association Task Force on Gender Identity, Gender Variance, and Intersex Conditions, and chairman of the American Psychiatric Association working group on "Sexual and Gender Identity Disorders" for the 2013 edition of the *DSM-5*.[416 417]

Based on all of this, Dr. Kenneth Zucker is the darling of many anti-LGBT hate groups and pro-reparative therapy organizations. These include Focus on the Family,[418] NARTH,[419] Courage,[420] Alliance Defending Freedom,[421] Life Site News,[422] American Family Association,[423] Liberty Counsel,[424] Americans for Truth About Homosexuality (AFTAH),[425] Parents and Friends of Ex-Gays and Gays (PFOX),[426] and others. His work has been cited repeatedly in amicus briefs filed by right-wing groups opposed to LGBT rights.[427]

If Dr. Zucker is opposed to his research being used this way by such organizations, he has been quiet about it.

He's also one of the leading proponents of a school of thought which describes the vast majority of children who exhibit gender non-conforming behaviors as just juvenile gay men and lesbians who need to be prevented from growing up to be transgender, because he regards being cisgender as a better outcome than being transgender. In the past, he has hinted to their parents that his methods might prevent them from being gay, too.[428]

The treatment these children receive should be familiar; it has striking similarities to the methods used by notorious "ex-gay" therapist George Rekers in the 1970s as part of his efforts to prevent children from growing up to be gay by punishing effeminate behaviors.[429] NPR described Dr. Zucker's methodology:[430]

> So, to treat Bradley, Zucker explained to Carol that she and her husband would have to radically change their parenting. Bradley would no longer be allowed to spend time with girls. He would no longer be allowed to play with girlish toys or pretend that he was a female character. Zucker said that all of these activities were dangerous to a kid with gender identity disorder. He explained that unless Carol and her husband helped the child to change his behavior, as Bradley grew older, he likely would be rejected by both peer groups. Boys would find his feminine interests unappealing. Girls would want more boyish boys. Bradley would be an outcast.
>
> It does seem to be the case that, at least in the short term, Carol's son Bradley is struggling in some ways with Zucker's therapy. Carol says it was particularly hard at the beginning.
>
> "He was much more emotional... He could be very clingy. He didn't want to go to school anymore," she says. "Just the smallest thing could, you know, send him into a major crying fit. And...he seemed to feel really heavy and really emotional."
>
> Bradley has been in therapy now for eight months, and Carol says still, on the rare occasions when she cannot avoid having him exposed to girl toys, like when they visit family, it doesn't go well.
>
> "It's really hard for him. He'll disappear and close a door, and

we'll find him playing with dolls and Polly Pockets and...the stuff that he's drawn to," she says.

"He's still a bit defensive if we ask him, 'Do you want to be a girl?' He's like 'No, NO! I'm happy being a boy.' ... He gives us that sort of stock answer... I still think we're at the stage where he feels he's leading a double life," she says. "I'm still quite certain that he is with the girls all the time at school, and so he knows to behave one way at school, and then when he comes home, there's a different set of expectations."

When compared with Dr. George Rekers's infamous (and ultimately fatal) methods with his patient "Kirk," there are similarities.[431]

"There was a one-way mirror or one-way window—and some days they would let him choose which table he would go to," said Maris, who has read about the experiments.

At one table Kirk could choose between what were considered masculine toys like plastic guns and handcuffs, and what were meant to be feminine toys like dolls and a play crib. At the other table, Kirk could choose between boys' clothing and a toy electric razor or items like dress-up jewelry and a wig.

According to the case study, Kaytee Murphy was told to ignore her son when he played with feminine toys and compliment him when he played with masculine toys.

"They pretty much told him he wasn't right the way that he was, but they never really explained to him what the issue was. They did it through play," Maris said.

Rekers wrote that Kirk would cry out for attention, even throwing tantrums, but Kaytee Murphy was told to keep going.

How is this not "reparative therapy"?

Someone might wonder how Dr. Zucker escapes the label of sexual orientation change effort (SOCE) with his "Drop the doll!" methodologies, when his techniques and goals seem so similar.[432] There is one semantic difference: Zucker does not claim to be trying to make gender non-conforming kids straight, he just claims to make them straight-*acting*. Somehow this nuance has mostly inured him from mainstream criticism.

It hasn't gone completely unnoticed, though: a 2003 letter in the *Journal of the American Academy of Child and Adolescent Psychiatry* called his techniques "something disturbingly close to reparative therapy for homosexuals."[433]

Dr. Zucker attributes gender non-conformance (what he calls "pre-homosexuality") to the same things "ex-gay" activists say cause homosexuality:[434]

> [Zucker] urges parents to steer their children toward gender-typical toys, clothes and playmates and advises them to prohibit behaviors associated with the other sex. Zucker's academic articles assert that while biology may predispose some children to gender nonconformity, other factors—like trauma and emotional disorders—often play a role. *Other contributing causes he cites include overprotective mothers, emotionally absent fathers or mothers who are hostile toward men.* [Emphasis mine.]

You might also ask how this isn't trying to change someone's gender identity. To Dr. Zucker's mind, it is because there is no such thing as gender identity.[435] To him, gender is learned, and it is plastic and malleable (no matter how badly John Money's experiment with David Reimer went) in pre-pubescent children.[436] [437]

There are no transgender children, just "confused" gender non-conforming (almost always gay) children who need behavior modification therapy.[438]

Twenty years ago, though, Zucker was pushing hard for reparative therapy of children who were too effeminate, in order to prevent them from growing up to be gay. In Zucker and Bradley's 1990 article on gender non-conforming youth and the motivations of reparative therapy he wrote:

> Two short-term goals have been discussed in the literature: the reduction or elimination of social ostracism and conflict, and the

> alleviation of underlying or associated psychopathology. Longer term goals have focused on the prevention of transsexualism and/or *homosexuality*. [Emphasis mine.][439]

For over 25 years, Zucker has seemingly been concern trolling the LGBT community. Everything he does is for the sake of the children, because he believed in the 80s and 90s that society would never accept gay people. Now, he uses the same argument for why gender non-conforming children should be prevented from being transgender.

Dr. Zucker is dismissive of efforts to create a more tolerant society, where gender non-conformance and homosexuality are accepted. In the 1995 book Zucker co-authored with Bradley, they wrote that "a homosexual lifestyle in a basically unaccepting culture simply creates unnecessary social difficulties."[440]

In other words, there's no point in trying to make society more open and tolerant—the only option is to learn to act (or be) straight unless you want to be mistreated.

On top of all of this, Zucker was the editor of the *Archives of Sexual Behavior* when Dr. Robert Spitzer's infamous article supporting reparative therapy efforts was published in 2001.[441] The article itself was not subjected to the usual peer-review process, and ultimately Dr. Zucker refused to retract it, despite Spitzer asking him to.[442] [443]

Zucker himself plays coy on whether or not he believes orientation can be changed, and he supports the rights of parents to subject their children to SOCE. In his 2004 book, he quotes his mentor Dr. Richard Green:

> The rights of parents to oversee the development of children is a long-established principle. Who is to dictate that parents may not try to raise their children in a manner that maximizes the possibility of a heterosexual outcome? If that prerogative is denied, should parents also be denied the right to raise their children as atheists? Or as priests?

Dr. Robert Spitzer always regarded homosexuality as a "sub-optimal" outcome, and given Zucker's close association with Spitzer, it is not hard to believe that Zucker still sees being gay as sub-optimal to being straight. Other things Zucker has said and written support this supposition. Zucker also quietly nudges the parents of gender non-conforming youth to put them in reparative therapy, by broadly hinting via correlation that changing their behavior might also change their orientation:[444]

> Dr. Zucker says that clinicians have an ethical obligation to inform parents of the relationship between GID (Gender Identity Disorder) and homosexuality. Clinical experience suggests that psychosexual treatments are effective in reducing gender dysphoria and that individual counseling and parental counseling are both effective methods of treating GID.

And Zucker promotes his methods' efficacy in fixing the problem (gender non-conformance) that he implies causes the other (homosexuality):

> It has been our experience that a sizable number of children and their families achieve a great deal of change. In these cases, the GID resolves fully, and nothing in the children's behavior or fantasy suggest that gender identity issues remain problematic... All things considered, we take the position that in such cases a clinician should be optimistic, not nihilistic, about the possibility of helping the children to become more secure in their gender identity.

When asked directly about the efficacy of SOCE, Zucker again waffled until recently. "At this point, I cannot make any statement about how therapy affects later sexual orientation," Zucker says, clearly choosing his words carefully. "But certainly, many parents bring their children to me because they would prefer that they not grow up to be gay."

He also claimed that all the evidence isn't in yet:

> Zucker says that the ethical issues in providing treatment "are moot until we can know whether treatment can alter the natural history of a child's sexual orientation."[445]

When his practices were investigated, it led to his firing. The results were highly damning, finding that:

- the methods being used were 30 years out of date
- the clinic assumed that all gender variant children need to be clinically "fixed" (i.e. they used coercive behavior modification on queer kids to make them act straight)
- children were pressured into being photographed without clothing
- the clinic emphasized tests, treatment, and methods with no scientific basis in evidence-based medicine
- Centre for Addiction and Mental Health (CAMH) staff asked pre-pubescent children questions that were highly sexual in nature
- former patients, parents, and therapists of former patients described the treatment as "disturbing" and "harmful"
- CAMH hid affirming community and medical resources from patients
- Dr. Zucker regarded being cisgender, heterosexual, and gender conforming as the "best" outcome
- Dr. Zucker and his team could not conclusively demonstrate that what they were doing was not reparative therapy.

In a 2014 German study, 13 experts in treatment for gender identity were asked if CAMH's methods were ethical. Eleven said no. The two who said yes were Dr. Zucker and another CAMH staff member.[446]

Despite this, anti-transgender concern trolls came out in force defending Dr. Zucker.[447] They couldn't actually refute the key findings of the investigation enumerated above, so instead they played the concern troll card and falsely claimed that non-transgender children will be coerced into medically transitioning if therapists allow children to explore their gender expression and identity.

One has to wonder where Dr. Zucker's desire to make children fit in, fade away, and escape the attention of bullies and religious zealots by acting straight comes from. One key passage about his past seems to provide a crucial insight.

His "intellectual, left-winger" Jewish parents were victims of McCarthy-era witch hunting—his dad lost several jobs, Zucker says, because he refused to "rat on his Commie friends." In Zucker's telling, they ultimately decided that "for the sake of their children, they needed to become conformist," and they moved to the suburbs to "disappear from the scene—trapped in middle-class consumer subculture for the good of the cause."

No one can say for certain what Dr. Zucker's motivations are. It could be a misplaced desire to help, it could be animus, or it could be concern trolling. In any event, with laws prohibiting reparative therapy on minors being introduced across the US, his theories are now held by very few professionals.

Ray Blanchard: right-wing darling

There is a long and rocky history between feminism and the transgender community, which is discussed in greater detail in Chapter 11. This book also discusses the different sorts of political attacks made by right-wing organizations against the transgender community in Chapter 7. There is an interesting convergence between radical feminists, the religious right, and bad science, and it lies at the point of Dr. Ray Blanchard.

Blanchard is responsible for a great deal of harm to transgender people in North America—and he seems proud of it. He admits abusing his power within the psychiatric community to make political points. Blanchard bragged in an interview about how he used his position to create a fake diagnosis in the *DSM-5*, and to resorting to unethical means to push his pet theories. He also believes that homosexuality should never have been removed from the *Diagnostic and Statistical Manual*.[448]

Blanchard's theories have been picked up by radical anti-transgender feminists,[449] who use them to justify their claim that transgender people are perverts who cannot be trusted.[450] Anti-LGBT hate group organizations also love Blanchard. The National Association for the Research and Therapy of Homosexuality (NARTH) based much of its anti-transgender manifesto on Blanchard's writings.[451] Blanchard's work is also used in the right-wing anti-transgender campaigns being waged by the Pacific Justice Institute and the like. Indeed, the Family Research Council[452] and the American Family Association[453] cite his theory as a reason that transgender people are sick and should be institutionalized rather than protected. Anti-trans pundits like Dr. Keith Ablow rely on Blanchard's theories to deny that transgender people even exist.[454]

All of these individuals and groups attempt to deny legal protections and medical care to the community.

Dr. Ray Blanchard is a psychologist who specializes in paraphilias. These are also known as sexual perversion and sexual deviation, and are the experience of intense atypical sexual arousal.[455] Blanchard also worked with sex offenders and pedophiles in the 1970s and 80s, and tended to view transgender people through the same lens. While best known for promoting anti-transgender theories, he has other odd ideas about human sexuality, including being a proponent of the idea that homosexuality is a disorder, and denying that bisexuals exist (or at least, denying that they are any different from heterosexuals).[456] He also believes that (cisgender) women can never have fetishes or kinks.

Dr. Ray Blanchard first proposed the theory of autogynephilia in the late 1980s—it asserts that there are two fundamentally different types (a taxonomy) of transgender women. The first group is "extremely feminine gay men" who believe life, and sex, would be easier as a heterosexual woman than as a gay man.[457] The second type, which Blanchard termed "autogynephiles," are transgender women who experience sexual arousal or fantasies involving the "thought or image of oneself as a woman," and transition to fulfill those fantasies. According to Blanchard's theory, all transgender women fall into one of these two categories, with no exceptions.[458] Blanchard also states that transgender identity is a sexual orientation, and that cisgender women never have autogynephilic fantasies.

In short, according to Blanchard, gender identity isn't real. It is a sickness. All transgender women are either self-hating gay men or heterosexual men with an out-of-control paraphilia.

But the problem is that in every single one of Blanchard's research studies he found a significant number of subjects who defied his two-subtype model and his assumption of causality,[459] that is, he found transgender women who were attracted to other women who did not have sexual fantasies about being a woman, and transgender women attracted to men who did have such fantasies.

Rather than question his model, Blanchard dismissed these many exceptions by accusing those research subjects of "misreporting" (lying about) their experiences, and other proponents of autogynephilia theory have subsequently followed suit.[460] [461] [462] [463] This makes the theory unfalsifiable, since assuming all his subjects who gave answers that didn't fit the model were liars allowed him selectively to throw out any data that would have contradicted his theory. This methodological failure makes the theory unscientific at its core.

The nail in the coffin for Blanchard's theory was a study by Dr. Charles Moser. In Dr. Charles Moser's first study on the subject, "Autogynephilia in women," he administered a survey almost identical to the one Blanchard used to cisgender women and found that:

> By the common definition of ever having erotic arousal to the thought or image of oneself as a woman, 93% of the respondents would be classified as autogynephilic. Using a more rigorous definition of "frequent" arousal to multiple items, 28% would be classified as autogynephilic.

It should be noted that Blanchard's own theory description states that cisgender women never have autogynephilic fantasies, stating:

> Autogynephilia does not occur in women, that is, biological females are not sexually aroused by the simple thought of possessing breasts or vulvas.[464]

In other words, Moser found that transgender women have almost the same sexual fantasies as cisgender women, which nullifies the hypothesis that being transgender is a paraphilia, since this arousal pattern is a normal one. He similarly violated one of the basic tenets of research in that he had no cisgender control group in any of his studies.

As for bisexual transgender women, he assumes they don't exist, or that they are no different from heterosexual ones. In essence, he has designed a theory that deliberately erases bisexuality as a legitimate orientation. Ironically, the implied narcissistic element of autogynephilia closely resembles the (discredited and outdated) narcissistic love theories regarding the roots of homosexuality.

Despite all these flaws and biases, it hasn't stopped anti-transgender people and groups from trying to use his theories to argue that transgender people should be discriminated against and denied health care. However, Blanchard refuses to take any sort of responsibility for this. In a 2013 interview, Blanchard claimed that he didn't believe his position caused any harm to the transgender community:

> **Q:** "Do you think that classifying transgender people as having a disorder does contribute to stigma against the trans community?"
>
> **A:** "No. I mean how many people who make a joke about trannies consult the DSM first?"[465]

In the same interview, he acknowledges that his work feeds the fires of those who wish to do transgender people harm, and that he doesn't care. The fact that his pet theories pop up in the Family Research Council's manifesto of how, and why, transgender people should be legislated out of existence exposes how this quote is disingenuous.[466]

> I'm certainly not in favor of saying things in a hurtful or mean way if there's an equally precise way of saying the same thing that is not hurtful or mean. I'm not one of these guys who goes out of his way to be politically incorrect. But I don't think we should promulgate untruths for the sake of political agendas, even if they are worthwhile political agendas.

First, is there a nice way of calling someone a deluded, self-hating homosexual, or a fetishist? Of course not, and he knows it. In fact, he has gone out of his way to describe transgender people as amputation fetishists.[467]

As a result, Blanchard is cited frequently by other anti-LGBT groups, particularly Catholic ones endorsing reparative therapy such as Courage (the group which the son of the late Antonin Scalia belongs to—Scalia was a vociferously anti-LGBT Supreme Court Justice) and the Catholic World Report.[468] And why not? Blanchard was raised Catholic, and he holds the very traditionalist Catholic view that any non-penis-in-vagina sex act is abnormal and should be pathologized. "[N]ormal sexuality is whatever is related to reproduction," Blanchard says.[469]

To date, there appears to be no evidence that Blanchard objects to either the radical right or radical feminists using his theories to spread their hate of the transgender community, nor of their use of it to attack access to civil rights protections or medical care. Indeed, he has posted repeatedly on anti-transgender websites in support of their positions.[470]

If Dr. Blanchard had no positional authority or credibility, it would be easy to dismiss him. But that is not the case—to the contrary, he was on the *DSM* committee in charge of paraphilias and sexual disorders. Blanchard has openly admitted to abusing that position to create diagnoses out of thin air—a serious breach of professional ethics—just to prove a political point:

> **Q:** "Do you think autoandrophilia, where a woman is aroused by the thought of herself as a man, is a real paraphilia?"
>
> **A:** "No, I proposed it simply in order not to be accused of sexism, because there are all these women who want to say, 'women can rape too, women can be pedophiles too, women can be exhibitionists too.' It's a perverse expression of feminism, and so, I thought, let me jump the gun on this. I don't think the phenomenon even exists."[471]

It is a testament to Blanchard's pull in the mental health community that the *DSM-5* nearly included autoandrophilia, the diagnosis he openly admits to making up out of whole cloth, just to show contempt for his critics and "political correctness." Given his power, what he said next in the same interview should scare every LGB person out there:

> I would say if one could start from scratch, ignore all the history of removing homosexuality from the *DSM*, normal sexuality is whatever is related to reproduction. Now you have everything else. I would distinguish between behaviors which are anomalous and benign vs. those that are malignant. So homosexuality would be not normal but benign. Whereas something like serious dangerous sadism would be a malignant variation.

As far as Dr. Blanchard is concerned, all non-reproductive sex should be pathologized. He is a radical Catholic who would go back to a time before 1972 and classify all lesbians, gays, and bisexuals as suffering from a paraphilia.

Given his history of pursuing his own aims regardless of professional ethical constraints, or concern for how his actions affect thousands of people in the LGBT community, Dr. Ray Blanchard holds a unique position: he is openly anti-LGBT, yet remains a Teflon version of Mark Regnerus (who cooked the books to create research saying lesbians and gays made bad parents).[472]

There is reason for hope, however. Blanchard has retired. His theories have been thoroughly discredited, and his life's work is a poorly regarded footnote in mainstream mental health. All of the accumulating evidence of the biological origins of gender identity undercut his own pet theory. As a result he is less and less frequently cited in academic literature, and his theories are now mostly found in non-peer-reviewed material being pushed by anti-transgender hate groups working to fight against protections for transgender people by demonizing them.

How to detect and debunk anti-transgender propaganda in the media on your own

There is no shortage of misinformation about transgender people to debunk these days. One could write articles dissecting material produced attacking transgender people as a class for a living, and still only touch a small fraction of them. At the same time, transgender people and parents of transgender people ask me all the time "Have you seen this?" every time a new one pops up.

It's better to teach a person to fish than to simply give them a fish. It's also better for readers to be able to critically dissect articles about transgender people for themselves than to rely on people like me to try and take all of them apart. Thus, here are the things you should ask yourself, and answer, every time you see one of these anti-transgender articles come up. The answers will allow you to effectively debunk the articles, and do so in a comprehensive way.

These questions should also help you think critically about almost any controversial topic, not just those related to transgender people.

1. Who wrote it?

Would anyone take an article on how to deal with racial issues written by David Duke (a former Grand Wizard of the Klu Klux Klan) seriously? Or an article on American Jewish history written by Richard Spencer? Of course not, unless they were a raging bigot to begin with. Therefore, look at who the authors of anti-transgender articles are.

When you find out that the author implies that transgender people were responsible for the rise of neo-Nazi riots, or that they generally agree with the statement that transgender people should be morally legislated out of existence, you can safely call them bigoted kooks who should not be taken seriously by anyone who isn't also a raging bigot.

2. Who does the author hang out with?

Let's apply the white-nationalist analogy again. Suppose someone claimed not to be a white nationalist. However, they just "happen" to write books and articles that white nationalists love and quote all the time. They hang out on white nationalist internet forums, and generally support the statements made by white nationalists in the comments section. They also give away links to free electronic copies of their works on white nationalist websites. Almost all of their followers on Twitter are white nationalists and people who really hate black people. Would you really take their claims of not being a white nationalist seriously?

If something looks like a duck, walks like a duck, quacks like a duck, and lives with a bunch of ducks in a pond, you would be pretty safe in assuming it is a duck.

The same applies to the concern trolls who claim not to hate transgender people, but who are the darlings of those who want to morally legislate us out of existence. The white nationalist example above also describes a number of prominent people who seem to make a living off of attacking transgender people.

If they walk like a bigot, talk like a bigot, and hang out with bigots, they're probably bigots.

3. Where is it published?

Would you ever take an article published on a neo-Nazi website about Jewish conspiracies seriously (besides someone who's obviously comfortable with their own anti-Semitism)? Obviously not—these sites have never had anything nice to say about Jews, and their bias isn't hidden.

So why on earth would you give any credence to an article about transgender people on The Federalist, The Daily Caller, Breitbart, or any other far-right-wing website seriously either? None of them has ever had a nice thing to say about transgender people, they are clearly biased, and have consistently treated us as a public health hazard that needs to be removed from the public consciousness.

4. Does it blatantly misuse (or cherry pick) real research?

One of the quickest ways to spot biased and unreliable articles about transgender people is when they misuse actual research. Most commonly this occurs when they cite a 2011 study by Dr. Cecilia Dhejne to argue that medical care for transgender people is ineffective, or that it makes them suicidal.[473] The problem is, the research says no such thing and Dhejne has gone on the record saying that attempts to use it to make these points are both wrong and unethical.[474]

As such, articles that deliberately misrepresent (lie about) the findings of actual academic work to support anti-transgender positions aren't just wrong, they are unethical from the start. I've met Dr. Dhejne, and she finds the use of her work to these ends disgusting.

5. Does it blatantly misrepresent the actual positions of people?
Dr. Kenneth Zucker is a problematic figure. He has been the biggest proponent of the 80 percent desistance myth, and been completely opposed to supporting pre-pubescent kids in any gender variant behavior whatsoever, even if the kids are otherwise emotionally healthy and happy.[475] This is why he is frequently cited by people and organizations opposed to letting transgender and gender variant kids be themselves. He is discussed in greater detail earlier in this chapter.

However, what they *never* acknowledge is that even Zucker supports the use of puberty blockers for adolescents (i.e. those who have started puberty) who are gender dysphoric, because in an interview with a conservative outlet he conceded that, "By age 11 or 12, trans kids are typically 'locked in' to their gender identity" and, for them, "I very much support that pathway, because I think that is going to help them have a better quality of life."[476] [477] (So even Dr. Zucker thinks that kids older than 11 or 12 are unlikely to desist and should go on blockers.)

As a result, any person or article that tries to apply the 80 percent desistance figure to transgender teens is either ignorant or lying. In either case, this makes the source unreliable and unworthy of further consideration.

6. Does it misrepresent the positions of mainstream organizations?
One of the most common examples of this is the breathless assertion that "They're giving hormones and sex-change surgery to 6-year-olds!" "They" in this case meaning medical practitioners who fall under the World Professional Association of Transgender Health (WPATH) Standards of Care.[478] WPATH sets the standards followed by the vast majority of health care providers who specialize in transgender medicine. These standards do not recommend blockers (a reversible intervention) until the beginning of puberty, followed by hormones as adolescence progresses (16 or older), and waiting for genital surgery until the patient reaches the age of majority.

Another blatant example of misrepresenting the positions of mainstream organizations is the assertion that care providers are railroading children into transitioning. Dr. Dan Karasic, a member of the Board of Directors for WPATH, states, "WPATH Standards of Care 7 supports allowing children to explore and express gender freely. Whether or not a young person needs to transition should be determined by that person."

7. What organizations does the author represent?

Ask what organizations the writer belongs to, or is representing. Do they belong to a hate group, as defined by the Southern Poverty Law Center?[479] Or speak for fake medical organizations that routinely produce recommendations driven by religious beliefs rather than peer-reviewed science and medical consensus?[480] If they do, they cannot credibly claim to be unbiased, and certainly are not acting in the best interests of transgender people.

(Seriously, if someone is a spokesperson for the Klan, you can't take their claims that they're acting in the best interests of blacks. Why should we think about it differently when the group being targeted is transgender people?)

8. Who does the article cite?

Does the article rely on sources that are biased and/or discredited? Dr. Paul McHugh would be an example of someone who is both biased and discredited as a source. You need to be able to describe why a source is biased or discredited.[481] For example, Johns Hopkins has implicitly repudiated McHugh's work by reopening the gender clinic, colleagues have publicly excoriated him, and no serious researcher cites the study he commissioned because it's poor quality and has non-reproducible results. If the article relies on biased and disreputable sources to make its point, its conclusions probably aren't valid either.

9. Does the article go against the scientific consensus?

There is currently an overwhelming consensus by professional organizations for mental and medical care providers on the necessity and efficacy of health care for transgender individuals.[482] These organizations include the American Medical Association, the American Psychological Association, and the American Psychiatric Association.

These organizations studied the matters in detail before taking these positions.

Thus, if the author contradicts all of these organizations, they must adequately explain why they are more qualified or smarter than the vast majority of experts who have studied the issue based on peer-reviewed evidence. Alternately, they must explain why all the peer-reviewed evidence is wrong in a way that would survive peer review.

Otherwise, it's merely an opinion piece with little in the way of (cherry-picked) research to support it, by someone with very few qualifications, and probably an ax to grind based on personal beliefs as well.

10. Does it substitute anecdotes for research?

Many of the articles that have come out recently about detransitioning and regrets are based on anecdotes, not actual research. This is because the actual research shows that when the Standards of Care for mental health care professionals treating transgender people are followed, regret rates are very low, and often caused by factors external to the patient (e.g. surgical complications, mistreatment and abandonment after transition).[483]

Often, anecdotes leave out or ignore key details as well, which brings us to the next question you should be asking...

11. Are crucial details left out or ignored?

Here are some facts about Senator John McCain. He joined the Navy, and tried to commit suicide as a direct result of joining the Navy. From this statement, one could be led to draw the conclusion that the Navy makes people suicidal, or that McCain was mentally unstable and should never have been allowed in the Navy in the first place.

However, it leaves out the key detail that he attempted suicide after being shot down, becoming a prisoner of war, held in solitary confinement for two years, and having his arms torn out of their sockets (leaving him permanently crippled) by his Vietnamese captors.

Similarly, most of the anecdotes about detransitioners leave out crucial details. Chief among these omissions is that there seems to be a common thread that most of them did not have access to competent mental health care before transitioning, or did not avail themselves of it. Others detransition, but do not regret having transitioned for a time. Another frequent omission is that people often detransition due to being abused for transitioning in the first place.[484] Systemic abuse can lead to very unhealthy mental states and poor decisions, whether by John McCain or a random transgender person.

12. Does it make unsupportable assumptions?

A prime example of an unsupportable assumption is that transgender people can (and should) just stop being transgender because of higher health risks, as if it were like quitting smoking or eating carb-loaded snacks before bedtime. This assumption first ignores that the medical and mental health care communities regard efforts to change sexual orientation[485] and gender identity as ineffectual and unethical.[486] It also ignores the fact that the only people promising to "fix" someone's gender identity are the same people who failed so miserably at "curing" gay people while using the same "embrace your God-given masculinity" snake oil.[487]

Or, conversely, it's a lot easier to reasonably assume based on the peer-reviewed evidence that if transgender people weren't ostracized, abused, and legally marginalized they'd have better mental health outcomes.[488]

Thus, any article on transgender people that assumes there is some sort of therapy that changes people's gender identity is engaging in sophistry.

13. Does it make unsupportable conclusions? (And ignore the supported ones?)

Examples of unsupportable conclusions in anti-transgender articles are myriad. Many of the anecdotes about detransitioners essentially conclude that no one should ever be allowed to transition (which ignores the peer-reviewed evidence showing that the vast majority of transgender people report improvement in quality of life after transition).[489] A far more logical conclusion would be that people should have better access to competent mental health care providers, which is something the APA is recommending anyway.

14. Does the article make wild accusations and/or predict ludicrous outcomes?

Wild accusations (that have actually been made) include that accepting transgender people will destroy humanity, destroy the nuclear family, cause people to forget how to procreate, cause hurricanes and terrorist attacks, destroy legal rights for LGB people, and destroy the LGB community by stealing all queer kids and forcing them to transition. If the material is making these sorts of assertions, it's not reliable.

15. Does the author make assertions that are outright falsehoods?

In Ryan T. Anderson's book of anti-transgender propaganda, he asserts that improvements in access to transgender health care in recent years are "not a consequence of any new scientific evidence" since the study commissioned by Dr. McHugh in 1977.[490] One has only to peruse the end notes of this book to see literally hundreds of peer-reviewed studies that have been conducted since 1977 that support the availability of affirming care for transgender people to realize that this is simply not true.

16. Does the article imply that religion is a cure for gender dysphoria?

This is a theological argument, and not a scientific one. If there was peer-reviewed evidence that prayer was more powerful than medicine, we wouldn't need hospitals. Indeed, they've actually extensively studied whether prayer is any good at curing people (hint: it's not).[491] But there is plenty of evidence that religious counseling and conversion therapy is harmful to queer people.[492]

Sound public policy is based on science, research, and analysis, not religious beliefs.

Chapter 6
LAW

Introduction to US Civil Rights Law

This chapter is meant to give you a basic understanding of how transgender rights have evolved from a legal perspective over the past 40-plus years. Over that time, more and more courts have decided that discrimination against transgender people is a form of sex discrimination, which is prohibited by the 1964 Civil Rights Act. Additionally, sex discrimination is also effectively prohibited (unless it furthers an important governmental interest by means that are substantially related to furthering that interest) under the Equal Protection Clause of the 14th Amendment.

When it comes to transgender civil rights, the courts play two crucial roles. First, the courts often must determine if government actions that affect transgender people are constitutional. An example of this that is currently in the news at the time of writing are the federal cases deciding if the attempt to ban transgender troops from the military is legal. The other area is determining if existing civil rights law applies to transgender people under the category of sex (e.g. is it legal to fire someone simply for being transgender?). The court system has a unique and historic role in protecting minority rights from majoritarian prejudices, distinct from the functions of the executive and legislative branches.

Before reading this chapter, though, there are several concepts you need to understand about the US court and legal system. These include state versus federal courts, court levels within each system, the Equal Protection Clause of the 14th Amendment, standards of review, levels of scrutiny, and how the 1964 Civil Rights Act works. Each is addressed below. These concepts are particular to the US legal system.

Additionally, some federal administrative agencies, like the Equal Employment Opportunity Commission (EEOC), Department of Labor (DOL), Department of Education (DOE), and Health and Human Services (HHS), have their own quasi-judicial tribunals presided over by administrative law judges. These rulings can have jurisdiction over federal agencies, as well as influence on state and federal court decisions. Two of these quasi-judicial decisions, *Macy v. Holder* and *Lusardi v. McHugh*, are discussed in this chapter and in the Appendix.

Basic legal concepts

The American court system[493]

There are both state and federal court systems. This chapter focuses primarily on decisions made by the federal system, since it is concerned with civil rights at the national level. Civil rights issues in state courts apply only to state laws, and can be appealed to the federal system only if there is a federal legal question. In other words, federal courts override state courts when there is a federal law or constitutional issue. Both federal and state court systems are hierarchical—a case enters the court system and proceeds up the hierarchy.

There are generally three court levels in the federal system. From lowest to highest they are the trial court (District Court), the intermediate appellate court (Circuit Court of Appeals), and the final appellate court (the Supreme Court). Federal cases start at a district court, and proceed upwards to circuit courts and the Supreme Court (in that order) if those higher courts agree to hear the appeals. The process of agreeing to hear appeals at the Supreme Court level is referred to as granting a writ of *certiorari* (or colloquially "granting *cert*," or "*cert*" for short). Federal bankruptcy courts exist in parallel to district courts, but are not a factor in this chapter.

The US district courts are the trial courts of the federal judicial system. There is at least one US district court in each state. There are also US district courts for the District of Columbia and 16 US territories, including Puerto Rico and the US Virgin Islands.

The US courts of appeals are the intermediate appellate courts of the federal judicial system. Their decisions are binding on US district courts within their areas of jurisdiction (i.e. district courts underneath a circuit court of appeals must abide by circuit court decisions, both past and present). There are 12 geographic courts of appeals (11 numbered circuits and the Court of Appeals for the DC Circuit) and a few other specialized district courts, such as the Court of Federal Claims, a specialized court with limited jurisdiction based in Washington, DC. Figure 6.1 shows the geographic regions covered by each of the circuits.

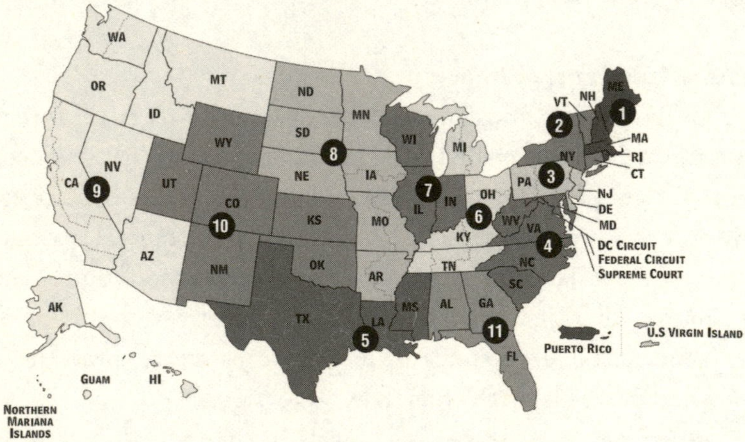

Figure 6.1: Geographic boundaries of US courts of appeals and US district courts

Source: Wikimedia Commons

The decisions of the US Supreme Court are binding on all federal courts and on state courts regarding the US Constitution, federal laws, and disputes between states.

After a case has been decided, the written decision can be applied to subsequent cases; it becomes precedent for future cases. This means that future cases deciding a similar issue must use this earlier decision as a guide. The process of using opinions this way is called *stare decisis*. Because of this reliance on previous relevant opinions, it is vital to find them and to make sure they are still good law.

However, not every opinion is precedential for every court.

A court must follow and is bound by an opinion that is mandatory authority (e.g. a district court in the 5th Circuit must abide by prior decisions made by the 5th Circuit Court of Appeals and the Supreme Court). Opinions issued by higher courts in a jurisdiction are generally considered binding on lower courts in that jurisdiction.

While opinions from other jurisdictions are not precedential, they may be persuasive. A court does not necessarily have to follow an opinion that is persuasive only, but may choose to do so if an opinion from a lower court, from another court within the district at the same level, or from another jurisdiction is at most persuasive only.

For example, US Supreme Court decisions are binding in the US Court of Appeals for the 2nd Circuit. However, a decision of the US Court of Appeals for the 3rd Circuit is not binding authority in the 2nd Circuit—it is persuasive authority only.

As a real-life example, the 6th Circuit ruled in 2004 that employment discrimination against transgender people was sex discrimination under the Civil Rights Act. In 2017, the 7th Circuit heard a case of a transgender employee who was fired for coming out. The 7th Circuit might consider the 2004 ruling by the 6th Circuit persuasive, but not precedential (because it came from another circuit).

The Civil Rights Act of 1964

The Civil Rights Act of 1964 is a landmark piece of federal civil rights legislation that forms the basis for most US federal civil rights law even today. It bars discrimination on the basis of age, color, religion, *sex*,[494] or national origin. The law was separated into 11 sections (Titles), which cover different aspects of the law.[495]

This chapter will primarily deal with Title VII of the 1964 Civil Rights Act. Title VII prohibits employers from discriminating on the basis of age, color, religion, *sex*, or national origin.[496]

Of all the Act's sections, Title VII is probably the most important to the transgender community as it deals with employment discrimination. The question that courts have been addressing since the 1970s is whether employment discrimination against transgender people is a form of sex discrimination. In the past decade, federal courts have overwhelmingly decided that it is. The Supreme Court has not heard a case on this issue, though it is generally regarded only as a matter of time before it does.

The Equal Protection Clause of the US Constitution

Section 1 of the 14th Amendment to the US Constitution states that:

> All persons born or naturalized in the United States, and subject to the jurisdiction thereof, are citizens of the United States and of the state wherein they reside. No state shall make or enforce any law which shall abridge the privileges or immunities of citizens of the United States; nor shall any state deprive any person of life, liberty, or property, without due process of law; nor deny to any person within its jurisdiction the *equal protection of the laws.*

The italicized portion is known as the Equal Protection Clause, and it implies that a state government cannot treat similarly situated groups of individuals differently. The federal government is considered bound to this principle by the 5th Amendment. As a practical matter, the Civil Rights Act generally covers discrimination by private entities (primarily businesses), and both the Civil Rights Act and the Equal Protection Clause cover various forms of discrimination by public (government) entities.

Levels of scrutiny

One of the key concepts in understanding how the Equal Protection Clause of the 14th Amendment applies to civil rights are the "levels of scrutiny" used in the US court system. Often the government makes laws and decisions that affect a group of people or abridge a right. For example, we don't let 12-year-olds have drivers' licenses, and felons are prohibited from owning firearms. Congress may treat groups of people differently so long as there is a rational basis for doing so. However, in cases involving a constitutional right, such as freedom of speech, or a suspect classification, such as race, there needs to be a "compelling" governmental interest. In the cases above, the rational basis for treating the groups differently is to prevent traffic accident deaths and violent crime.

Exactly how compelling the reason has to be is based on the right being infringed on or the class of people affected. In recent decades, legal protections for rights and classes of people have generally been divided into three levels by the courts, known as levels of scrutiny: strict (the highest), intermediate, and rational basis (lowest level of scrutiny). Each of these is discussed briefly below. More recently, courts have created a fourth level of scrutiny which is relevant to the LGBT community, often called "heightened scrutiny." Scrutiny is important, because it determines how hard it is legally for the government to discriminate against, or even affect, a class of people.

STRICT SCRUTINY

For a court to apply strict scrutiny to a case, the law or government action (such as an executive order) brought before the court for review must either have significantly impacted a fundamental right (such as freedom of speech or religion), or affect a suspect classification such as race, national origin, religion, or poverty.[497] To pass the strict scrutiny test, a law must further a "compelling governmental interest," and must be narrowly tailored to achieve that interest.

As an example, if a state passed a voter ID law that primarily affected African-Americans, making it much harder for them to vote, courts would be likely to apply the strict scrutiny test to determine whether this law was constitutional under the Equal Protection Clause of the 14th Amendment because it negatively impacted one specific race of people. If the law failed the strict scrutiny test, as it likely would in this example, the law would be struck down, and the state would not be allowed to enforce the law.

INTERMEDIATE SCRUTINY

For the intermediate scrutiny test to be applied, the statute before the court must negatively affect certain protected classes of people, less suspect as a classification than race or national origin (i.e. affect a class of people that is protected, but less so than race or national origin), including a quasi-suspect classification, such as sex (gender)[498] or legitimacy of birth. Rights (vice classes of people) protected by intermediate scrutiny include the 2nd Amendment (the right to bear arms) and some freedom of the press cases. To pass intermediate scrutiny, the law must further an important government interest and do so by means that are substantially related to that interest.

If a state government was requiring female employees to wear skirts or dresses as part of the dress code, intermediate scrutiny would probably be applied in court because this would impact only one sex of people. The rights being abridged are related to sex, as males and females are being held to a different standard by the government. It would likely fail the intermediate scrutiny test, since preventing women from wearing pants is not an important government interest.

RATIONAL BASIS SCRUTINY

To pass rational basis scrutiny, the challenged law must be rationally related to a legitimate government interest. Rational basis is the easiest of the tests to pass. Rational basis review is generally used in cases where no fundamental rights or suspect classifications are at issue. To pass review, the government action must serve a legitimate state interest and there must be a rational connection between how the law is enforced and what it is trying to achieve.[499]

An example might be a law requiring dentists pass an exam to practice dentistry. Dentists are not a protected class of people, and there is a legitimate governmental interest in ensuring people receive competent medical care. As such, a rational basis challenge of the law requiring dentists to pass an exam would be likely to fail under the US legal system, and the ordinance would remain in effect.

HEIGHTENED SCRUTINY

"Heightened scrutiny," or "rational basis with bite," most closely resembles intermediate scrutiny, and generally applies the same two tests (does the law further an important government interest and does it do so by means that are substantially related to that interest?). What separates this from intermediate scrutiny is that the suspect class has generally not been formally protected by law, which describes LGBT people in the US.

In *Witt v. Department of the Air Force* in 2008, the US Court of Appeals for the 9th Circuit ruled that the law commonly known as "Don't Ask, Don't Tell" (DADT) was subject to "heightened" scrutiny based on its analysis of *Lawrence v. Texas*, which struck down laws against sodomy.[500] The court created a three-pronged test for heightened scrutiny. To pass, the law "must advance an important governmental interest, the intrusion must significantly further that interest, and the intrusion must be necessary to further that interest." This differs from the "substantially related to important governmental interests" two-prong test for "intermediate" scrutiny.

The Supreme Court hasn't commented on heightened scrutiny or what tests to apply to it. The *Witt* test is somewhat random, and cobbled together from different tests.

In determining if a class of people is protected by heightened scrutiny, courts have often considered whether these people:

- have historically been discriminated against[501]
- possess an immutable or highly visible trait[502]
- are powerless to protect themselves via the political process[503]
- have distinguishing characteristic(s) that do not prevent them from contributing to society.[504]

In recent years, LGBT people, and particularly transgender people, have been increasingly seen to meet all four of these tests for belonging to a quasi-suspect class, and are thus entitled to heightened scrutiny. Some courts have said trans people are entitled to intermediate scrutiny, which is generally considered higher than heightened scrutiny. See *Adkins v. NYC*, 143 F.Supp.3d 134 9S.D.N.Y. 2015 as an example of where the courts found that intermediate scrutiny was applicable to transgender people. This has the effect of setting a higher legal hurdle for the government to discriminate against them even if LGBT people are not specifically protected by laws. It still allows for laws which, while not directly targeting LGBT people, adversely affect them.

Important case law related to transgender rights

Case law is where courts apply these concepts to real-life situations. It also shows vividly how the interpretation of laws and the Constitution changes over time, as well as how a bunch of cases can come together (like *Hopkins* and *Oncale*) to help create an entirely new legal concept. Sort of like chemistry for lawyers. This section provides a summary of the effects of the most important cases for transgender people in American history. Refer to the Appendix for a more complete list of court cases and descriptions of their impact.

Several early LGBT civil rights cases put before the court in the 1970s and early 1980s were brought by transgender employees fired for being trans. These plaintiffs argued that discrimination against transgender people, then referred to as transsexuals, should be covered by the sex discrimination clause in Title VII of the Civil Rights Act.

For many years, courts disagreed with this argument, relying on the presumed legislative intent of Congress that discrimination "because of sex" in Title VII was originally intended to cover discrimination against women by men. It was not meant to cover discrimination against men, effeminate men, transgender people, or others based on gender stereotypes. *Holloway v. Arthur Andersen* is one of the earliest and most cited cases as the 9th Circuit rejected the argument that transgender people were protected by the Civil Rights Act. As a result, transgender people were not considered to be protected by the Civil Rights Act in the courts until the early 2000s.

One important case, used for decades to defend transgender discrimination, was the 1984 case of *Ulane v. Eastern Airlines.* Kenneth Ulane, a pilot for Eastern Airlines for over a decade, transitioned to Karen Frances Ulane and was fired for it in 1981. Ulane filed a suit for sex discrimination under Title VII of the Civil Rights Act of 1964, alleging that she was 1) discriminated against as a female, and 2) discriminated against for being transgender.

The lower (district) court judge ruled in favor of Ulane on both counts and awarded her reinstatement as a flying officer with full seniority and back pay, plus attorneys' fees. Unfortunately, the 7th Circuit overruled the lower court on both counts, concluding that discrimination against Ulane was "not because she is female, but because she is transsexual." Essentially, the court ruled Eastern Airlines was not discriminating against her as a woman, but against her for the act of transitioning, which is not covered by Title VII.[505]

This case, and this novel rationale for justifying discrimination (namely that it had nothing to do with sex), had far-reaching effects, and was frequently cited in future Title VII cases involving transgender individuals. It was because of *Ulane* that many circuits rejected the argument that transgender people are protected by Title VII up until the 2000s. *Ulane* was effectively overturned in 2017, when the 7th Circuit decided that sexual orientation was protected in *Hively*, and then used the logic of *Hively* to sidestep *Ulane* in *Whitaker v. Kenosha Unified School District* (described later).

A case from 1985, *City of Cleburne v. Cleburne Living Ctr., Inc*, provided the first significant weapon in the arsenal of legal arguments against trans discrimination. When the City of Cleburne enacted an ordinance specifically to prevent a facility for mentally handicapped people from being built, the court ruled against them and found that the Equal Protection Clause prohibits any laws that are "arbitrary or irrational" or reflect "a bare...desire to harm a politically unpopular group." It also found when passing a law that targets a group adversely, the state must show that the law is rationally related to a legitimate governmental purpose.

Although this case had nothing to do with LGBT discrimination, *Cleburne* began to be cited by other cases that did involve transgender rights. *Cleburne* was used as the basis for rejecting laws or policies targeting transgender people, because it cogently stated that unpopularity is not a legitimate rationale under rational basis analysis, making such laws harder to defend in court.

Perhaps the most important case in this chapter is *Hopkins v. Price Waterhouse*. The plaintiff, Ann Hopkins (a cisgender woman), claimed she had had her promotion to partnership at the firm postponed for two years in a row based on sex stereotyping against her gender nonconformity. After her promotion was postponed for the first year,

Hopkins met with the head supervisor of her department, who told her that to increase chances of promotion she needed "to walk more femininely, wear makeup, have her hair styled, and wear jewelry." Hopkins was well qualified for partnership and frequently outperformed her co-workers. There were ample examples to show that she was denied promotion based on sex stereotyping. Many male employees at the firm even said they would not be comfortable having her as their partner because she did not act the way they believed a woman should.

Hopkins claimed that the postponement of promotion was based on sex-stereotyping against her gender non-conformity and that this violated her rights under the sexual discrimination clause of Title VII of the Civil Rights Act of 1964. Unlike many previous cases, this time the lower courts (District Court and the Appeals Court for DC) *did* find that discrimination based on gender stereotypes was prohibited under Title VII. What's more, when Price Waterhouse appealed, this decision was upheld by the Supreme Court and therefore could (and must when applicable) be used across the entire country.

This is perhaps the single most important case in the history of transgender case law. Virtually every case that found in favor of transgender plaintiffs in the past two decades cites Hopkins *as precedential, since the Supreme Court ruled that discrimination on the basis of sex stereotypes is a violation of Title VII.*

In 1996, a case concerning LGBT legal protections came before the Supreme Court. The cities of Aspen, Boulder, and Denver, Colorado, each had enacted ordinances which banned discrimination in housing, employment, education, public accommodations, health and welfare services, and many other transactions and activities on the basis of sexual orientation. In response, voters in the state of Colorado passed an amendment to the state constitution in 1992 (Amendment 2) that repealed these ordinances to the extent they prohibit discrimination on the basis of "homosexual, lesbian or bisexual orientation, conduct, practices or relationships." Amendment 2 also prohibited all future legislative, executive, or judicial action at any level of state or local government designed to protect LGBT citizens.

Amendment 2 was challenged in court as being unconstitutional for violating the Equal Protection Clause of the 14th Amendment.

After making its way through district and circuit courts, the case arrived at the Supreme Court of the United States (SCOTUS). SCOTUS agreed with the plaintiffs and ruled Amendment 2 to be unconstitutional because it violated the 14th Amendment. SCOTUS found that the law targeted a suspect class for no legitimate end, and that it did so out of animosity. It concluded that:

> Amendment 2 classifies homosexuals not to further a proper legislative end but to make them unequal to everyone else. This Colorado cannot do. A State cannot so deem a class of persons a stranger to its laws. Amendment 2 violates the Equal Protection Clause, and the judgment of the Supreme Court of Colorado is affirmed.[506]

This ruling drew on the same concept as *Cleburne*: one cannot use legislation to single out a specific group for unequal protection and rights. What separates it from other case law is that SCOTUS specifically addresses whether discrimination on the basis of sexual orientation should be allowed at the lowest level of scrutiny (rational basis), and found that it didn't. Thus, laws targeting people based on sexual orientation are generally not seen to pass even the test for rational basis scrutiny, much less heightened or intermediate.

A Supreme Court case in 1998 provided another tool for future court cases challenging transgender discrimination. In *Oncale v. Sundowner* a male cisgender oilfield worker (Oncale) was subjected to sexual harassment and humiliation on the job, and sued for discrimination under Title VII of the 1964 Civil Rights Act. In the past, arguments like this had failed, with the court finding that Title VII only applied to sexual harassment and discrimination against women. But this time, the Supreme Court ruled unanimously that original legislative intent must not be given controlling weight in interpreting the Civil Rights Act.

This ruling became key to future rulings on transgender issues. Over the course of the next 20 years, almost all previous federal court anti-transgender rulings on Title VII would be struck down using the combined Supreme Court precedents of *Hopkins* (finding that discrimination based on gender non-conformity was prohibited under

Title VII) and *Oncale* (finding that discrimination against both men and women was prohibited under Title VII).

In 2000, the first court opinion was published holding that transgender people are protected under a sex discrimination statute, using *Hopkins* and *Oncale*. In *Schwenk v. Hartford*, a transgender prisoner, Crystal Schwenk, sought damages for an attempted rape by Mitchell, a prison guard. Mitchell's defense argued that Schwenk was male and that the 1994 Gender Motivated Violence Act (GMVA) did not protect men who are raped or sexually assaulted by other men. They also argued that transgender people were not covered by the GMVA. These arguments were rejected by the district and circuit court of appeals, which ruled in favor of Schwenk.

This ruling was one of the first to affirm that a law prohibiting sex discrimination applies to discrimination against transgender individuals. It was also the first to apply *Hopkins* and *Oncale* in combination to reach this decision and, in the process, overturn previous case law. This is the point when courts increasingly begin to affirm protections for transgender people.

The case of *Smith v. City of Salem* in 2004 was the first federal appeals court case to specifically find (and be upheld) that discrimination against transgender people in employment was a form of sex discrimination under Title VII of the 1964 Civil Rights Act. Smith, a firefighter with the City of Salem for seven years, was fired after announcing her plan to transition. The court relied on *Hopkins* and *Oncale* to shoot down defense arguments that used older case law.

The trend continued in 2005, when *Barnes v. City of Cincinnati* built on this previous decision. Barnes, a transgender police officer, challenged her demotion from sergeant to corporal under Title VII. Not only did Barnes win, but the 6th Circuit Court of Appeals decision firmly established transgender individuals as a protected class and, as such, subject to Title VII *and* the Equal Protection Clause within the Circuit.

Additional cases that also succeeded in affirming protection from employment discrimination for transgender people include *Lopez v. River Oaks Imaging & Diagnostic Group Inc.* in 2008, and *Schroer v. Billington* in 2009. In *Schroer*, the DC Circuit Court of Appeals rejected arguments made in *Ulane*, that transitioning is not protected under sex discrimination laws. Schroer's legal team countered *Ulane* with the question, "If you hire Catholic employees and Jewish employees, but fire anyone who converts from Catholicism to Judaism, how is this not a form of religious discrimination?"[507]

Protection for transgender employees of government agencies under the 14th Amendment was recognized by the US 11th Circuit of Appeals in 2011. Vandy Beth Glenn was a legislative editor at the Georgia General Assembly in 2007. When she told her supervisor, Sewell Brumby, of her intent to transition, she was immediately fired. In *Glenn v. Brumby*, the 11th Circuit ruled that discrimination against an employee based on the employee's non-conformance to gender/sex stereotypes is a violation of the equal protection clause of the 14th Amendment to the US Constitution. This ruling used *Hopkins v. Price Waterhouse* as its primary guidance, stating:

> A person is defined as transgender precisely because of the perception that his or her behavior transgresses gender stereotypes... There is thus a congruence between discriminating against transgender and transsexual individuals and discrimination on the basis of gender-based behavioral norms.[508]

The Equal Employment Opportunity Commission (EEOC) helped to confirm this trend for transgender people at the federal level by siding with the transgender plaintiffs in *Macy v. Holder* (2012) and *Lusardi v. McHugh* (2015).[509] This was a formal federal position that discrimination against transgender people in employment is a violation of Title VII of the 1964 Civil Rights Act.

Lusardi was particularly important. The EEOC found that deliberately misgendering transgender people in the workplace is a form of harassment and creates a hostile work environment. Similarly, it found that denying Lusardi access to facilities unless she had "the surgery" violated Title VII and that doing so because she was transgender was a violation of Title VII as well. The EEOC ruling is binding on all federal agencies and persuasive in other courts.

This was also affirmed in 2017 with the 7th Circuit case, *Whitaker v. Kenosha Unified School District*. The plaintiff, a transgender boy named Ashton Whitaker, was prevented from using the boys' restroom at his school. His family sued the school district. In the end, the 7th Circuit ruled in favor of Whitaker both on the grounds of sex discrimination under Title IX of the Education Amendments of 1972, and the 14th Amendment's Equal Protection Clause. In the process, they also sidestepped the longest-standing anti-transgender court ruling remaining at the circuit court level (*Ulane v. Eastern Airlines*). In combination with the 7th Circuit *Hively* decision, holding that sexual orientation is a form of sex discrimination under Title VII, it seems fairly clear that not much remains of *Ulane* in the 7th Circuit. In 2018, a district court judge in Maryland reached a similar conclusion in the case of *MAB v. Board of Education of Talbot County*.

Adverse circuit court rulings that have not been overturned

A few adverse rulings (*Etsitty v. Utah Transit Authority* and *Kastl v. Maricopa County Community College District*) remain on the books at the circuit court level, however. Both predate *Macy*, *Glenn*, *Lusardi*, and *Whitaker*, and thus would be less likely to be upheld in a challenge now. These are examined separately from the chronology above, as they represent ongoing legal issues.

In 2007, the 10th Circuit Court of Appeals heard the case of Sandoval Etsitty, a bus driver for the Utah Transit Authority (UTA). Etsitty was in the process of transitioning but had not undergone gender confirmation surgery at the time. Her job had been terminated because UTA administrators believed "it would be impractical to arrange for a unisex restroom for one operator." Transit authority officials also expressed concern about potential UTA liability based on complaints that may result from the plaintiff using a female restroom, whether in a UTA facility or out in the field. They understood that Etsitty was required by her doctors to live full time as a woman before undergoing GCS.

The court denied both claims to Title VII and 14th Amendment protections. In deciding against Etsitty, the court rejected the notion that transgender people were protected by *Hopkins*, rejected *Smith*, and cited the now overturned *Ulane v. Eastern Airlines* as persuasive. In the process, the court created a legal roadmap for terminating the employment of transgender persons; simply state that the employer has no suitable bathrooms, then terminate their job because it would cost money to provide one.

As of 2017 (when *Ulane* was overturned), however, *Etsitty* is now the lone circuit court-level decision left standing holding that transgender people are not protected by Title VII of the 1964 Civil Rights Act. The court did, however, explicitly note that a transgender plaintiff might be able to bring a sex stereotyping case. As of the time of this writing, at least one district court in the 10th Circuit has found that, despite the *Etsitty* opinion, sex stereotyping claims by transgender plaintiffs are permitted.[510]

In 2009, the 9th Circuit heard the case of *Kastl v. Maricopa County Community College District*. The college banned Rebecca Kastl, who was transgender, from using the university's women's bathrooms. While the 9th Circuit recognized that transgender people are protected from discrimination in employment under Title VII, the court ruled that those protections do not extend to access to facilities. The court agreed with the college's argument and it had "a compelling interest in protecting privacy rights of other individuals...by maintaining the sex-segregation of the restrooms." The plaintiff had provided her driver's license (which had an "F" for sex) but did not provide proof that she had had any kind of gender confirmation surgery.

Case law summary

Over the past four decades, courts have moved from rejecting nearly all claims that transgender people are protected by existing law to the vast majority of courts accepting transgender people as protected by Title VII of the 1964 Civil Rights Act. This is by no means the end of the case law road. The Supreme Court has yet to hear a case that determines what, if any, protections transgender people have under Title VII and the 14th Amendment, although they nearly took on a case involving the similar Title IX of the Education Amendments of 1972 in the case of *Grimm v. Gloucester County School Board.*[511]

The fact that SCOTUS granted cert in this case indicates they believe the matter is ripe and, as such, America will likely see a case involving transgender civil rights reach SCOTUS in the next few years. A single adverse ruling could undermine every positive circuit court case to date. The results would be devastating for the transgender community. Given the uncertain composition of the Supreme Court going forward, the outcome of a hypothetical case involving a transgender person is unpredictable.

For transgender people, however, the stakes couldn't be higher, given that a majority of states have no legal protections for transgender individuals, and religious organizations are demanding that their followers discriminate.

The (social conservative) empire strikes back

People tend to regard history as a stream of progress that only flows one way. The LGBTQ rights movement has experienced great success over the past 35 years passing laws and fighting court cases to make discrimination against LGBTQ people illegal.[512] The crown jewels of these achievements are marriage equality, state and local non-discrimination laws, and the legal interpretation of Title VII of the 1964 Civil Rights Act to protect transgender people on the basis of sex.[513] [514]

Now, remember the end of the first *Star Wars* movie, where the Rebels blow up the Death Star, celebrate like crazy, and hand out medals like they just won the war? Then in the next movie, the good guys spend the entire film getting an ass-whooping from one end of the galaxy to the other?

I cannot think of a better metaphor for what's probably about to happen in the legal arena for LGBTQ people. The battle for marriage equality is over (for now). When the Supreme Court torpedoed the thermal exhaust port of the Defense of Marriage Act (DOMA) via the landmark *Windsor* marriage equality case, it set off a chain reaction that ended the bans on same-sex marriage across the nation.[515]

But it is not over yet. As mentioned in the case law section, SCOTUS has never actually ruled on whether the 1964 Civil Rights Act applies to transgender people or what level of scrutiny should be applied to transgender individuals under the Equal Protection Clause of the 14th Amendment. In the next five years, all of that is probably going to be decided. If the transgender community loses—which is probable—there will not be a path to reclaim that case law progress for at least a generation, if not two or three. It took 75 years to overturn *Plessy v. Ferguson* (which created the legal doctrine of separate but equal racial discrimination), while *Korematsu* (which allowed the internment of Americans of Japanese descent during World War II) still stands over 70 years later.

A series of devastating legal challenges to the LGBT community, particularly to the transgender community, are in the works. These challenges are primarily mounted by the Alliance Defending Freedom (ADF), a coalition of over 3000 anonymous conservative Christian lawyers providing over $208 million dollars-worth of *pro bono* legal work dedicated to instituting biblical law in the United States. They are designated by the Southern Poverty Law Center as an anti-LGBT hate group.[516] Defeating these will be more difficult since Justice Kennedy announced his retirement on June 28, 2018. The subsequent nomination (and confirmation) of ultra-conservative Brett Kavanaugh to replace him gives hardline conservatives on the Supreme Court a 5–4 advantage. This advantage is likely to rise to 6–3 if the Trump Administration also replaces Justice Ginsburg or Justice Breyer due to their retirement or death.

Thus, these upcoming legal challenges include:

- laws that make LGBT people ineligible for civil rights protections
- religious Freedom Restoration Act (RFRA) challenges to LGBT protections
- the Trump Administration's attempts to ban transgender people from the military
- weakening *Obergefell v. Hodges* (marriage equality) to the point of being meaningless
- the constitutionality of bathroom bills, particularly for transgender students.

The conservative plan to effectively end the LGBTQ rights movement has snapped into clear focus based on these legal challenges. It is not a short-term plan, but it is one that will inevitably take place over the next five to ten years. The scary part is that the right-wing plan to tear down 40 years of civil rights progress using the court system is not just feasible, but also highly likely to succeed.

At the macro level, social conservatives have two high-level goals in the court system. The first is to get rulings via impact litigation that LGBTQ people are not protected by existing law or even the 14th Amendment beyond a bare minimum level of rational basis scrutiny.[517] This helps create a legal framework under which businesses and government have wide latitude to discriminate against LGBT people, and have little legal impetus to protect these same people from discrimination (e.g. we'd like to help you, but we cannot).

The second is to lay the groundwork for the RFRA of 1993 to nullify almost all legislation, case law, policies, and regulations protecting LGBTQ people. Once this is accomplished, the protections for transgender people under the 1964 Civil Rights Act will almost inevitably fall, along with protections for women and other minorities.

To achieve both, all organizations like the ADF have to do is keep planting the seeds of their arguments in dissents to court opinions and wait for a more conservative balance at the Supreme Court. Kennedy's replacement has a legal philosophy even more conservative than Justice Gorsuch, and is endorsed by anti-LGBT groups like The Heritage Foundation, Family Research Council, and The Federalist Society. The Senate is likely to confirm whomever is nominated since the "nuclear option" was invoked under former Speaker Harry Reid, and as a result only a simple majority is now required to confirm judicial nominations.

So, what does the legal path to the LGBTQ civil rights Armageddon look like? If these legal challenges to civil rights protections succeed, here's what's probably in store.

Nullifying state and local LGBT protections

In 2011, Tennessee passed a law that nullified all county and city ordinances that protect people based on sexual orientation and gender identity.[518] So far, that law has avoided being struck down as a violation of *Romer v. Evans* because it does not specifically say that sexual orientation and gender identity cannot be protected, just that the local ordinances cannot protect more groups than are protected by the federal government.[519] Arkansas and North Carolina have followed suit, and now there are no local protections for LGBT people in any of these states.[520] [521] So far, all of these laws have stood up to court challenges.

Expanding RFRA to create a license to discriminate: the New Death Star

Expansion of the interpretation of "religious freedom" laws is probably the most direct threat to LGBT civil rights in the US. The religious right has been quietly constructing a new Death Star, and it came in the form of *Burwell v. Hobby Lobby* and *Zubik (aka Little Sisters of the Poor) v. Burwell*, cases in which the Supreme Court ruled in favor of the religious right.[522] [523]

Hobby Lobby relied in great part on *Citizens United*, a case which gave corporations personhood for purposes of freedom of speech.[524] Based on *Citizens United*, the Supreme Court decided that corporations have the same religious freedom rights as private citizens. *Zubik*, in turn, relied on *Citizens United* and *Hobby Lobby* to decide that any imposition on the religious beliefs of a corporation, no matter how slight (in this case, signing and dating a waiver stating that the plaintiffs would not provide birth control to their employees), was an intolerable burden on their constitutional right to religious freedom.

While the *Hobby Lobby* and *Zubik* cases applied to a corporation having the right to refuse birth control coverage to employees for religious reasons, these decisions could easily be extended to discrimination against LGBT employees. This would essentially nullify employment protections for LGBT people in every city, county, and state that currently has them. It could make passage of a federal non-discrimination statute a moot point.

The potential parade of horribles under a broad expansion of RFRA is nearly limitless. It could allow employers to refuse partner benefits in states with marriage equality. It could negate all the rulings favorable to the transgender community that equate discrimination against transgender employees with sex discrimination under Title VII. Indeed, this argument has already successfully been made at the district court level in the 6th Circuit where an employer (Harris Funeral Homes Inc.) claimed that, not only did RFRA allow it to discriminate against transgender employees, it could *ignore the 1964 Civil Rights Act prohibition on discrimination on the basis of sex.*[525]

Thankfully, the 6th Circuit overturned the district court in March 2018.[526] The three-judge panel was unanimous in rejecting the claim that "religious freedom" is sufficient to overcome the government interest in preventing sex discrimination. However, it remains to be seen if the Alliance Defending Freedom will successfully appeal the 6th Circuit decision to the Supreme Court.

Thus, this is a direct and dangerous attack on LGBT Americans enabled by opening up the aperture of RFRA as a legal justification to ignore civil rights laws. In previous years, the Supreme Court did not have the votes to take up cases involving vendors refusing to serve LGBTQ people in states where LGBTQ people are legislatively protected from such discrimination. These cases usually involved a 1st Amendment claim that the government was forcing them to express themselves in a way that violated their religious beliefs. For example, in 2014 the Supreme Court declined to hear the case of *Elane Photography v. Willock*, in which a New Mexico photographer for hire refused to take pictures at a same-sex wedding.[527] [528]

That changed after the death of Justice Scalia, and the addition of Justice Gorsuch. This is why SCOTUS has heard the case of *Masterpiece Cakeshop, Ltd. v. Colorado Civil Rights Commission*, which is basically the same as *Elane Photography*, but with cakes.[529]

The Masterpiece Cakeshop claim will succeeded on the basis that one of the civil rights commission members noted the role of religion in past gross violations of human rights, and Kennedy interpreted it as unallowable hostility (even if what was said was true.) Justices Alito, Thomas, and Gorsuch all seemed primed to carve out a giant religious exemption to civil rights laws in their concurring opinions, and Chief

Justice Roberts has never sided with LGBT people in a court case. Even though Kennedy decided *Masterpiece Cake Shop* for the plaintiffs on narrow grounds, it was hailed as a victory by the religious right, and it left the door open for future courts to create a religious exemption to nearly all civil rights laws. Given the composition of the court after his retirement, this is a near certainty.

Gorsuch has a history of interpreting RFRA extremely broadly, to the point that, in Gorsuch's opinion, even signing a piece of paper opting out of the ACA's provisions on birth control was an unconstitutional burden on the free exercise of religion.[530] [531] While Chief Justice Roberts has not been supportive of 1st Amendment claims, he did vote with the majority in *Hobby Lobby* and *Little Sisters of the Poor Home for the Aged v. Burwell*.[532] He also dissented in *Obergefell* and has expressed the view that, in his opinion, the LGBTQ lobby is so powerful that it does not need government protections from discrimination.

After President Trump's inauguration, the Department of Justice (DOJ) actively began trying to strip the LGBT community of legal protections. Over a few weeks in mid-2017, the DOJ came out against protections for LGBT people in two separate briefs.[533] It has also argued in favor of Trump's ban of transgender people in the military and has produced two more memos describing how the DOJ intends to broadly interpret RFRA so that anyone anywhere can discriminate against LGBT people for almost any religious reason.[534]

One of these memos is entitled "Federal Law Protections for Religious Liberty," and is guidance directed at "all executive departments and agencies."[535] The document outlines 20 principles of religious liberty, asserting not only that religious liberty is a "fundamental right of paramount importance" but that "free exercise of religion includes the right to act or abstain from action in accordance with one's religious beliefs," and that this right extends to both "persons and organizations."

The memo also states that "Religious employers are entitled to employ only persons whose beliefs and conduct are consistent with the employers' religious precepts."

The second memo, titled "Implementation of Memorandum on

Federal Law Protections for Religious Liberty," was addressed to all DOJ attorneys, and "direct[s] all attorneys within the Department to adhere to the interpretative guidance set forth" in the first memorandum.[536]

It also had an immediate effect: the US Department of Agriculture (USDA) released a related memorandum only a few weeks after the DOJ's directives in November 2017.[537] This USDA document allowed employees to specifically preach their religious views about LGBT people at work. Any attempts to stop such speech are punishable under this new equal opportunity policy.

While LGBT people aren't directly mentioned, the message of these two memos is clear: the DOJ will do nothing to stop anti-LGBT discrimination and will do everything it can to allow it under the auspices of "religious freedom." The potential fallout from this is both extensive and devastating. Here are some examples of plausible consequences:

- Imagine a federal employee who files an RFRA claim that paying into health insurance that provides same-sex partner benefits and transgender health care violates his religious beliefs. To accommodate these beliefs, LGBT federal employees would have to buy separate, more expensive, policies.
- If a Catholic hospital receiving federal funding refuses to treat an LGBT person, refuses spousal visitation, or refuses to use a transgender person's legal name and gender, their funding would probably be protected per the DOJ. In many parts of the country, religious hospitals are already the only medical facilities available for hours in any direction. Overall, one in six hospitals in the US are now owned by the Catholic Church. This could result in LGBTQ people having to either lie on their paperwork to receive treatment (which could lead to medical problems based on incomplete sexual history, incorrect name use, and other issues) or LGBTQ people having to either start their own facilities, travel many hours to an accepting facility, or, most likely, forgo health care even in emergency situations. This could lead to long-term medical problems or death.

- If a public-school principal refused to educate LGBT students or allow them to attend classes, the DOJ has indicated it would support an RFRA claim over the previous Supreme Court ruling in *Plyler v. Doe* that requires all children to be provided with access to education. In addition, students could claim that it violates their religious beliefs to attend classes with openly LGBT people and be permitted not to attend or they could claim a right to relentlessly pressure and mock such classmates to make them stop being LGBT by accepting Jesus.

Similarly, if a federal employee stated that it violates his religious beliefs to work in the same building as a LGBT person, the Department of Justice has indicated that it would likely support such a claim. This could effectively clear most LGBT people out of federal service if it were upheld at the Supreme Court level.

There is additional bad news. The Family Research Council (FRC) and Alliance Defending Freedom (ADF) are already looking for clients to attempt impact litigation. Once a more conservative Supreme Court is in place after Justice Kennedy's retirement, the damage that the FRC can do is limited only by the minds of the 3000 lawyers doing *pro bono* work for the ADF.

In the long run, the goal of the FRC and ADF is to drive LGBT people back into the closet through legalized, protected, crowd-sourced intimidation and discrimination. If they are able to create a society where coming out means almost certain financial and career doom, many people will be forced to stay in the closet.

Make no mistake: the religious right wants to legalize and protect discrimination against LGBT people. They are also likely to get away with it.

The transgender military ban

On July 26, 2017 President Trump wrote in a series of tweets that:

> After consultation with my Generals and military experts, please be advised that the United States Government will not accept

> or allow Transgender [sic] individuals to serve in any capacity in the U.S. Military. Our military must be focused on decisive and overwhelming victory and cannot be burdened with the tremendous medical costs and disruption that transgender in the military would entail.

The Secretary of Defense and Joint Chiefs of Staff were caught completely off guard by these tweets and were not in support of the statement made.[538] [539] Indeed, Secretary of Defense James Mattis had been quietly lobbying the House of Representatives to leave the policy allowing transgender people to serve in place.[540] Despite this, on August 25, 2017, the White House followed up on the tweets with an executive order directing the Department to "return to the longstanding policy and practice on military service by transgender individuals that was in place prior to June 2016 until such time as a sufficient basis exists upon which to conclude that terminating that policy and practice would not have the negative effects discussed above." (In other words, the White House directed the Pentagon to revert to the previous policy banning transgender people medically, unless the Pentagon could convince the White House that allowing transgender people would not be expensive or prejudicial to good order, morale, and discipline.)

Four lawsuits led by national civil rights organizations such as the American Civil Liberties Union (ACLU), National Center for Lesbian Rights (NCLR), GLBTQ Advocates & Defenders (GLAD), Lambda Legal, and the Transgender Legal Defense and Education Fund (TLDEF) quickly followed.[541] [542] [543] [544] NCLR and GLAD struck first, winning a DC District Court ruling that barred enforcement of most of the executive order. While the DC ruling did not include accessions, the next three rulings barred enforcement of the entire executive order.

The DOJ and White House are appealing this ruling, claiming that, since the decision on how to remove transgender service members has not been made yet, no legally recognizable harm has been done. This seems like arguing that one cannot appeal a death sentence until it has already been carried out. Unsurprisingly, the argument did not persuade the DC District Court judge, who found that the policy was already disrupting the lives and careers of transgender service members.

The executive order poses some enormous legal questions: namely can the federal government single out transgender people for disparate treatment without much of a rational basis? Can it renege on a pledge it made to allow them to serve openly (also known as the reliance doctrine or promissory estoppel)?[545] By demanding that transgender people must prove there is a benefit to them serving, they are being treated differently under the law from other groups of people who do not have to prove that their service is beneficial.

In the end, the executive order banning transgender service members is likely to become a case hinging on what level of scrutiny should be given to transgender people, and how far executive branch power extends, that will be decided at the Supreme Court. While initial rulings have been promising, the expected composition of the Supreme Court if and when this case makes it there means the long-term outlook is uncertain at best.

Weakening marriage equality

The conservative plan for tearing down marriage equality is essentially the same as their plan for *Roe v. Wade* (abortion rights): chip away at it little by little until it is a right that exists on paper but is functionally useless or irrelevant. What is the point of getting married if no one in a conservative state will sign a marriage license, or if that license confers no actual rights?

On June 26, 2017, the Supreme Court issued a *per curiam* (see definition in end notes) decision in the case of *Pavan v. Smith.*[546] In *Pavan*, the state of Arkansas argued that married lesbian parents could not have both women's names on the birth certificate of their children because the children were conceived by anonymous sperm donations.[547] [548] A heterosexual married couple who conceived in the same way would legally be allowed to have both parents' names on the birth certificates and thus differential treatment was clearly occurring.

The US Supreme Court reversed the Arkansas state Supreme Court ruling favoring the state, finding that "Arkansas may not, consistent with *Obergefell*, deny married same-sex couples that recognition."[549] Gorsuch, Alito, and Thomas dissented, arguing that *Obergefell* is not settled law, and only applies to the issuance of marriage certificates and death certificates. While Justice Roberts did not join the dissent, it is unknown if he supported the decision either, since individual justices do not have to sign onto a *per curiam* decision.

What this tells us is that we have at least three, if not four, Supreme Court justices ready to roll back marriage equality by allowing states to reduce the legal rights of same-sex partners to a relatively worthless piece of paper that does not have to be honored for any legal purpose except death certificates.

This exact same argument was also successfully used on June 29, 2017 at the Texas Supreme Court, in the case of *Pidgeon v. Turner*.[550] Pidgeon, a conservative pastor in Houston, Texas, argued that since the Texas state law forbidding recognition of same-sex marriage was merely overturned rather than repealed, it was illegal for city government to offer city employees in same-sex marriages the same benefits as heterosexual employees.[551] [552] The Texas Supreme Court agreed with Pidgeon 9 to 0, accepting the argument that *Obergefell* didn't specifically say anything about employee benefits.

This indicates that one can expect *Obergefell* to be continually challenged until eventually religious conservatives get one or two more votes at SCOTUS, whereupon the Supreme Court will issue an opinion that *Obergefell* can be interpreted narrowly. If Chief Justice Roberts balks at such a blatant attack on *stare decisis*, all conservatives have to do is wait for Justice Breyer or Justice Ginsburg to step down or die before the end of the Trump Administration. Given that, as of 2018, Justice Ginsburg is 85 years of age, and Justice Breyer is 79, the odds that at least one of them leaves the bench before the end of 2020 is high.

Upholding bathroom bills like HB2

In 2016 North Carolina passed HB2 which banned transgender people from public bathrooms matching their gender identity as well as negating all local laws in the state that protected LGBT people.[553] The bill was absurdly declared an "emergency measure." It passed with almost no debate, over the objections of the North Carolina business community. In the end, it cost the state hundreds of millions of dollars in lost revenue. Governor Pat McCrory lost his job in the 2016 election when he failed to win re-election against an opponent promising to repeal HB2. The bill was later partially repealed, including the bathroom provisions.[554] It left in place the prohibition on laws protecting LGBT people, however.

Still, the bill was never about bathrooms (see Chapter 7 for a longer discussion of the politics surrounding bathroom bills). HB2 would likely have allowed discrimination against anyone who violated any sort of gender stereotypes, and didn't happen to be carrying their birth certificate on them.

The bill made it perfectly legal to tell non-transgender women and men (cisgender women and cisgender men) that they cannot use the bathroom if they do not meet some arbitrary standard for femininity or masculinity. Butch lesbian?[555] Take a hike. Have polycystic ovarian syndrome or acromegaly?[556] [557] No loo for you. Teen boy who wears his hair long? Go use the women's facilities and hope your friends do not ever find out. Wearing sweat pants and a hoodie instead of a house dress?[558] To the men's room you go.

It is not hard to see how this bill had potential for abuse.

Most people would wonder how on Earth such a thing could be constitutional. They would be right. It probably is not. (Or, at least not as we understand the constitution today. Justice Gorsuch actually supported a corporation that ordered an employee to commit suicide or be fired.[559])

There is a clear analogy between Amendment 2 in Colorado (which resulted in *Romer v. Evans*), and HB2. Given the lack of incidents where gender non-conforming people have caused harm in public spaces and the evident animus of the bill in attempting to single out a group, HB2 would seem to fail both constitutional tests miserably.

The landmark case of *Glenn v. Brumby* in the 11th Circuit has also established that the Equal Protection Clause applies to transgender people, although the 4th Circuit, where North Carolina is located, has not yet ruled on this. Additionally, many other cases have established that, as a class, transgender people are subject to "intermediate scrutiny." Intermediate scrutiny is just a fancy legal way of saying that if something affects transgender people as a group, it has to serve an important state interest (see the earlier section on intermediate scrutiny). Given that cities in North Carolina had public accommodations protections for years without incident, such a reason is very hard to discern.

Another pertinent case is *Lusardi v. McHugh*, which found that denying access to facilities, or limiting transgender people to separate and unequal ones, is a violation of Title VII. Whether this holding can be expanded to other public accommodations remains an open question, however.

Title VII does not include "sex" as a protected class with regards to public accommodations. Any government action based on sex, however, must pass the test of intermediate scrutiny. Keeping women who dress differently, wear their hair differently, have a medical condition, who are too tall, whose hips are too narrow, or who are too broad in the shoulders out of bathrooms clearly does not meet the requirement of serving an "important state interest." HB2 likely violated the intent of *Hopkins v. Price Waterhouse* that holding people to a gender stereotype, without a compelling governmental interest, does not meet the intermediate scrutiny test.

That leaves the question: how does one enforce a bathroom law targeting transgender people? This is perhaps the biggest reason why bathroom bills are likely to be unconstitutional; they are vague, intrusive, non-uniformly applied, and essentially unenforceable. This would seem to violate the vagueness doctrine.[560]

Having people show identification will not catch all the transgender people either. Many primary forms of documentation (drivers' licenses, passports, and, in the case of some states, birth certificates) can have gender markers amended with a letter from a doctor, even without surgery. Other methods of identifying transgender people are equally fallible as well as a violation of constitutional rights: such as strip searches, TSA (transportation security administration) body scanning machines, posting guards at bathroom entrances, and DNA testing. All up, doing so would cost *trillions* to implement nationwide, and none is guaranteed to "catch" all transgender or intersex people using the "wrong" bathroom without catching some cisgender people in the net as well. This will result in costly lawsuits.[561]

There is an alternative to this *reductio ad absurdam* list of options: continue letting all people use the facility corresponding with their gender identity.[562] It costs nothing, does not result in gross civil rights violations, and all the sane people can simply get on with their lives.

Conclusion

Over the past 40 years, transgender people have increasingly gained protection under the 1964 Civil Rights Act and the Equal Protection Clause of the 14th Amendment at the district and circuit court level. To date, the Supreme Court of the US has not heard a case which directly addresses a legal question about transgender people. Given how many legal challenges are being mounted right now by conservative organizations (such as the ADF), this is likely to change in the next few years. Given Justice Kennedy's retirement and presumable replacement with arch-conservative nominee Brett Kavanaugh, any ruling is unlikely to favor transgender people.

Consequently, many legal observers believe that transgender people may well see a series of rulings that allow governments, businesses, and individuals to discriminate based on nearly any excuse (religion, public safety, record keeping, etc.). Given *stare decisis* and the longevity of Supreme Court justices, it is unlikely these will be overturned in our lifetimes.

Transgender people being forced to spend the rest of their natural lives as second (or third, or fourth) class citizens seems to be the most likely outcome at the time of writing. While a reader might think this cannot possibly be constitutional, remember, it is only unconstitutional if the Supreme Court says it is unconstitutional, and that what the Supreme Court believes is constitutional changes with every new justice, and at times with each new case.

Chapter 7
POLITICS

Transgender people make a great political dog whistle for conservatives. They are a tiny minority that the public has had a hard time empathizing with. It's harder to empathize with people whose experiences you don't understand. That lack of understanding allows conservatives to fill in the gaps with their own explanations of the transgender experience. It is relatively easy to demonize a group of people you don't know or understand, and social conservatives have done so with gusto in recent years.

Since the Supreme Court decided *Obergefell* in 2015, transgender people have been at the center of most political debates about LGBT people in society. This is due more to conservative pushback than the sudden appearance of transgender people on the national scene; transgender people have been part of public consciousness since Christine Jorgensen in the 1950s. Indeed, recent articles have shown that conservatives made this shift as part of a deliberate and calculated effort.[563]

Many observers saw this coming. As early as 2014, we started to see legislation targeting transgender people. We also saw anti-LGBT hate groups changing their messaging strategy, from rallying their base against the imaginary consequences of same-sex marriage ("people will be marrying their lawnmowers!") to rallying the base against the imaginary consequences of even tolerating transgender people ("people will pretend to be transgender to do all sorts of bad things!"). Much of this shift also had to do with increased public acceptance of LGB people over the past decade.

The Republican Party Platform of 2016 included opposition to letting transgender students use bathrooms in accordance with their gender identity.[564] In February 2018, the Republican National Committee (RNC) voted to endorse President Trump's ban on transgender people in the military.[565] In 2018 the Kansas Republican Party passed a resolution opposing "all efforts to validate transgender identity." The resolution also "affirms God's design for gender as determined by biological sex and not by self-perception," and condemns affirming medical care intended to align transgender people with their "perceived gender identity."[566]

The Republican Party has now clearly embraced opposition to transgender people as an issue they are willing to stand on. One might question why people seem so passionate about transgender issues, given the fact that transgender people have so very little impact on most Americans' lives, and only a small percentage of Americans even know a transgender person.

Why do they care? Why do they believe this is an issue they should put front and center even as the long tide of history seems to be swinging towards acceptance of LGBT people? Why is this an issue they think they can win on? Or, do they feel it is an issue they would rather avoid, but are forced to?[567]

This chapter attempts to answer these questions. It looks at why transgender people have become a focus for social conservatives and how that makes transgender people a convenient political target. It explores how religious-based hate groups intend to make life as a transgender person nearly impossible via a combination of law and policy. The chapter explores how efforts by the social conservatives to legislatively ban transgender people were never about public safety, and always a part of their plan to keep transgender people in the closet by making life as difficult as possible for them.

This chapter also addresses one of the stranger questions in politics: why would a transgender person vote for conservatives who have shown nothing but hostility to the community? Finally, this chapter discusses why the political and legal situation for transgender people is likely to get worse for a long time before it gets better.

Trans: the perfect political storm

In 2014, *Time* magazine featured transgender actress Laverne Cox on its cover with the headline, "The Transgender Tipping Point."[568] It was the first time an out transgender person had ever been on the cover of the venerable publication.

Response from the right was swift, with popular Tea Party website editor Matt Drudge posting an image of the cover on his page and religious right author Kevin Williamson penning a particularly nasty piece in the *National Review* called "Laverne Cox is Not a Woman," which the *Chicago Sun-Times* inexplicably reprinted, then quickly retracted.[569]

In this same week, the Houston Equal Rights Ordinance (HERO) was debated for almost nine hours by the city council.[570] Nearly all the opposition focused on the inclusion of gender identity in the ordinance and there was almost no debate on including sexual orientation.

Transgender people are now a consistent dog-whistle issue for social conservatives.[571] [572] They are baselessly accused of being rapists and child molesters, of being delusional and mentally ill.[573] Social conservatives in very public positions have offered many "solutions" to the perceived transgender menace, ranging from mistreatment until they self-deport back to their birth gender, to forced institutionalization, to shooting transgender people on sight in bathrooms, to "putting them in camps."[574] [575] [576]

The out-of-proportion reactions by social conservatives are likely because transgender issues manage to hit so many conservative issues simultaneously: a rejection of science as liberally biased, opposition to the bodily autonomy of women, expectation of conformance with gender stereotypes, and general antipathy towards LGBT people. Transgender people manage to be at a three-way intersection of things conservatives are diametrically opposed to.

When Louisiana Governor Bobby Jindal told Republicans to "stop being the stupid party," with reference to science, it didn't seep into their analysis on transgender people.[577] Socially conservative commentators like Williamson approach transgender people from a perspective of "this is what I think based on nothing in particular other than my own personal disgust" rather than "this is what the bulk of research shows and what the consensus of the medical community believes."

Conservative commentators cherry-pick the fact that gender dysphoria is in the *DSM-5* to claim that all transgender people are, by definition, mentally ill. They fail to note that the American Psychiatric Association (APA) does not list being transgender as a disorder, that the condition of gender dysphoria is only diagnosable if there is "clinically significant distress," and that the main reason why the diagnosis was included is because medical professionals need diagnostic codes for providing treatment. Indeed, the APA specifically states that "gender nonconformity is not in itself a mental disorder."[578]

Social conservatives frequently mock transgender people's gender identities, claiming that "physical reality" trumps delusions.[579] Arriving at this conclusion requires ignoring all of the most recent research into the origins of gender identity while also ignoring the fact that transgender people are well aware of their own biology; that's why they are dysphoric in the first place. While they may say "biology isn't bigotry," as a way to excuse hostility towards transgender people, calling for people to harass and discriminate against transgender people based on personal religious beliefs certainly is.

Along the same lines, for social conservatives, transgender health care evokes the same visceral reactions as women's reproductive rights, for many of the same reasons. Bodily autonomy is great...unless someone decides their religion has something to say about it.

Social conservatives are morally opposed to any sort of coverage of transition-related care—even though transition-related care has been shown for decades to be the most effective way of dealing with something that is, at its core, a medical issue. The same people who complained about "Obamacare" and government not letting doctors decide what is best for patients also conveniently ignore the fact that medical organizations are essentially unanimous in their support of access to transition-related medical care.[580]

Several US courts have likewise shown a willingness to agree, ruling on multiple occasions that transition-related care is medically necessary and that completely withholding it from prisoners violates the 8th Amendment.[581]

When confronted with these facts, social conservatives slip into the same sort of cognitively dissonant excuses they deploy on issues like global warming and evolution: "Research can say anything," "Researchers are all liberals," "Doctors are all liberals," "Medical organizations are liberal," "It is just a few activist judges." Any potential for discussion is blocked by their confirmation bias, which is the tendency people have to interpret information in a way that confirms one's pre-existing beliefs.

Fundamentally this is just a continuation of the all-but-lost cultural war on gays, lesbians, and bisexuals. Twenty-five years ago, social conservatives were making the same accusations that LGB people are psychologically damaged sexual predators who recruit children. These same conservatives oppose societal acceptance of LGB people as much as they did 25 years ago but it has become a political and legal liability to express it openly. Targeting transgender people does not (yet) carry the same political penalties.

In their 2012 election post-mortem, the Republican Party identified a lack of inclusiveness of women, minorities, and the LGBT community as a primary cause of their failure to unseat President Obama.[582] Only token outreach efforts were made to women and minority communities during the 2016 election, however. The Republican Party focused more on suppressing these voters than convincing them to vote for Republicans, and no real attempt was made to woo LGBT people.[583] The Republican social conservative wing has made it clear that that sort of LGBT inclusion is unacceptable. Thus, the 2016 Republican Party platform was more anti-LGBT than ever before.[584]

I believe Republicans are worried, though. Transgender issues have become perhaps the last socially acceptable way of "kicking the dog" when it comes to the LGBT community.[585] If social conservatives cannot use transgender people as bogeymen anymore, they'll have a hard time finding another target that touches so many of their hot-button issues at once while riling the base so effectively. They have convinced the GOP (Grand Old Party, another name for the Republican Party) faithful that, if transgender people gain acceptance, it will be the end of everything: freedom of religion, freedom of speech, the destruction of health care, the end of the nuclear family, and an end to personal privacy.[586] [587]

It remains to be seen who will replace transgender people as the right wing's whipping boy when absolutely none of this happens.

Why they hate us

"Why do people spend so much time and energy hating transgender people?"

Most transgender people have asked this question a thousand times over. We do not pose a threat to anyone as an impoverished, persecuted minority representing about 0.7 percent of the general population. While many might say they don't hate transgender people, or claim they're "saying it with love," transgender people certainly aren't feeling it.

To transgender people, it feels like hatred. We are accused of being a threat to women and children. We are accused of being sexual deviants who should never be allowed around children, when in reality we love ours as much as anyone. Religious conservatives argue that not only should they be able to discriminate against transgender people in all aspects of life, but that such discrimination is a moral obligation. We are threatened with losing our military careers, when all we want to do is serve our country.

At the same time, we see examples of local communities rallying around the cause of forcing a transgender kindergartner out of school.[588] While support for transgender people is highest among Millennials and Generation Z, in a few places, students have held anti-trans rallies against their classmates.[589] Conservative religious and political figures have called on like-minded individuals to shoot transgender people they find in bathrooms.[590] [591]

We are a small minority that is treated as an existential threat, and social conservative organizations are spending an immense amount of time and money in an effort to stigmatize and marginalize us while spreading harmful and misleading information. The Alliance Defending Freedom is at the forefront of impact litigation designed to make life more difficult for transgender people, while granting a special right to discriminate against LGBT people on the basis of religion.[592] Perhaps they do not see it as hatred, but it certainly looks and feels like it from where transgender people stand.

Thus, here are ten reasons why I believe some people seem to hate transgender people so much.

1. Hate is easy

Hate requires little effort. No one has to step out of their comfort zone, they do not have to learn anything, deal with nuance, or put themselves in anyone else's position. No one has to challenge their friends, family, or people at the church. Americans increasingly live in a bubble or an echo chamber, where they self-select what information they want to be exposed to, and social media algorithms prevent them from being exposed to new ideas and different people. Thus, they just go along with everyone else and make assumptions that feel safe and intuitive.

2. Sympathizing with transgender people is hard

Transgender identities are often a very alien concept to people. Empathizing with people based simply on their humanity is hard. Having empathy for someone who is very different is even harder.

3. Most people do not know a transgender person

Most studies say that, at best, only 16 percent of people personally know someone who is transgender, yet approximately 75 percent know someone who is lesbian or gay.[593] Studies also show very strong correlations between knowing an LGB person, and being supportive of LGB issues. The transgender community lacks that vital component of acceptance because there are not enough transgender people to be as ubiquitous as LGB people can be due to their larger numbers.

4. Transgender people often look/sound different

It has always been easier to ridicule people who look or supposedly sound different. For example, look at the caricatures of blacks, Latinos, Native Americans, Japanese, gays, and many others from the past.[594] [595] [596] [597] [598]

If an unpopular group of people looks different, it can and will be used to caricaturize and demean them.

5. It is assumed to be a choice

The short answer is that it is not a choice, in the same way that LGB people do not "decide" between being completely celibate or being with the ones they love.[599] Acceptance of LGB people is highly correlated with belief in a biological origin of sexual orientation and gender identity. Though the role of biology in gender identity is becoming better understood by scientists, most of the public is not aware of these advances (or they disbelieve them).[600]

6. There has been a lack of positive representation in the media

The number of positive examples of transgender characters in the media remains limited. Existing transgender characters usually fall into one of three categories: a pathetic transgender person (Brie in *Transamerica* or Rayon in *Dallas Buyers Club*), a trap for straight men (*The Hangover* 2), or a sex worker (*Anything*). While there have been a few more positive portrayals in recent years, it is worth remembering that portrayals of LGB characters took decades to evolve into the more nuanced and complex ones we see today.

Since the Trump Administration's attempt to ban transgender people from the military on July 26, 2017, there has been an increase in positive portrayals of transgender people in the news, showing transgender service members in a positive light. This is a relatively recent and potentially transient event. It remains to be seen if this has a long-term impact on public perception, though there is a strong argument to be made that it will.[601]

Chapter 10 includes a longer discussion of transgender representation in the media.

7. Transgender people challenge deeply held paradigms and that makes people very uncomfortable

Transgender people challenge people's deeply, and unconsciously held, beliefs about sex and gender. Things that contradict a person's set of paradigms are typically either rejected outright or they elicit a fight or flight reaction.[602]

It does not help that the human brain is very finely calibrated to evaluate faces and categorize them based on very subtle cues as either male or female. The mind recognizes, though often not consciously, when someone does not fit the paradigms of the gender binary. When people do not fall neatly into one of those two groups, it may cause a visceral reaction ranging from discomfort to fear, disgust, and anger.

8. Hating those who are different is an evolutionary advantage

When it was tribe against tribe, one's genetic survival depended on banding together for the common defense. The ability to use hate to unite the group makes the defense of their genetics more likely to be successful. Intellectually or emotionally humanizing one's "enemy" is not a successful evolutionary strategy.

In modern times, being transgender or intersex is one of the more visible ways a person can be quickly identified as different. When a transgender person is assaulted, the attacker is much more likely to carry the violence all the way through to murder.[603]

9. Transgender people are portrayed as a perversion

Transgender people are both implicitly and explicitly accused of being perverts, fetishists, and likely rapists. The reasons for this are discussed extensively in Chapter 5. Chapter 4 discusses why transition isn't about sexual attraction or behavior.

This is largely why the social conservative tactics against non-discrimination ordinances have been so successful; they tell people that it is a choice between protecting their wives and daughters, and a tiny group of "perverts." In recent years, as societal acceptance of transgender people has increased, hate groups have backed off from the outright calling of transgender people perverts and freaks and now instead falsely allege that people will pretend to be transgender in order to commit crimes. (More on why this is a smoke screen later in this chapter, but wouldn't it be much easier to just pretend to be a janitor?)

10. Transphobia is more socially acceptable than homophobia now

Using transgender people as the butt of a joke is still common.[604] Urging violence, demanding trans people be sent to concentration camps, calling trans people rapists and perverts, and using slurs to describe trans people are all still socially acceptable in a way that they are not for the LGB population.[605] [606] [607] [608]

So, what are the answers to all this? Some are cultural: there must be more positive portrayals of transgender characters in the media. That also means no more Rayons or Bries—they are as much a stock character as a *Star Trek* redshirt.

Transgender people coming out publicly is helpful in reducing overt transphobia and bias. The more people know transgender people, the better it makes it for the rest of the community. There is also a clear need for better science being put out to the public, and for the LGB community to actively debunk anti-trans science the way they did the Regnerus study, which used shoddy science to try and prove that LGB people were worse parents than straight people. US courts eventually rejected his research as "entirely unbelievable and not worthy of serious consideration."[609] The same must happen for anti-transgender studies of similarly low quality.

It is necessary to emphasize the actual science which shows biological origins, that this is not a choice, and that gender identity is an immutable characteristic like sexual orientation. People need to understand that this is neither a lifestyle choice, nor a sexual perversion. Lastly, people who collectively push virulent anti-transgender ideology need to be called exactly what they are by the wider media: hate groups.[610] The Southern Poverty Law Center does not designate groups as such lightly; there must be a pattern of "rhetoric and harmful pseudoscience that demonizes LGBT people as threats to children, society and often public health." Simply being religious or opposed to marriage equality is not enough, the key element to being designated a hate group is defamation.[611]

A straight, non-transgender friend and ally summed up what we need the most though:

I cannot comprehend what a person who identifies as transgender endures. As a human being, I do not have to comprehend to feel compassion and acceptance. It is okay to not understand. It is not okay to demean and belittle because of your own personal shortcomings and inability to understand.

Transgender people are being demonized the same way gays were

Since before the end of the fight for marriage equality, social conservatives have realized that they were going to have to move on from using opposition to lesbians and gays as a rallying cry. As a result, conservatives were left rummaging through the junk drawer of anti-gay tactics and propaganda from the past five decades to see what they could use against transgender people.[612]

The most regressive of recent anti-transgender voices have actively called for deliberate systematic discrimination against transgender people in order to force them back into the closet, along the lines of the "celibate gay" movement among religious conservatives.[613] In Ryan T. Anderson's anti-transgender book, he concludes that society should "avoid adding to the pain experienced by people with gender dysphoria, while we must present them with alternatives to transitioning."[614]

In other words, their goal is to keep transgender people from transitioning, which is treated as a sin equivalent to homosexual acts or abortion. In this same book, Anderson proposes removing all legal recognition of transgender people, providing broad religious protections for people who discriminate, banning transgender people from bathrooms, and protecting the moral rectitude of such discrimination and opprobrium.

They see this as "helping" transgender people by not cooperating with the "delusion." This is an idea that dates back to the 1960s. Similarly, in the 1960s, homosexuality was also still considered a mental disorder and individuals expected LGB people to remain in the closet for the good of all concerned. They also expected gay men and lesbians who couldn't stay completely in the closet to seek conversion therapy of some sort.

Similarly, transgender people are expected to resist temptation, and not transition in order to save their souls, and to avoid people around them feeling uncomfortable by becoming invisible.

For example, a 2014 incident revolved around Laura Klug, a transgender public school substitute teacher in Texas who was fired simply because she was transgender and a parent objected to her presence.[615] There was no allegation of misconduct; some parents simply did not want children exposed to transgender people. This is eerily reminiscent of the fight that surrounded the Briggs Initiative in 1978, which would have banned gays and lesbians from being teachers in California had it been successful.[616]

The majority of propaganda against Houston's Equal Rights Ordinance in 2015 was directed against the inclusion of gender identity, with very little of it directed at the protection of sexual orientation.[617] The talking points against transgender people have been rooted in the same sexual predator narrative that was so prevalent in the vintage anti-gay propaganda of the 1980s. For example, in 1980s conservative propaganda cartoons, adult gay men are shown "recruiting" children into the gay "deathstyle." This implied both that gay men were child molesters, and that the cause of homosexuality was being molested as a child.[618]

Social conservatives are also pushing the thoroughly discredited "transgender people (or people pretending to be transgender) are potential predators in bathrooms" myth as hard as they can.[619] This scare tactic is designed to appeal to the paranoia and fears of rape that already exist in gender-segregated spaces, exactly the same way they did with their claims as far back as 1993 that "gays will rape men in showers if we pass 'Don't Ask, Don't Tell.'"[620] Oddly enough, conservatives also argued (and Jon Stewart lampooned) that gay men would become sexual predators in showers if we repealed DADT in 2010.[621] It was also used in the 1970s to oppose the Equal Rights Amendment.[622]

Likewise, the "ex-gay" myth of the 1990s was repackaged to promote "reparative therapy" for transgender people. A few hardy (read: immune to all evidence) souls keep pushing the narrative that there are no transgender people, just gender-confused individuals who need to be "fixed" through therapy.[623] [624] However, the presumed causes of being transgender, and the therapies these people recommend, are either incredibly light on details or are exactly the same as those they recommend for "curing" homosexuality.[625] These cures apparently involve screaming and beating the crap out of pillows with tennis rackets.[626] Other reparative therapies involve shaming the patient, or coercive behavior modification meant to enforce gender stereotypical behavior.[627] The chapter on transgender medical and mental health describes in detail why reparative therapy should be banned as harmful quackery, and has no support from science or mainstream professional organizations.

Finally, one relatively new tactic against LGB people has recently been employed against transgender people as well. In 2012, the Human Rights Campaign got ahold of internal National Organization for Marriage memorandums which outlined a race-baiting strategy of "driving a wedge between gays and blacks." This strategy was visible in the efforts to repeal the Houston Equal Rights Ordinance, where opponents have relied heavily on appealing to black churchgoers to drive turnout at events that demonize transgender people.[628] Ultimately, the divide and conquer strategy of the opposition using transgender people worked, as the right wing successfully appealed to Spanish-speaking voters and minorities.[629]

This may be a last gasp, though. It is somewhat understandable given that many conservatives see societal acceptance of transgender people as a complete descent into Satanism, anarchy, madness, and fascism, while demographics paint a bleak picture for the future of social conservatives.[630] [631] [632] Millennials and Generation Z are uninterested in LGBT-baiting tactics, and are becoming more and more solidly aligned with the Democratic Party. It is to be hoped that this shift in zeitgeist means that the bargain-bin tactics of the social conservatives will be put right back there.

The social conservative plan for transgender people

In 2015, the Family Research Council laid out a five-point plan to legislate transgender people out of public life by making the legal, medical, and social climate too hostile for anyone to transition, or exist, in.[633] The basics of the plan are as follows:

1. States and the federal government should not allow legal gender marker changes.
2. Transgender people should not have any legal protections against discrimination, nor should anyone be required to respect their identity.
3. Transgender people should not be legally allowed to use public facilities in accordance with their gender identity.
4. Medical coverage related to transition should not be provided by the government or any other entity.
5. Transgender people should not be allowed to serve in the military.

Stop for a moment here, and imagine a world where you cannot get an accurate government ID, a world where you cannot vote (because you can't get accurate government ID), cannot drive without risking arrest, and cannot get a job. You cannot prove that you are who you are, because no one will believe your ID is real. You will never be treated as your correct gender by any government agency. What ID you have will constantly out you as transgender, inviting discrimination. With Religious Freedom Restoration Act expansions at the state and federal level acting as an aggressive attempt to carve out a right to discriminate based on religious or other personal beliefs, any government employee can discriminate against you at any time, as long as they claim a "sincerely held religious belief."

Now imagine being constantly outed as transgender in this world where the law explicitly states that you are a target. Imagine having that scarlet letter of an incorrect gender marker on every ID you possess, making it clear that the bearer of this card has no enforceable civil rights. Anyone can legally fire you, kick you out of a home rental, refuse to serve you, take your children away, refuse to teach you or your children, verbally abuse you for their own amusement at work—it is all legal and protected behavior. The religious "liberty" to abuse, harass, and humiliate transgender people would reign supreme in the Family Research Council's march back to the 1950s.

These are real concerns. Surveys have shown that transgender people not only self-report discrimination, but independent organizations have found it as well in employment, housing, and other areas. In one such study, when employers were presented with resumes that outed qualified applicants as transgender, 48 percent of businesses preferred less qualified cisgender applicants.[634]

Now imagine being transgender and that, on top of being legally un-personed via lack of government recognition, jobless, homeless, harassed, and hated, you'll be arrested for using a bathroom. Use one bathroom and it is a felony. Use the other, and you're likely to be beaten, maybe to death.[635] If you fight back against your attackers, you'll go to a prison for people of the opposite gender, which all but guarantees you will continue to be raped, beaten, and denied medical care while serving time.[636] [637]

On top of all of this, you cannot get treatment for gender dysphoria other than (medically debunked, ineffective, counter-productive) religious-based reparative therapy or "pray away the gay" style camps. Unable to medically transition (the only proven treatment for gender dysphoria), you're marked constantly as being transgender. To add insult to injury, you cannot even join the military to escape the nearly inevitable poverty and homelessness that accompanies being transgender under their plan.

Given all of these factors, the goal of the Family Resource Council could not be clearer: transgender people must be pushed out of American life and forced to either stay in the closet or attempt to exist in a world where they have no legal recognition. Transgender people who do decide to transition will be marginalized in every facet of life and shoved towards the underground economy, where 11 percent of trans women find themselves doing survival sex work due to lack of anything else being available.[638] The FRC and anti-transgender conservatives know quite well that most transgender people, when faced with the certainty of personal ruin, will remain alone, in the closet, for life. However short that may be.

The end state goal of the social conservatives is to effectively eradicate transgender people legally and legislatively by preventing them from participating in public life. Call it cultural genocide if you will; it means the forced disappearance of a class of people.

The most frightening part is that the FRC, ADF, and other religiously based anti-LGBT hate groups have had unprecedented access to the White House since the beginning of the Trump presidency.[639] Vice President Mike Pence has long had a cozy relationship with the FRC, which wholeheartedly endorsed Pence's "license to discriminate" RFRA bill in Indiana. Pence claims that he does not advocate discrimination against transgender people, but refused to answer if he thought discrimination should be legal.[640] He supported a law that allowed people to do exactly that, however, and make it impossible to protect LGBT people against religious-based discrimination. In addition, Pence belongs to a religious denomination that demands that its followers discriminate.[641]

In July 2017, United States Attorney General Jeff Sessions gave a closed-door speech to the Alliance Defending Freedom. It is aligned with the FRC and its goal is to create a biblically based legal system in the United States.[642] This includes making being openly LGBT illegal.[643] Sessions also consulted with the ADF prior to releasing a pair of Department of Justice memorandums on "religious liberty," effectively allowing federal employees to preach being anti-equality at work and encouraging discrimination against LGBT people without fear of repercussions.[644]

The idea of a government controlled by people who want to make being LGBT illegal is shocking.

It is even more so when it has become a reality.

Analyzing anti-trans bills

For decades, most of the social conservative legal and legislative efforts on LGBT issues were based around support for the "Don't Ask, Don't Tell" policy, and opposition to same-sex marriage. The latter was successfully used as a wedge issue in the 2004 Presidential election. However, in 2010 DADT was repealed. After Proposition 8 and the Defense of Marriage Act were overturned by the Supreme Court in 2013, social conservatives recognized the writing on the wall that they were in danger of losing their top-remaining anti-LGBT issue with which to rally their base.

By 2015, nationwide marriage equality looked all but inevitable, and social conservatives made a deliberate shift in focus to transgender people, and particularly transgender people in bathrooms.[645] These were successfully used in the fight against HERO in Houston, re-using ads labeling transgender people perverts and predators that had previously been tested in campaigns against LGBT rights in Gainesville, Florida and Anchorage, Alaska.[646] [647]

Thus, by 2015 the focus of social conservatives had shifted to religious freedom laws and impact litigation (discussed in the chapter on law), and to either repealing laws protecting transgender people, or passing laws targeting transgender people for discrimination. This section focuses on the laws targeting transgender people either directly or indirectly.

In 2015, there were 20 state-level bills intended to target (and therefore harm) transgender people. All of them were either defeated or carried over to the next legislative session. In 2016, that number increased to 55 bills in 26 states, of which three were passed.[648] In 2017, 61 bills targeting transgender people were introduced in state legislatures, of which another three became law.[649] Going forward, we can expect to continue to see anti-transgender bills at the state level, and that some of them will be passed. It remains to be seen if they will be found constitutional, but the increasingly conservative lean of the court suggests this to be likely.

These bills fall into one of several categories, explored below.

1. Bills targeting transgender students in education and sports[650] [651] [652] [653] [654]

More than half of the anti-transgender bills filed in 2017 targeted transgender children and youth in schools. While the Obama Administration Departments of Education and Justice clarified that Title IX protections against sex discrimination apply to transgender students, the Trump Administration has revoked the guidance now and these bills are meant as a further challenge.[655] An increasing number of school districts and state departments of education have adopted policies and guidance to protect transgender students from bullying and discrimination, and opponents hope to use fear-mongering tactics to reverse them. Some of the bills were designed to prevent transgender student athletes from competing unless they did it based on the sex listed on their birth certificate. For most transgender student athletes, this makes it impossible to compete in the division which matches their gender identity, creating situations in which no one wins.[656]

Some school districts are considering school policies that would exclude transgender students from using gender-segregated facilities in accordance with their gender identity.[657] Unlike the state bills, several of these school district policies have passed, forcing transgender advocates and allies to bring lawsuits to stop them. Transgender students are often subjected to increased bullying, harassment, social stigma, and discrimination as a result of these and discriminatory efforts. Others suffer from medical conditions such as kidney and urinary tract infections because they are unable to access bathrooms. This makes protection necessary for the success of transgender students.[658] [659]

2. Limiting access to gender-segregated public facilities[660] [661] [662]

After the Houston Equal Rights Ordinance (HERO) debacle, and based on polling data, conservatives zeroed in on bathroom access for both children and adults as an area where they could potentially roll back basic human rights for both the LGBT community and other marginalized people.[663] [664] [665] For example, the defeated measure in Houston provided protections against discrimination on the basis of 15 characteristics, including race, sex, disability, sexual orientation, and military status. To kill HERO, opponents falsely claimed that allowing trans people to use the bathrooms that match their gender identity—one small aspect of HERO—would lead to women being sexually assaulted in bathrooms. That lie was used to drum up big crowds at local hearings, and conservative legislators have used the same claim to rally their base against LGBT protections, regardless of any proof of this ever happening at any time.[666]

This emphasis was taken even further in North Carolina with HB2, and the Texas legislative session of 2017 where the Lieutenant Governor was willing to call the legislature back into session to push through a transgender "bathroom bill" he was dead set on passing. While corporations have opposed such laws, it seems likely they will continue to be introduced.

3. Prohibiting transition-related treatment for prisoners[667]

These bills are a reaction to recent cases in Georgia, Massachusetts, and California in which courts ruled that transition-related care for transgender prisoners is medically necessary and withholding it is a violation of the 8th Amendment.[668] [669] Wisconsin passed a law banning transition-related treatment, and it was struck down in 2011 in the case of *Fields v. Smith*.

4. Preventing transgender people from amending their birth certificates[670]

One bill, defeated in 2015, would have prevented transgender people born in Virginia from changing their birth certificates to match their lived identities.[671] Tennessee passed a similar law in 1977, and recent attempts to change the law through legislative and legal action have failed.[672] In 2017, the Kansas Department of Health changed its regulations to make it effectively impossible for transgender people to revise their birth certificates.[673] At the time of writing, Tennessee, Kansas, Idaho, and Ohio do not allow transgender people to change their birth certificates, although Idaho is currently being sued to change this.

Far more only allow a change of gender markers on birth certificates if the individual has had GCS. Many transgender people do not want GCS. Others cannot have GCS for financial or physical reasons, thereby making a change in government ID impossible.

This has a significant impact on transgender people since many states base driver's license gender markers on a person's birth certificate.[674] Additionally, many jobs require submission of a birth certificate as identification. Outing oneself as transgender during the hiring process significantly reduces job opportunities, even in cities and states with strong LGBT protections.[675]

5. Obstacles to marriage[676]

One bill addressed the non-existent problem of transgender people marrying cisgender people without disclosing their surgical history. The number of people who would be affected by bills like this is negligible—it serves little purpose except to stigmatize transgender people and label their marriages as artificial. It also legally requires transgender people to disclose medical information to the government, which is unnecessary, intrusive, and not required of other individuals.

6. Defining "sex" so as to exclude transgender people from state and local legal protections in employment and education[677]

These laws would prevent transgender people from making claims under state and local bans on sex discrimination. It is a response to the nearly overwhelming number of court decisions holding that discrimination against transgender people is sex discrimination under Title VII of the US Civil Rights Act of 1964 and Title IX of the Education Amendments of 1972 (see Chapter 6 and the Appendix). If these sorts of laws are passed, transgender people will need to make all discrimination claims in federal court, which often requires more time, money, and effort than a state-level claim. A similar bill has been introduced at the federal level as well.[678]

Why are these bills being filed?

These bills are being filed primarily by social conservative lawmakers, many of whom are linked with the Family Research Council, Liberty Counsel, and the Alliance Defending Freedom.[679] [680] [681] They are following the legislative templates laid out by the ADF and FRC to deny transgender people basic access to the workplace, schools, and public accommodations like restaurants and gyms, and to prevent legal recognition.

What will happen with these bills?

Fortunately, the majority of these bills will not move forward. They are often introduced by lawmakers who are at odds even with other members of their caucus and there is frequently little political will to focus on such a non-issue rather than more important legislative priorities. These bills are not popular with the public, either, who oppose laws allowing religious-based discrimination. In 2015, 2016, and 2017, most of these bills died in committee, as bills usually do. However, there were pitched battles in places like Texas and Georgia between moderates and businesses on one side and social conservatives on the other.

In 2016 in South Carolina, Nikki Haley said a bathroom bill was not needed. Also in 2016, Georgia Governor Nathan Deal vetoed a bill expanding RFRA. In Texas, Speaker of the House Joe Straus blocked a 2017 bathroom bill, stating he didn't want "a single suicide on his hands."[682] In 2016 South Dakota Governor Dennis Daugaard vetoed a bathroom bill targeting transgender students, stating, "this does not address any pressing issue concerning the school districts of South Dakota."[683]

These bills have tended to be poorly written, vague, and broadly worded, which can lead to substantial unintended consequences and legal challenges that have a high probability of success. Additionally, some of the bills were likely to run foul of district or circuit court rulings on Title VII and Title IX, meaning that they were even more likely to be overturned when challenged in court. All of this made many lawmakers hesitant to move them through the legislative process.

Transgender people in many states and national LGBT organizations are working to oppose the kinds of laws described above through community organizing and outreach to their members and from behind the scenes through discussions with lawmakers.

What will happen if some of these are actually passed?

HB2 was passed in North Carolina in 2016. Among the many effects it had, HB2 effectively banned transgender people from state government-owned bathrooms (such as rest stops, schools, universities, and government buildings). It also nullified all local laws protecting LGBT people. It was challenged in court immediately, and immense pressure put on North Carolina by businesses and the NCAA to repeal HB2. Ultimately, HB2 was repealed and replaced with a law that didn't ban transgender people from bathrooms, but left the provisions nullifying local protections for LGBT people in place.

Thus, HB2 represents what happens when one of these bills is passed. The bill was immediately challenged in court by legal groups like the American Civil Liberties Union or National Center for Lesbian Rights, and a stay would be requested, meaning that the law cannot go into effect until the challenges have been decided on.[684] If the law is unconstitutional or clearly conflicts with federal law and if it does immediate harm to a group of people that belongs to a suspect class, it is more likely to be struck down by a court. Because HB2 was partially repealed, we still do not know how this would play out if fought to the finish.[685]

Finally, as seen in Indiana and North Carolina, passage of an anti-LGBT law can be very costly. Indiana lost $60 million revenue in 2015 because of its passage of a measure that would allow discrimination against LGBT people based on religious objections (later amended to ostensibly prevent discrimination).[686] North Carolina is estimated to have lost $395 million due to HB2, with that number still growing.[687]

As a result of these losses, businesses in Texas were adamantly opposed to adoption of a "bathroom bill" in 2017. Economic concerns are likely the main reason why the Texas Speaker of the House, Joe Straus, and other moderate Republicans refused to let the bill come up for a vote twice (despite being passed in the Texas Senate).[688]

What's the verdict?

Religious conservatives hope to play on unfounded fears regarding transgender people to energize their base and reignite the culture war against the LGBT community after the marriage equality victory. Opponents of equality believe they have found a vulnerable target in transgender people. However, the bills they are advocating for often conflict with federal law, the Constitution, and common sense.

Trans people are more likely to be the victims of violence in gender-segregated spaces including public restrooms and there has never been any evidence to indicate that transgender people or mythical "people claiming to be transgender" enter these spaces to engage in illegal or improper behaviors.[689] Significant numbers of transgender people report being denied access to facilities, or being physically or sexually assaulted in them. Almost 60 percent of transgender people in a national survey report having avoided going to the bathroom at least once in the last year for fear of harassment or assault.[690] Regardless, if a transgender person ever did engage in improper actions in a bathroom, there are already laws to prohibit such conduct; thus these laws do nothing but stigmatize transgender people.

However, given that the number of anti-transgender bills has increased every year since 2013 and that the Department of Justice under Attorney General Jeff Sessions dropped the lawsuit against HB2 in North

Carolina, there are likely to be a high number of anti-transgender bills being introduced for the foreseeable future.[691]

Social conservatives have made transgender youth their number 1 target

In 2015, the South Dakota legislature passed a law banning transgender students from bathrooms, enacting part of the FRC's plan to make life nearly impossible for transgender people. While Governor Daugaard vetoed the bill, North Carolina followed with a bathroom bill (which mostly targeted students) shortly thereafter.[692]

While these bills called for "reasonable accommodations," this has resulted in separate and unequal situations for transgender students, wherein inconvenient facilities are offered as a false compromise. The results are students who either miss class, are punished for being tardy, or suffer kidney and urinary tract infections as a result of "holding it" or deliberately dehydrating themselves.[693] Other students have suffered the humiliation of being treated like potential sex offenders, being followed around by school staff to make sure they use a separate bathroom, or even faced plans to issue them wrist bands identifying them as transgender so other students can report them.[694] These consequences of "separate but equal" facilities have been observed in North Carolina and across the country where transgender students are banned from facilities.[695]

The South Dakota bill, as was written, considered it a reasonable accommodation to make a transgender child "hold it" until a teacher is available to escort them to a single-stall bathroom like some sort of suspected 7-year-old sex offender. Where similar policies were implemented, younger students suffered the humiliation of urinating all over themselves because the teacher was too busy to escort them to the bathroom.[696] If a school principal decided he simply did not want to have a transgender student at school, many of these laws would legally protect them if they told the student, "There are no bathrooms here that you are allowed to use, so you will have to leave school permanently."

This will cause a student to choose between losing access to education or attempting to conceal and repress their gender identity at school. One South Dakota state senator cited the desistance myth in his support of the bill, remarking that these kids are probably just going to change their minds anyway, so why not encourage them to not be transgender?[697] [698] Never mind that rejection and isolation didn't work out so well for Leelah Alcorn, and the 57 percent of trans kids who attempt suicide in unsupportive environments, according to one study.[699] Chapter 4 describes the close relationship between discrimination, stigma, minority stress, abuse, and suicide attempts in transgender youth.

If anyone thinks for a moment that very few adults would do such horrible things to transgender kids, try watching the 14-year-old transgender teen Jazz Jennings read the parade of online threats from adults to torture and murder her.[700] Talk to most parents of transgender children and they can share all about the threats they receive from community members threatening to kill a transgender child if the parents or their children find the transgender child in the "wrong" bathroom.[701] Other parents of transgender youth have told me how parents and students have told their child they should kill themselves.

Now consider again, how far of a stretch of the imagination is it to envision a social conservative school administrator forcing a child to leave school in comparison?

It is time to stop calling these "bathroom bills" and anti-transgender bills. Instead, call them what they are: an attempt to make it impossible to be a transgender student in America.

HB2 and bathroom bills aren't about public safety

During the fight over HB2 in North Carolina, and others like it, we have heard high-profile defenders of them claim that these bills were passed as a matter of "public safety."[702] [703] [704] However, here are nine facts that demonstrate why these sorts of bills are never about public safety and why they have always truly been about targeting transgender people.

1. Law enforcement officials say it is not about public safety

Public accommodations non-discrimination laws just like Charlotte, North Carolina's existed for decades in over 200 cities and 18 states.[705] When law enforcement officials in areas with laws protecting transgender people have been asked if those laws endanger public safety, they have been unanimous in stating that such laws do not cause a public safety hazard. You can read literally dozens of testimonials from police spokespeople, commissioners, and chiefs in states with non-discrimination ordinances saying the same thing: public accommodations laws protecting transgender people do not endanger public safety.[706] [707] [708] Most of these statements come from police officers in conservative states like Texas, Florida, and Iowa. Minneapolis has had a non-descrimination ordinance since 1993, and police spokesman John Elder stated that it is "not even remotely" a problem.

2. Victims' advocates say it is not about public safety

In 2016, the National Task Force to End Sexual and Domestic Violence Against Women and 250 other local, state, and national organizations that advocate on behalf of survivors of sexual assault and domestic violence signed a joint statement opposing legislation that bans transgender people from public restrooms. They also opposed other bills that codify discrimination against transgender people.[709]

The joint statement reads:

> Those who are pushing these proposals have claimed that these proposals are necessary for public safety and to prevent sexual violence against women and children. As rape crisis centers, shelters, and other service providers who work each and every day to meet the needs of all survivors and reduce sexual assault and domestic violence throughout society, we speak from experience and expertise when we state that these claims are false.

This statement was signed by these organizations in response to conservative individuals and organizations claiming that people concerned with women's rights and safety should oppose laws protecting transgender people in public accommodations.[710]

3. Businesses say it is not about public safety

While retailing giant Target has been attacked for reiterating its transgender inclusive policy, the truth is that 83 percent of all Fortune 500 companies have similar policies allowing transgender employees and customers to use facilities in accordance with their gender identities.[711] [712] An op-ed highlighted how boycotting every transgender-friendly business in America would essentially require an individual to be locked in a closet and die of starvation.[713]

Think of it this way: most corporate lawyers are very risk averse. If they thought that transgender inclusive policies were likely to result in sexual assault and potential liability, they would certainly advise their clients not to institute them. One can infer from the 83 percent figure that the vast majority of companies, and their lawyers, who looked at this issue decided that it was not a realistic risk. Other studies have found that non-discrimination protections are good for business, good for LGBT employees, and even good for their straight co-workers.[714] [715] [716]

Conservatives frequently say that the market should decide. Clearly, it has.

4. 18 states, DC, and 200+ cities say it is not about public safety

Public accommodations laws that include transgender people have been around since 1993. City managers, administrators, and mayors' offices who have implemented public accommodations non-discrimination ordinances have not found them to be an issue.[717] [718] [719]

"To our knowledge, Miami-Dade County has not experienced an increase in sexual assaults or rape in women's restrooms since the passing of the new ordinance or as a result of it. Nor do we have any knowledge of men pretending to be women to enter women's restrooms," says Mike Hernandez, Director of Communications for Miami-Dade County Office of the Mayor.[720]

"Austin incorporated gender identity into our non-discrimination ordinance in 2004; the only notable change is that those who are transgender have a legal remedy should they be denied a public accommodation... I can say that I have not heard of such incidents in my years of service on the Austin City Council," adds Kathie Tovo, former mayor pro-tempore of the Austin City Council.[721]

5. Non-partisan fact checkers say it is not about public safety

Politifact is a non-partisan media outlet that impartially examines claims and statements by politicians. When it looked at the claim by North Carolina Lt. Governor Dan Forest that Charlotte's ordinance would create a "bathroom free-for-all" that endangered public safety, it rated it as false.[722]

Conversely, Politifact rated the statement that "There have not been any public safety issues in cities that allow transgender people to use the bathroom of the gender they identify as" as mostly true, stating: "We haven't found any instances of criminals convicted of using transgender protections as cover in the United States. Neither have any left-wing groups or right-wing groups."[723]

6. If it was about public safety, why did they exempt businesses?

We have established that official experts on non-discrimination ordinances all agree that they do not endanger public safety.

But let's suppose that the people who passed HB2 might really have believed this myth. If they did, why did they let private businesses (like Target) continue to set their own policies? If they thought that transgender inclusion would lead to sexual assaults of women and children, did they believe that it somehow becomes an "acceptable risk" as long as it is not on government property? In their minds, is the principle of *laissez faire* capitalism more important than the lives of the women and children they claim to cherish so much?

It seems more likely that conservatives always knew that these bills were never about public safety and thus they did not want to interfere with the corporations' donations to their campaigns.

7. If it was about public safety, why did they exempt janitors?

Ostensibly, HB2 was about preventing people from pretending to be transgender in order to gain access to women's bathrooms for unlawful purposes. Though HB2 banned transgender people from using the restroom they preferred, they also put in an exemption that would (using their own logic) allow anyone pretending to be a janitor to cause harm within restrooms. Ironically, janitors attract far less attention and are far less stigmatized than transgender people, making such a ruse theoretically more plausible.

Thus, if this was about public safety and the authors of HB2 really believed that people would play dress-up in order to do nefarious things, why did they include a loophole for janitorial staff (which would theoretically allow predators to pretend to be janitors in order to do bad things)? One explanation is that the lawmakers actually believe people would be perfectly willing to pretend to be transgender to do nefarious things, but the same perpetrator would never pretend to be a janitor in order to cause harm to others.

A more plausible explanation is that this was never actually about safety and was instead all about targeting transgender people.

8. If it was about public safety, why didn't they legislate against actual sex offenders?

If you were going to write a bill that tried to protect the public against sexual predators, wouldn't you want to include people who are actually registered sex offenders in the bill's language? It would make a lot of sense. Yet, nothing in HB2 actually targeted sex offenders. If this were really about safety, why were legislators terrified of transgender people using bathrooms at the same time as children, but were okay with kids sharing a bathroom with people who have actually been convicted of sexual assault?

Unless, this was never actually about public safety at all...

9. If HB2 was never about going after transgender people, why are anti-transgender hate groups its biggest backers?

Who are the people backing HB2? Lots and lots of Southern Poverty Law Center designated hate groups. The Family Research Council was one of HB2's biggest backers.[724] Liberty Counsel (another hate group) offered to defend HB2 in court *pro bono*.[725] Meanwhile, Liberty Counsel's President, Anita Staver, publicly threatened to shoot any transgender people she found in a bathroom.[726]

The Alliance Defending Freedom appears to have written the model legislation for HB2.[727] It has a long history of anti-LGBT animus, and has been pushing dozens of anti-transgender bills across the country.[728] These bills include jail time, multi-thousand dollar fines, bounties, and registry as a sex offender for any transgender person who uses a bathroom of the sex with which they identify.

Thus, it is not a coincidence that the organizations most in favor of HB2 also want to legislate transgender people into the closet, shoot them, or jail them for existing.[729] This also makes the claim that HB2 is about public safety, and not about harming transgender people, all the more unbelievable.[730]

Why would a transgender person vote Republican?

In a 2016 interview with transgender journalist Dawn Ennis, Caitlyn Jenner came out supporting presidential candidate Ted Cruz.[731] This was disappointing for most transgender people; Ted Cruz is one of the most virulently anti-transgender politicians in the nation.[732] He regularly appears with, and takes endorsements from, "kill-the-gays" pastors.[733] He is in ideological lock step with the Family Research Council (FRC) and has been endorsed by it.[734] Cruz has publicly endorsed most of the positions in the FRC's five-point plan.[735]

Cruz is also a Southern Baptist, a faith that retains a consistently stated position that accepting a transgender person's identity is a sin which endangers one's salvation.[736] [737] The Southern Baptist Convention has also endorsed legislating transgender identities out of legal existence, literally.[738]

Jenner's near-endorsement of Cruz for President was (rightly) met with howls of protest by the transgender community. It was recognized that a Cruz Administration was likely to be very hostile. They felt anger, frustration, and bewilderment; how on earth could a transgender person support a candidate who openly wants transgender people to have no legal rights?

Others in my social media feed noted that there are some transgender people who identify as Republican. Many of them would never vote for Cruz and prefer pro-LGBT Republicans like Senator Mark Kirk of Illinois or Representative Ileana Ros-Lehtinen of Florida.[739] [740] Transgender Republicans I spoke with (also rightly) point out that not all Republicans are like Cruz.

Discussions about LGBT issues with Republicans are necessary and inevitable, especially when they control 75 percent of all state legislatures (as of 2018), and will likely continue to control a majority due to gerrymandering and voter ID laws.[741] Republicans who are motivated more by the Chamber of Commerce's recommendations than personal religious beliefs are crucial to moving the ball forward on pro-LGBT legislation. These Republicans recognize the benefits of a diverse workforce and the productivity of happy, secure workers. They can be convinced that LGBT people will pick up and leave, taking their skills and money with them, when their work environment is hostile.

Conversations were crucial to convincing South Dakota Governor Dennis Daugaard to veto HB1008 which would have banned transgender students from school facilities.[742] [743] So were the policies and case laws protecting transgender people, which helped emphasize the legal and economic consquences of discrimination.[744] While most of the people who are hostile to transgender people are Republicans, not all Republicans are hostile.

Some of them can even be convinced. Take, for instance, New Hampshire, which was the last state in New England without transgender protections. In 2018, it has a Republican House, Senate, and Governor, and yet passed a state law protecting transgender residents in employment, housing, and public accommodations.

Ted Cruz is almost certainly not one of those people who can be convinced. He depends on anti-LGBT hate groups for money and political support. Changing his stance on transgender people would literally require him to renounce his religion. Voting for Ted Cruz and hoping he can be convinced not to support anti-transgender initiatives is betting on a long-shot.

Still, a few transgender people agreed with Jenner in her support of Cruz and desired to engage him on transgender issues. Thus, the question remains, how could a transgender person support Ted Cruz? As I scrolled through their comments, I realized almost all of the transgender individuals supporting Cruz had a common set of demographic traits. I later followed on with a set of interviews of transgender people who supported President Trump well into his first 200 days in office.

The most prominent feature was security. All were white, as are most Republicans. They also tended to have a high level of income security (such as military retirement pay) and consistent access to health care (such as through military retirement, Veterans Affairs, academic institutions, or parent.). One said he saw himself as "normal," meaning that somehow transgender people who do struggle with discrimination are to blame for their problems. For the transgender men that responded, they had a high degree of passing privilege and were "stealth" in their daily lives. Many replied that they were not "single issue voters," implying that the concerns for most of the transgender community were things they did not have to worry about.

Another sub-set were transgender people who do not live their day-to-day lives as a transgender person; their identity remains a secret, they aren't planning on coming out or transitioning. These people live as their birth gender in public, and only come out in the privacy of their own homes, at conferences, or in support groups. Often, they live in terror of being outed, or suffer because they feel as if they are stuck in the closet. They are effectively already where the Family Research Council wants them, and their risk calculations tell them to stay in the closet, no matter how bad it seems.

The other common undercurrent was a lack of empathy for other transgender people. They themselves were fine, so why is everyone else not? One older transitioner with a military background expressed a belief that since her transition was hellish, everyone else should have to "punch their ticket" the same way.

This is a lot to think about, but when taken together, it paints a very clear picture: the transgender people who supported Cruz (and Trump) generally do not have skin in the game. They were conservative before transition and remained so after transition because having conservatives in office does not endanger them personally. They live in safe places with safe incomes.

These conservative transgender people escape cognitive dissonance in a lot of ways. They did not believe that a conservative administration would do all the horrible things the FRC has promised to do. They believe that the most important thing to transgender people is "a good economy" that offers more job opportunities. They claim to be "looking at the bigger picture," or say that they are "single-issue" voters, with an implication of self-perceived moral and intellectual superiority.

Even assuming the Republican platform in general, or the policies of the current administration in particular, would actually foster a strong economy, it is hard to see how a good economy would be sufficient to overcome living somewhere where it is nearly impossible to get an education, ID, a place to live, or a job. Yet they continue to hold these views, even as the administration has pursued the policy goals of the FRC and ADF, including expanding RFRA to nullify protections for LGBT people, dropping legal cases and policies supporting transgender people in schools and the workplace, and the attempt to ban transgender people from the military.

These transgender conservatives think the situation described above is still better than the presumed economic havoc caused by a Democratic administration. They seem to envision a nation that devolves into a North Korea-like hellscape under a Democratic administration, where everyone's prospects look worse than a transgender person's under a theocratic administration.

This Democratic-induced doomsday scenario defies any sort of rational thought. After eight years of a Democratic President and six years of congressional gridlock, U3 unemployment (the official unemployment rate) stood at 4.9 percent, and the U6 unemployment (unemployment including discouraged and underemployed workers) rate at 9.7 percent.[745] Both were at the lowest point in nearly ten years. Presidents have only moderate influence on the economy and external factors (like the sub-prime mortgage crisis) play a much larger role than a President's budget (which gets largely ignored anyway, regardless of the administration).[746]

This belief that a Democratic president would destroy America so completely that transgender people would be better off under a socially conservative administration stretches credulity. For most transgender people who work on transgender rights, 2017 was a catastrophe. Alternately, some of these conservative individuals believe that it does not matter what happens to the rest of the transgender community, because they are safe and see themselves as one of the good, "normal" people.

The reason that the vast majority of transgender people do not vote for Republicans is that they understand that living as a transgender person in an America run by people beholden to the FRC and ADF is far worse than life under a Democratic President. The current administration has carried through with many of the policies and legal positions advocated for by the FRC and the ADF, and it is a frightening prospect.

Fifty percent of transgender people live in the 32 states where there are no explicit legal protections.[747] A quarter of transgender people cannot afford health care, and 55 percent are subject to health care exclusions targeting them. One in six has been fired for being transgender. A similar number have been mistreated or harassed at work for being transgender in the past year. Most gender non-conforming youth (77%) have been subjected to bullying and harassment. Most of us need correct government ID, and employment, to survive. Transgender people in the military are fighting desperately for their careers after the attempt to ban them.[748]

Thus, what sort of transgender person votes for conservatives? Ones who have misjudged the relative risks to the community at large, don't care what those risks are, and have very little personal skin in the game.

It is going to get worse before it gets better for transgender people

Years ago, Federal Reserve Chairman Alan Greenspan warned against "irrational exuberance." This phrase sprang to mind in 2015 when reading an article in an LGBT publication, titled "7 Reasons to Be Hopeful in 2015."[749] The author did not appear to be living in the same world as the rest of us.

Things are going to be rough for a while, and here's why.

1. Republicans are in charge for the foreseeable future

As of December 2017, Republican-controlled states outnumber Democratic-controlled ones, 26–6. They also control 66 state legislatures (out of 99) and 35 governorships. They control the US House of Representatives, the US Senate, and the Oval Office. After Supreme Court Justice Kennedy's 2018 retirement, Republicans will control the Supreme Court outright. Gerrymandering in most red states ensures that, even in a blue-wave election, Democrats still might not be able to retake the House even if they win by seven points. One example of this is in 2017 when Democrats in Virginia were unable to reclaim the state house there despite winning the popular vote by nine points.[750] While Democrats will likely make gains in 2018, most state governorships and legislatures will remain Republican as a result.

2. The few states controlled by Democrats already have the basics covered

Someone might look at the few states that Democrats control and say: "Well, I'm sure there's a lot we can get done in those blue states." The problem is that those "true blue" states have already done all the basics that can be done legislatively within their own cities and states, including protections in housing, public accommodation, credit, and the workplace. Most of the things that can be done in blue states are items very specific to the transgender community, such as removing surgical requirements for birth certificates, banning reparative therapy, or banning exclusions in health insurance targeting transgender people. This juxtaposes red states' laws, which are created and passed by conservatives.

3. Religious conservatives have no shortage of (horrible) options

There is almost no end to the number of ways conservatives can make life difficult for LGBT people who live in the red states they control. The LGBT movement will undoubtedly contest these in court, but a post-Kennedy Supreme Court is likely to uphold the constitutionality of many, if not nearly all, of these anti-transgender laws.

License-to-discriminate laws, papers-to-pee bills, laws barring state employees from issuing marriage certificates to same-sex couples, laws banning transgender people from getting accurate birth certificates, repealing state protections for transgender people by executive order, overruling all local protections for LGBT people, allowing RFRA licenses to discriminate, and making "reparative therapy" the only type of treatment available to LGBT people are all laws Republicans have passed or tried to pass in the last few years to ensure that their states are as uninhabitable as possible for LGBT people.[751] [752] [753] [754] [755] [756]

4. Conservatives have unfathomable amounts of money to throw at their policy goals on transgender issues

The Heritage Foundation, in part led by a former board member of the FRC by the name of Kay Cole James, has an annual budget of nearly $100 million. The Alliance Defending Freedom has a budget of $43 million per year, and access to an army of 3000 lawyers doing *pro bono* work worth $208 million. The Family Research Council has a budget of about $13 million, and the Federalist Society has about $18 million per year to work with.

In comparison, the largest transgender non-profit organization in Washington DC is the National Center for Transgender Equality (NCTE), which has had a budget of about $2 million per year since 2016.[757]

With the IRS no longer enforcing the Johnson amendment (which gave churches tax exempt status as long as they didn't endorse candidates or support their campaigns), under the Trump Administration churches can now receive, and give out, essentially unlimited amounts of dark money for political purposes. Additionally, the IRS rarely audits legitimate churches.

5. The livability gap between red and blue states will continue to widen

While LGBT folks in deep-blue areas are moving on to genderqueer/gender-fluid acceptance, LGBT people in red states are fighting just to prevent legally enforced second-class citizen status, even if an individual has some form of passing privilege and expresses their gender in a binary way.

As a result, LGBT people with the option of getting the hell out of red states (usually younger people) are doing just that at their earliest opportunity. A 2014 study by the Williams Institute reinforces this, finding that LGBT people suffer far higher economic and health disparities in the regions with worse overall climates, which strongly incentivizes them to get out of that state. As a result, there are even fewer LGBT people remaining in red states to push their political representatives toward change.[758]

6. The Supreme Court will likely be a rubber stamp for religious conservatives' policies

As was stated in the legal section, something is only unconstitutional if the Supreme Court says it is unconstitutional. As of 2018, conservative members of the Supreme Court (who have full control after Kennedy's retirement) have endorsed the following as constitutional:

- Corporations can order employees to do something that would obviously result in their own deaths and the corporation can fire the employee if they refuse to complete this request.[759]
- Justice Clarence Thomas effectively endorsed the legality of the internment of Japanese Americans during World War II.[760]
- Corporations have the same rights as people, including freedom of religion.

Additionally, in 2018, we will see rulings on the constitutionality of a voting system that is rigged so that only one party can ever control the government, and whether everyone has a right to ignore laws protecting LGBT people, women, disabled people, and so on, if their religion tells them to (per the Masterpiece Cakeshop Supreme Court case, discussed in the previous chapter). Progressive court watchers were justifiably less than optimistic on both, as the court gave narrow rulings in favor of political gerrymandering and a religious right to discriminate.[761] [762]

After Kennedy's retirement, no one is counting on the Supreme Court to stop social conservatives from doing anything, no matter how outrageous, directed at LGBT people.

7. Republican voters do not care about LGBT issues

While many individual Republicans are not hostile to LGBT people, it does not prevent them from voting for candidates who are incredibly hostile towards LGBT people, to the point of being off the deep end. In 2014, Colorado voters overwhelmingly elected Gordon Klingenschmitt to the state's House of Representatives.[763] Representative Klingenschmitt was, by every verifiable account, a nutjob, liar, and serial filer of nuisance lawsuits, and unashamedly and vocally homophobic and transphobic.

Klingenschmitt once bragged of having once tried to rid women of the "foul spirit of lesbianism" through an exorcism. He also openly proclaimed that "American law needs to reflect God's law" and that our foreign policy must also be based on the Bible.[764] [765] [766] Klingenschmitt believes that gay people "want your soul" and that they may sexually abuse their own children, which is why he says LGBT people should face government discrimination since only people who are going to heaven are entitled to equal treatment by the government.[767] [768] [769] [770]

Klingenschmitt also declared that the "Don't Ask, Don't Tell" policy should never have been repealed since gay soldiers cannot serve effectively in combat because they are constantly "taking breaks on the combat field to change diapers all because their treacherous sin causes them to lose control of their bowels."[771] He also proclaims that those who are not welcome in the church should not be entitled to use public restrooms.[772]

Finally, Klingenschmitt has said that "Obamacare causes cancer," that the Bible commands people to own guns in order to "defend themselves against left-wing crazies," that ISIS is a sign of the End Times, and that the Federal Communication Commission (FCC) is allowing demonic spirits to "molest and visually rape your children." [773] [774] [775] [776]

Despite a poorly run campaign in 2014 though, he nonetheless managed to defeat his Democratic opponent by nearly 40 points...[777] [778] This dossier of anti-LGBT craziness was not enough to keep people from voting for him. It illustrates that many Americans couldn't care less if a politician would, in the words of Bayard Rustin, "castrate us or put us on an island and drop an H-bomb on us."[779]

As long as there is an "R" next to their name, many Republicans will vote for Republicans, even if that Republican is unqualified and running on a platform that says LGBT people shouldn't exist.

Klingenschmitt's election served notice that extreme anti-LGBT animus wouldn't be enough to sway Republican voters away from a manifestly unqualified individual. No matter how awful or outrageous a position on LGBT people a Republican politician takes, it is unlikely to dissuade other Republicans from voting for him or her.

Given how much focus there is on transgender people by social conservatives, and how much control of government they will have for the foreseeable future (including the Supreme Court), it signals difficult times ahead for transgender people in the United States, even if social acceptance continues to grow.

Chapter 8

RELIGION

As you have probably noticed, transgender people face a lot of adversity and social stigma. Arguments against transgender people having a place in society have come from medical experts with an ax to grind, social conservative politicians, and a handful of vocal, radical anti-transgender feminists (more on them later in Chapter 11).

Religion, however, is perhaps the greatest cultural source of stigma for transgender people in the US. According to an international poll conducted by Ipsos in 2017, Americans are more likely to believe that being transgender is a sin than any other nation in the survey. The US population is also the most likely of any of the countries surveyed to believe that society has gone too far in accepting transgender people.[780] Most of the conservative politicians and medical professionals supporting anti-transgender hate groups like the Family Research Council and Alliance Defending Freedom have evangelical or Catholic backgrounds in common.

This chapter is meant to explore the interaction of transgender identities and religion inside the US, along with the power imbalance between the two, and the goals of conservative religious organizations inside the US regarding transgender people. It also looks at how these denominations plan to achieve these goals, while exploring why Americans, and LGBT ones in particular, are dropping out of organized religion *en masse*.

Religion: benefit, hazard, or both when it comes to LGBT people?

In the classic future-noir film *Blade Runner*, Deckard describes his philosophy on replicants as "They're either a benefit or a hazard. If they're a benefit, it's not my problem." While the character of Deckard applies this to machines, it also works for many other things, including religion. Religious faiths are both potentially hazardous and beneficial for LGBT people. However, in times like these, when headlines tell us that yet another gay teen was bullied to death in the name of religion, it is much harder to see the benefit of religion for LGBTQ people.[781] [782] [783] The same applies to the religious voices claiming that their beliefs give them a special privilege to discriminate against LGBT people.

Religious attitudes towards lesbians and gays tend to be correlated with attitudes towards transgender people. Attitudes towards transgender people and their issues also tend to lag a few points behind LGB in most polls that consider the groups separately. For the sake of this section, we will consider them together, as there is more data on the whole community than on just transgender people.[784] When it comes to LGBT people, religious communities are deeply divided. Most religious organizations with conservative views are actively opposed to marriage equality, employment protections, medical care for transgender people, equal access to housing, and public accommodations.[785] [786] [787] The vitriol often goes too far, leading to gross stereotyping, demonization, and sometimes outright calls for genocide.[788] [789] [790] A survey of the 100 largest churches in the US in 2017 found that not one of them was inclusive of LGBT people.[791]

The evangelical community in particular tends to have an eschatological (apocalyptic) view of "us vs. the gays."[792] Ironically, according to one study, LGBT people are almost as likely as other Americans to see themselves as Christians.[793] The same study also shows that anti-LGBT views are a minority opinion among non-evangelical Christians.[794] Religious groups like the Metropolitan Community Church, Unitarian Universalist Church, the United Church of Christ, and the Episcopal Church actively try to create a safe space for LGBT people.[795]

LGBT people often find comfort and strength in their religious faith. Other times, Christian faith allows straight people to find compassion for LGBT people in the Bible's teachings of tolerance, love, and acceptance. Such was the case with my mother-in-law. With guidance from her pastor, she came to believe that there is a purpose for everyone. During my transition, she saw a potential for teaching lessons in love and a chance to help others in a similar situation.

Even within conservative religious organizations, there is disagreement between members regarding how LGBT people should be treated. Kathy Baldock, an outspoken straight, cisgender evangelical Christian author, has made it her mission to convince other evangelicals around the country to embrace the LGBT community.[796] At one LGBT conference for members of the military after DADT, I was surprised to meet a Pentecostal chaplain who was trying to reach out.

Nevertheless, conservative religious organizations continue to alienate even their own straight members with their treatment of LGBT people. Parents of a 14-year-old girl in Ohio told me a harrowing story. Their daughter had come out as lesbian, and the church had given the family two options: put her in a reparative therapy program or be stripped of all their positions in the church. They chose to leave the church that they'd grown up in.

Almost all the data shows that conservative religious propaganda against LGBT people is becoming less effective. According to a 2017 Gallup poll, 64 percent of Americans now support marriage equality after the *Windsor* and *Obergefell* decisions, and a vast majority supports employment protections for LGBT people. Meanwhile, an ever-diminishing minority believes homosexuality is a sin.[797] [798] [799] Despite doctrine by the Southern Baptist Convention, the Ethics and Religious Liberty Commission, and the Nashville Statement,[800] 44 percent of self-identified evangelicals between the ages of 18 and 29 support marriage equality.[801] This makes sense, given that 77 percent of Americans now know someone who is lesbian or gay, younger people are more likely to know someone who is LGBT, and knowing an LGBT person has a strong positive correlation with both tolerance and acceptance.[802]

This brings up the question of why conservative religious organizations and individuals continue to preach a doctrine of exclusion. One obvious reason is that it is very lucrative. Anti-LGBT religious groups are very well funded.[803] Apocalyptic scare tactics cater to a population fearful of societal changes that they aren't comfortable with.[804] These resources have allowed the aggressive and hostile voices to drown out the more numerous moderate and progressive religious voices in our cultural conversation.[805]

One result of this well-funded campaign is that it is driving younger people away from religion altogether. Almost a third of people between 18 and 29 have no specific religion ("The Nones"), according to a recent study by Pew.[806] Most still have religious beliefs, and the vast majority of them hold tolerant views of LGBT people and their issues, but when it comes to fighting back against the exclusionary practices of the religious right, most Nones seem to take the attitude of "not my circus, not my monkeys." In other words, it's not my religion, I'm not gay, so it's not my problem. They seem to trust that cultural evolution and demographic shift will solve the problem over time.

This is a tragedy for LGBT youth. They don't need things to get better in 20 years. They need it *now*. Forty percent of today's homeless teens are LGBT.[807] LGB teens are five times more likely than the general population to attempt suicide.[808] The rate is even higher for transgender youth.[809]

LGBT teens need help and a more accepting society and home life. Affirming religious organizations provide a framework to promote both, though the number of open and affirming denominations are small in comparison with faiths that exclude LGBT people. These LGBT-friendly churches are seeing their membership decline, as well as those more conservative faiths, though. Given how out of step with science and culture the beliefs of religious conservatives are today, from birth control to climate change to human sexuality, they appear to be poisoning the well from which they drink.

I once asked an ordained transgender woman how she reconciled being who she is with her Christian beliefs. She had concluded that LGBT people were never broken; we are exactly as we were meant to be and don't need fixing. However, many LGBT youth are left to grapple with their sexual orientation or gender identity in isolation because of conservative religious dogma. Unfortunately, most LGBT youth don't have the theological resources of an accepting and supportive adult in a graduate-level theology program. Most religious leaders have no experience with transgender people, little understanding of the research surrounding their issues, and come from faiths which reject and exclude transgender people out of tradition and Biblical literalism.

In the process of passively waiting for culture to change, we are breaking children who didn't need fixing in the first place.

What makes this even more tragic is that there aren't Bible verses that are directly applicable to transgender issues, and in those few that might be indirectly there are contradictions and a lot of room for interpretation. The most commonly cited Bible verses used against transgender people deal with these:

> So God created man in his own image, in the image of God created he him; male and female created he them. (Gen 1:27)

> But from the beginning of the creation God made them male and female. (Mark 10:6)

Claiming that transgender people don't exist but allowing that intersex people do based on these passages requires a significant amount of mental gymnastics (or cognitive dissonance). While they can blame intersex conditions on "the fall," this is essentially layering a creation story on top of a scientific reality: namely that sex is not purely from binary.

Then there's this Old Testament verse:

> A woman shall not wear a man's garment, nor shall a man put on a woman's cloak, for whoever does these things is an abomination to the Lord your God. (Deuteronomy 22:5)

Strictly speaking, anyone who has worn a kilt or gone to a toga party could be deep trouble. Maybe women in pants. Additionally, what sorts of clothing are considered masculine and feminine has varied greatly over time. Social conservatives are not fighting to pass legislation which prohibits women from wearing pants, suggesting this is more about a distaste for transgender people than Biblical literalism. It's also worth noting that the next verse in Deuteronomy goes on to forbid taking birds out of their nests.

This verse can also be interpreted to condemn Christian faiths that ordain women. Some Biblical scholars believe that this was originally a prohibition on women wearing the religious vestments of men; in effect a prohibition on women taking male roles in religion. These reasons may be, in part, why the verse is hardly referenced anymore in opposition to transgender people.

Another Old Testament verse used against transgender people is the following:

> No one whose testicles are crushed or whose male organ is cut off shall enter the assembly of the LORD. (Deuteronomy 23:1)

If this really is about the Bible, and not about transgender people, many veterans of the wars in Iraq and Afghanistan would be banned from churches. Thousands of troops injured in these wars suffered traumatic perianal injuries and amputations.[810] Indeed, decades ago this concept of "whole body" was primarily used to prevent disabled people and amputees from being ordained, and not to prevent transgender people from participating in church.[811] Thus, is the Southern Baptist Convention (SBC) going to strip search everyone with a purple heart? Or perhaps just rely on a doctor's note? Additionally, many transgender people choose not to have surgery anyway.

Regardless, the New Testament seems to overrule Deuteronomy 23:1 for Christians who believe in a new covenant anyway:

> For there are eunuchs who have been so from birth, and there are eunuchs who have been made eunuchs by men, and there are eunuchs who have made themselves eunuchs for the sake of the kingdom of heaven. Let the one who is able to receive this receive it. (Matthew 19:12)

While Genesis 1:27 and Mark 10:6 echo each other in the sentiment that "God made male and female," the Bible also states:

> There is neither Jew nor Greek, there is neither slave nor free, *there is no male and female,* for you are all one in Christ Jesus. (Galatians 3:28)

On the whole, scripture seems to apply to transgender people in an indirect way at most. If you were to apply it uniformly, though, you would have to exclude a lot of non-transgender people from church as well. Claims that transgender people are undoubtedly an affront to God and must be crushed as the pre-eminent cultural evil are not backed up by scripture. To arrive at such a conclusion, scripture must be cherry picked, interpreted in the most literal and radical way possible, done while ignoring contradictory verses, and then applied unequally to transgender people.

Oddly enough, the SBC acknowledges that intersex people exist, and that they can have valid gender identities, but blame intersex conditions on "the fall." But for transgender people without ambiguous genitalia, our gender identities are invalid. Additionally, we know that some intersex conditions cause people with a XY karyotype to have identities and primary sexual characteristics that are unambiguously female.[812] In other words, chromosomes and genitals aren't 100 percent indicative of sex or identity.

It is also worth noting that children, and the races, also are a result of the fall, and the SBC isn't denouncing either of these as innately sinful. One might ask if there is an official list of things that are "good" and "bad" after the fall. (Hint: there isn't.)

Some people of faith deeply disagree with such treatment of LGBTQ youth. A few, particularly the parents of LGBTQ youth, are willing to take a stand against it.[813] However, when people stand idly by, faith will continue to be a more of a hazard than a benefit.

> What does it profit, my brethren, if someone says he has faith but does not have works? Can faith save him? If a brother or sister is

naked and destitute of daily food, and one of you says to them, "Depart in peace, be warmed and filled," but you do not give them the things which are needed for the body, what does it profit? Thus also faith by itself, if it does not have works, is dead. (James 2:14–17, New King James Version)

LGBT and the rise of the "Nones"

One of the most profound interactions between the LGBT community, the public, and religion is how it is contributing to the decline of most religious demographics in the US, particularly among white Catholics, mainline Protestants, and evangelicals.[814] At the same time, the fastest growing religious group in the US is the "Nones"—those who do not identify with any particular religion. It is not a coincidence that the Nones are growing fastest among Millennials, and that Millennials and Generation Z are consistently the age group with the most pro-LGBT attitudes.

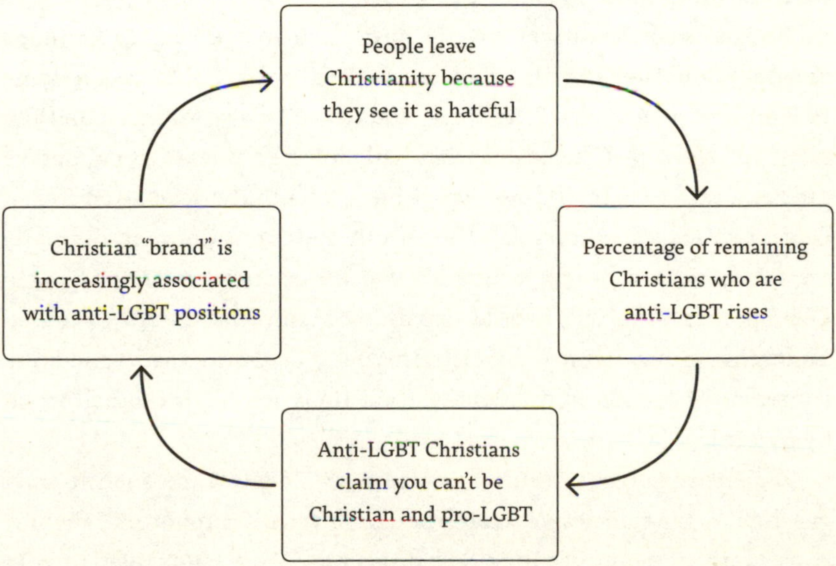

Figure 8.1: The Christian identity downward spiral

There are now approximately 56 million religiously unaffiliated adults (those identifying as agnostic, atheist, or "nothing in particular") in the US, according to Pew Research. In light of this group's "none of the above" attitude toward existing organized religion, the group is sometimes referred to as the "Nones." The number of atheists may be even higher than is commonly thought as well. A 2017 study estimated that 26 percent of Americans are atheists, but that many of them do not say so even in anonymous polls as a result of social stigma.[815]

The Nones are more numerous than either Catholics or mainline Protestants, according to Pew's latest survey. Indeed, the unaffiliated are now second in size only to evangelical Protestants among major religious groups in the US, and growing faster than any other group. The Nones are more likely to be young, white, and educated. However, growth is occurring across almost every demographic.

The Nones also tend to be one of the most solidly Democratic and pro-LGBT demographics as well.[816] [817] This isn't coincidental; prior studies from the Public Religion Research Institute have shown that up to a third of Millennial Nones left traditional faith communities because of religious intolerance toward LGBT people.[818]

Religious conservatives have harmed their image with Millennials based on how they handled their own sexual scandals. In 2015 it came to light that Josh Duggar, the eldest son of the family followed on their television show *19 Kids and Counting*, had molested at least five underage girls as a teenager, including two of his sisters.[819] The revelation forced Duggar to leave his job with the Family Research Council, officially an anti-gay hate group, where he vocally opposed laws protecting LGBT people.[820] [821] (But, in 2017, when Roy Moore was credibly accused of forcing himself on teen girls in the 1980s, and threatened the conservative agenda in the Senate, the Family Research Council stood by Moore.)

The entire Duggar family has also been deeply enmeshed in anti-gay, right-wing politics. Notably, they have vocally supported religious conservatives including Rick Santorum and Mike Huckabee. In 2015, Michelle Duggar recorded a robocall that accused transgender people of being child molesters, as part of the campaign to repeal Fayetteville's law protecting LGBT people from discrimination.[822] [823]

The Duggars have held themselves up as a model of Christianity in America. They wear their religion on their sleeves; the family is politically active, deeply conservative, anti-LGBT, patriarchal, and anti-science.[824] Some members of the family have adopted the position that if you aren't as conservative as the Duggars, you're not real Christians.[825]

"Real Christians" like the Duggars think they are doing God's work. But if they are judged by their effect on how Americans view Christianity (which they believe is the only version that doesn't result in damnation), they have instead helped drive people away from churches. Research indicates that their entrenched, anti-LGBT positions and apparent hypocrisy on sexual morality are part of why Americans are abandoning the faith in record numbers—and not coming back.

When the Pew Research Center released its latest survey results on religion in America, it highlighted a trend that has been quietly ongoing for decades: people are leaving organized religion in droves.[826] In response, churches have been attempting to combat this declining attendance, "jazzing up" services in ways that include engaging youth pastors, rebranding efforts, and doing anything else they can think of to get Millennials back—apparently to no avail.[827] The number of people who identify with *any* religious denomination keeps shrinking.

Certainly, there are other factors at play. Generational replacement is failing to happen—for every person who has joined a religion having been raised unaffiliated, there are more than four people who have become religious "Nones" after having been raised in some religion, revealed Pew.[828]

Many Nones cite organized religion's lack of relevance to their lives as a key reason they have left the flock.[829] A generalized set of beliefs that remains outside of churches has been called "Moralistic Therapeutic Deism," in which the individuals hold a belief of a need for people to be good to one another in a general sense as a way of making oneself feel good, and that God remains in the background.[830] In European countries there are clear correlations over time between wealth, education, and religiosity. As wealth and education rates grow, religiosity tends to drop. The US has long been something of an outlier as a wealthy and religious nation.[831] It could be argued that what we are seeing is simply a regression towards the mean.

With Millennials leaving religion faster than any other age demographic, this suggests that some powerful non-economic factors are driving them away. And on a broader scale, the factors leading to the rise of the Nones in the US appear strong enough to overcome the social and cultural influence of growing wealth inequality.

Dr. Brittney Cooper, an Assistant Professor of Women's and Gender Studies and Africana Studies at Rutgers University, summarized the problem posed by conservative Christianity to Millennials like herself in a powerful essay alleging that white social conservatives have concocted a bigoted "white supremacist Jesus."[832]

"I cannot stand in a church and worship on Sunday alongside those who on the very next Monday co-sign every kind of legislation that devalues the lives of black people, women, and gay people," writes Cooper. "I am a firm believer that our theology implicates our politics. If your politics are rooted in the contemporary anti-black, misogynist, homophobic conservatism, then we are not serving the same God. Period."

Some religions have attempted to reverse this trend, with varying degrees of success. This chapter provides a brief overview of several important religious demographics.

White evangelicals (and the Southern Baptist Convention)

The SBC is both evangelical and the largest Protestant denomination in the country. Where it goes, other evangelical denominations follow. Under President Russell Moore over the past few years, the SBC has made a significant attempt at rebranding on lesbian and gay issues.[833] Transgender issues, however, are another matter, and the SBC has taken a harder line than ever before.

For example, the Convention has abandoned its longstanding claim that there is no such thing as gay people, and formally disavowed reparative therapy for sexual orientation, though activists criticized a lack of action behind those words.[834] [835] The SBC also recognizes the existence of intersex conditions, and has issued a resolution rejecting "gay-bashing."[836] [837]

Overall, this is effectively window dressing, says Jacob Lupfer, an editor at *Religion News Service* and doctoral candidate at Georgetown University, who attended the SBC Ethics & Religious Liberty Commission (ERLC) Conference in 2014. His report from that conference was tellingly titled "Southern Baptists change their tone but not their substance on homosexuality."[838]

"Differences of tone and nuance notwithstanding, the message to gay Christians was clear," wrote Lupfer in 2014. "Either they believe same-sex erotic expression is a sin and commit to a life of celibacy, or they can give in to their impulses, thus living in willful rebellion against God."

Even this small change in tone was resisted by a significant number of evangelical theologians, and the SBC continues to work closely with anti-LGBT hate groups.[839] The SBC opposes all legal protections for LGBT people, and strongly supports expanding the Religious Freedom Restoration Act (RFRA) to allow it to bypass non-discrimination laws and court rulings.[840] As recently as 2013, SBC leaders said they believe gay people are gay because they were molested as children.[841] Southern Baptist military chaplains are not only prohibited from ministering to lesbian and gay troops, but also from associating with chaplains who do.[842]

In 2014, the SBC held a National Conference on "The Gospel, Homosexuality, and the Future of Marriage."[843] The Conference made headlines when the President of the SBC, Dr. Russell Moore, disavowed reparative therapy and instead encouraged choosing life-long celibacy.[844] Encouraging life-long celibacy is a bad idea to begin with; humans are social beings who benefit physically and mentally from intimacy and companionship. It's even worse in light of how well celibate priests and abstinence-only education worked out for the Catholic Church.

While this is still incrementally better than their previous stance that all LGBTQ people are unwelcome, setting conditions for inclusion that require LGBTQ people to harm themselves psychologically is little better.[845]

However, the SBC's position on transgender individuals has become even more regressive. In June 2014, the SBC passed a resolution essentially saying that transgender people:

- are crazy ("Transgender people perceive a conflict between their biological sex and their gender identity")
- are delusional ("Gender identity should be determined by biological sex, and not by one's self-perception")
- are in opposition to the will of God ("We affirm God's original design to create two distinct and complementary sexes, male and female"; "We affirm distinctions in masculine and feminine roles as ordained by God")
- are rejecting God's plan ("We affirm that male and female designate the fundamental distinction that God has embedded in the very biology of the human race")
- should just pray the trans away ("We invite all transgender persons to trust in Christ and to experience renewal in the gospel")
- should not be protected by law ("We call upon all judges and public officials to resist and oppose the efforts to treat gender identity as a protected class"; "We commit ourselves to pray for and support legislative and legal efforts to oppose the Employment Non-Discrimination Act and other legislation like it that would give gender identity the same legal protections as sex and race")
- should not in any way ever be validated by the law ("We continue to oppose steadfastly all efforts by any court or state legislature to validate transgender identity as morally praiseworthy")
- should never have access to transition-related care ("We condemn efforts to alter one's bodily identity [e.g. cross-sex hormone therapy, gender reassignment surgery] to bring it into line with one's perceived gender identity")

- should never be represented in a positive way in the media or schools, because they are a threat to children ("We oppose all efforts by media and entertainment outlets and public schools to mainstream transgender identity in the eyes of our children")
- should be shunned and denounced by all real Christians ("Our love for the gospel and urgency for the Great Commission must include declaring what God's word teaches about God's design for us as male and female persons created in His image and for His glory").[846]

Transgender people are not welcome in the churches aligned with the SBC or the Nashville Statement unless they stop being transgender.[847] It is worth noting that this series of resolutions is completely in line with the FRC's plan to make life as difficult as possible for transgender people (including having no churches to go to), and thus encouraging them to self-deport to the closet.

During the October 2014 Biblical Marriage Conference, the SBC went a step further. It took positions on transgender people similar to where they were on gay people 20 years ago.[848] According to official doctrine, transgender people are not part of God's plan.[849] At the conference the SBC endorsed reparative therapy for transgender people, and told parents that accepting the identity of your transgender child will send you to hell.[850] [851] Prominent members still actively promote the false narrative that transgender people are sexual predators and amputation fetishists.[852]

The organization appears to recognize that its cultural influence and size are waning. Despite the SBC's efforts to change its tone on gay (but not transgender) people, the core theology and positions have changed very little. Indeed, some observers see the SBC's hard line on transgender people as a last stand in the culture wars. According to Dianna Anderson at Reproductive Health Reality Check:

> Such a belief is so dependent upon a number of evaporating cultural assumptions—straight marriage that will always produce children, gender and sexuality as fixed states, the idea

> that men are leaders and women are followers—that it's fairly easy to see why representatives of various Christian organizations are panicked at the idea of affirming transgender identities. That affirmation, after all, would be a devastating blow for the house of cards upon which they've built their faith. Accepting the very existence of trans people is an act that threatens their image of God—because God, in conservative Christians' eyes, only created (and called "good") male and female in a compulsory heterosexual binary.[853]

Strikingly, the SBC seems to have found a successful strategy for holding total membership numbers (roughly) steady, but shrinking as a percentage of the US population. Evangelicals have seen the slowest rate of decline in market share—in fact, the total number of people in the US who identify as such increased slightly between 2012 and 2015, according to Pew; however, the mean age of white evangelicals is 55 years old.[854] The 2016 election showed that there remains a market for selling fear of outsiders (such as transgender people, immigrants, and Muslims). White evangelicals were certainly buying it, and were President Trump's most reliable supporters at the polls.[855]

Roman Catholic Church

The Catholic Church's shift on lesbians and gays has been hard to read, leaving the world guessing at what the words and actions of Pope Francis really mean. Was the Church moving toward acceptance when Pope Francis said "Who am I to judge?"[856] regarding pious gay clergy? Or when he demoted the vociferously anti-gay Cardinal Raymond Burke?[857]

Other times the Catholic Church seems to be drawing a line in the sand, calling same-sex marriage a "threat to the family."[858] The Church also called transgender rights a threat to humanity comparable to nuclear weapons, and seems to be gearing up for a cultural war on transgender issues.[859]

While Pope Francis has been hailed as a moderate, particularly on LGB issues, the rhetoric he and other Catholic leaders have used about transgender people has become increasingly inflammatory. He was quoted in a 2016 meeting with Polish Bishops as saying, "Today, in schools they are teaching this to children—to children!—that everyone can choose their gender... We are living a moment of annihilation of man as image of God."[860] He accused Western countries which tolerate transgender people of "ideological colonizing," stating: "One such colonization, I'll say it clearly with its first and last name—is gender." This was said, without a trace of irony, at about the same time Pope Francis canonized Junípero Serra, who was an actual colonizer.[861]

Other high-level Catholic officials have also made recent statements that leave little doubt that the Church has decided transgender people, and acceptance of them, are a dire threat to civilization. In 2015, Pope Francis stated that transgender people are a "threat to the order of creation," and compared the danger of transgender people to nuclear weapons, stating: "Let's think of the nuclear arms, of the possibility to annihilate in a few instants a very high number of human beings. Let's think also of...of the gender theory, that does not recognize the order of creation."[862]

Pope Benedict called being transgender one of the worst sins, and the existence of transgender people as a threat to man and God alike, telling Pope Francis, "'Holiness, this is the epoch of sin against God the Creator, He's intelligent! God created man and woman, God created the world this way, this way, this way, and we are doing the opposite."[863]

Other high-level Catholic officials have also advocated against the world tolerating the existence of transgender people. American Cardinal Raymond Burke said in 2012, "With gender theory, it is impossible to live in society. Already today, in certain places in the United States, anyone at all can change identity and say, 'Today I am a man; tomorrow I will be a woman.' That is truly *madness*. Some men insist on going into the women's restrooms. That is *inhuman*."[864]

At the 2016 National Catholic Prayer Breakfast, which was attended by Speaker of the House Paul Ryan, Cardinal Robert Sarah also described tolerance of transgender people a threat to life, the universe, and everything.[865] "The death of God results in the burial of good, beauty, love and truth... Nowhere is this clearer than in the threat that societies are visiting on the family through a *demonic* 'gender ideology,' a *deadly impulse* that is being experienced in a world increasingly cut off from God through *ideological colonialism*."

One must ask: if the Catholic Church's position is that transgender people will annihilate man and God, what is its position on what is to be done with transgender people? This potentially implies that the Church's position is that removing transgender people from society is an act of self-defense and a moral imperative. Indeed, the Pope's own comparison of transgender people to nuclear weapons is illustrative. The Catholic Church's position on nuclear weapons is that they should be banned, abolished, and legislated out of existence, for the good of humanity.[866] What then of transgender people?

The references to "colonialism" are another hint of its intent: it is nudging nations towards laws like the Ugandan "Kill the Gays" legislation. The Catholic Church in Africa has been highly supportive of laws in Africa designed to kill, imprison, or otherwise drive lesbians and gays underground in an act of legislative cultural genocide.[867] Charles Martin Wamika, Bishop of Jinja, Uganda, told parents of gays and lesbians that they would be rewarded in heaven if they turned over their children to the state for punishment.[868]

This is terrifying for transgender people.

The Catholic Church has a long, sordid history of standing idly by during genocide...or even encouraging it. Athanase Seromba, a Catholic priest, was convicted of crimes against humanity in 2014 for his role in the Rwandan genocide where Catholic churches were used as extermination centers.[869] The Catholic Church cannot attempt to pretend that its position on transgender people is about the sanctity of people's reproductive organs or protecting youth without descending into complete hypocrisy. For hundreds of years, the Catholic Church castrated boys to keep its top talent in choirs and didn't ban the practice until the beginning of the 20th century.[870] It castrated gay men to "cure" them well into the 1950s.[871]

At the same time, the Church continues to try to cover up, hide, and otherwise dodge the consequences of Catholic priests abusing children. Indeed, the Church even blamed the children for being abused.[872] Thus, efforts to condemn transgender people on the basis of the Catholic Church's tattered authority on human sexuality seem tone deaf at best.

In the US, the Catholic Church has now joined the largest Protestant denomination, the Southern Baptist Convention (SBC), in the positions that transgender people should have neither legal recognition nor protection.[873] There is an irony that two religious groups who would never worship together, and label each other as apostates, would find common cause in labeling a tiny minority as a threat to humanity.

However, the Catholic Church's positions may not be for a US audience for several reasons.

First, there is little cause to believe that the Catholic Church can stop the growing cultural acceptance of transgender people in the US any more than it could get its members to accept other unpopular bits of dogma. Fifty-seven percent of US Catholics now support same-sex marriage according to one poll.[874] Others put it above 60 percent.[875] Eighty percent of US Catholics now think birth control is morally acceptable, and 98 percent of US Catholic women have used it.[876] The majority of US Catholics also reject the Church's teachings on co-habitation, divorce, and premarital sex according to Pew Research.[877] Thirty-four percent of Catholics believe that society has not gone far enough to accept transgender people, while significantly fewer Catholics believe that society has gone "too far."[878] Additionally, majorities of Catholics see bullying of LGBT people as a problem, oppose discrimination against them, and believe that intolerance of LGBT people is driving young people from the Church.[879]

Some social conservatives have suggested that because the Hispanic Catholic population is growing compared to white Catholics, the overall membership of the Catholic Church in America should become more conservative over time. However, this does not seem to be borne out by the data, which shows that white Catholics and Hispanic Catholics support LGBT issues at about the same rate.[880] Thus, there is little reason to believe that the change in demographics over time in the American Catholic Church is likely to align the beliefs of the members with the teaching of the Vatican on social issues like LGBT people and birth control.

As such, it seems highly unlikely that US Catholics as a whole will accept the narrative that transgender people are a dire threat to humanity who should be excluded from public life now or in the future.

Where the real danger lies is in places that are already hostile to lesbians and gays, have large Catholic populations, and have weak human rights laws and/or enforcement. However, it also lends credibility to conservative politicians in the US looking for the moral authority to pass draconian anti-transgender policies (such as HB2 in North Carolina).

The rhetoric being used demonizes transgender people, while the repeated use of "colonizing" language is a dog whistle to politicians in nations where past colonialism is still a source of anger and resentment. The apparent goal of some leaders in the Catholic Church is to goad these countries into legislating their transgender populations out of existence, while not directly telling them to do so. Thus, in the aftermath of the human rights disaster, they will have some degree of culpable deniability because they never actually told them to do it, nor suggested specific laws.

At the same time, local Catholic leadership is often allowed to set the tone for individual parishes throughout the entire nation. This may be a simply pragmatic approach, given that US Catholics themselves have moderate views on social issues. Their support for marriage equality has consistently been similar to that of the US population as a whole.[881] However, even this local flexibility doesn't seem to be enough to stem the tide of Millennials leaving the Church as a whole.

The Pew survey shows the American Catholic Church's numbers are in almost as steep a decline as mainline Protestants. Reactions to the trends detailed in the survey vary greatly across church leaders and devout members. Given the Catholic Church's stance on issues such as birth control, LGBT people, and divorce, it is not hard to see why Millennials would see it as out of touch and not really relevant to the actual moral issues facing them and the country.

"The religious landscape is reflecting popular culture and the news," said Jeff Cavins, Director of Evangelization and Catechesis for the

Archdiocese of St. Paul and Minneapolis.[882] "People are becoming bored with mainline religion and looking for alternative ways of satisfying their spiritual needs. Americans are turning to social causes as a way of expressing their inner priorities."

Other observers see the decline of the Church's influence in the US as inevitable. They see a pattern similar to Europe, with the organization's structures becoming "little more than tourist attractions," to borrow author and spiritual teacher Steve McSwain's phrasing.[883]

Meanwhile, more conservative Catholic commentators like Anne Hendershott, Professor of Sociology and Director of the Veritas Center for Ethics in Public Life at Franciscan University of Steubenville, take more of a "good riddance" approach to the exit of LGBT people and their allies from the Church.[884]

"While the LGBT community does not want to be reminded of biblical injunctions or of sin, it appears—ironically—that the churches which refuse to acknowledge sin are not deemed worth attending," wrote Hendershott for *Catholic World Report*. "Indeed, that may be the problem: if there is no creed or doctrine beyond 'we are all good,' there is no good reason to attend church; any group activity will suffice."[885] Hendershott perceives the exodus of the Church's socially progressive members as strengthening the institution by making it more homogenous.

Across the ideological spectrum, though, demographers generally agree on one thing: the Nones are not coming back to the fold any time soon.[886]

Mainline (non-evangelical) Protestants

This broad categorization includes Christian denominations such as Lutherans, Episcopalians, Methodists, and Presbyterians. In times past, the Northeast United States was overwhelmingly Mainline Protestant, but not anymore. There are 20 states in which the Nones are the largest religious group, concentrated on the Pacific Coast and the Northeast.[887] Identification with Mainline Protestant Churches have fallen faster than for any other group in the Pew survey.

Mainline Protestant Churches have varying degrees of acceptance for transgender people. Some, like the Metropolitan Community Church, United Church of Christ (UCC), and the Episcopal (Anglican) Church, have explicit policies and positions supporting transgender people.[888] Programs like the UCC's "Open and Affirming" (ONA) and organizations such as the Episcopal Integrity USA work to bring LGBT people back to their churches.

In other cases, the matter of transgender people is left deliberately vague. Mennonites leave the question of whether one can be Christian and transgender up to individual congregations. The Presbyterian Church (US), United Methodist Church, and Lutheran Church similarly have no specific policies excluding transgender people, yet no policy for inclusion either.[889] Some have taken steps to show that being transgender is not an insurmountable barrier to participating in the church, such as the United Methodist Church ordaining a transgender deacon in 2017.[890]

A few remain generally hostile to LGBT people. The African Methodist Episcopal Church forbids same-sex marriage, but says nothing on transgender issues. Similarly, the Presbyterian Church declares "homosexual practice" a sin, and will not ordain transgender people as ministers, though there is no explicit policy. The Presbyterian-affiliated "Harvest USA," however, declares "gender distortions" to be a "sexual sin."[891]

It is worth taking a moment to discuss primarily black Protestant denominations in America with relation to LGBT issues. Membership in black Protestant Churches (such as the African Methodist Episcopal Church) has been relatively stable, remaining at around 8 percent across generations.[892] Most polling data over the past decade shows that black Protestant support for same-sex marriage (which acts as a proxy for many LGBT issues), while increasing over time, is significantly less than it is with Catholics and white Mainline Protestants. However, black Protestant support for same-sex marriage is also significantly higher than it is with white evangelicals.[893]

Anti-LGBT hate groups have attempted to use LGBT people as a wedge issue with black churchgoers for years.[894] While this has worked at times in a tactical sense (HERO in Houston), it has not had the intended strategic effect. Black Mainline Protestant support for same-sex marriage has increased at about the same rate as it has for the general population. Only 3 percent of blacks identify as Republican, and that number has dropped sharply in recent years, according to Pew Research.[895] There is also anecdotal evidence that black churchgoers are leaving traditionally white, evangelical denominations.[896]

We can infer that Democratic support for LGBT issues has not been a political deal breaker to people in predominantly black Protestant Churches, nor has it translated into support for current religious conservative wedge issues. Black Protestants are strongly opposed to the creation of a religious right to refuse service to LGBT people, presumably because they were on the wrong end of such "rights" in the not-so-distant past.[897] Thus, while a few prominent black church leaders have aligned themselves with white evangelical political organizations such as the Family Research Council, they remain outliers within the black community.[898]

While there is no overwhelming consensus position on transgender people within Mainline Protestant denominations, in general, they are more accepting or tolerant of transgender people than evangelical Christian denominations and the Roman Catholic Church's positions. In terms of membership attitudes towards transgender people, mainline Protestants are slightly more conservative than Catholics, but significantly more liberal than evangelical Protestants.[899] Still, these positions and attitudes have not had a noticeable effect in the rate of membership decline: it has been faster than that of evangelical denominations hostile to LGBT people.[900]

Both evangelical and Mainline Protestant leaders are keenly aware of these statistics. Some, particularly those in conservative denominations, blame the declining attendance on the liberalization of these churches, saying they have watered down Christianity into moral relativism, with no clear delineation of right and wrong.[901] Some sociologists hold that demographics, such as differences in birth rates, are the real reason why the ranks of Mainline Protestants are declining faster than evangelicals.[902]

Others point to a groundbreaking 2010 study by Putnam and Campbell, which argues there is a strong link between Millennial disenchantment with Christianity and the rise of evangelical conservatism in the 1980s and 90s.[903] That study hypothesizes that Millennials have come of age in an environment where being Christian means being conservative (and Republican).[904] More socially progressive Millennials—which is most of them—view the choice as an ultimatum of sorts: choosing between one's political identity, or their religious identity. When it comes down to brass tacks, Millennials are apt to change the latter, given how little effort it takes to drop out of organized religion, and how little price there is to pay for it outside rural areas. In short, when there is a conflict between religious and political identity, people are giving up the religious one.

The solution, from Putnam and Campbell's perspective, would be to sever the link between religion and politics. But recent polling indicates that 57 percent of Republicans want to see Christianity as the official religion of the United States.[905] Additionally, greater religious involvement in government is a core tenet for many evangelicals. But given the shrinking number of Mainline Protestants compared to the stable membership of the evangelical community, the researchers' hope that the divide between church and state will be reasserted seems forlorn.

The blurring of the lines between church and state appears to have accelerated under the Trump Administration. The Supreme Court ruled in *Trinity Lutheran v. Comer* that churches cannot be excluded from public funding.[906] President Trump has ordered that the IRS not enforce the Johnson amendment, which says that churches cannot contribute to campaigns or endorse candidates if they want to keep their tax-exempt status.[907] At the same time, almost half of the voters of Alabama decided that having any Democrat in office is worse than a Republican (Roy Moore) who stalks 14-year-old girls.[908] As such, it appears that churches will play an even greater role in politics going forward, and further cement the impression that religion = Republican = anti-LGBT.

Latter Day Saints (Mormons)

The Church of Jesus Christ of Latter Day Saints (also known as the Mormon Church) hired several marketing firms to revamp its image after the Church lobbied hard for Proposition 8, which had banned same-sex marriage in California.[909] The Mormon Church also brought in experts on LGBTQ youth to develop messaging specifically aimed at preventing suicide in Mormon youth.[910] It hasn't worked; the Church has continued to harden its positions on LGBTQ people, excluding children with LGBTQ parents, and the result has been skyrocketing teen suicide rates.[911]

While being one of the most solidly Republican denominations, the Mormon Church has taken several steps to appear less anti-LGBT, including supporting statewide non-discrimination legislation in Utah (with a huge, "religious freedom"-shaped caveat and a lack of protections in public accommodations), and setting up a website for "conversations" about "same-sex attractions."[912] [913] [914]

But anyone hoping that the Church would also take a more affirming view toward LGBT people saw those hopes dashed at a press conference about Utah's non-discrimination law.

"To those who follow the Church closely and who are familiar with its teachings and positions on various social issues, it will be apparent that we are announcing no change in doctrine or Church teachings today," said Elder D. Todd Christofferson in January 2015.[915] "The Church of Jesus Christ of Latter-Day Saints believes that sexual relations other than between a man and a woman who are married are contrary to the laws of God."

The caveat in the Church's support for statewide non-discrimination protections was an exemption that allows individuals to discriminate on religious grounds.[916] This religious exemption allows for a myriad of abuses. "Doctors would still be allowed to deny medical care," reported the Human Rights Campaign in a statement about the Utah law.[917] "Pharmacists would still be allowed to refuse to fill valid prescriptions. And landlords, as well as business operators, would still be allowed to reject LGBT people. All in the name of religion."

Further, the Church still expects transgender people never to transition. Lesbians, gay men, and bisexual people are expected to either remain celibate their entire lives, or enter into a mixed-orientation marriage (i.e. a gay person marrying a straight person of the opposite sex). Mixed-orientation marriages (a straight person married to a gay person) are subtly encouraged, despite new research that shows such relationships are likely to fail, and the quality of life for Mormon men in these marriages is worse than people suffering from chronic autoimmune disease.[918 919 920] The Church also quietly supports so-called ex-gay therapy to suppress gay men's identities, by taking no formal position on the scientifically discredited practice, but reminding members it sure is easier to get into heaven if you're not gay.[921]

This messaging took a significant hit in 2018 when the Church's poster child for mixed-orientation marriage, Josh Weed, announced that he was divorcing his wife, getting a boyfriend, and was very sorry for endorsing mixed-orientation marriages as a viable option.[922]

Despite aggressive proselytization, though, and having the largest families of any denomination, Mormon identification rates in the US remain flat.[923] Missionary conversion rates continue to decline, as do retention of new members, average Mormon family size, and retention rates for young people born into the faith.[924 925 926] Mormons were excited during recent presidential election cycles to have Mitt Romney as a hugely well-known example.

The Mormon cultural characteristics of education, moderation, restraint, and civility are at odds with the image promoted by the Trump Administration. This led to an independent candidate credibly challenging Trump in Utah in 2016, and Mitt Romney opposing Trump's candidacy.[927] Higher educational attainment and exposure to world cultures via missionary work may be part of why Mormons are more likely to support marriage equality than white evangelicals (37% to 31%).[928]

Other major world religions in the US

While the focus of this book is on the US, and this chapter on the religious denominations most central to the discussion of transgender issues, a brief discussion of how other major world religions relate to transgender people in the US is warranted. It is worth noting that polling data in the US on transgender rarely separates out by religions such as Judaism, Islam, Hinduism, and Buddhism. As such, proxy data points (such as views on same-sex marriage, or whether homosexuality is a sin) will have to be used for comparison, since attitudes on these issues tend to be highly correlated with attitudes towards transgender people.

Data from the Pew Research Center also shows that Hindus, Jews, Unitarian Universalists, and Buddhists are the most educated groups in the country.[929] Education has also been found to be highly correlated with key indicators of LGBT acceptance, such as support for same-sex marriage.[930] Thus, it is unsurprising that Jews (Reformed and Conservative), Hindus, Buddhists, and Unitarian Universalists are the strongest supporters of same-sex marriage of any group discussed; more so than even Catholics or Mainline Protestants.[931]

It is worth noting that atheists, agnostics, and Nones have, on average, less education than any of the four religious groups mentioned above. However, they support marriage equality at a rate greater than that of Jews and Hindus, but less than that of Buddhists and Unitarian Universalists.

The reasons why these religions support transgender people go beyond just educational attainment. Hinduism has a long tradition of recognizing three genders based on a belief in reincarnation. As such, Hindus believe gendered distinctions are based on psychology, not on genitalia or biology.[932] Reformed and Conservative Jews have explicit positions affirming transgender people.[933] [934] (Orthodox Judaism is not affirming, but is still trying to reach an official position.[935]) Buddhism has no position on transgender people specifically (either for or against), but is generally considered one of the most tolerant where transgender people are concerned.[936]

Islam in the US differs from Judaism, Buddhism, and Hinduism in its attitudes towards LGBT people. Muslims in the US are more educated than the general population average, but also culturally have stricter sexual mores. As a result, Muslims in the US are less supportive of same-sex marriage than average, but more so than Mormons, white evangelicals, and Jehovah's Witnesses. While this statistic does not directly address attitudes towards transgender people, generally they are highly correlated with attitudes towards gays and lesbians. It is worth noting, however, that some Islamic countries (Iran and Pakistan) have official positions that recognize transgender people, while allowing them to medically and legally transition. Thus, these two countries are to the left of the Republican Party on transgender issues.

In terms of political affiliation, each of these religious groups (Muslims, Jews, Hindus, and Buddhists) favor Democrats over Republicans by at least a two or three to one margin.[937] While this doesn't necessarily mean support for transgender people, these groups generally support a party that has a platform which supports transgender people.

Thus, as a result of their size, beliefs, and party affiliation, none of these groups (except perhaps Judaism) is at the forefront of the battle for or against transgender inclusion and acceptance in our society. Despite attempts by the religious right to enlist these groups in support of RFRA expansions, all of them are generally opposed to laws allowing people to discriminate against LGBT people on the basis of religion.[938] Indeed, Jews, Buddhists, and Hindus are among those most strongly opposed to such exemptions from civil rights law.[939]

For the most part, Hinduism and Buddhism could be described as passive supporters, while Reformed and Conservative Judaism is much more active. Orthodox Judaism and Islam are less supportive, but leaders in these communities have not been aligning themselves with the American religious right (such as the ADF and FRC). The reason for this is not hard to discern: these organizations have a stated goal of making the US a "Christian nation." This is hardly a selling point for rabbis and imams.

While it would be preferable if these religious groups were active allies to the transgender community, history has shown how difficult it can be to engage cisgender people on these issues on a good day.

The LGBT community and religion

The LGBT community is somewhat less likely to be religious than the American population as a whole, according to a recent Gallup poll.[940] Given the dearth of LGBT-affirming faiths, how often LGBT people have been mistreated by the faith communities they were born into, and the link between anti-LGBT religions and politics, this is unsurprising. That hasn't stopped national organizations like the National LGBTQ Task Force and the Human Rights Campaign (HRC) from having dedicated religious outreach campaigns.[941] [942] These organizations see such efforts as essential to their missions. Chad Griffin, HRC's President, describes religious outreach as one of the group's top priorities in fighting for LGBT equality:

> There's sort of two pieces of this work. Number one, and first and foremost, is changing hearts and minds. You change hearts and minds by building bridges and by having a conversation with business leaders, with faith and religious leaders, with community leaders, and also with elected officials at the community level and at the state level.[943]

These religious outreach efforts have several purposes. According to a National LGBTQ Task Force Report on inclusive religious organizing, "Pro-LGBTQ faith-based leaders and leadership structures bring significant resources to the fight—the ability to speak with moral authority to large numbers and through a variety of communication vehicles."[944]

The ability to have religious leaders testify in favor of LGBT inclusions significantly alters the perception that religion is unanimous in condemning LGBT people, according to the report. It also allows for greater reach into communities where people of color suffer the most from the confluence of multiple forms of discrimination and oppression.

Unfortunately, the influence of LGBT-affirming churches is waning as their membership declines. While there are some members working very hard to change the most hostile denominations from within, these denominations (and their leaders) continue to take a harder line on transgender issues. Relatedly, research shows that increased internet access helps tighten the spiral of religious de-identification by consistently pointing out the link between conservative religions and politics.[945] [946]

"For people living in homogeneous communities, the internet provides opportunities to find information about people of other religions (and none), and to interact with them personally," wrote Allen Downey, a computer science professor at Franklin W. Olin College of Engineering who studied the impact of web access on religious identification.[947]

Atheists and agnostics within the LGBT community often see this tightening as a necessary step toward isolating the radical right from the general population, building what *Salon* recently labeled a "New American Secularism."[948] [949] Some even believe that traditional Christian faith needs to be torn down before it can be built back up.[950]

No matter what angle you look at the demographic data from, the decline in denominational identification is accelerating. So is the decline in church attendance. It seems likely that this trend will continue for the foreseeable future.

While the end result is uncertain, current shifts in religious messaging imply that a segment of conservative religions will hold on to a core constituency for a long time to come, without moving toward greater acceptance (both in part because they do not, and in spite of it). A contrarian social outlook (no matter how unpopular) will always have adherents, and individuals who hate LGBT people will find a place for their views long after they are no longer socially acceptable and will have a home in evangelical denominations for a long time to come. For example, interracial marriage has been legal across the US for more than 50 years. Approximately one in six Americans is still opposed, according to a Pew survey.[951] Put another way, anti-LGBT positions are a feature, not a bug.

One argument against inclusion, acceptance, or even tolerance is the relative shift in demographics. Right-wing pundits who support the Church maintaining its anti-LGBT stance have seized on to the fact that evangelical groups are holding on to members better than denominations that affirm LGBT people.

In an August 2014 op-ed for *The Federalist*, Alex Griswold sardonically concluded that the fastest way to "Shrink your church in one easy step" is to become LGBT-affirming.[952] "A number of Christian denominations have already taken significant steps towards liberalizing their stances on homosexuality and marriage, and the evidence so far seems to indicate that affirming homosexuality is hardly a cure for membership woes," wrote Griswold. "On the contrary, every major American church that has taken steps towards liberalization of sexual issues has seen a steep decline in membership."

Griswold fails to note, however, that while 25.4 percent of people in the US are white evangelical Protestants, only 8 percent of people between 18 and 29 identify this way. The average age of a white evangelical Protestant in the US is 55 years old, and growing. Sixty-two percent of white evangelicals are over 50 years of age now. Thus, while being progressive isn't saving faiths, neither is hostility to LGBT people in the long run.[953]

So, Griswold's article misses the bigger picture. Conservative faiths are declining more slowly while moderate progressive ones are shrinking more quickly, but Pew's research suggests that it's actually conservative faiths that are making *all* of Christianity toxic to moderate and progressive Millennials.

LGBT rights aren't the only social issue where conservative theology drives younger moderates and progressives away. As prominent atheist blogger Hemant Mehta noted at CNN, those conservative faiths are "antigay, anti-women, anti-science, anti-sex-education and anti-doubt, to name a few of the most common criticisms."[954] The fact that the vast majority of white evangelicals in Alabama supported Roy Moore while condemning LGBT people in the same breath was appalling to most of the rest of the country.[955]

Churches that dig in their heels on anti-LGBT positions might hear more about how that issue is driving away new members, but that's because public opinion on LGBT people has shifted faster than any of the other issues the church is refusing to evolve on.[956]

A 2007 study by the Barna Group found the most common word used by Millennials to describe Christianity was "antihomosexual." For a staggering *91 percent* of non-Christians, this was the first word that came to their mind when asked about key Christian qualities. The same was true for 80 percent of young churchgoers. The next most common negative descriptors were "judgmental," "hypocritical," and "too involved in politics," according to David Kinnaman and Gabe Lyons' book *UnChristian: What a New Generation Really Thinks About Christianity... And Why It Matters.*[957]

While this research is a decade old, this perception has remained since then. A 2012 Public Religion Research Institute (PRRI) study found that 64 percent of Millennials say that "anti-gay" describes present-day Christianity somewhat or very well, and 62 percent of Millennials also believe that present-day Christianity is "judgmental."[958] PRRI also found in a follow-up study that 34 percent of Millennials who left their religion did so because of their religion's anti-gay teachings or treatment of LGBT people.[959]

What we do know is that the rise of the Nones and the increasing acceptance of LGBT people are linked.

And neither is likely to be undone.

Evangelicals and religious-based therapy for transgender people

The 2015 Association of Certified Biblical Counselors conference in Louisville, Kentucky, hosted a special plenary session on transgender people, and followed up with a wider conference on transgender issues.[960] The counselors group is drawn from conservative Christian denominations, especially the Southern Baptist Convention. This section describes ten of the messages it had about transgender people, and why they were likely to do harm.

It should be noted that these counselors are not part of mainstream professional organizations, which have universally opposed conversion therapy efforts. This is an organization which believes that all counseling should be based on a conservative interpretation of the Bible, and not peer-reviewed best practices. The Association of Certified Biblical Counselors has its own credentialing, and does not follow the more stringent requirements of mainstream professional organizations. Still, religion masquerading as science was bound to do great harm with the stigmatizing attitudes it takes towards transgender people.

1. Rejection is godly

After the 2014 Southern Baptist conference, where the denomination urged people with transgender children to reject their children's identities, the counselors' conference doubled down. Members have now made it clear that under no circumstances should you accept your child's identity if they are transgender. They have hinted that it is okay to reject and cast out your children for being gender non-conforming.

They took the position that it's okay to cut off relationships with a transgender child who is transitioning, because the act of transitioning means they (the transgender person) rejected you (and by extension God) first.

As evangelical theologian Andrew Walker wrote, "If I affirm transgenderism, I am actually doing an unloving thing. I am withholding truth because I value my own reputation or my own friendships or my own comforts more than I value the eternal happiness of the person made in God's image who stands in front of me."[961] There was no discussion of the actual statistics and research on the effects of rejection.

2. Transgender people are abominations

They made it clear that all transgender people who accept their identities are in rebellion against God and are going to hell. It doesn't matter what they believe, how they worship, or how they behave; as long as they remain gender non-conforming, they are damned. You cannot be transgender and Christian. You cannot be transgender and saved.

3. Transgender people are disgusting

Speakers at the conference made it clear just how they feel about transgender people, calling it "a culture that is really full of sexual darkness and decay."[962] When confronted with this, their followers on Twitter responded that of course sin is disgusting, and transgender people are basically sin, abomination, and a rejection of all of God's plans personified.

Meanwhile, the number of transgender people murdered in the US has risen for five consecutive years.

4. Transgender people are a bigger threat to Christianity than gays

Somehow, the conservative Christian belief that they are the most oppressed group of people in the US has become bad enough that the conference members claimed that acceptance of transgender people—and transgender people themselves—represent the direst threat ever to Christianity.[963] Such a belief is out of alignment with reality: 70–75 percent of the US identifies as Christian, while only a tiny and impoverished minority are transgender.

They're also a little fuzzy on how acceptance of transgender people will end Christianity in America, but they seem really certain transgender people are part of why Millennials are leaving religions in droves. They can't quite seem to come to grips that when Millennials are forced to choose between loving their friends and family, and staying with a church urging them to reject someone they love, Millennials are choosing love.

5. "Pray away the gay" is back...as "pray the trans away"

The group has completely rejected the notion of "conversion" or "reparative" therapy, or at least the therapy part of it. They rejected applying any psychological or therapeutic theory towards gender dysphoria. Members also rejected the notion that some trauma causes people to be transgender or that being transgender can be cured with some sort of talk therapy.

Instead, it's all because of sin. Since the only cure for sin is prayer, and because Jesus can cure anything, religion can cure both homosexuality and gender dysphoria through praying. And Bible study. And Jesus.

What about people who don't succeed in praying the transgender away? According to these Biblical counselors, they just didn't pray hard enough or have enough faith, and as a result are going to hell for it.

After decades of lesbians and gays trying this and breaking themselves into a million pieces in the process, who here thinks it will end well for transgender people?

6. All of the experts on the 2015 Association of Certified Biblical Counselors panel were white, heterosexual, cisgender men

This conference about transgender people was hosted entirely by people who aren't transgender, dislike them intensely, and were arguing that marginalizing, demonizing, and discriminating against a minority group was what's best for said minority group. The result was what you would expect: it looked like a "conference" about the civil rights movement hosted by white supremacists.

7. None of the experts had a degree in mental health care or medicine

All of the people speaking at the panel had a degree from a theological school. None of them had degrees in medicine, psychology, gender studies, or psychiatry. When the topic of actual medical consensus came up, they claimed that it wasn't one. Or they cherry-picked a factoid, or misused or misrepresented clinical opinions. They hand-waved away the consensus of the American Medical Association, American Psychiatric Association, and American Psychological Association, claiming they are all biased liberal organizations.

8. The Bible is scientific and science is biblical

The speakers at the conference resorted to another bizarre logical sleight of hand when they claimed there is no gap between a biblical view and a scientific view. Their logic was essentially a tautology: the inerrancy of the Bible means that everything in the Bible is scientifically valid, and that science confirms everything in the Bible. Therefore, they believe that their beliefs about transgender people are 100 percent correct scientifically, because the Bible is science, and science totally agrees with the Bible (as they interpret it), because the Bible is always right.

As long as people interpret it exactly the way they do.

9. Rejected and dead is a better outcome than loved and accepted for trans kids

They don't see a difference between being dead by suicide and alive and transgender: you end up in hell either way. These folks are telling parents that, sure, the suicide statistics on rejected transgender children may be right, but if you don't shame and reject them into not being transgender anymore they're going to hell either way.

However, if you accept your transgender child, you're all going to hell, not just your kid.

The message is pretty clear, and evangelical parents are taking it to heart. According to the court testimony of a transgender teen boy who was seeking to terminate his parents' guardianship, his father told him to go kill himself because "he was going to hell anyway."[964]

The message is it is better for you to end up with a dead kid than a transgender one.

10. You can come to church with us if you come as someone else

In a rather ineffective attempt to show they're not a hate group, the conference panelists said they'd love for transgender people to come to church with them...as long as they went back to their birth gender, conform with societal and religious gender norms, and generally be straight-acting and looking.[965] According to Andrew T. Walker, transgender people are "a settled rejection of God's purposes for us as male or female cannot be reconciled with following Christ."[966] This means he believes that transgender people who do not stop being transgender cannot be Christians, and are irredeemable.

In other words, transgender people are welcome as long as they're not transgender. Or at least pretending not to be transgender for the sake of everyone who doesn't want to share space with "one of those people."

This is quite possibly the worst welcome mat since the Claymore anti-personnel landmine.

Convert, cure, closet, or kill: the religious right's plan for transgender Americans

Given that leadership at the two largest religious groups in America (the Southern Baptist Convention and the Roman Catholic Church) regard transgender people as an existential threat not just to their religions, but to humanity, one would expect them to have strategies and tactics on how to deal with this. It is no coincidence that these are essentially re-toolings of their failed strategies to push gays and lesbians back into the closet.

In 2012, an article by legal professor and civil rights lawyer Tobias

Barrington Wolff was published in the *Harvard Law & Policy Review* titled "Civil rights reform and the body."[967] In many ways, he was prescient, predicting that transgender people and bathrooms would become the central fight in the LGBT movement. Wolff pointed out in his article that unlike the right's strategy during the Civil Rights Movement, it is possible to erase LGBT people from our culture by four basic methods: convert, cure, closet, or kill. These four observed strategies were used for decades against lesbian, gay, and bisexual people, and Wolff suggested similar strategies would be used by the religious right against transgender people in the next great social debate.

They have indeed been used, some more than others, and with greatly varying degrees of success. Let's look at each of them in turn.

Convert

There has been a significant shift in the messages conservative religious organizations are sending on inclusion of LGB people, including those of Southern Baptists and Mormons.[968] [969] The new view by the SBC and Mormons on sexual orientation is that people don't choose to be LGB, reparative therapy doesn't work, and that lesbians and gays can be included if they are willing to renounce their "lifestyle" and become celibate for life (unless Jesus makes them straight if they pray hard enough). Few LGB people seem to be taking these organizations up on their offer, but it at least sort of looks welcoming.

For transgender people, such an offer is nearly meaningless. In order to be welcome, they would have to stay closeted (either pre- or post-transition), or detransition if they have already transitioned. This is one of the most hardline stances, but it is the dominant one endorsed by conservative Christianity today. To understand why the positions of these churches are far less welcoming to transgender people than lesbians, gays, or bisexuals, let's take a hypothetical case.

Suppose you have two identical men: one a cisgender gay man (let's call him Bob), and a transgender man (say...Doug). Both dress the same way at church (suit and tie), look the same, are celibate, and both are indistinguishable but for their sex assigned at birth. Under the current policy of conservative churches, Bob would (theoretically) be welcome, but Doug would not because his gender expression did not match his sex at birth. Essentially, the transgender man fails to renounce the "transgender lifestyle" unless he completely alters his gender expression for the entire time, detransitions, and essentially attempts the near impossible task of re-transitioning in the other direction. Bob merely has to forego sex, which would otherwise take up a tiny fraction of his day, if at all.

Nor would the church particularly want Doug back even if he did try, given how out of place he would look trying to cram himself into a gender role (and expression) that fits neither his outer appearance, nor his inner identity.

Thus, it is unsurprising that non-affirming churches have put little effort into appearing more welcoming to transgender people, or that transgender people have been making little effort to be a part of these churches. With 30 percent of Millennials not identifying with any denomination, there is no longer a cultural expectation that everyone, much less transgender people, needs to find a place within a church.

Cure

Unlike LGB people, the religious right is still pushing the myth that transgender people are mentally ill and are best served by seeking a cure.[970] They take different approaches based on whether the transgender person is an adult or juvenile.

Their "proof" that *transgender adults* can be cured is Walt Heyer, who transitioned back in the 1980s and then detransitioned about a decade ago.[971] Heyer admits he suffered from dissociative disorder (colloquially referred to as multiple personality disorder in popular media), and that his psychiatrists didn't pick up on it when he started transition. Indeed, he admits lying to his therapists at the time.[972] Heyer then makes the unsupportable assumption that *all* transgender people have dissociative disorder, and no one should transition. In the process, Heyer has become a poster child for the ex-gay/ex-trans movement, and a close ally of religiously motivated anti-LGBT hate groups.

The religious right tries to back up Heyer's claims with Dr. Paul McHugh, a self-described conservative Catholic who has been involved in the cover-up of sexual abuses of children by priests and the assassination of abortion doctors, and who participates in gatherings of anti-LGBT hate groups as a guest of honor. McHugh uses his status as a professor emeritus at Johns Hopkins University to support these hate groups and organizations promoting reparative therapy, and promote the narrative that transgender women are sexual deviants who should be "cured." (A longer description of Dr. McHugh's activities can be found in Chapter 5.)[973 974 975]

Both Heyer and McHugh promote reparative therapy with the excuse that, because transgender people have difficulty functioning in a society which reviles and abuses them, they should therefore seek a cure (rather than making society more accepting).[976] The problem with both Heyer and McHugh's position is that the treatments they recommend are provided by *exactly* the same ex-gay organizations, with *exactly* the same people, using *exactly* the same religious perspective, and using the *exact* same methods (and theories) as were performed on gays for decades (with absolutely no success).[977 978 979 980] They ignore that no evidence exists to suggest a treatment that can change a person's gender identity.

In fact, the leading body of experts on transgender care, the World Professional Association of Transgender Health, has standards of care which explicitly state: "Treatment aimed at trying to change a person's gender identity and lived gender expression to become more congruent with sex assigned at birth has been attempted in the past, yet without success, particularly in the long-term. Such treatment is no longer considered ethical."[981]

In other words, the "cure" for transgender is the same religious "ex-gay" snake oil with a different label.

Transgender children are primarily targeted by the religious right by the myth that the vast majority of transgender youth will spontaneously stop being transgender (the "desistance myth" referred to in Chapters 4 and 5), especially if coercive behavioral modification is applied to their gender non-conforming behavior.[982] The primary purveyor of this myth is Dr. Kenneth Zucker, the disgraced former head of the youth gender clinic in Toronto (who is also discussed extensively in Chapter 5).[983]

For the purpose of this section, it is worth reiterating that, for decades, Zucker told desperate parents his 1970s vintage behavior modification on effeminate boys could prevent kids from growing up to be gay or transgender.[984] After the professional community rejected reparative therapy on lesbian and gay youth, he claimed that he only cured transgender kids because he believed that transgender people will never be accepted by society (just as he stated gay people would never be accepted back in the 90s), and being a transgender adult is thus a bad outcome.

Zucker claimed he doesn't perform reparative therapy; but he also now refuses to practice anywhere that has banned it.[985] As a result of all of this, Zucker is cited more often by anti-LGBT religious organizations or hate groups when trying to justify their attempts to cure transgender people than anyone except Paul McHugh.[986] [987]

Chapter 4 describes in great detail why the desistance narrative is junk science, but it can be summarized by noting that multiple independent reviews of the studies showing "desistance" found that 90 percent of the children being treated under the old *DSM-IV-TR* standards for "gender identity disorder" would not meet the criteria for gender dysphoria under the *DSM-5*, because they did not actually have any sort of cross-gender identity.[988] [989] In short, you cannot legitimately claim to cure someone of being transgender who was never actually transgender in the first place.

With marriage equality resolved, the religious right needed a new cause to claim they were "protecting children." As a result, the religious right is increasingly targeting transgender youth. The plurality of anti-transgender bills introduced target transgender youth, and some even cite the desistance myth as a rationale. At a local level, churches are being used as the staging area and headquarters for rallying people against transgender children. The religious right is far more frightened of transgender children than it is of transgender adults, and for good reason.

Nothing damages the narrative that transgender people need fixing more than studies which show that transgender children and teens who transition early are every bit as healthy as other children and teens. Just as bad for the right wing is the fact that these children grow up to be healthy adults, who cannot be spotted (and targeted for hate) as being visibly transgender. The latest research and treatments are almost universally going against anti-LGBT forces.

The latest research shows that socially transitioned youth who live in supportive families have mental health outcomes equal to their cisgender (non-transgender) peers.[990] A Danish study on the use of puberty-blocking medication on transgender youth showed that the test group had mental health outcomes equal to their peers, no medical complications, and that none of the cohort expressed regrets.[991] A separate US study released in 2015 had the same results.[992]

Because the outcomes for youth who are supported by their families in their gender identity and expression appears vastly better than those who are rejected, the American Psychological Association's guidelines for treating transgender youth rejected Zucker's approach, stating, "Attempts to force gender diverse and transgender youth to change their behavior to fit into social norms may traumatize the youth and stifle their development into healthy adults."[993]

The end of reparative therapy was in sight, however briefly. After winning the case against the for-profit ex-gay organization JONAH, a coalition of the National Center for Lesbian Rights, the Human Rights Campaign, and the Southern Poverty Law Center filed a complaint with the Federal Trade Commission alleging that practitioners of reparative therapy are committing consumer fraud.[994] However, under the Trump Administration, there is almost zero chance this complaint will survive.

Given how the approach of "curing" transgender people appears to be either laughably infeasible or actively imploding, the religious right is focusing mostly on the next option: forcing transgender people back into the closet.

Closet

It is possible to drive sexual minorities underground via legislation. Theocracies such as Iran and Saudi Arabia have effectively done so with draconian punishments, including execution.[995] [996] While such punishments would probably not pass constitutional muster in the US, there are perfectly legal ways to make being a transgender person in the US functionally impossible (unless you're independently wealthy to begin with, and never need to hold a job again).

As discussed in detail in Chapter 7, the Family Research Council (FRC) (a religious political group whose purpose is to make American law and policy conform with their Biblical worldview) laid out a five-point plan on how to effectively legislate transgender people out of existence, by enacting laws and policies designed to make it impossible to function on a day-to-day basis.[997] The (paraphrased) points are as follows:

- The government should not recognize gender changes legally.
- No laws should protect transgender people from discrimination.
- The government should not provide transgender-related medical coverage.
- No insurer should be required to provide transition-related medical coverage.
- Transgender people should not be allowed to serve in the military.

These points are reiterated here, since the FRC is a religious-based hate group. Thus, while the means are political, the ends are religious. This also serves to illustrate how modern conservative political and religious goals firmly overlap. There is nary a difference between the position statement of the Southern Baptist Convention on transgender people, the Kansas Republican Party statement, and the document put forth by the FRC—indeed, they frequently use language that is nearly identical.[998] [999] [1000]

Implicit in the first point is that transgender people should not be allowed to use bathrooms in accordance with their gender identity, regardless of surgical status. One element missing from this plan, but certainly supporting it, is the creation of "Super Religious Freedom Restoration Acts (RFRAs)" like the First Amendment Defense Act and Mississippi's "Religious Freedom" law (HB1523).[1001] [1002] Additionally, the Department of Justice's 2017 memorandums on "religious freedom" give wide latitude for employees of the deferral government to discriminate against LGBT co-workers, and even private citizens.[1003] Broad interpretations of religious freedom laws and policies make it impossible for the government to punish anyone (public or private) who discriminates against LGBT people based on their religious beliefs.

As described in Chapter 7, the desired outcome of these laws, policies, and court decisions is to make it nearly impossible to function in society on a day-to-day basis, thus forcing transgender people to either stay in the closet, detransition, or end up in the underground economy.[1004]

Almost 60 anti-transgender bills were introduced in 2016 (most of which targeted transgender youth), restricting access to public accommodations, defining "sex" in non-discrimination laws to exclude transgender people, or permitting health care providers to refuse to treat transgender patients.[1005] [1006] [1007] Another six states introduced laws banning protections for LGBT people, which would join Tennessee and Arkansas in nullifying local non-discrimination ordinances.[1008] Twenty-two states introduced "Religious Freedom" laws making discrimination against LGBT people legal and consequence-free.[1009]

The vast majority of these laws were not passed, but HB2 in North Carolina was. It functionally accomplished two of the Family Research Council's goals by nullifying all legal protections for transgender people, and effectively banning them from public bathrooms, while setting a nearly impossible bar for obtaining legal recognition of a gender change.[1010] [1011]

Also noteworthy is that while North Carolina required sex change surgery to change a gender marker, it was adamantly opposed to state-provided insurance covering such procedures. Additionally, many transgender people do not want such surgery, or are physically unable to have it. Most simply cannot afford it.

This is why the transgender community reacted so vehemently to HB2: it is the realization of many of the goals of religiously motivated hate groups intended to legislate a community out of public life. This is something that has not generally been pointed out in the mainstream media, though it should be.

For example, how would the media have reacted if North Carolina had passed a law targeting black people that was explicitly proposed and endorsed by the Klan? Or that required black people to pay $25,000 for government-issued ID, but not white people? Such blatant discrimination on the basis of race would be completely unacceptable, yet somehow there is a debate on whether this is justified when applied to transgender people.

Mississippi's religious freedom law was initially struck down by a federal judge just before it took effect, with the court stating that "The State has put its thumb on the scale to favor some religious beliefs over others. Showing such favor tells non-adherents that they are outsiders, not full members of the political community, and...adherents that they are insiders, favored members of the political community... [T]he Equal Protection Clause is violated by HB1523's authorization of arbitrary discrimination against lesbian, gay, transgender, and unmarried persons."[1012] However, the 5th Circuit reversed the lower court ruling, and upheld the constitutionality of Mississippi's law based on standing. It went into effect in 2017.

Similarly, the fate of HB2 looked grim prior to its partial repeal.[1013] Legal observers suggested several ways it would not pass constitutional muster. The 4th Circuit Court (which presides over North Carolina) had previously ruled in *Grimm v. Gloucester County Schools* that transgender students must be allowed to use facilities in accordance with their gender identity.[1014] The Supreme Court agreed to take up the case, but it was rendered moot when the Trump Administration struck down the Department of Education guidelines protecting transgender students, and Gavin Grimm graduating from high school.

HB2 itself was probably doomed based on all the other precedents it seems to violate. Mark Joseph Stern, who covers LGBT law at Slate, points out that HB2 likely violated *Romer v. Evans, Arlington Heights v. Metropolitan*, and *Reitman v. Mulkey*, based on animus and disparate impact on a disfavored class of people.[1015] [1016] [1017] [1018] Given how the HB2 bill and its conservative backers were also trying to force a particular class of students to use facilities which are demonstrably inferior to those available to other students, it is also hard to see how this does not run foul of *Brown v. Board of Education* either.[1019]

Because of the Trump Administration's positions and Kennedy's retirement it appears increasingly likely that attempts to legislate transgender people out of public life may succeed. A religious right to discriminate would establish transgender people as permanent second-class citizens. Other laws designed to force transgender people into the closet are also increasingly likely to survive legal challenges as well.

In short, the future for transgender people as a class in the United States looks bleak, particularly in conservative states looking to pass anti-transgender laws.

Kill

The religious right's disdain for the lives of LGBT people in the past is undeniable. The reaction to the AIDS crisis of the 80s and 90s was typified by the belief that it was a "gay" disease, and they were thus happy to ignore it as long as it was only killing "those people."[1020] Worse, religious right leaders have expressed sentiments to the effect that HIV is "God's punishment" for the sin of homosexuality, or that "gays deserved it," or that HIV was a solution to the "problem" of homosexuality.[1021] [1022] [1023] In the process of justifying "let them die" they cited Romans 1:32: "Who knowing the judgment of God, that they which commit such things are worthy of death, not only do the same, but have pleasure in them that do them."

Such expressions are now generally considered beyond the pale by the public, an embarrassment by more mainstream figures in the religious right, and generally limited to something thought but not said publicly by lay members.[1024]

Religious leaders advocating killing gays are generally fringe figures, and even the Family Research Council has all but abandoned the notion of re-criminalizing gay people (in the US at least, Uganda is another matter).[1025] [1026] [1027] Now, the religious right has moved on to transgender people as the new primary target.

Transgender people are portrayed as hypersexual predators and perverts: threats to women and children. This is the same tactic used to demonize blacks, Jews, and gays in the past, before such accusations came to be widely considered offensive.

One way of killing transgender people indirectly is suicide, where attempt rates are extraordinarily high already.[1028] Places where transgender people have less protections and more discrimination also see a higher observed suicide attempt rate.[1029] Thus, anti-transgender legislation serves two lines of effort at once: it kills transgender people (even if indirectly), while helping to reinforce the narrative that transgender people should be forced back into the closet for their own good via legislation and moral opprobrium.

Still, some of the effort to encourage physical harm to transgender people is far more overt.

After declaring transgender people a threat to women and children, figures within the religious right have stepped up their calls for violence against transgender people.[1030] Anita Staver, the President of Liberty Counsel (a theocratic law firm behind anti-LGBT bills in 20 states), posted a tweet suggesting she would shoot transgender people entering the ladies' room.[1031]

The most egregious example of calls for violence against transgender people came from James Dobson, founder of Focus on the Family (the nation's largest evangelical organization) and the Family Research Council. He lamented in a 2016 World Net Daily article that people weren't murdering transgender people for using the bathroom often enough in modern times, writing: "If you are a dad, I pray you will protect your little girls from men who walk in unannounced, unzip their pants and urinate in front of them. If this had happened 100 years ago, someone might have been shot. Where is today's manhood? God help us!"[1032] Less than two weeks later Dobson reiterated his call for action against transgender people: "I mean, where is manhood that we don't stand up and defend our own families? And I think that we're going to be responsible before the Lord if we don't do it."[1033]

Some popular, mainstream conservative commentators have also jumped onto violence as a solution to "the transgender people." Matt Walsh promoted the idea that if transgender people don't want to be beaten to death, they should simply stop being transgender.[1034] Simply put, this is an ultimatum not far removed from that seen in Iran or Saudi Arabia, though it is a call for vigilante justice, as opposed to governmental.

Some have asked why comments such as James Dobson's are legal. The answer lies in the 1969 case of *Brandenburg v. Ohio*.[1035] This Supreme

Court case found that a member of the Klan who suggested "revengance" against "Jews" and "n*ggers" at a Klu Klux Klan rally was protected by the 1st Amendment because his words were not likely to incite "imminent lawless action." It is telling that the case law protecting Dobson's language today protected the Klan during the Civil Rights Movement.

In the meantime, more transgender people are being murdered in the US every year.[1036] While most of these cannot be directly traced to the religious right's fear mongering against transgender people, cisgender women are being accosted as a direct result of this sort of fear mongering. Self-appointed potty police have harassed cisgender women with short hair in Texas, Connecticut, and Michigan for using the bathroom. They assumed that their hair length indicated that the women were transgender, and thus violence was an option on the table.[1037] [1038] [1039] Lesbian women have been thrown out women's bathrooms by actual police in the past year, including one on a video that went viral.[1040] [1041]

Still, these attempts to either kill or terrorize transgender people do not appear to be preventing people from coming out. The Williams Institute at UCLA recently published a new report finding that twice as many people identify as transgender as they did five years ago, increasing the total to 1.4 million Americans.[1042] If the goal was to drive transgender people into the closet, it appears to have failed; and killing 1.4 million people in America is simply unthinkable.

In the final analysis, all of the tactics described by Wolff are being used to some extent by the religious right. The tactic of forcing transgender people into the closet via targeted legislation is the one that they are currently leaning on the hardest. It also appears to be the most viable long-term strategy.

Converting transgender people is unlikely when many Millennials don't feel a need to be a part of any church, much less one that despises them.

"*Curing*" transgender people looks doomed as well because it is the same ridiculous ex-gay "therapy" promoted by kooks and charlatans who were a joke already.[1043]

Forcing transgender people into the *closet* by legislating them out of public life may work. Laws are only unconstitutional if the Supreme Court says they are, and the current administration is filling the courts with people hostile to LGBT people.[1044] There is also proposed legislation to pack the courts to guarantee that conservative social legislation can be achieved and upheld.[1045]

Killing transgender people is no more likely to drive transgender people out of public life, or eradicate them, than it did anyone else hate groups have incited violence against.

In the end, the attacks on transgender people come from the same playbook the religious right used against lesbians, gays, and bisexuals. It is probably going to fail, in the long run, for the same reasons as well. The only real question is how many transgender people and their families will be harmed along the way.

Chapter 9
MILITARY

A short history of the fight for an open transgender military service

After "Don't Ask, Don't Tell" was repealed by Congress in 2010, lesbian, gay, and bisexual service members were finally able to come out in the military. Not so for transgender troops, who remained barred from serving based on Department of Defense (DOD) medical regulations. Most people remained unaware that transgender people were still unable to serve, including many leaders within the LGBT movement. Thus began an effort, led by an organization I belong to, SPARTA, to lift this ban and implement a policy allowing transgender people to not only serve, but to transition while in the service and receive appropriate medical care.[1046]

Our only viable strategy was to convince the DOD that a new policy needed to be implemented. The Republican-controlled Congress was not going to pass legislation allowing us to serve. The DOD would have pushed back hard if President Obama's White House had ordered them to do it, but there is a longstanding tradition of the White House not interfering in DOD personnel policy. There was also little belief that the courts would intervene or agree with us in a lawsuit; the legal concept of deference to the military on policy decisions would almost certainly make impact litigation a waste of time.[1047]

In 2013, we at SPARTA began trying to build awareness of transgender people in the military, first by reaching out to movement leaders and politically active LGBT people. At the same time, we began gathering data and building a body of policy analysis and research that would serve as recommendations to the Pentagon on how to implement an open service policy for transgender people. From there, we began pushing stories of transgender service members into national media outlets. Our first major success was getting a front-page story in *The New York Times* in February 2014.[1048] The next big hit was a Sunday cover story in *The Washington Post* in April 2014, which featured a member of SPARTA.[1049] Shortly thereafter, then-Secretary of Defense Chuck Hagel told reporters he supported the study of changing medical policy on transgender service members, stating that it "continually should be reviewed" and "I'm open to those assessments because, again, I go back to the bottom line: every qualified American who wants to serve our country should have an opportunity if they fit the qualifications and can do it."[1050]

By then, it wasn't just SPARTA working on transgender military service. The Palm Center had received a grant from the Tawani Foundation and was producing a steady stream of research and policy papers examining the issue.[1051] National LGBTQ organizations had come around, and now saw transgender military inclusion as an achievable policy goal. They began quietly making it known to allies on the Hill, in the White House, and at the Pentagon that this was a high priority.

SPARTA continued to work with the media to ensure that the issue didn't drop out of the picture. At the same time, we began circulating research on potential policy solutions to the Pentagon. These policy recommendations were presented to the Pentagon as a long form report in the spring of 2015.[1052] A shorter FAQ based on this report was also distributed, and is the basis for much of the rest of this chapter. Shortly thereafter, in June of 2015, the then-Secretary of Defense Ash Carter announced that the Pentagon would be forming a working group to study how a policy allowing transgender people to serve should be crafted.[1053] Additionally, he announced that all discharges of personnel for being transgender were to be immediately halted.

After some delays, Ash Carter announced on June 30, 2015, that

"Effective immediately, service members may no longer be involuntarily separated, discharged or denied re-enlistment solely on the basis of gender identity. Service members currently on duty will be able to serve openly."[1054] Carter also announced that a policy would be put in place by October 1, 2016, to cover all aspects except accessions (people joining the military). The policy that emerged closely resembled the policy researched and recommended by SPARTA in most respects.[1055] The accessions policy was intended to be in place by July 1, 2017, but was later delayed by Secretary of Defense Mattis in June 2017 until January 1, 2018.

Following the election of President Trump, there were concerns regarding whether his administration would accede to the policy goal of the conservative religious organizations that strongly supported his candidacy. On July 10, 2017, Tony Perkins of the Family Research Council reportedly broached the idea of banning transgender people from the military with President Trump.[1056] On July 26, 2017, President Trump tweeted:

> After consultation with my Generals and military experts, please be advised that the United States Government will not accept or allow...Transgender individuals to serve in any capacity in the U.S. Military. Our military must be focused on decisive and overwhelming...victory and cannot be burdened with the tremendous medical costs and disruption that transgender in the military would entail. Thank you.[1057]

These tweets caused a great deal of confusion. Did that tweet constitute a lawful order? The Chairman of the Joint Chiefs of Staff concluded it did not.[1058] Which generals was the President referring to? Secretary of Defense Mattis was surprised by this; he was on vacation at the time of the tweets and was reportedly "appalled."[1059] The Joint Chiefs of Staff were also unaware that this was in the works.[1060] The top officer in the Army, Chief of Staff 4-star General Mark Milley, first found out about it when asked about it by the press at a luncheon.[1061] The DOD leadership also correctly feared that such an order would result in lawsuits.

There were also the matters of cost and readiness. The RAND Corporation had studied this question for the DOD Working Group and concluded that "covering transgender-related care for service members will increase the U.S. military's active component health care spending by only 0.038–0.054 percent." RAND also concluded that the estimated effect of inclusion of transgender service members on military readiness was "negligible."[1062]

On August 25, 2017, the White House issued an executive order stating, "I am directing the Secretary of Defense, and the Secretary of Homeland Security with respect to the U.S. Coast Guard, to return to the longstanding policy and practice on military service by transgender individuals that was in place prior to June 2016."[1063] Lawsuits by the American Civil Liberties Union, National Center for Lesbian Rights, Lambda Legal, and Equality California challenging the legality of the tweets and the executive order quickly followed.[1064]

As of the time of writing, three federal judges have ordered a halt to the executive order. The first preliminary injunction came on October 30, 2017, when US District Judge for the DC Circuit Colleen Kollar-Kotelly blocked most of the executive order, except the ban on accessions. She found, in a "strongly worded" opinion, that the policy "does not appear to be supported by any facts."[1065]

A second federal judge in Maryland halted the entire executive order, including accessions, on November 21, 2017. US District Judge Marvin J. Garbis, a George H.W. Bush appointee, was also harshly critical in his opinion: "The lack of any justification for the abrupt policy change, combined with the discriminatory impact to a group of our military service members who have served our country capably and honorably, cannot possibly constitute a legitimate governmental interest."[1066]

A third judge also halted the executive order in its entirety on December 11, 2017: US District Judge Marsha Pechman. In her opinion, she concluded that "all of the reasons proffered by the President for excluding transgender individuals from the military [are] not merely unsupported, but [are] actually contradicted by the studies, conclusions, and judgment of the military itself."[1067]

Pechman rejected government claims that retaining transgender service members burdened the military, finding that, "While Defendants raise concerns about transition-related medical conditions and costs, their concerns appear to be hypothetical and extremely overbroad." Additionally, she found the ban likely violates the plaintiffs' rights to due process and to equal protection under the law without advancing any government interest, and that the plaintiffs are likely to succeed in their claims.

With these injunctions in place, the last piece of the transgender military policy (accessions) went into effect on January 1, 2018.

On March 23, 2018, the Pentagon released a "study" which supported the executive order by the Trump Administration, and recommended the separation of transgender service members, and banning of any transgender people from joining.[1068] According to reports, the "study" had been written by members of anti-LGBT groups, including the Center for Military Readiness, The Family Research Council, the Alliance Defending Freedom, and the Heritage Foundation, and the outcome was foreordained.[1069] [1070] The talking points "study" bore a striking similarity those in a book released by an anti-transgender theologian at the Heritage Foundation, and the American Medical Association, American Psychological Association, and American Psychiatric Association all put out statements in support of transgender service.[1071] [1072]

The American Psychological Association blasted the Pentagon "study" calling it a "misuse of psychological science to stigmatize transgender Americans and justify limiting their ability to serve in uniform and access medically necessary health care."[1073] Similarly, the American Medical Association wrote that the study, "mischaracterized and rejected the wide body of peer-reviewed research on the effectiveness of transgender medical care."[1074]

As of the time of this writing, the ban on transgender military service in the United States will go to trial on April 19, 2019 in the 9th Circuit Court of Appeals. From there, it will almost certainly be heard by the Supreme Court, given that the DoD's arguments have gained little traction in lower courts. Given the composition of SCOTUS after Kennedy's retirement, the outlook is somewhat bleak for transgender service members.

How transgender military policy is implemented

This section is primarily based on an FAQ produced by SPARTA in 2015 and updated for this book. The FAQ was written originally as a quick read for policy makers to help them understand that the issues related to the inclusion or transgender service members were not irreducible. Instead, most could be addressed within the military administrative and medical system as it stood. The FAQ attempted to answer almost all the immediate questions people would have regarding implementation of a policy in plain language. A full "deep dive" into how transgender military policy is constructed can be found in SPARTA's *Transgender Military Service: A Guide to Implementation*.[1075]

Leaders needed to know that transgender people and their medical treatment are not a new phenomenon; the first successful gender reassignment surgeries were performed in the early 1930s. The last decade has seen a dramatic increase in the visibility of transgender Americans and in public awareness and understanding of the issues they face. Nevertheless, there remain widespread and persistent myths and misconceptions about the lives and experiences of transgender people.

For example, many still believe that transgender identities are inherently disordered or unstable, or that the medical care required by transgender individuals is more costly, complex, and burdensome than other kinds of medical care. These misunderstandings have led directly to widespread bias, prejudice, and discrimination against transgender Americans.

When the Department of Defense prepared to review its policies relating to the recruitment, readiness, management, and retention of transgender service members, it was critical that such myths and misconceptions be replaced with accurate, up-to-date information. This FAQ, prepared by SPARTA's Transgender Military Service Task Force, was designed to do just that—provide leaders and policy makers in the DOD and elsewhere with a factual basis for considering the question of whether and how transgender Americans should be allowed to serve their country openly. This section:

- provides basic, concise answers to questions about transgender phenomena, transgender medicine, and the gender transition process
- analyzes the impact of gender transition on individual readiness and performance
- addresses commonly held concerns about the practicalities of allowing transgender people to serve, such as uniforms, billeting, and privacy
- provides concrete examples of how transgender-inclusive policies function in allied militaries
- includes first-person accounts of transgender service members currently serving in the US Armed Forces and of their counterparts in the UK, which has allowed transgender people to serve openly since 2000 and is one of 18 nations that currently do so.

Q: How many transgender individuals are there in America? In the US military?

A: There are approximately 1.4 million transgender people in the US.[1076] Transgender people are twice as likely to have served in the military as the general population;[1077] 15,450 were estimated to be serving currently in the active component, reserves, National Guard, and Individual Ready Reserve (IRR), by the Williams Institute at UCLA.[1078] The RAND Corporation, a non-profit government-funded think-tank, estimated that there are between 1320 and 6630 active duty transgender service members, and between 830 and 4160 in the selected reserves.[1079] RAND did not attempt to estimate the number in the IRR.

Q: Are transgender individuals, by definition, mentally ill?

A: They are not. In May 2013, the most recent (fifth) edition of the *Diagnostic and Statistical Manual of Mental Disorders* of the American Psychiatric Association was released (DSM-5), which de-pathologized gender non-conforming behavior and identities, removed the earlier gender identity disorder diagnosis, and placed gender dysphoria in its own distinct category. The American Psychiatric Association states:

"It is important to note that gender nonconformity is not in itself a mental disorder."[1080] It is only if there is a clinical level of distress due to dysphoria that there is anything to diagnose.

Q: What types of medical care do transgender service members require?

A: Treatment for gender dysphoria may include a variety of therapeutic options ranging from psychotherapy to surgery.

Treatment options may include the following:

- Psychotherapy (individual, couple, family, or group) for purposes such as better understanding one's gender identity, role, and expression; addressing the negative impact of gender dysphoria and stigma on mental wellness; alleviating internalized transphobia; enhancing social and peer support; and promoting resilience.
- Changes in gender expression and role (which may involve living part time or full time in a gender role more consistent with one's gender identity).
- Hormone replacement therapy administered via pills, intramuscular injections, or transdermal patches or gels.
- Surgery to change primary and/or secondary sex characteristics (e.g. breasts/chest, external and/or internal genitalia, facial features).[1081]

As with many conditions, the individual decides on a course of treatment based on the recommendation of his or her doctor and other consulting specialists. The number and type of these interventions and the order in which they are received varies from person to person.[1082]

Standards of Care and Ethical Guidelines for treatment are published and maintained by the World Professional Organization for Transgender Health (WPATH), an international professional organization established in 1979.[1083] WPATH is recognized by the AMA as "the leading international, interdisciplinary professional organization devoted to the understanding and treatment of gender identity disorders."[1084]

Q: What are the projected costs of providing appropriate medical care for transgender service members?

A: A recent study by the Williams Institute of UCLA showed that, in civilian contexts, the cost to employers of providing transgender individuals with appropriate health care raised gross premium costs by no more than 0.4 percent (four tenths of a percent) for large companies, and as little as 0.04 percent (four one-hundredths of a percent) for smaller organizations.[1085] The RAND Corporation estimated it to be "between $2.4 million and $8.4 million annually—an amount that will have little impact on and represents an exceedingly small proportion of health care expenditures (approximately $6 billion in the fiscal year 2014) and overall DOD health care expenditures ($49.3 billion)."[1086] A related study published in the *New England Journal of Medicine* reached a similar conclusion, and estimated the total costs to be $5.6 million annually.[1087] It is also worth noting, for comparison's sake, that the DOD spends nearly $84 million annually on erectile dysfunction medications, and $437 million on military bands and concerts.[1088] [1089]

Applied to the military context, providing appropriate health care is significantly more cost effective than discharging transgender service members without cause. For example, it cost over half a million dollars to train CT3 Landon Wilson,[1090] a US Navy Cryptologic Technician discharged in 2014 for being transgender. Replacing him cost far more than what it would have cost simply to treat him.[1091]

Q: Will the Department of Defense be able to provide the medical expertise necessary to care for transgender service members?

A: Most of the care transgender service members require can be handled by a general practitioner.[1092] DOD doctors already perform some of the surgical procedures transgender service members may need, such as breast reconstruction, augmentation, reduction, and hysterectomy.[1093] In the few cases where DOD medical professionals lack proper expertise or DOD medical facilities are not properly equipped, there are already administrative systems in place, such as TRICARE (the military health insurance program), to allow service members to obtain access to appropriate specialists outside the DOD.[1094] The DOD is training medical and mental health providers on how to treat transgender service members, establishing centers of knowledge on the east and west coasts.

Q: Don't transgender individuals require a lot of extra, specialized medical care after transition?

A: No. Post-transition, most transgender individuals who are otherwise healthy see a general practitioner once or twice a year for routine blood work and prescription renewal.[1095] [1096]

Q: Are transgender people deployable to forward locations and other austere environments, like Afghanistan or on a ship?

A: Yes. There are no special medical requirements that would prevent a transgender service member from deploying to any location where US troops serve today.[1097]

In fact, DOD has been deploying transgender individuals for over a decade as civilians and contractors to Afghanistan, Iraq, and the Persian Gulf and embedding them with US forces there.[1098] [1099] [1100] In this capacity, transgender Americans have served openly in forward locations such as Camp Anaconda and Balad Air Base in Iraq, New Kabul Compound and Kandahar Air Base in Afghanistan, and aboard US Navy ships operating in the Persian Gulf. Additionally, our allies have successfully deployed transgender service members for more than 20 years and into every theater.[1101]

Q: Will providing transgender service members with access to necessary medications place an additional burden on the military health care system?

A: No. The military health care system already provides the medications commonly used for HRT to non-transgender service members as treatment for other conditions. HRT for transgender service members would not require new pharmaceuticals, logistics, or significant cost.[1102]

Q: What if a transgender service member is prevented from accessing their medications due to logistical or tactical circumstances?

A: Such a situation is highly unlikely. Allied militaries in which transgender individuals serve openly have found the rate of such occurrences to be extremely low. In those circumstances where temporary loss of access to HRT medications is truly unavoidable, the effects are neither debilitating nor life threatening.

> I was on oral HRT from day one as this was prescribed by my NHS endocrinologist, and simply stocked up from my medical center before deployment. When I suddenly found myself extended for 2 months in the Falklands in 2011, I ordered more through the medical center there.[1103] *Flight Lieutenant Ayla Holdom, RAF*

Q: Will transgender service members spend a lot of time in a non-deployable status (i.e. unable to be deployed for long periods of time while transitioning)?[1104]

A: No. Transgender service members in other countries report spending less than six months in total in a medically non-deployable status. Typically, the medical elements of transition that might affect readiness are scheduled so as not to impact unit readiness (i.e. while the unit is on a home cycle). The recovery time for most transgender surgeries is six to eight weeks before resumption of full activity.[1105] This is a short interval compared with many of the conditions the DOD allows people to be non-deployable for (e.g. the DOD doesn't discharge everyone who breaks their arm or tears their meniscus).

> I was kept at G1 A1 Z1 [physically fit for flying and ground deployment without any restriction] and retained my flying category throughout, with the exceptions of having a month off flying duties when I began my HRT (which is the standard time-period for any long-term medication) and six months off flying in total, following my gender reassignment surgery, during which time I was medically downgraded to P7 (non-deployable)... Shortly after I began HRT though, before my public transition, I was deployed for seven weeks to the Falkland Islands in a flying role and again for nine weeks towards the end of my transition, a few months before my GCS.
>
> I am now A1 P2, which means there's no restriction to my flying or my deploying and is simply a marker to show I am on long-term medication.[1106] *Flight Lieutenant Ayla Holdom, RAF*

Q: What about uniforms?

A: In most countries where transgender individuals serve openly, regulations stipulate a timeline within which a service member's transition will take place. The service member works with his or her chain of command to customize the transition timeline so that it best suits the particular circumstances of both the service member and the unit.

The transition timeline centers on the date on which the service member's gender is changed in his or her military records. From the date of that change, transitioning service members are held to the same grooming and uniform standards as others of that gender.[1107] For many individuals, their daily uniform is unisex and little change is required.

> I picked up my new uniform a few days before I began to present in work, as I had arranged a date to begin with my line management, the medical staff on unit and the admin staff.[1108] *Senior Aircrewman, RAF*

> The uniform didn't change as it's the same for everyone (unisex). There is a set of dress uniforms which is specific to gender but is not compulsory.[1109] *CPL Rebekah Anderson, RAF*

Q: What about housing and billeting of transgender service members?

A: There is no reason transgender service members cannot be billeted with others of their officially recognized gender post-transition. In the UK, during the period between the official change of gender and the completion of transition, single living accommodation (SLA) is often used.[1110] In many circumstances, no change is needed (when individuals live off base, for example).[1111] Troops in the field already often share tents, and find ways of ensuring privacy.

> I was placed into an ensuite room of my own within a mixed sex block. This is to separate myself from others so as not to make people uncomfortable when using shared ablutions [bathroom

and shower facilities] and also to prevent my being uncomfortable when placed into that type of situation."[1112] *Senior Aircrewman, RAF*

I lived in my own home, so this wasn't really an issue."[1113] *Flight Lieutenant Ayla Holdom*

Q: To what physical fitness (readiness) standards should transgender service members be held?

A: It takes about a year for HRT to take its full effect and the transitioning individual's physiological characteristics (such as muscle mass) to become analogous to those of the gender to which they are transitioning. After that year, transgender individuals hold no significant competitive advantage or disadvantage over their non-transgender counterparts.[1114] For this reason, the National Collegiate Athletic Association (NCAA) requires transgender women to undergo one year of HRT before competing on women's teams; transgender men are no longer allowed to compete on women's teams after beginning HRT.[1115]

In allied militaries where transgender service members serve openly, they often skip one physical readiness cycle during transition while they gain or lose muscle mass as a result of HRT. After this cycle, they are held to the standard of their newly recognized gender. The point at which an individual is considered to have completed gender transition may vary from person to person, depending on medical treatment and other factors, and thus each case should be considered on an individual basis.[1116] In the US, an Exception To Policy (ETP) letter may be granted to service members who need time to build up to the new standards.

I maintained sufficient fitness while on HRT in my first year to pass the "male" fitness standard (though of course, not to the high level that I had in the past). Once I'd transitioned publicly, prior to GCS, I simply passed to the female standard. This wasn't even questioned and seemed fairly straightforward as all my records had changed to read female by then. It was a simple administrative change in that sense."[1117] *Flight Lieutenant Ayla Holdom, RAF*

Q: How should privacy in places like bathrooms and locker rooms be handled for transitioning service members?

A: In most situations outside basic training, open bay showers and bathrooms no longer exist. In those cases where additional privacy is needed in fixed facilities, the solution can be as simple as adding shower curtains. For transgender service members living in their own private housing, such concerns are lessened. On completion of transition, no special accommodations are needed.

Privacy in the field is a common concern even in the current regulatory environment, and service members have developed various means of ensuring privacy is maintained in these contexts. Mixed-gender groups of service members who share field quarters often hang blankets or improvise other means of protecting one another's privacy. Where there is only one field shower facility available for both genders, use of the facility takes place on a gender-segregated schedule.

Transgender service members should only be asked to utilize separate facilities on a purely temporary basis to facilitate transition.[1118]

> The day I transitioned, I moved my locker into the female changing facilities. It was fairly black and white for my colleagues (being a close-knit unit).
>
> I deployed to the Falklands twice during my transition; once while still presenting as male (though on HRT) and once just prior to GCS. This presented minor issues due to the communal bathroom facilities, shared with a corridor of people (all SAR [search and rescue] crews). This is a hangover from many years ago and there is now a sign on the door which is turned to either "male" or "female"... With the few colleagues I was deployed with, it was no secret and I simply chatted with them about the situation, resolving to turn the sign to a neutral position whenever I was using the showers.[1119] *Flight Lieutenant Ayla Holdom, RAF*

Q: What about situations like basic training where there is no privacy?

A: In allied countries that allow transgender individuals to serve openly, those desiring to join the service who are still in the process of transitioning are asked to complete their transition and re-apply when they have finished.[1120] The DOD is requiring individuals applying for accession to have been stable in their target gender for 18 months to address this.[1121]

Q: Will transgender people join the service just to get access to surgery?

A: Unlikely. Our allies have not experienced significant adverse selection, as this phenomenon is known, nor have US civilian organizations that provide insurance coverage for transition-related medical care.[1122] Here in the US, if an individual wants coverage for transition-related medical treatment, there are far easier ways to obtain it than joining the military. About three out of five Fortune 500 companies already offer such benefits to their employees. More and more small companies, colleges, universities, states, and municipalities are offering transgender-inclusive health care plans. Even entry-level employers such as Walgreens, Kroger, and Target include transgender health care coverage in their policies.[1123]

Q: Will service members be allowed to switch genders back and forth at will?

A: No. Only those who have received appropriate counseling and expressed a clear, consistent, and persistent gender identity different from the sex they were assigned at birth can transition and change their official gender. The process put in place by the DOD ensures that the gender transition process is methodical, planned, and done in concert with the service member, their medical team, and the member's chain of command.

Q: Will other troops accept transgender service members?

A: Prior to the policy, many transgender SPARTA members were open to some degree in their units about their condition and being received favorably by peers and the chain of command. Most are accepted by their units now, and DOD leadership has repeatedly emphasized the need for treating individuals with dignity and respect as core values of our armed forces. Their colleagues and superiors judge them on how they perform their duties. Both President Obama[1124] and the former Chief of Naval Operations unknowingly met and interacted with transgender service members and treated them as their affirmed gender.

Most SPARTA members who have come out in the past few years since Secretary of Defense Carter halted administrative discharges for transgender personnel in 2015 have been accepted by their units, and treated with dignity by their chain of command. DOD leadership has repeatedly emphasized the need for treating individuals with dignity and respect as core values of our armed forces.

We regularly heard reports of commanders who desperately didn't want to lose their best people just because they were transgender. Similarly, in the UK, transgender service members have by and large been accepted and embraced by their units.

> I was struck by how, shortly after my coming out, it went "nuclear." I had old and bold Warrant Officers coming to me to shake my hand and offer their heartfelt support. These were colleagues who grew up in a military where being gay or transgender would at best result in the loss of your job and dignity, and at worse would result in a "bit of a kicking behind the bike sheds." It really struck me, with not a small amount of pride, how over just a decade this significant change in military policy was reflected in genuine change of ethos as well.
>
> This was also highlighted the day I drove in to pick up my new ID card. Naturally, to get onto the base I had to use my old ID card, which didn't really match my appearance. The grizzled guard on the gate checked my ID, then just smiled warmly and said, "Don't worry, Ma'am, you're not the first and you certainly won't be the last. Good luck to you." *Flight Lieutenant Ayla Holdom, RAF*

> I have had no negative comments regarding my transition and the support from my work colleagues has surpassed my expectations. Considering the military environment, I was dubious and actually scared as to how people would react before I came out about it. Looking back, I realize that probably the most difficult step of

my entire transition was having to step forward to people I knew quite closely and tell them that I was trans, what that means, and how it would affect them. *Senior Aircrewman, RAF*

When they pinned the Army Commendation Medal on me, my regimental commander, full bird infantry colonel, told me "I just want you to know that I am proud of your accomplishments here and you have left a lasting mark on this unit...Jacob." *Transgender man in the US National Guard, on his commanding officer using his male name*

So by the time I got out everybody knew I was trans and the overall attitude was that it was a shame I had to end my military career in order to make it happen for me. When our squadron commander came by the watch floor one day, we happened to have a nice conversation about it and she was also really cool about it. She even bemoaned the fact that she was losing talented airmen because of such an awful policy. *Recently separated US Air Force Chinese linguist*

Overall, their reaction was extremely positive. My Chief pulled me aside. He told me that it was up to me to tell or not tell anyone I wanted, but that no matter what, he would wield the EO policy with extreme prejudice against anyone who tried to use this against me. His exact words were, "They'll be out of the section before their ass hits the ground." *United States Marine Corps Reserve E-4*

Q: Why should we retain policies allowing open service?

A: First, *the old regulations burdened and eliminated good people for bad reasons.* During down cycles, it becomes all the more imperative to retain the best people. Indiscriminately separating highly trained, motivated, and capable individuals who are more expensive to replace than to retain disrupts units and wastes taxpayer dollars. Additionally, the old policy discourages "closeted" transgender service members from reporting a range of issues that might affect their performance, from health problems to sexual assaults. Transgender troops returning from multiple combat tours are reluctant to talk to mental health professionals because being fully honest will also result in losing their careers.

Second, *the old regulations kept the US Armed Forces from recruiting and retaining the best talent.* The DOD ranked 40th out of 108 nations in LGBT inclusion according to a 2014 study by the Hague Centre for Strategic Studies—behind countries like Albania, Cuba, South Africa, and the former Soviet State of Georgia.[1125] This was in large part due to the old medical policy on transgender service members. Being viewed as backward, behind the times, or biased costs our military the top recruits.

Lastly, *the old regulations denied integrity to thousands of transgender service members.* Previous policies forced transgender service members to hide who they are from their fellow service members, their leaders, and the medical personnel charged with supporting them and maintaining their readiness. Of even greater concern, however, is the fact that we forced them to disregard one of our highest shared values: our honor. Former Chairman of the Joint Chiefs of Staff Admiral Mike Mullen addressed this issue in testimony before Congress near the end of DADT. His words are just as true today when applied to transgender service members as they were then:

> No matter how I look at this issue, I cannot escape being troubled by the fact that we have in place a policy which forces young men and women to lie about who they are in order to defend their fellow citizens. For me personally, it comes down to integrity—theirs as individuals and ours as an institution.[1126]

Transgender service members simply want to serve with honor and integrity. We owe it to them to give them that opportunity.

Chapter 10

MEDIA AND POPULAR CULTURE

Transgender people in the US, and elsewhere, are being included in popular culture and in the media more than they ever have been in the past. We're in the news with the attempt at banning us from the military. TV shows such as *Orange Is the New Black*, *Transparent*, and *Sense8* have featured prominent transgender characters played by transgender actors. In general, these have been portrayals that were well received by critics. *Transparent* features two transgender actors as recurring characters. Actress Laverne Cox won an Emmy for her work as an executive producer on MTV's *Laverne Cox Presents: The T Word*. *Tangerine* was centered around the lives of transgender women of color, featured transgender actors in the lead roles, and received critical acclaim. Jazz Jennings has helped dramatically re-shape the narrative about transgender youth in America with her reality TV show I Am Jazz, which has been described by critics as "engaging", "heartfelt", and "sensitively constructed."

The *TransMilitary* documentary, directed by Fiona Dawson and Gabriel Silverman, which was first screened at South-by-Southwest in 2018, received the audience choice award for best documentary, and was named one of "The best 8 films we saw at SXSW 2018" by Rotten

Tomatoes."[1127] Top critic John DeFore at *The Hollywood Reporter* described the documentary as "affecting," and described how "*TransMilitary* introduces several outstanding trans service members whose peers and superiors are totally unfazed by their situation, knowing that being able to count on someone in the field is infinitely more important than what's in his or her pants."[1128]

These are just a few of the positive and well-received recent media representations of transgender people playing (or being) themselves. However, when it comes to big budget movies, most still fail to cast transgender people in transgender roles, and both film and TV still frequently repeat inaccurate, outdated tropes about transgender lives.

While P.T. Barnum once said, "There's no such thing as bad publicity," not everyone would agree. While most people know what "transgender" means, that doesn't mean they encounter us on a routine basis. Eighty-seven percent of Americans know someone who is lesbian or gay, but only 16 percent know a transgender person.[1129] Thus media portrayals of transgender people are likely to have a disproportionate effect on how cisgender people perceive a transgender person when they meet them.

For example, if when a transgender person goes to a job interview, and the interviewer's only exposure to transgender people is characters who are prostitutes, serial killers, or flaming human wreckage, this probably doesn't work in the transgender applicant's favor. The characters "Brie" in *Transamerica* and "Rayon" in *Dallas Buyers Club* were both played by cisgender actors. While Brie was a lead character played by a cisgender woman, and Rayon was a side-kick character played by a cisgender man, they were similar in that neither was competent in their gender presentation, both were leading disastrous lives, and neither was the sort of person you would hire for more than an entry-level job, if at all.

The characters themselves are essentially human wreckage, and played alternately for laughs and for pity.

This chapter examines the most pernicious ways that transgender people are harmed by media representation. This includes an examination of "the pathetic tranny," "the transsexual serial killer," and "the trap" tropes about transgender people. It also looks at how being played as freaks and jokes who could never be loved by "real" people takes a devastating emotional toll. Finally, it discusses how to improve representation.

"Rayon" in *Dallas Buyers Club* did not help the transgender community

Some people who are otherwise sympathetic to transgender people have had a hard time understanding why Jared Leto's character is so infuriating to the transgender community. He won an Oscar for portraying a transgender woman in *Dallas Buyers Club* and his character, Rayon, was the empathetic comic relief that everyone cried for. That's a win, right?

No. Not at all.

When most media portrayals of a transgender woman for decades are of someone who is either a serial killer or an incapable, sad, and/or pathetic prostitute, it makes it that much harder for transgender people to be taken seriously. In many ways, it's not so different from the way film used to treat gay men as pathetic closet cases: tragic, tormented, and miserable.

Still, there was a lot of apologetics on this issue. "That was the 80s, not today," one person said. "There are Rayons out there," wrote another. "This is a positive portrayal because Rayon ends up being an empathetic character," another claimed. Never mind that for the past 30 years, almost all portrayals of transgender people look like Rayon (i.e. incompetent, drug-using sex worker).

The blow-back for objecting to portrayals of transgender people this way forces our allies underground. One family member emailed me regarding Rayon, writing:

> I did not want to put this on Facebook and open myself up to public mocking and ridicule, but I did want to comment... Historically, anything I have seen coming from the entertainment industry about transgender people has been mocking, demeaning and cruel.

This also isn't the 80s anymore. It hasn't been for nearly 30 years. However, movies like this shape public perceptions of the transgender community *today*. And in case you hadn't noticed, it sucks out there for transgender people right now; it's getting worse as social conservatives ramp up legal attacks on us and work to convince the public that transgender people are a threat to pretty much everything people hold dear.

I'm sure there were Rayons out there, but according to Hollywood, transgender people are *all* Rayons. Virtually every media depiction of a transgender person fits in the category of "pathetic tranny," "serial killer," or "trap for heterosexual men." The former means never being taken seriously, the latter means being the target of violence.

Perhaps if there were a diversity of transgender characters in media, this wouldn't be particularly harmful. But this has ensconced the most notable transgender character in movie history as firmly in the territory of negative stereotype.

There are practical consequences to these stereotypes. I cannot tell you the number of times that I have been the first openly transgender person someone has met. In almost every case, I get the same response: "You aren't at all what I expected."

What they did expect was someone who couldn't hold down a job. They expected a flake who didn't know how to dress or present themselves professionally, and a caricature of exaggerated femininity with no emotional control. They don't expect someone with a supportive, loving family and a stable life.

In short, they expected a hot mess, and not someone who looks and sounds like a scientist, officer, and soccer mom. They didn't expect someone with their life together. These stereotypes put me, and everyone I know, at a huge disadvantage even as I advocate for transgender rights.

Jared Leto is a good actor. But the stereotypes perpetuated and reinforced by the character of Rayon are a big part of a vicious catch-22: the transgender community is one of the most disenfranchised, marginalized, and stigmatized communities in America, but fighting back and changing people's minds is all the harder because media portrayals make it difficult to be taken seriously, due to the stereotypes that are harming us in the first place.

Never go "full tranny" when casting transgender roles

In 2016 news broke that Mark Ruffalo had produced a movie (*Anything*) co-starring Matt Bomer (a cisgender, gay man) as a transgender prostitute.[1130] When people asked why a transgender person wasn't cast, actress and transgender activist Jen Richards alleged that Ruffalo didn't even consider anyone else for the role.[1131] Richards did audition for a supporting role in the movie, but was turned down because she "doesn't look trans enough."[1132] Many in the transgender community were appalled by this.

Ruffalo implied on Twitter that he was surprised by the transgender community's response, stating: "To the Trans community. I hear you. It's wrenching to see you in this pain. I am glad we are having this conversation. It's time."[1133]

However, the transgender community had this conversation over two years prior to *Anything* with Jared Leto and the *Dallas Buyers Club*.[1134] The problem is that Mr. Ruffalo wasn't listening then and it's too late now, given that the movie has already been completed and released. Yet again, a film was made about transgender people without actually casting a transgender actor in the role of a transgender character. Again, those in control of the film seem to have zero cultural awareness of the history between the transgender community and cinema.

There is so much wrong with this movie, and others like it, on so many levels. First, there's the idea that transgender women are just buff, good-looking dudes in women's clothes and bad makeup. This also implies that who we are is performative, rather than that this is who we are. It implies that transgender women are really men and should be treated as such. This leads to people disregarding the lived experiences of transgender people, and feeds into the social conservative narrative that being transgender is simply a "bad lifestyle choice."

There are more than enough Rayons already. In turn, actual transgender people are seen as sex workers and/or sex objects, thus contributing to the bigoted beliefs that cause transgender people to suffer appalling levels of unemployment, poverty, and violence.

Worst of all, this sort of casting and stereotyping is just plain lazy. It is giving audiences what they expect and what they want when it comes to transgender people. They expect transgender people to look and sound like linebackers in house-dresses stumbling around in high heels. They expect characters who are incompetent at not just makeup, but life in general. They want to watch portrayals of transgender people as the flotsam and jetsam of society to feel better about themselves, the same way they watch television shows about hoarders. The general public simply does not want the truth about transgender people, and when we fail to perform, they get angry.[1135]

There are a few exceptions to how transgender characters and actors are treated which demonstrate how successful such portrayals can be. *Her Story* with Jen Richards is amazing and richly deserving of the Emmy it was nominated for based on how it handles real issues, such as queer dating and the place for transgender people in women's spaces.[1136] *Sense8* by the Wachowski sisters succeeds in crafting a likable, competent transgender character for whom being transgender is just part of the backstory, not the whole story.[1137] *Tangerine* handled sex work in the transgender community well by casting actual transgender people, making the characters fully developed, and highlighting how sex work wasn't a choice: it was survival.[1138]

In 2008, the movie *Tropic Thunder* came out and satirized a lot of Hollywood tropes, including bad and offensive casting choices.[1139] *Tropic Thunder* featured Robert Downey Jr. in black-face playing an African American soldier in a movie about Vietnam. It also featured Ben Stiller playing an actor whose career stalled following a cringe-worthy performance as a mentally disabled man, which attempted to pander to the Oscars. (This was mocking Sean Penn's actual cringe-worthy Oscar pandering in *I am Sam*.[1140])

These two characters exchanged some biting dialogue that is as applicable to the aforementioned situation with Ruffalo and Bomer.

Kirk Lazarus (Downey): Everybody knows you never go full retard.
Tugg Speedman (Stiller): What do you mean?
Kirk Lazarus (Downey): Check it out. Dustin Hoffman, *Rain Man*, look retarded, act retarded, not retarded. Counted toothpicks,

> cheated cards. Autistic, sho'. Not retarded. You know Tom Hanks, *Forrest Gump*. Slow, yes. Retarded, maybe. Braces on his legs. But he charmed the pants off Nixon and won a ping-pong competition. That ain't retarded. Peter Sellers, *Being There*. Infantile, yes. Retarded, no. You went full retard, man. Never go full retard. You don't buy that? Ask Sean Penn, 2001, *I Am Sam*. Remember? Went full retard, went home empty handed..."[1141]

Anything combined two of the worst of the excesses lampooned by *Tropic Thunder*—an actor playing someone who is part of a class of people to which they do not belong and pandering for Oscars by playing "pathetic" characters of a particular class of people. Thus, I propose a new term for what *Anything* was doing: "going full tranny." (And yes, "tranny" is every bit as offensive as "retard.")

And what do I mean by "full tranny"? Like the Bechdel Test for whether a movie is inclusive of realistic female characters, the "full tranny" test is indicative of whether a movie is inclusive of realistic transgender characters. The conditions of the "full tranny" test are:

1. cisgender actor playing a transgender person
2. character is a sex worker (or other work implied to be demeaning)
3. character is worthy of pity but not respect
4. character is not "passable" in their gender presentation.

If the movie meets all four of these conditions, it has gone "full tranny," and was undoubtedly shopping for film awards at the expense of good taste, like *I am Sam*.

Given Bomer's physique, given the obvious Oscar pandering happening here, and given Ruffalo's apparent ignorance of the history between the transgender community and how they are portrayed in movies, Ruffalo went "full tranny."

In the end, it is highly likely that people will someday look back at *Anything* the way they do *I am Sam*, where the conventional wisdom of Hollywood exclaims, "Everybody knows you never go full tranny."

The hackneyed trope of transgender villains

For six seasons, the freeform tween-drama *Pretty Little Liars* had been leading up to a reveal of who the hiding-in-plain-sight-all-along arch-villain was. Finally, in 2015, the show revealed the psychotic antagonist to be Charlotte "CeCe" DiLaurentis.

"CeCe" was born Charles DiLaurentis...

...and is crazy, and transgender, and crazy because they're transgender and spent time in an asylum because they're crazy. Because transgender. While the show's producers did some hand-waving to explain that CeCe comes from a crazy family and that all this has nothing to do with her being transgender, this claim is simply not credible. The rest of the "crazy" family members aren't doing the things that make CeCe the "Big Bad" of the show. They're not spending time in mental institutions.

First, this "twist" was already cliché when *Ace Ventura* did it in 1994, three years after *Silence of the Lambs* did it in 1991, 11 years after *Dressed to Kill* did it in 1980, and 20 years after Norman Bates cross-dressed his way through *Psycho* in 1960.[1142] [1143] [1144] [1145] Using transgender people and their transitions as a twist, and a way to explain psychotic behavior, is just plain lazy writing and has been for a very long time. It's the "big-bad unmasking" equivalent to revealing that all of the ninth season of *Dallas* was just a dream.

If George Lucas had made Jar-Jar Binks a crack dealer, it would be about as hackneyed and offensive as what the writers of *Pretty Little Liars* did.[1146] Even the name they chose is insensitive: CeCe McDonald is a transgender woman of color who went to a men's prison for 19 months defending herself against a drunken neo-Nazi.[1147]

So let's look at all the stereotypes they hit:

- Transgender people are crazy. Check.
- Transgender people are deceivers. Check.
- Transgender people's identities aren't real (because they're crazy). Check.
- Transgender people are dangerous. Check.

It's impressive really. They managed to create a character that simultaneously exemplifies most of the negative stereotypes that prevent transgender people from getting jobs, receiving health care, finding housing, and being accepted as who they are by their families, and that can get them killed by heterosexual men. It did manage to reaffirm the messages transgender people are probably dangerous, should be locked in asylums, are lying about who they are, and are an acceptable target for violence.

In the process, the producers of the show managed to reinforce the talking points of social conservative, anti-LGBT hate groups working against the basic human rights of transgender people in the US.

What's worse is that the producer should know better. From the 1870s onwards, the concept of "female hysteria" was used to dismiss anything women thought, did, or said, as well as their objections to being labeled as such.[1148] Donald Trump's odious comments about Megyn Kelly in 2015, alleging that she was crazy because she was having her menstrual cycle, echoed those same 19th-century labels. It demonstrates that when you categorize an entire group of people as mentally incompetent, it sticks around for generations.[1149]

It's also not as if the writers weren't warned this was a really bad idea in the months before the big reveal.[1150] It was noted that the show had already handled pronouns badly, and clearly had no idea how transgender people live, given the character they were speculating about.[1151]

And therein lies the problem. It isn't as if there aren't tons of transgender people to talk to. It's not like transgender studies, journal articles, blogs, authors, actors, activists, or reality TV shows are hard to find these days. The shows' writers weren't interested in telling a new or different story, they were telling the story that people want to hear; the story that they have heard over and over before.[1152]

There's comfort in imagining people who are different from you being uncomfortable and dangerous. Them versus us. It's an easy narrative, and it's one transgender people struggle to fight back against. Everyone knows transgender people are mentally ill, right? Or are a threat to women and children. Of course, the crazy people deny being any of these things.

When transgender people struggle in the face of discrimination, portrayals like these allow observers to look at us and say, "Well that's just what happens to crazy people. Sad." It's this sort of crass logic that lets the privileged look at everyone else in America who is suffering from systemic violence, oppression, and silencing and say, "They probably deserved it."

Looking at yourself in the mirror and saying "I'm part of the problem" is much harder than labeling others whom you see as broken, inferior, or deserving of what befalls them as a class.

The writers of *Pretty Little Liars* were a part of this systemic problem. We all can do better.

The killing joke

One of the many problems with the *Pretty Little Liars* reveal was that it demonstrated a profound lack of understanding of how transgender people live. Trivializing and misrepresenting the experiences of transgender people is harmful both directly (mental health) and indirectly (they can't find work).

When Sarah Silverman created a video for the National Women's Law Center, it wasn't a mean-spirited jab.[153] It was a comedic attempt to suggest that women could reduce the gender wage gap by simply "getting a penis" surgically. In the video, it is implied that she could do this on a whim, without identifying as male, and that simply having male genitalia (without identifying as male) makes you male.

Some have called it transphobic, others have spoken out that they see nothing wrong with it, and that it was just meant to be absurdist to be funny.[154] I wasn't outraged over this. I just felt tired and exasperated.

This video reinforces a number of false stereotypes about medical care that are harmful to the transgender community. It is not surprising that these persist: when this was made less than 10 percent of Americans had a friend or family member who they knew to be transgender. However, the assumptions in the video are part of the cultural narrative that makes it so hard for transgender people to get access to medical care.

And lack of access has been repeatedly shown to be a predictor of poor mental health outcomes in the transgender community.

Without further ado, let's break down exactly what the video got wrong.

1. It assumes people can get gender confirmation surgery whenever they want

People who undergo GCS must endure a rigorous process beforehand. This includes many hours of counseling, letters from at least two evaluating mental health professionals, and living continuously in their desired gender for at least a year before surgery.

These minimum standards are set by the foremost body of transgender health experts (the World Professional Association for Transgender Health) in the Standards of Care 7.[1155] No reputable surgeon will perform GCS on an individual who has not met these criteria.

2. It assumes gender is based on genitals

Gender is between the ears. Even with a penis, Sarah Silverman would just be perceived as a woman with a penis by both herself, and by others. In reality, the wage gap comes from gender stereotypes, not from sex itself.

3. It assumes that GCS would close the wage gap

The video states that women earn 78 cents to a man's dollar. Another study found that transgender men increase their pay by 7.5 percent when they transition.[1156] That bumps the 78 cents up to 84, still well short of what men earn.

In short, you're still paying the transgender tax, and the female-assigned-at-birth tax. It's also worth noting that transgender women lose 32 percent of their income when they transition.

There is clearly sexism here, but no matter how you look at the numbers, the gender non-conformance tax is far larger than the benefit of being seen as male.

4. It assumes changing one's gender wouldn't drop their salary to zero

It's currently legal to fire someone for being transgender in 32 states, and it happens frequently when they transition. Even when people fight these firings and win, it marks them as someone who sues their employer and makes it very difficult to find work again. Ask some of the pioneers in transgender workplace discrimination suits how difficult finding work became after they won their lawsuits.

5. It assumes Sarah would be okay with having a penis

In reality, this would almost certainly result in gender dysphoria, and she would experience mental trauma and reduced quality of life. Existing halfway between genders is stressful. Chloë Sevigny, who played a transgender assassin on *Hit & Miss*, found wearing a prosthetic penis unbearable. "I cried every day when they put it on," she said in an interview. This, for a prosthetic that she knows isn't real, and comes off when the day is over. When lesbian journalist Norah Vincent tried to live as a man as a social experiment, it took less than a year before the strain caused her to have herself voluntarily committed.

In short, if Sarah somehow did get GCS, it would probably have a severe, negative impact on every aspect of her life and mental health.

6. It assumes female-to-male GCS is easy

The video handled GCS as if it were something easy enough to be done on a whim. In truth, there is a dizzying array of surgeries available utilizing different techniques, some of which require multiple skin grafts and several rounds of surgery. I also know, from my FTM (female-to-male) friends who have undergone some versions of GCS, that recovery can be challenging.

This is part of the reason why many transgender men choose not to undergo GCS. They still experience all the pros and cons of being a transgender man at work regardless.

For a review of transgender male GCS myths, I highly recommend Mitch Kellaway's excellent essay, which is included in Chapter 4 of this book.[1157]

7. It assumes she could afford GCS and/or get coverage for it

Obtaining access to medically necessary care is usually a tremendous challenge for transgender people. Many health plans exclude all transgender-related health care, or reimburse at a rate that many doctors refuse service. Many transgender people end up paying for most of their health care needs out of their own pockets, and not just those related to GCS.

In all likelihood, someone able to get GCS would have to start with a great salary and transgender-inclusive health coverage to begin with.

8. It implies GCS is cosmetic or medically unnecessary

Neither assumption is true. Every major medical, psychological, psychiatric, and therapist organization in the US has issued statements supporting the medical necessity of GCS.[1158] GCS isn't cosmetic either. AMA Resolution 122 states:

> An established body of medical research demonstrates the effectiveness and medical necessity of mental health care, hormone therapy and sex reassignment surgery as forms of therapeutic treatment for many people diagnosed with GID... Health experts in GID, including WPATH, have rejected the myth that such treatments are "cosmetic" or "experimental" and have recognized that these treatments can provide safe and effective treatment for a serious health condition.[1159]

9. It assumes people watching the video know all of the assumptions above

Satire can be incredibly socially progressive when the audience is somehow wiser than the characters in the skit. They have to know *why* something is a dumb idea, or wrong, or enforcing a misguided stereotype in order for the satire to be effective. Whether it's *Saturday Night Live*, Mel Brooks' movies like *Blazing Saddles*, or *In Living Color*, great comedy and satire clearly illustrate biases and perceptions in a way that highlights their stupidity and shows how much damage that stupidity causes.

Most people, though, know very little about GCS, and even less about trans masculine people. Instead of breaking down stereotypes, the video reinforces them. It takes existing confirmation bias and tells the audience, "Yeah, run with it." Great satire doesn't come at the expense of a group that's already the butt of jokes and stigmatized to the point of poverty.

Access to medical care for transgender people isn't a joke. It can be a matter of life and death. It improves mental health, and greatly improves quality of life. There are already so many myths about GCS out there that are used to deny us access to health care, and this video perpetuates many of them."[1160]

Thus, I'm not outraged, I'm just exasperated and tired. Exasperated that allies missed the point; tired of explaining over and over again how myths, misconceptions, and confirmation bias are a lethal combination to the transgender community.

And Sarah Silverman's video is part of the killing joke.

To those who laughed

Being stereotyped as an incompetent drug-addled sex worker is bad. Crazed serial killer is worse. But perhaps nothing hurts more than being seen as nothing more than an object of disgust and ridicule for people to laugh at. Which is why this section is about a little song on *America's Got Talent* about a man finding the perfect girl for him (except she's got a penis). It went viral, and most cisgender people laughed.

Most transgender people I knew felt crushed. This section is a letter to those who laughed.

You know who you are. You tittered, guffawed, and otherwise found Ray Jessel's song on *America's Got Talent* about drawing the line at dating a transgender woman hilarious.[1161] You chortled because of the unspoken implication that "that one little flaw" is actually a huge problem. You went along with the notion that no normal person could really romantically love a transgender woman, no matter what other attributes they have.

You never stopped to think about what it might be like to be that transgender person, rejected always for things we have no control over, because nothing in our culture actually teaches or encourages people to have empathy for us. We are ogres and untouchables, to be both laughed at and feared. We are not supposed to have feelings, marry the prince (or princess), or have happily ever afters.

Except we do have feelings, we do need love, and we need hope for a better future, just like everyone else.

Over 400 years ago, it was observed in *The Merchant of Venice*, "If you prick us, do we not bleed? If you tickle us, do we not laugh? If you poison us, do we not die?" It was meant as an observation that we are all human, with thoughts and feelings and biology like any other. But somehow that famous wisdom doesn't reach as far as transgender people today.

Laverne Cox rightly observed that loving a transgender person is a revolutionary act.[1162] Being transgender is widely seen as so vile that our partners, parents, and children reject us. We learn that love isn't unconditional, that in fact we cannot be loved by the people who mean the most to us. It means being told by the person who promised to love you no matter what that they can't love you through this.

This charming ditty reminds transgender people that no one could love us as romantic partners, and if they do, there is something wrong with them. It also reinforces the validity of this narrative to everyone else. The message is both gratuitous and cruel, because it is already so omnipresent in our lives.

We are treated by pop culture as disgusting things and "its" for having the body we were born with. However, the culture dominated by everyone else makes it nearly impossible for most transgender people to obtain transition-related medical care which might take care of "that one little problem." Even if we do want GCS, and somehow manage to obtain care, we are still labeled as less than real and therefore still unworthy of love and companionship. You label us, and then make it impossible to remove the label.

We cannot win. We cannot hope. We cannot be loved. But we can quit the game. And we do.

In droves.

When you poison us, we die. The toxic themes are absorbed from the environment you create: no one could love us, we are disgusting, we are freaks, we do not deserve love, we deserve to be alone, and that there is something fundamentally wrong with anyone who could love us. We die in poverty, loneliness, and despair: 41 percent of all transgender people have attempted suicide at least once, and those are just the ones who survived.[1163]

Or we die at the hands of those who might have loved us were we other than transgender. When people find out our biology or history, they murder us for it and claim they panicked. Accidental attraction to a transgender person is so horrific that it is seen as a viable excuse for homicide.

So, if it isn't perfectly clear already if you laughed, you were punching down.

Hard.

When you laughed, it told every transgender person watching that we cannot be loved because the thought is just that disgusting. Laughing was the moral equivalent of mocking someone for their stutter. Or telling a gay kid that he should never find love because you find that kind of sex icky. Or cheering on the police as they take a homeless veteran's shopping cart away, because you just want them to disappear.

It. Was. Punching. Down.

Most people have just enough empathy to accept themselves. Extending your empathy beyond that minimum requires effort. Maybe after reading this you'll be able to empathize with people who have been so systematically cut off from love, affection, family, and even human dignity that almost half choose to die rather than live without them. Maybe you'll be able to break away from what society says is an acceptable level of ridicule of a group of people who are already reviled, mocked, impoverished, beaten, and murdered.

Maybe you'll realize that when you laugh, we die a little more on the inside, until the outside finally follows.

Maybe.

Most people can't handle the truth about what it's like being transgender

When Caitlyn Jenner disclosed that she was transgender in an interview with Diane Sawyer, it lit up the media on transgender awareness like

I have never seen before—even more than Laverne Cox's *Time* cover.[1164] The quality of the coverage exceeded my meager expectations as well.[1165] What was most surprising though was that despite the great coverage and how Jenner came across, our authentic stories still aren't generally being told (*TransMilitary* to the contrary).

Barely a week after Jenner's relatively nuanced responses to Sawyer's thoughtful questions on the ABC News special, the media machine of Jenner's extended Kardashian family seized on the Olympian's story.[1166] NBC's *Today* breathlessly aired a clip showing Jenner "bonding" with stepdaughter Kim Kardashian about nail polish, teasing a special two-part episode of E!'s *Keeping Up with the Kardashians,* subtitled "About Bruce."[1167]

One day after Jenner's interview aired, a person from my past in Ohio perfectly illustrated the ways broader society isn't interested in hearing the authentic stories about being transgender—unless those include the stereotypical images of weeping families, shopping for dresses, and yes, sharing nail and makeup tips.

The woman from Ohio who highlighted this emailed me about a presentation I had given at a university on the science behind transgender medical issues. This individual expressed disappointment that my presentation (again, at a university) was more academic than personal. "We wanted to hear the things we heard last night on that program," she wrote. "Like what it *feels* like and how the struggle is personally. I never felt like you wanted to let yourself be open."

I could only sigh.

People want to get what they expect, including transgender stereotypes. They want the clichés and the tearful stories. They want transgender people to expose the most intimate details of their lives for the supposed education of others. They want all the stuff that made the "transgender documentary drinking game" a reality.

This game requires the participants to take a shot every time an interview features footage of a trans woman poignantly painting her face with makeup, pulling stockings up her legs, trying on high heels, uncomfortably reflecting on the infamous "before" and "after" trope, or any one of the dozens of tropes found in most such productions.[1168]

In most cases, even a five-minute documentary would prove lethal to the contestants.

"The media is a business, and just like any other business it is about making money," Allyson Robinson rightly explained in an op-ed explaining why networks give cisgender/non-trans audiences what they want in trans stories.[1169] "It has to show pictures of a trans woman putting on mascara or doing the laundry in a skirt and heels or dramatic 'before and after' shots, because society's desire to leer at those things is what gets eyeballs on the screen."

I first witnessed this phenomenon several years ago when I was asked to review a draft of a transgender documentary. It was generally good, but occasionally fell into the tropes of depicting acts of overly stereotypical femininity. I asked the producers if they could take out those B-roll close-in shots of putting on lipstick and earrings, and they recoiled in horror.[1170] "Oh no, we can't take those out," they exclaimed. "They're the part the focus groups liked the most!"

Which leads me to my point: we still can't tell the truth. We can't tell our stories. The only truths that generally seep into the media are the ones people wanted to see and hear in the first place. They want confirmation that their hunches are correct.

When I deliberately gave that university-level presentation at that university, one full of citations, examples, and information, people were in fact seeing the real me. I am a researcher, who writes and researches, studies and publishes, presents and lectures—sometimes even on transgender issues. I gave them the intelligent, prepared, professional woman I believe I am.

The public doesn't want that though: they're looking for a train wreck to spill their guts onstage. It doesn't matter that the material was well researched and presented. They want to feel better about themselves by comparison. It's as though they invited Stephen Hawking to speak, then were annoyed at him for talking about physics instead of how much Lou Gehrig's disease sucks.

There is a double standard at play here. Transgender people are routinely expected to bare their souls in ways that others aren't. There are some things people will only share with their doctor, therapist, or partner. In fact, the things I don't want to share with the public are the same sorts of things I believe cisgender people don't like sharing with anyone besides their doctors or partners either.

This desire for some minimum level of privacy and dignity isn't a transgender thing. It's a human one.

But here's the real kicker: When we do tell the truth, and it's not one the public wants to hear, people can get angry.

People don't want to hear how the tolerance they mistook for acceptance is its own soul-crushing hell.[1171] They get very angry when they are told their outreach efforts to the transgender community are failing.[1172] [1173]

They don't want to know about the costs and compromises required to make a newly minted mixed-orientation marriage work.[1174] [1175] That involves even more acceptance than they're comfortable with, because the solutions some transgender people and their spouses find to survive the uncharted terrain of an entire family in transition interfere with messaging on marriage equality. After all, pro-equality arguments at the Supreme Court recently went out of their way to avoid linking same-sex marriage with even tacit consideration of non-monogamy.[1176]

Thank the powers that be for Janet Mock, Laverne Cox, and Angelica Ross, because without them, the media probably wouldn't give any trans women of color a platform to tell their stories. This isn't because of deliberate malice or conscious racism, but simply because the revenue-risk justification isn't there. Look no further than the buzz caused by Jenner's interview compared with Cox's multi-magazine cover tour last summer.[1177] [1178] Which did you hear more about?

The stories and awareness of transgender men certainly aren't out there either. If they were, there would be more groups like the Family Research Council riling up the base about the dangers *transgender men* pose to the population. As it is, the talking points of the FRC and its transphobic contemporaries fail when confronted with the reality of trans-masculine individuals; they flop about like a fish at the bottom of a boat when facing this reality.[1179]

Nowhere was the absurdity of transphobic arguments better laid bare than in Minnesota transgender man Michael Hughes's bathroom selfie campaign revealing the sinister agenda of trans people in public restrooms: #WeJustNeedtoPee.[1180] [1181] [1182]

It seems that the public doesn't want to see or hear the totality of transgender lives and experiences. They want the same stories, framed the same way, with the same sorts of people, repeated *ad nauseum*. Society's struggle is not about becoming comfortable with transgender people; it's about becoming comfortable with narratives that go beyond a very specific set of stereotypes.

So, when confronted with narratives and framings that explode these stereotypes, the public gets upset—and instructs trans people to tell their stories in a way that confirms biases and props up the pre-existing paradigms.

Visibility is not enough

There has been a narrative for years that visibility is what would finally allow transgender people to be accepted. Tell our stories, be heard, and then people might start believing we're real people. GLAAD board member Jennifer Boylan has frequently quoted her mother as saying, "It is impossible to hate anyone whose story you know."[1183] She's right, but it is not enough to accept people, and therein lies the rub.

Never have transgender people been so visible in our culture. With Caitlyn Jenner, Laverne Cox, athletes, runway models, *Transparent*, and more, we're seemingly everywhere, and it is still not enough. The ubiquity of anti-transgender "bathroom bills" and the attempt to re-institute the ban on transgender people in the military shows how much a significant portion of the population still loathes and fears us. When the word "transgender" comes up, "sexual predators" is seemingly never far behind.

Some people may no longer feel comfortable actively and vocally hating us, but they still don't want to share space with us. In restaurants, bathrooms, locker rooms, sports teams, schools, and the workplace, the omnipresent message is "You're not wanted here."[1184] [1185] [1186] [1187] [1188]

We can tell our stories and even be heard, but it changes nothing. School board members in Gloucester, Virginia, praised transgender student Gavin Grimm for telling his story to them. Minutes later they voted 6–1 to ban him from most school bathrooms.[1189]

The American public knows very well we're here. They just don't *know* us. A pair of surveys in 2015 found that people are more likely to have "seen" a ghost than met a transgender person.[1190] Ninety percent of people know an LGB person, but only 16 percent know someone who is transgender. It doesn't help that the only stories the public wants to hear about transgender people are the ones they have come to expect and which spawned the transgender documentary drinking game.[1191] Apparently, we're no fun if you can't point and laugh at us.[1192] People would much rather watch a train wreck of a life than someone different doing just fine.

One of the very few things that can break this mindset and make cisgender people more willing to stand up for transgender people is actually having a close friend, family member, or partner who is transgender. This was illustrated in the Web series *Her Story* when a group of cisgender people talk about transgender people in episode 2.[1193] What comes out is a lot of transphobia, with the one character who is sympathetic to transgender people remaining silent.

It wasn't until that cisgender woman entered into a romantic relationship with a transgender person that she was willing to stand up to transphobia. Until a transgender person matters to you in a personal way, most people will treat transgender issues as "Not my circus, not my monkeys."

This is why the fiercest transgender allies in America are the parents of transgender children. Wayne Maines and Debi Jackson were both conservative, religious Republicans before their children turned out to be transgender girls.[1194] [1195] Suddenly, with their own loving, beloved, and vulnerable children under attack from the same conservatives they used to agree with, they turned and fought. In the process of loving, accepting, and protecting their children, they were finally able to empathize with transgender people as a whole.

These anecdotes encapsulate why polling suggests that a plurality of people are still against sharing a bathroom with a transgender person.[1196] They have been told over and over again by the social conservatives that men will pretend to be transgender in order to sexually assault women and children. When activists (correctly) point out that this is groundless fear-mongering, the public doesn't know who to believe.[1197] So they do a mental calculation: do I protect people I know from a danger that (probably) isn't real or protect people I have never met, never will, and can't empathize with?

As a result, transgender people almost invariably lose when our basic human dignity is put up for a popular vote.[1198] Why? While we may be visible, we are only 0.7 percent of the population. This means that forging enough close relationships with people to motivate them to stand up for us *en masse* and trying to create a bloc of trans allies exceeding 50 percent of the population is a difficult exercise at best mathematically.

If that's true, then what is the answer? Three-quarters of statehouses are controlled by Republicans. The districts of the US House of Representatives have been so effectively gerrymandered by the Republican Party that we may not see trans-friendly politicians in charge until the 2030s.[1199]

We can hold the line with what allies we have and create new ones by being visible in our communities; we can put forward allies who are authority figures like the police, military officers, and sexual assault victim advocates who will help negate some of the most outrageous narratives. We can go places where we have protections and work to pull other queer folks out of the places where people think WWJD stands for "Who Would Jesus Destroy?"

We can reach into those spaces too, with authentic representations of transgender people in media, as were shown in *TransMilitary*, and casting actual transgender people for roles of transgender characters. We can work with writers, producers, and directors to build more realistic portrayals. We're here and more than willing to provide that guidance.

We can pursue a science-based movement that holds the line or even moves it forward through targeted policy change and impact litigation where poll numbers hold little sway.[1200] In places where we are losing ground, we will make them pay for every inch by using litigation and peaceful direct action.

A mentor of mine once remarked that we cannot just be "those people who sue you." We must strive to be the people you know: parents, children, friends, mentors, and partners. We must be the people who hold the moral high ground. We must be the people who fight these battles smartly, and utilize cost-imposing strategies. We must be the people who speak up, act out, and do not go gentle into that good night when our human rights and dignity are threatened.

Failing all that, we *will* be "those people who sue you."

Chapter 11
GENDER/ FEMINISM

The relationship between the LGBT community and feminism is a long and complicated one. In the 1960s, the National Organization for Women (NOW) attempted to exclude lesbians because they were afraid lesbians would hurt their image as a respectable, mainstream organization representing most women.

In the 1970s, a strain of Second Wave Feminism hostile to transgender people emerged. Academic Janice Raymond's book *The Transsexual Empire* is an example of this line of thinking.[1201] Much like religious conservatives, some of these feminists reject the idea that gender identity is separate from sex. Other anti-transgender feminists argue that sex is biology and that gender (and by extension gender identity) is purely a social construct. Both religious conservatives and anti-transgender feminists reject the concept of an innate gender identity that is independent of sex and social conditioning.

Regardless, their primary policy objectives with regards to transgender people are also indistinguishable from religious conservatives: namely, to prevent any legal recognition of transgender people, remove all legal protections for transgender people, and block access to transition-related medical care for transgender people. Often, these anti-transgender individuals, sometimes called transgender exclusive radical feminists (TERFs), believe that transgender people are such a dire threat to women that they will ignore their other principles and considerations to achieve their anti-transgender policy goals.[1202]

(Note that TERF is a more recent term, and despite protestations that it is somehow a slur despite being wholly descriptive, it was originally coined by anti-transgender feminists to describe themselves.)[1203]

This has led to a very strange alliance between a handful of (ostensibly) radical feminists and right-wing religious organizations like the Family Research Council (FRC) and the Alliance Defending Freedom (ADF).[1204] This is despite the FRC's and ADF's hostility toward feminism in general, as well as toward bodily autonomy for women.[1205]

Thankfully, these individuals represent a small, if vocal, minority. Today, the vast majority of feminist thought is inclusive and accepting of transgender people and of diverse gender identities and gender expression. Third-wave feminism, championed by older women of color like bell hooks and Audre Lorde, and younger ones belonging to Generation X, embraced individualism, diversity, intersectionality, and bodily autonomy. Fourth-wave feminism, built on social media and electronic communication by the Millennial Generation, is focused on battling sexual assault, harassment, workplace discrimination, rape culture, and misogyny.

This chapter provides responses to some of the most public discussions regarding the intersection of feminism, gender, and transgender identities.

For a more comprehensive academic exploration of how all of these modern issues are directly applicable to the transgender community, I highly recommend Julia Serano's seminal work, *Whipping Girl*. It argues effectively that most of the animus directed at transgender people is directed at transgender women, and is thus a form of misogyny.[1206] Her book is an excellent way to take a deeper, graduate-level dive into the relationship between feminism and transgender people.

Some things you should know about gender

There have been an increasing number of attacks on the legitimacy of transgender and gender non-conforming people coming from both the left and the right.[1207] Most of these attacks stem from either a flawed understanding of gender, misrepresentation of evidence, or deliberate obtuseness. Often, the arguments proffered in response to these attacks have failed to address their underlying causes.

Gender and gender expression are complicated, but not nearly so much as critics would like to claim. They are also not inherently contradictory, nor anti-feminist. Indeed, they can be liberating for everyone. Here are the things a person needs to know about gender and gender identity to find their way through the misinformation on the topic.

1. Just because you don't understand something doesn't invalidate it

Many of the most recent attacks by right-wing outlets can be summarized as: "This gender theory stuff doesn't fit my worldview; I totally can't wrap my head around it, so it must be wrong."

An inability to understand something doesn't make it wrong. The family dog will never understand the internal combustion engine, but still likes to go for a ride in the family mini-van. Just because someone doesn't understand physics doesn't mean they should start an argument with Neil deGrasse Tyson. The fact that transgender people seem to exist throughout human history across multiple cultures is enough to demonstrate that gender, and transgender people, are a reality.

This leads to the second point.

2. It is not a fad: gender non-conforming people have been around for millennia

There is extensive archaeological evidence that transgender and gender non-conforming people have existed for millennia. In Eastern Europe, 5000-year-old graves were found with female skeletons buried with male warrior accoutrements.[1208] There are records of Norse women going Viking (raiding), and a Norse warrior grave was found containing a female skeleton buried with weapons, armor, and traditionally male garb. The *Kama Sutra* describes a third sex, and the Bible talks of "self-made eunuchs." The *kathoey* of Thailand have a place within Buddhist writings. Other cultures have long traditions of gender non-conforming individuals, such as the *hijra* of Hinduism and India, the *fa'afafine* of the Pacific Islands, and two spirits in some Native American cultures.

The reason we see more of this phenomenon now is due to greater cultural awareness of such people, and changing cultural norms that allow transgender people to be more visible. People are much more likely to identify as LGBT in socially tolerant US states than in conservative ones,[1209] and there are many more out gay people in California than there are in Iran or Saudi Arabia. As attitudes about LGBT people have changed for the better in the United States, more people are openly identifying as LGBT as well.[1210]

3. Gender fluid expression is something a lot of straight cisgender people do (to a degree) already[1211]

The cutting edge of gender-related cultural change right now is coming in the form of gender fluid and non-binary people. This is something that conservatives have the hardest time with, but is actually an extension of something a lot of people already do subconsciously.

Women in American society can (and do) express their gender in ways that change from day to day, if not from hour to hour. They can put on a business suit to feel commanding and strong at work or an interview, both of which are stereotyped as masculine traits, or mix a jacket with a dress to convey more femininity in the office. When going to a party they can dress in ways that make them feel attractive, which often means much more stereotypically feminine attire.

Alternately, there are times when gender expression is completely irrelevant or gender neutral. Most parents have had days when everyone in the house has the flu, and their gender expression is: "Screw it. I'm wearing tennis shoes, sweat pants, and a hoodie to the drug store for more Pedialyte."

Women generally have much greater scope for varying gender expression than men do, which bolsters the underlying point: given the option, straight cisgender people will change their gender expression to fit how they want to feel about themselves in that moment, whether it is strong, sexy, or comfortable. While these feelings may be tied to stereotypes of masculinity and femininity, they are a deeply ingrained part of how we see ourselves.

Gender fluid people simply take this day-to-day and moment-to-moment variance in expression we see in cisgender people, and expand on it. It is not something new, but rather something which has evolved and become more visible in the expanding cultural space for such expression.

So, is transgender identity based on nature or nurture? Conservative pundits like to ask this as a black or white, yes or no, one or the other question. The truth is a bit more complicated.

4. Gender has components of both nature and nurture

Demonstrating that gender is partially a social construct is relatively easy. The colors pink and blue are not intrinsically gendered; they are merely frequencies of light. Dresses and skirts are not intrinsically gendered either; they are simply bits of fabric any human being can drape over themselves. (The fact that some people are willing to defend the morality of hurting or killing someone for wearing the "wrong" bit of fabric says a lot more about us than it does about the fabric.)[1212]

At the same time, people seem to have an innate gender identity, whether female, male, or somewhere in between. Anecdotally, we can see this in Dr. John Money's failed experiment with David Remer. The *guevodoces* of the Caribbean similarly appear female until puberty and are raised as such as a result of 5-alpha-reductase deficiency.[1213] However, at puberty their genitals descend and they are thereafter treated as male. While usually infertile, *guevodoces* almost universally identify as male, despite their upbringing.

These examples effectively contradict the notion that gender, and gender identity, are purely social constructs. However, neither is it purely biological; there are components that are cultural. Both are significant, and observing transgender children helps square this circle. Anecdotally, we see children as young as 2 or 3 asserting a gender identity different from their sex despite all prior conditioning.[1214] They assert their gender from a very early age, and choose cultural artifacts (e.g. using a towel to make a dress) to express how they see themselves. Other research seems to show gendered preferences for toys seems hard-wired as well.[1215]

Thus, gender has interacting biological and social components. The fact that there are both does not invalidate the concept of gender identity.

5. How you were raised does not determine the reality of your gender identity

One line of argument that tries to further segregate transgender people is that they are not "real" women or men because they do not have the exact same experiences as most cisgender people.[1216] This is dangerous in the sense that it invalidates the lived experiences of a threatened minority group, while othering them and opening the door for "separate but equal" legal marginalization. It's also wrong on a number of levels.

Transgender people are held to a double (read: impossible) standard for asserting the validity of their gender identities. David Reimer was raised as a girl, but no one questioned whether he was a "real" boy when he asserted his gender identity. The same is true for the *guevodoces*. In this, we can see that when someone asserts a gender other than the one they were raised in, it is only treated as valid if the individual's eventual identity is perceived as cisgender.

Similarly, many transgender children are now socially transitioning at an early enough age that they will likely have almost no memory of having lived in a different gender role. Even in my case, as a "late" transitioner (mid-30s), when I die I will likely have spent more than half my life as a woman. On top of that, there's the issue that male privilege is not monolithic.[1217]

Finally, the argument that you're only a "real" woman if you have menstruated, are fertile, or have had children is reductionist and vaguely creepy, in a *Handmaid's Tale* kind of way. There are cisgender women who never had a period, are infertile, or choose not to have children, yet they do not have to defend the validity of their gender identity and expression the way that transgender people do.

6. Transgender people do not intrinsically reinforce gender stereotypes

Transgender people, by definition, go directly against societal norms for how a person should dress or act based on their perceived sex and gender. Virtually every circuit court in the US has agreed with this interpretation of what it is to be transgender. However, the argument made by anti-transgender conservatives attempting to appeal to women and feminists is that when transgender people transition, they do so by adopting cultural norms and stereotypes of their target gender, thus reinforcing them.

Both cisgender and transgender people change their gender expression to match how they feel about their gender, and themselves, at any given moment and over the course of their lives. My grandmother gave up on heels in her 50s; she hardly wore anything but tennis shoes for the last 35 years of her life. However, transgender people have traditionally had even less space to express their gender than others.

In the past, transgender people (particularly transgender women) were not allowed to medically transition unless they looked, sounded, and acted in a stereotypically feminine manner. In recent years, people who are visibly gender non-conforming have been at a much higher risk of violence and discrimination than those who conform.[1218] Religious conservatives continue to urge violence against transgender people, and the easiest way to avoid this is to adopt an appearance and mannerisms that blend in.[1219]

As such, if transgender people have done anything to reinforce stereotypes, it is a result of the patriarchal culture over which they have no control, a culture that severely punishes anyone who is seen to violate these stereotypes.

The final nail in the coffin of this flawed argument is that as medical culture reduced gatekeeping, and as our culture is making more room for diverse gender expressions, gender non-conforming transgender people are becoming more common. This is perhaps one of the most gender-transgressive developments in our culture today, and is a direct result of the work transgender activists have done to begin opening this space up.

Far from reinforcing the gender binary and gender stereotypes, the transgender movement is actively working to deconstruct them.

Transgender issues are feminist issues

In 2014, the president of the National Organization for Women, Terry O'Neill, published a blog post on *The Huffington Post* titled "Why transphobia is a feminist issue."[1220] It was an excellent and timely piece given debates about where transgender issues fit with feminism. It also followed the trend of feminists who were previously ambivalent, or even hostile, to transgender issues now embracing them.[1221]

This is a logical development. Intersectional feminism recognizes that equality isn't just for women who look like me: it is equality for all. If we only work on behalf of the "right" kinds of women, it diminishes the movement and repeats mistakes of the past.[1222] By denying intersectionality, past feminisms effectively excluded women who were marginalized in more than one way—including trans women, but also lesbians, women of color, Latinas, immigrants, and others. In addition to simple solidarity, though, it shows that many of the core issues of feminists and transgender people are the same.

1. Fighting gender stereotypes

In 1989, the US Supreme Court heard the case of Ann Hopkins, who claimed that her promotion to partnership at her firm was postponed for two years in a row based on the fact that she did not conform to gender stereotypes. The head supervisor of her department, Thomas Beyer, told her that to increase chances of promotion, she needed "to walk more femininely, wear makeup, have her hair styled, and wear jewelry." Many male employees said they would not be comfortable having her as their partner because she did not act the way they believed a woman should. On appeal by Price Waterhouse, the Supreme Court upheld the lower court's ruling that making employment decisions based on gender stereotypes is sex discrimination and therefore a violation of Title VII of the Civil Rights Act of 1964.[1223]

While *Hopkins* was a seminal case in establishing women's rights in the workplace, it is not a coincidence that virtually every court case that has ruled in favor of transgender protections in the workplace since has relied on the *Hopkins* case as a foundational argument. Arguing that transgender people should be held to some patriarchal set of gender norms, without applying those expectations to everyone else, requires that you accept that transgender people exist somewhere below both men and women in a legalized caste system. Such an argument should be anathema to anyone who considers themselves a feminist.

We recognize that gender stereotyping is harmful to everyone and resolve to work against it together. Defining ourselves, our roles in life, and how we express our gender is a universal human right.

2. Bodily autonomy

Social conservatives wrote radically anti-transgender pieces for the national media. In June 2016, Dr. Paul McHugh wrote of his opposition to current medical standards for transgender individuals in *The Wall Street Journal*.[1224] Kevin Williamson similarly wrote a vitriolic and ill-informed piece attacking the identities of transgender people in the *National Review* the same month.[1225]

McHugh and Williamson also radically oppose reproductive justice efforts. Dr. McHugh is a self-described orthodox Catholic whose outlandish views, and role as an apologist for church scandals, are well documented.[1226] [1227] [1228] McHugh opposes abortion in all cases, and supported forcing a pregnant 10-year-old girl who had been raped by an adult relative to carry to term, even if it killed her.[1229] Kevin Williamson recently called for the hanging of any woman who has an abortion, along with the doctors or nurses who perform it.[1230]

Access to medically necessary care and a right to choose what we do with our bodies are fundamental issues for both feminists and transgender people. If we allow other people's beliefs to get between a transgender person and their doctor, what excuse do we have when those same people try to come between anyone else and their doctor?

3. Opposing patriarchy/kyriarchy[1231]

The structures that are meant to keep women in their place are exactly those that work to ensure that transgender people self-deport to the closet. Religious institutions that prohibit women from positions of influence within the church universally regard transition as a sin. The glass ceilings that women collide with are the same ones that transgender women (in particular) face. Women and transgender people in the military are still fighting to be fully included. Women, and transgender women, continue to fight against their sexuality being pathologized or categorized within false dichotomies (slut v. frigid, gay man v. fetishist).[1232] [1233] [1234]

Transgender people represent a fundamental threat to many patriarchal power structures, and to the arguments that support them.[1235] They blur the lines of what it supposedly "means" to be a man or a woman, obliterating conventional definitions of sexual orientation and sexuality. They lie at the intersection of so many forms of oppression (sexism, homophobia, and racism) that successfully taking on transgender issues makes inroads into many patriarchal strongholds.[1236]

Similarly, the same entities trying to enforce gender stereotypes also defend the indefensible when it comes to justifying their oppression. Vilification and blaming of victims of violence, calls for "right to discriminate" laws against gays and lesbians, defenses of horrific child abuse in the name of discipline, the defense of Roy Moore, and calls for an end to the concept of separation of church and state—all of these come from power attempting to preserve itself by any means necessary.

Feminist and transgender issues are interdependent. Bodily autonomy for all or for none. Enforcement of gender stereotypes applies either to all of us or to none of us. You cannot oppose the overarching system of oppressions while giving it a free pass to perpetuate itself against one disadvantaged class.

We will only succeed together, because feminist issues are transgender issues.

Femmephobia in the LGBT community

Misogyny is expressed in many ways. As Serano wrote in *Whipping Girl*, fear of anything seen as feminine (femmephobia) is one of them. Not even the LGBTQ community is immune to this, just as it is not immune to racism, Islamophobia, or any other bias.

Someone once said that most people only have just enough empathy to accept themselves. That is often true, even within the LGBT community.

While working on transgender military issues, some lesbian and (mostly) gay people who suffered under "Don't Ask, Don't Tell" turned right around and opposed an open transgender service, even when transgender people stood shoulder to shoulder in solidarity with them against DADT.[1237]

The same talking points against transgender people (mostly transgender women) were, and are, also used against LGB people:

- They're gross.
- They're a distraction.
- The military isn't a social experiment.
- Showers.

The talking points and opposition to transgender people were almost never focused on transgender men. It was nearly universally focused on transgender women, and the underlying cause was femmephobia.[1238]

This does not only affect transgender women negatively; it can be found across LGBT communities, and all of them are harmed by this expression of misogyny. The transgender community seems to absorb the brunt of the backlash, though.

A direct result of femmephobia is the oppression of anyone (men, women, and other genders) whose gender presentation is in any way classified as being on the feminine end of the gender binary, due to their clothing, behavior, or mannerisms.[1239] [1240] [1241]

One recent article summed up how femmephobia starts early and is deeply ingrained in our culture: "I can't tell you the number of parents I've seen who think they've somehow failed at feminism because their daughters like lace and Barbie dolls; it's much rarer to see the parent of a boy upset because his love of Batman and Star Wars doesn't sufficiently challenge gender roles."[1242]

Femmephobia seems like something that would be much more endemic to a straight, cisgender, heteronormative culture. The problem, though, is that femmephobia is alive and well within every facet of the LGBT community—and it negatively affects each and every one of them.

Here's a taste of how.

1. Gay men are affected by external and internalized femmephobia

It's been noted for over a decade that gay men's singles ads frequently say "no fats, no fems."[1243]

Passing as straight is valued, and being seen as effeminate in any way is often viewed as an embarrassing stereotype by a large portion of the gay community.[1244] Being anything but 100 percent stereotypically masculine is viewed by many as weakness, and believed to show a lack of leadership qualities.

While the LGBT community is quick to jump on religions that tell gay men they can only be loved if they stop being gay, it's no less damaging to be told by your own that no one will ever love you if you are effeminate.

Some have attributed this to the movement's attempt to mainstream queerness by playing an exaggerated form of respectability politics. There's a fear that if LGBT+ people don't look and sound like everyone else, we'll be rejected for being too "different" to be palatable to the public.

Another speculation is that some gay men adopt misogynistic attitudes as a defense mechanism to demonstrate that they're "real men," too.[1245] At some level, femmephobia in the gay community is a self-defense mechanism: those who blend in are far less likely to be targets of violence or discrimination.

Thankfully, some elements of the LGBT movement (like the National LGBTQ Task Force) have tried to reject this narrative, embracing the motto "Be You."

2. Femmephobia confines lesbians

Both gay men and women are encouraged to be more masculine, but for very different reasons.

In lesbian circles, femme invisibility can be a byproduct of femmephobia. There can be pressure to "butch it up" to establish one's queer credentials. Lesbians who express their gender in a more stereotypically feminine way are often assumed to be less radical, less feminist, more assimilationist, and more invested in pandering to and sustaining the patriarchy.

Sometimes, a femme gender expression is used to question the validity of a lesbian's expressed sexual orientation or to claim that their orientation is "just a phase."[1246] A more femme gender expression can be used to call a lesbian's sexual orientation into question, labeling her as potentially bisexual.

This is an illogical stigmatization of both lesbian and bisexual women based on gender expression, and plays on biases against polysexual people.

These artificial constraints on acceptable gender expression don't make life any easier for queer women, and they coerce people into living inauthentically—which is what we were fighting against in the first place.

3. Femmephobia is part of bisexual erasure

Femmephobia impacts women who are bisexual as well. One of the biggest issues facing the bisexual community, and bisexual women in particular, is erasure and invisibility.

Many lesbians assume that all femme women are either straight or bi.[1247] One lesbian friend of mine put it this way: "When she's wearing wingtips and a pompadour, there's a better than 50–50 chance I can flirt with her without being smacked down."

Additionally, because femme lesbians are suspected of being bisexual, some lesbians avoid dating them because there is the suspicion they might just go back to dating men (even if they've never been with one in their life). If all femmes are assumed to be bisexual, and all bisexual people (and particularly women) are assumed to actually be straight, femmephobia leads directly to bisexual erasure.[1248]

Bisexuality is the largest part of the LGBT spectrum, and a part of the human spectrum of sexuality as a whole. Femmephobia stigmatizes bisexual women in particular, who are already nearly invisible and marginalized. Yet it is not addressed nearly often enough in the discussion of how to combat these systemic harms.

4. Femmephobia contributes to the invisibility of transgender men

It's no secret that transgender women absorb the brunt of hate that comes from femmephobia.

It's ironic, however, that this single-minded focus on transgender women leads to transgender men being something of an afterthought in all the debates over LGBT equality. When was the last time a social conservative had a spittle-spraying freak-out over transgender men in men's bathrooms?

When transgender men transition, their salaries increase on average by 7 percent. When transgender women transition, it drops on average by 32 percent.[1249]

Neurobiologist (and transgender man) Ben Barres saw this effect first hand.[1250] He noted that people regarded his work far more highly if they didn't know he was transgender. After giving a presentation of his work, he heard an audience member remark, "Ben Barres gave a great seminar today; his work is much better than his sister's." This individual did not know that Barres had transitioned, and did not realize Ben and his "sister" were the same person.

While this might seem like a good thing for transgender men, it also provides a perverse incentive to stay in the closet and remain isolated. Transgender men are often able to "blend" more than transgender women, and thus have the option of going "stealth" more frequently. I know of some transgender men (some of whom are teachers) who have remained deep in the closet because of the stigma of being transgender, and the fear of being seen as anything less than a "real" man.

Maintaining this requires strict discipline, like severely limiting the number of people who know your history. This can often include shutting out other members of the LGBT community.

It may not be coincidental, then, that transgender men may attempt suicide at a rate higher than transgender women.[1251] Social isolation has repeatedly been shown to be a risk factor for suicidality, and femmephobia creates a perverse incentive for transgender men to isolate themselves.

5. Transgender women are the nexus of femmephobia—and the results are devastating

Perhaps no segment of the LGBT community suffers from femmephobia more than transgender women. Transgender women are the subject of a disproportionate amount of hate and vitriol directed at LGBT people. Of the 23 transgender people murdered in the US in 2015, all were transgender women.[1252]

Queer feminist pioneer Judith Butler[1253] observed in a 2015 interview that:

> Killing is an act of power, a way of re-asserting domination, even a way of saying, "I am the one who decides who lives and dies." So killing establishes the killer as sovereign in the moment that he kills, and that is the most toxic form that masculinity can take. Trans women have relinquished masculinity, showing that it can be relinquished, and that is very threatening to a man who wants to see his power as an intrinsic feature of who he is.[1254]

Also, the rejection of anything feminine by many gay men has sometimes led to vituperative attacks by gay leaders in the movement made against transgender women.

Jim Fouratt, an early leader of the Gay Liberation Front and participant in the Stonewall Riots, accused "gay academics and pop journalists" of "embracing this new push to make gay men and lesbians straight by leading them to endure painful physical body manipulation and dangerous hormonal injections to take on the topography of the conventional definition of what is male and what is female."[1255]

Similarly, during the debate on whether to include gender identity in the language of the Federal Employment Non-Discrimination Act (ENDA) in 2007, bill sponsor and gay Democratic Representative Barney Frank reportedly screamed "Never!" at the interviewer in a crowded restaurant when asked about whether he would support inclusion. He went on a rant about "penises in showers," despite ENDA specifically excluding bathrooms.[1256]

In 2007, Human Rights Campaign Executive Director Joe Solmonese broke his promise to only support ENDA if it included gender identity, and followed Frank's lead in dropping gender identity from ENDA.[1257] In 2015, an HRC internal report was leaked which found the organization's culture was "rooted in a white, masculine orientation which is judgmental of all those who don't fit that mold."[1258] One staff member interviewed was even more blunt: "I see femophobia—feminine men and women are not considered as important."

In the past, and sometimes today, finding safety in queer women's spaces has also been difficult for transgender women, but perhaps less so for trans masculine individuals.

Transgender men, many of whom initially identified as lesbians, were often still accepted (or revered) in queer women's spaces.[1259] One queer woman I know described the spectacle of a trans man holding court to an adoring crowd at a lesbian bar.

Transgender women, however, are sometimes not welcome at all in such spaces, regardless of passability or surgical status.[1260] They are frequently accused of caricaturizing women if they present as too femme, but have their identities questioned if they present in a less femme way, with considerable overlap between the two zones of unacceptability.

As a result, transgender women often have no way of safely expressing their gender without it serving as a basis to reject them either way.

6. Femmephobia is internalized misogyny

Femmephobia represents a rejection of the notion that anything about being feminine is valuable or strong. While it has been argued that femininity only exists to please the male gaze, that theory fails in this context when one asks if the male gaze is also pleased by feminine men.

Femmephobia doesn't further the cause of equality. It divides us, sets us against one another, and diminishes the value of others in the community. In a movement based on the concept of universal human worth, this is unacceptable. It's time for us to make a conscious effort to stop devaluing anything, or anyone, who doesn't meet some societal stereotype of perfect masculinity.

Who decides what makes a woman?

When Caitlyn Jenner came out in 2015, it seemed that everyone had an opinion and was in a rush to express it. Elinor Burkett published a long-form op-ed in *The New York Times* that set up numerous straw man arguments that echoed (somewhat more politely) those seen on anti-transgender websites by anonymous posters and trolls.[1261] Burkett's article made a number of unsupported assumptions, and misrepresented transgender people as a whole.

I found that I agreed with her on one point, however. I too thought that the small minority of transgender people objecting to the "Vagina Monologues" were needlessly reactionary. It painted the transgender community with far too broad a brush, though, as most of the community is fine with the play. I have friends who have been part of all transgender productions of the "Monologues"; these productions have been happening for over a decade, and Eve Ensler has been a supporter of the transgender community.[1262] [1263]

However, unlike Dr. Burkett, I recognized that this minority was just that: the minority.

Throughout the article, transgender people are represented as some monolithic entity. Additionally, she makes sweeping generalizations and assumptions that can be disproven by both science and simple anecdotes. These are also some that are commonly proffered by anti-transgender feminists. Let's look at some of the issues with the article one by one.

1. Male privilege is not monolithic and universal

As will be discussed in the last section in this chapter, privilege is a multilayered and intersectional phenomenon.[1264] While Dr. Burkett says she does not want to play the oppression Olympics (competing to prove who is more oppressed), it is also a gross oversimplification to use Caitlyn Jenner to imply that all men have more privilege than all women. There's race, religion, wealth, ability, region, sexual orientation, gender identity, gender expression, and many more factors at play. Men have more privilege than women on average, but there are clearly some women who have more than some men because of these other factors.

2. The female experience is not universal...or limited to non-transgender (cisgender) women

Many "gold-star lesbians" have never woken up in the morning worried that they're pregnant.[1265] The girl next door to me when I was growing up needed a hysterectomy at 12 and never had a period. Many cisgender women have been told that unless they have had kids, they don't really know what it's like to be a woman.

Conversely, transgender women also definitely have to worry about being beaten or raped. We can have our breasts stared at, or suddenly become the "coffee wench" for men at meetings. My last job paid me a fraction of what the male programmers who theoretically worked for me made.

If being female is a checklist of experiences, then a lot of cisgender people would be left off it, too.

3. Caitlyn Jenner is an outlier within the transgender community

Caitlyn Jenner is representative of all transgender women in the way the Kardashians are representative of all cisgender women.

Which is to say, not at all.

Many transgender women have very little safety, money, or privilege pre-transition, especially as people perceived as effeminate men. After transition, transgender women are highly susceptible to extreme poverty, violence, incarceration, HIV infection, homelessness, and unemployment. To imply that transgender women usually carry over a large portion of prior male privilege post-transition flies in the face of every demographic statistic we have. Additionally, many Generation Z transgender girls and women socially transitioned very early, and will never have experienced male privilege in their conscious lives. They do, however, experience discrimination both for being seen as female, and at other times for being transgender.

4. Sex hormones do affect transgender people emotionally

Burkett mocked Jenner for describing how taking hormones affected her emotionally. But let's be real here: hormones do affect our emotional state. This one is common sense, to an extent. Doctors almost do not need to say that sex hormones are one reason why teenagers are moody pains in the butt, many women experience ups and downs during their cycle, testosterone is correlated with aggression (it's one of the reasons why people get their pets fixed), and changes in emotional response are often a sign of the onset of menopause.

So, why should it come as any surprise that when transgender people begin taking hormone replacement therapy (HRT), many see some changes in how they experience events around them? Or more importantly, why should they be shamed for expressing how they experience these changes?

5. Judging an entire class of people based on anecdotes is bigotry

Dr. Burkett's article took great umbrage at a few transgender academics and activists who got into online squabbles over language. I have no problem with the word vagina, or "The Vagina Monologues," and neither do the vast majority of transgender people. But based on these interactions with a (very) small but vocal portion of the transgender community online, she has decided that the entire transgender community is a threat to all women.

While a minority of trans people object to the word vagina, or "The Vagina Monologues," the same is true for a minority of cisgender women who oppose the word and/or the play. And no group should be defined/stereotyped by a subset of their population. It's not unlike pointing at terrorists who were Muslim, and using it to describe why you think all Muslims are bad.

Ascribing a universal set of beliefs to transgender people based on a small subset of that community is a form of stereotyping. Using those stereotypes to condemn an entire community is bigotry.

6. Human dignity is not a zero-sum game

Accepting transgender women as women does not fundamentally detract from the rights, dignity, or value of cisgender women. The argument that calling transgender people women or men in accordance with their gender identities somehow dilutes or pollutes the meaning of these words is effectively the same argument used by those opposed to marriage equality. They claim that adding same-sex unions to the definition of marriage will destroy it, devalue the worth of straight people's marriages, or render the meanings of man and woman meaningless.

Accepting a transgender woman as female doesn't devalue the institution of womanhood any more than accepting gay spouses devalues the institution of marriage.

7. Dr. Burkett's anti-trans arguments are the same as those used by right-wing misogynists who hate feminists

Stella Morabito is a writer over at *The Federalist*, and comes from the Phyllis Schlafly school of anti-feminist thought.[1266] These beliefs include opposition to abortion under any circumstances, no-fault divorce, sex before marriage, women working outside the home after they have children, and same-sex marriage. Morabito also supports abstinence-only education, thinks feminism is a form of communism, and that feminists are waging the "real war on women."[1267] [1268] Morabito represents the far right, social conservative view of feminists and where women belong in American society.

But Dr. Burkett and Ms. Morabito agree on one thing: they both get really, really angry about transgender people calling themselves men or women. In fact, Morabito wrote an article titled "How the trans-agenda seeks to redefine everyone," that makes almost the exact same points as Burkett's article "What makes a woman?"[1269]

Rather interesting intellectual company for a "feminist" to keep.

8. Transgender women are held to an impossible standard for gender expression

It's hard to believe Dr. Burkett's claims that she has nothing against transgender people when she finds Caitlyn Jenner's *Vanity Fair* photo so offensive, but hasn't also written 2000 words in *The New York Times* decrying all the other similarly clad (and Photoshopped) women who have graced the cover in the past. Therein lies the rub.

Transgender women are accused of not being "real" if they don't express themselves in a way that is stereotypically feminine enough, and also accused of being fake or caricatures if they present in a stereotypically feminine way. This leaves a narrow to non-existent window of "acceptable expression."

For example (true story), both I and a co-worker at my last job coincidentally owned identical business suits. However, it was hinted to me by different people that the suit was both too masculine (because of how it was cut), or too feminine (because it came with a skirt, and is a warm tan in color). My co-worker who owned the same suit did not have her gender questioned in the same way.

9. Gender confirmation surgery isn't about gender stereotypes

Dr. Burkett's article states that transgender women have GCS more often than transgender men because of gender stereotyping. This seems highly unlikely, given that transgender women outnumber transgender men to start with based on the data in the latest national transgender survey.[1270] Additionally, GCS for transgender men is far more complicated, more expensive, and often produces a less functional result than GCS for transgender women.[1271] In short, if gender stereotypes play any role in the statistic she cites, it is a small one.

10. Feminism isn't just for the "right" kinds of women

Past acceptability politics in feminism included the National Organization for Women disowning its lesbian members in the 1960s because Betty Friedan feared that outspoken lesbians were a threat to the feminist movement.[1272] Setting up lesbians as a "Lavender Menace" created a rift that ultimately weakened the movement for women's rights, and hurt queer women in particular. Even today, lesbian, bisexual, and transgender women suffer the most from economic disparities.[1273]

Now, transgender people are told by Dr. Burkett and others that they are only welcome in the movement if they give up their claims to their intrinsic identity for which they have fought so hard, and to only express their gender in ways that people like Dr. Burkett find acceptable.

Can there be any serious expectation that anyone would find such terms for inclusion acceptable?

11. Language evolves over time

Language evolves as culture changes.[1274] American cultural understandings of marriage, gender, sex, and basically anything LGBT are in flux. Additionally, the English language has a very hard time with non-binary gender concepts.[1275] How does American language include transgender men who are pregnant? How do Americans have language that doesn't "other" people who identify as women, but transitioned to get there?

The meanings of words change over time, and often there is intense disagreement over what precisely words *should* mean. Individuals should regard the meanings of those words more poetically, and be open to others using them differently. Over time, it is reasonable to assume that common meanings will become more generally agreed on, and language will adapt to cultural changes with regards to gender and sexuality.

12. People don't choose to be transgender

Dr. Burkett hints that she thinks being transgender is a choice, when she writes, "What we do with those genders—the roles we assign ourselves, and each other, based on them—is almost entirely mutable."

Ummm...no.

No one chooses this life because they think it will be fun or easy. Every statistic, survey, and study completed have said this is a hard road, and we know it. Transgender people transition not because it is easy or fun, but because it is easier than continuing to live a lie.

13. Labeling transgender people as not real men or women is part of the problem

In our binary society, when transgender people are labeled not "real" men or women, it implies they are things, "its," or simply not human. The results of being seen as fake, or as non-human, are devastating.

From Gwen Araujo, to Brandon Teena, to Angie Zapata, to Jennifer Laude, to Cemia Dove, our lack of ownership of our bodies and identities has meant being forcibly stripped, groped, raped, strangled, stabbed, drowned, burned, and bludgeoned.[1276] [1277] [1278] [1279] [1280] It means that transgender panic defenses live on in court, and sometimes even win. After Brandon McInerney shot Larry King (who was genderqueer) twice in the back of the head in the middle of a crowded classroom, the jury became deadlocked on the case. Some even sympathized with the murderer.[1281] "[Brandon] was just solving a problem," one juror said.

At the same time, religious leaders have used the assertion that transgender people are not "real" women and men as the basis for urging their followers to murder transgender people for using bathrooms consistent with their gender identity.[1282] [1283]

While Dr. Burkett claims she abhors violence against transgender people, she is adding to the problem when she tries to deny them the right to self-identify as men or women by adding a left-wing veneer of academic respectability to anti-LGBT hate groups.

Examining male privilege post-transition

Transgender people often have a cultural one-way mirror with which to observe the cultural aspects of gender, misogyny, and discrimination. At the same time, we also gain insights into the effects of intersectional identities by eliminating one of the variables: namely our externally perceived sex and gender.

The reality of male privilege is well established. Women struggle to get into positions of power within business or politics.[1284] Women make 5–7 percent less than similarly situated men, even when all other variables are accounted for, leaving discrimination as the primary culprit.[1285] The epidemic of sexual assault in the military is longstanding, getting worse, and a national shame.[1286] The #MeToo movement has highlighted the epidemic of sexual assault and rape culture in the United States. There is no question that being female carries a significant "life penalty" with it. There's no denying that male privilege exists.

However, sometimes it feels taboo to ask how far male privilege goes. Who better to ask, though, than transgender men and women who have lived on both sides of the divide?

Years ago, I came across a post by a transgender man of color who asked whether trans men really have it easier.[1287] It explored the intersectionality of gender and race in his experience. He concluded that being seen by society as a black man carried more disadvantages than being seen as a black woman, thanks to the prevalence of racial profiling. When I shared this blog post with other transgender people, the responses were mixed.

A white transgender man who read this blog post observed:

> I'm hesitant to say that either side of the spectrum has it easier than the other, because a struggle is a struggle. But 99 percent of the time, trans men definitely do have it easier.

A transgender woman of color who is also a veteran observed that the intersection of being a person of color and a transgender woman was even worse from her perspective:

> I was stopped for looking like a drug dealer by the local police. It didn't help when the local addicts would walk up to me and ask for their stuff. However, I haven't read a single story when a trans woman of color was attacked and lived. I've slowly accepted the fact that my chances of surviving in Afghanistan were higher than my chances being out in America. Once I transition, life expectancy goes out the window.

Her observations are in line with the statistics we have. According to the National Coalition of Anti-Violence Programs, 68 percent of all LGBT people murdered in hate crimes in 2016, outside the Pulse Nightclub massacre, were trans women. This was despite their being only about 6 percent of the LGBT community.[1288] Of those transgender persons murdered, 95 percent were transgender women of color. My friend was even right about the level of violence: trans people who survive hate crimes are 1.76 times more likely to require significant medical attention than other LGB victims. Economically, transgender people are twice as likely to be unemployed and four times as likely to live on less than $10,000 per year.[1289]

As a result, when an individual is perceived by others as a male-assigned-at-birth (MAAB) transgender person, you more than forfeit whatever privilege you had in terms of susceptibility to violence and poverty.

My own personal experiences also suggest that male privilege is not a constant value but can vary depending on where you are. I was often at a huge disadvantage as a small, slightly built, somewhat effeminate "man" in a very type-A, masculine military culture.

In most situations, the male way of showing who is boss is to see who gets the omega to roll over fastest. Being the automatic omega dog in any given situation means either taking the abuse, or standing up to it. In my experience, standing up to it generally meant taking even worse abuse as a result.

As a civilian researcher, I still worked within a military environment. The pilots I worked with were uniformly polite, proper in their bearing, and professional in their approach to the work we were doing. They also tended to pay more attention to the adjustable briefing room chairs they sat in than to me or any of the other women I worked with. There was often more than a whiff of patronization when my military past comes up.

From my white-collar perspective, given the choice between active abuse and being treated like a picture hanging in a hotel room, the option of being ignored actually seems preferable. I somehow doubt, though, that I would feel better off post-transition if I had been the one on the top of the heap physically and socially pre-transition.

Environment is a variable as well. I went to a high school with a very tight-knit, gifted group of people that was diverse and egalitarian. If you looked at our resumes today, you would be very hard-pressed to tell which ones belong to women and which ones belong to men.

A cisgender, straight (and very funny) feminist friend had her own thoughts on all of this:[1290]

> Many feminists would respond by saying "that's patriarchy." The system of male privilege winds up harming men. The pressure to exert domination, particularly physical domination, over other men is a result of patriarchy's strict gender roles. Similarly, the horrible treatment of trans or gender non-conforming people who were designated male at birth could actually be seen as a manifestation of patriarchy/misogyny. They are hated for their rejection of male privilege, their embracing of femininity. It's almost as if the only thing worse than being a woman is "choosing" to be a woman when you don't have to.

Another queer feminist writer sums the concept up well:

> Really, everyone is affected by patriarchy. And, patriarchy looks different, takes different forms, and has different effects in different places, times, classes, religions, and races.[1291]

Male privilege undeniably exists. However, it does not seem to be the monolithic power some might assume. It isn't the be-all-and-end-all existing as someone perceived as male, and it also has a flip side that harms some men even as it privileges them as a class. It varies based on race, work environment, cultural setting, and whether someone is perceived as gender conforming. Pinning down how much it is actually worth depends on many factors and interactions besides simply sex.

Chapter 12

WHERE WE GO FROM HERE

The cultural, political, and legal landscape for transgender Americans is changing more rapidly than at any point in history. In many ways, these changes are signs of the progress being made. At the same time, the negative focus on transgender people by social conservative organizations and politicians is also a sign of cultural change.

As the rhetoric ratchets up and increasingly hyperbolic claims about transgender people are made, the hostility may counterintuitively accelerate acceptance. The propaganda being used today closely resembles that used against lesbian, gay, and bisexual people 20 years ago. The American public has largely rejected narratives that LGB people "recruit" children, that they shouldn't be allowed to teach, and that they prey on people in bathrooms, that they will disrupt military good order and discipline, or that they are innately sinful and should be marginalized within society. Still, while these attitudes are still held by even a shrinking percentage of people, it can make life difficult for transgender people.

Even though transgender issues have been increasingly in the news and acceptance is growing, there are still topics that haven't yet entered popular discourse. These include issues related to non-traditional relationships, sexuality, immigration, and prisoner rights.

Given that the fight is ongoing, and how much has yet to be addressed, the struggle for acceptance and legal protection is likely to be a long one. Indeed, things are likely to get worse for years, if not decades, before they get better. This chapter explores how the attacks on transgender people are a sign that transgender people are winning the culture war, that many structural challenges remain which will impede progress, how lack of conversation is one of those impediments, and what the future holds for transgender people and the movement.

The hate means we're winning the culture war (for now...)

Nearing the end of the battle for marriage equality, the right wing set their sights on the transgender community. We saw it coming, and it's as ugly as you would imagine.[1292] Some leaders in law enforcement, government, and the conservative movement are all threatening to personally assault or kill any transgender person they see in a bathroom.[1293 1294] Right-wing figures in the media like Curt Schilling are posting ugly memes about transgender people.[1295] Republican candidate for President in 2016, Senator Ted Cruz, even went so far as to say that transgender people shouldn't be allowed to use any public bathroom, and that they should only be transgender inside their own homes.[1296]

This sort of discourse isn't likely to end any time soon.[1297 1298] The people responsible for House Bill 2 in North Carolina vowed not to repeal it and sent the bill to repeal it to a committee that never meets.[1299 1300] In the end, the bill was partially repealed, leaving in place a ban on legally protecting LGBT people from discrimination. In Texas, Lt. Gov. Dan Patrick and other politicians have vowed to run retailer Target out of the state for allowing trans people to use the bathroom consistent with their gender identity, and Republican leaders there have indicated a desire to pass statewide anti-transgender laws.[1301 1302] Oxford, Alabama, has already passed a citywide version, and Rockwall in Texas is considering one.[1303 1304]

The only way these sorts of laws will be struck down in the near future is through lawsuits. In 2016, the US Court of Appeals for the 4th Circuit ruled in favor of access to appropriate accommodations for transgender students to use facilities in accordance with their gender identity.[1305] The American Civil Liberties Union and Equality North Carolina challenged HB2 in court on similar grounds.[1306] At the same time, the Supreme Court has declined to hear a case challenging a Mississippi law protecting anyone who discriminates against LGBT people.[1307] Thus it appears these anti-transgender laws are going to have to be challenged and overturned in court, one by one.

It will be long. It will be hard. It will be painful.

Counterintuitively, it is also a sign that we are winning.

Most signs point to a slowly growing cultural acceptance of transgender people. The best quantitative measure of this is the Human Rights Campaign Corporate Equality Index's measurement of companies offering trans-inclusive benefits, since this represents businesses putting (a little) money where their mouths are. In 2002, not a single Fortune 500 company offered transgender-inclusive health benefits.[1308] In 2018, 58 percent of them do so and this number is rising quickly.[1309] Despite the right-wing freak-out over Target allowing transgender people to use restrooms consistent with their gender identity, 83 percent of all Fortune 500 companies have similar non-discrimination policies.[1310]

While corporations are increasingly recognizing transgender concerns, the overall cultural landscape is moving more slowly. Visibility is not sufficient, given how transgender issues are already high profile and how many anti-transgender laws are being passed.[1311] Having friends and family who are LGBT makes acceptance much more likely. The bad news is that only 16 percent of Americans personally know someone who is transgender;[1312] the good news is that this is up from just 8 percent in 2008. This is likely a result of the additional visibility in media, and transgender people more willing to be "out."

Unfortunately, it's possible to win hearts and minds and still lose the war if social conservatives pass laws and policies designed to drive transgender people underground, and put judges in place to uphold them.[1313] In 2010, transgender issues were barely on conservatives' radars. The strategy of the LGBT movement then was to quietly build favorable cultural conditions for the time when the right wing came for transgender people, so that we could control the battle space when the fight came. Because most LGBT organizations were still in a "we'll deal with transgender rights later" mindset as the marriage equality decision[1314] galvanized the right and shifted them to transgender people, the opportunity was squandered.

It's too late for that now. The fact that the movement is relying on legal challenges to turn back laws designed to drive transgender people out of entire states is indicative of the failure to win in the cultural arena before the situation became this dire. As a result of this failure to adequately prepare, the LGBT movement is functioning mostly in a reactionary, crisis-driven mode. To use a military metaphor, the transgender community is in the middle of a desperate, last-stand firefight with the enemy well inside their perimeter, and simultaneously conducting psychological operations (PSYOP) in the middle of this firefight just adds another degree of difficulty.[1315]

However, all of this has happened before. In the 1970s, Anita Bryant led the charge to repeal ordinances protecting lesbians and gays as part of the Save Our Children campaign, the exact same tactics that are being used against transgender people today.[1316] [1317] The consequences of the Save Our Children campaign were also eerily similar to the hyperbolic threats of violence recently made against transgender people.

Fifteen years after Bryant's heyday, the opposition to allowing lesbians and gays to serve in the military was primarily about bathrooms and showers.[1318] The panicked predictions of the US military disintegrating under a wave of gays and lesbians raping people in bathrooms and showers proved to be every bit as dumb (and improbable) as it sounds.[1319]

In the end, keeping people permanently in a state of fear over something irrational and baseless is impossible.[1320] In the long run, the fact that experts on sexual assault, law enforcement, and respected media outlets all conclude that the anti-transgender arguments are baseless hysteria will seep through to the public consciousness.[1321] [1322] The fear of transgender people, or people pretending to be transgender, will ebb away. This will accelerate as more Americans have a friend or family member who is transgender. This will accelerate as accepting Millennials and Generation Z come to dominate the cultural and demographic landscape.[1323] Transgender people are winning the fight for cultural acceptance, even if it is slow and ugly.

It may take years and we're going to lose a lot of good people along the way, but eventually the zealots won't be able to fear-monger about transgender people anymore. They will have to find someone else to demonize, just as they did with lesbians and gays. Who will it be next? Left-handed dentists?

Fear and hatred never needed a rational basis.

Twelve things the trans community still isn't talking about

Years ago, a spouse of a transgender woman wrote an article about the difficulties of suddenly becoming the other half in a non-traditional family unit.[1324] It was immediately met with howls of protest by a number of transgender people who felt that there were already too many narratives out there about life as a transgender person being one filled with pain and torment and that adding a focus on spousal trauma only made things worse.

In another instance, a transgender woman was found to be into kink. This was used to discredit her by people who claimed that, because of it, she wasn't really transgender.

These incidents illustrate the phenomenon whereby transgender people feel compelled to stick to a script, as was described in Chapter 10. Much of this is due to various stigmas and a lack of acceptance being placed on transgender people by culture, psychology, and medicine.

When the pressure comes from sources internal to the transgender community, it is often the result of acceptability politics and internalized transphobia.

As was discussed in Chapter 11, examples of acceptability politics include the National Organization for Women (NOW) disowning its lesbian members in the 1960s.[1325] Setting up lesbians as a "Lavender Menace" created a rift that ultimately weakened the movement for women's rights, and hurt queer women in particular. Even today, lesbian, bisexual, and transgender women suffer the most from economic disparities, while at the same time transgender people are expected to have a particular narrative in order to meet the demands of respectability politics.[1326]

Because of internalized transphobia, social stigma, and the pressure to deliver homogenized socially acceptable narratives, many issues related to the transgender community are rarely addressed. The following is a short list of things we should be talking about as a culture, or will be soon.

1. Marriage and relationships

Something that is rarely talked about is how difficult it is even for supportive spouses as their partner transitions.

Some of the best-known success stories in the transgender community of relationships that survive transition gloss over the grieving process, the pain, the loss, the questions, and the lack of available support for non-transgender (cisgender) spouses. Those partnerships that *do* survive the initial transition often face the daunting question of what to do now that they are a mixed-orientation couple (i.e. a marriage in which one person is lesbian or gay and the other is straight, and thus there is a lack of sexual attraction).[1327]

Trans people often avoid sharing these stories because they are already commonly accused of being selfish for transitioning. The truth is far more complex and follows the inexorable arc of a classical Greek tragedy: the end is inevitable from the beginning act and actions taken by characters to avoid their destiny only drive them more inescapably toward their fate.

What makes Greek tragedies and transgender marital issues all the gloomier is that the players often exhibit remarkable nobility, far beyond that of most mortals; yet at the same time their human flaws end up creating a darker fate than that enjoyed by others of lesser character.

Both parties are suffering and both do what has to be done at every step. The only real solution is to greatly reduce the stigma of being transgender so that people are able to come out much earlier and avoid entering into unsustainable relationships that will collapse when they do come out.

2. Alternate relationship structures, non-monogamy, and polyamory

When a marriage does survive transition, the sex life often disappears. This leaves many couples with only a few options: divorce, a sexless marriage, or some form of an alternate relationship structure.

The first is often unacceptable due to the existence of children, a sense of duty to each other, or finances. The second is frequently something neither party is willing to settle for. This leaves the third option as the most viable solution for many.

Unfortunately, given the continuing stigma of even ethical polyamory (the non-possessive, honest, and responsible philosophy and practice of loving multiple people simultaneously), many transgender people in these situations feel like they have jumped right from one closet into another.[1328] [1329] The irony of this is that up to 72 percent of all men in traditional marriages cheat on their wives, yet acceptance of polyamory is only 14 percent.[1330]

Then there's the pressure—especially for public transgender figures—to sustain an image of a "happy mixed-orientation marriage," hiding relationship issues in order to be effective in the public arena.[1331]

3. Sexual orientation

Because of lingering belief in 1970s vintage psychiatry, there are still some within the community who reject the identity of any transgender person whose identity is not binary, and their sexual orientation "straight" after transition. They have latched onto Blanchard's theory and weaponized it against other transgender people, and used it as a way to validate themselves.[1332]

This is disturbing on many levels.[1333] First, wasn't the whole point of the LGBT movement to *stop* shaming people for their sexual orientation and gender identity? Second, these attacks are eerily similar to the ones used by people whose goal is to "morally mandate it [transsexualism] out of existence."[1334]

So why is being a transgender woman who is attracted to women stigmatized? It comes down to the use of Blanchard's Autogynephilic Theory to label all transgender women attracted to women as fakes and perverts.[1335] Transgender women are still terrified of being labeled like this, even more so as conservatives try to use it to legislate transgender people out of existence.[1336] At the same time, internalized transphobia (self-hatred due to unconscious acceptance of social stigma) creates a situation of lateral violence wherein some members of the community will use their heterosexual orientation as a way of labeling themselves as "real women" or "real transsexuals," and labeling those attracted to women as "fakes."

4. Kink and BDSM

When the transgender woman at the center of a right-wing freak-out over locker rooms at Planet Fitness in Michigan was revealed as a participant of the kink/BDSM scene, some self-appointed leaders within the transgender community took it on themselves to deny her gender identity.

Much of this stigma comes from both Blanchard (again) and social conservatives and others pushing the false narrative that transgender people are perverts and predators.[1337] Although the transgender person at the center of this did absolutely nothing wrong, some members of the transgender community wanted to disown her because they felt she reflected badly on the community for her interests.[1338] They were repeating the mistakes of prior generations in playing respectability politics, much as NOW excluded lesbians for their sexuality in the 1960s.

It is also ironic is that the kink/BDSM community has often been one of the few welcoming safe spaces for transgender people.[1339]

The truth is that straights, gays, lesbians, bisexuals, and transgender people (among others!) can all be kinky. When straight people are kinky, it makes over 160 million dollars at the box office and sells 100 million book copies.[1340] [1341] When transgender people are kinky, it's grounds for excommunication from the community.

5. The age at which people knew they were transgender

Much as there is a "born this way" narrative for queer people, so there is for transgender people. Acceptance of LGBT people is highly correlated with the understanding that sexual orientation is inborn.[1342] This leads to transgender people feeling highly pressured to say "I always knew" rather than admitting that they didn't feel dysphoric until puberty or that they always felt different from others but that they didn't figure out what the conflict was until later in life.

Failing to say "I always knew" unfairly casts doubt on the validity of a transgender person's gender identity. This pressure to conform is constant, even if multiple lines of research indicate the biological origins of gender identity regardless of when someone becomes aware. Worsening this situation for transgender women is Blanchard's typology (also again), which labels anyone who "didn't know" from birth a fetishist and probable pervert.[1343]

6. Sex work

According to the 2011 National Transgender Discrimination Survey (NTDS), 11 percent of transgender people have done sex work to survive.[1344] Their involvement in the sex industry was found to be highly correlated with familial rejection, youth homelessness, bullying in school, and job discrimination.

In other words, people who are rejected by their families, thrown out of their homes as teens, beaten while at school, and can't find jobs are much more likely to resort to the sex industry for survival. These are the most innocent victims of cultural and religious discrimination against transgender people, yet we hesitate to share their stories because of the stigma of the sex industry.

Due to the media's frequent portrayal of transgender people as sex workers, transgender people are often profiled by police as sex workers and subject to violence.[1345] At the same time, the assumption that all transgender people are sex workers leads to our culture devaluing the lives of transgender people. It also leads the general public to wrongly assume that transgender sex workers are doing this by choice, thus allowing society to ignore the needs of transgender people, including minors, who are subjected to this in order to earn the money to maintain stable housing and access to necessities.

We need to be talking about the conditions that force transgender people into sex work, and not simply depicting transgender people as sex workers.

7. Transition regrets

First, here are the most important facts: strong regrets about transition are rare, and every major professional health organization considers access to transition-related care a medical necessity.[1346 1347]

However, there are a still a few people (1–4%) who regret medically transitioning. This is far lower than almost any other medical procedure.

Risk factors for regret mentioned in studies include lack of support from the patient's family, poor social support, late-life transitions, severe psychopathology unrelated to gender dysphoria, unfavorable physical appearance, and poor surgical results.

Anecdotally, I personally know of one case where a transgender woman who ended up with regrets was given an ultimatum by her medical team: undergo gender confirmation surgery or lose access to hormones. This incident violates everything that the World Professional Association of Transgender Health (WPATH) recommends.

Why regret happens and how to prevent it, though, simply isn't discussed. This has a great deal to do with Walt Heyer, who had undiagnosed psychological co-morbidities, wasn't actually transgender, and who now advocates against anyone having access to transition-related medical care.[1348] His position is extremely harmful because it is frequently used by conservatives who really don't have transgender people's best interests at heart.

The position that, since a small percentage regret transition, no one should transition is logically flawed. It's a bit like saying "I'm lactose intolerant, so no one should drink milk." It also ignores the fact that the vast majority benefit from it, and do not regret it. Preventing everyone from transitioning would do far more harm than good.

"Transition regret" has become the rallying cry of social conservatives determined to ensure that no one ever transitions, and, as a result, anyone who publicly discusses their detransition risks having their story misused by people with an anti-transgender agenda.[1349] Thus, instead of talking about lack of education for mental health care providers, cultural discrimination, familiar rejection, and limited surgical training increasing what regret cases we do see, we say nothing at all, and people with regrets are reluctant to talk about it.

8. Mental illness

Transgender people and cisgender people can all suffer from mental health struggles and mental illness diagnoses. The general public is loath to talk about mental illness in general, but for transgender people, this taboo is even more pronounced. Because conservatives push the narrative that all transgender people are, by definition, mentally ill, it is difficult to talk about actual instances of mental health struggles or to seek help for them.

Conservatives also often push the narrative that since transgender people suffer from psychological co-morbidities at a higher rate than the general public, their identities are just a product of these co-morbidities, and they should be treated for these rather than gender dysphoria. It is also used to make the argument that transgender people shouldn't be allowed to transition. All of these arguments ignore the central fact that these co-morbidities are primarily due to stigma, discrimination, and abuse for being transgender in the first place.[1350]

Admitting that you have a problem is made even more difficult; it forces you to grapple with whether the haters are right about other things too. Similarly, it isn't something the community as a whole is comfortable discussing, given we're still fighting against the narrative that we're all suffering from a disorder even when individuals are perfectly healthy and happy.

9. Which medical treatments (if any) a transgender individual pursues

In many states, a transgender person's legal rights specific to their identity are based on their surgical status.[1351] There are also cisgender and transgender people who reject other people's gender identities if they have not had, or do not want, particular medical interventions. Often, cisgender people express that transgender people are only welcome in spaces (bathrooms) and activities (sports) if they have had GCS (bottom surgery).

As a result, there is heavy pressure for a transgender person to at least claim to want medical intervention. Denying a desire for medical transition gives transphobes an excuse to say that transgender people don't want to play by the same rules as everyone else, to deny our identities, or to use this as a pretext for discrimination.

Ignoring for a moment that most transgender people don't have the money to pay for these procedures, much less insurance that covers them, the ideas behind this are chilling. A person's human rights should never be contingent on undergoing unwanted massive surgery.

We have been down this road before, and it doesn't end well.[1352]

10. Non-binary, gender fluid, genderqueer, and gender non-conforming identities

Our society thinks about gender as a binary. As a result, the LGBT movement's messaging is that transgender women are women, and transgender men are men.

When non-binary, gender non-conforming, or gender fluid people enter the conversation, it disrupts well-tested talking points about transgender people and invites a lot of questions. We, as a movement, are not yet good at answering questions about gender non-binary people, such as: *What bathrooms should they use? Will gender identity and expression change from day to day? Does this make it a choice? What about gender markers on ID? What about gendered dress standards at work? Is gender identity fixed, or can it be changed via reparative therapy?*

The LGBT movement often avoids talking about these types of identities because it complicates our efforts for acceptance, even though everyone's identity should be respected. However, we risk painting ourselves into a legislative and legal corner down the road if we ignore gender non-conforming identities now.

Answering identification questions cannot be put off indefinitely. More and more high school and college-aged people identify as somewhere on the gender non-conforming spectrum and they deserve to have their narratives shared as well, without facing a barrage of daily questions.

11. Asylum and immigration

Many immigrants who are transgender flee to the United States hoping for a better, safer life. For all the challenges transgender people face in the US, their lives are far better here than in many countries, where being openly LGBT is criminalized and sometimes punishable by death.[1353] In other countries, such as Brazil, being transgender isn't illegal but social stigma leads to extremely high levels of violence directed at the transgender community.[1354]

When these individuals seek asylum, they are often faced with immigration judges who know nothing of transgender issues and who are openly contemptuous of their identity and the danger these individuals face if they return to their country of origin.[1355] Other times, transgender immigrants are denied due process, such as when they aren't informed of their right to claim asylum or to consult attorneys.[1356]

Transgender people who are detained by Immigrations and Customs Enforcement (ICE) are disproportionately likely to be mistreated. Only 1 in 500 ICE detainees is transgender, yet 20 percent of all detainees who are raped while in custody are transgender.[1357] The perpetrators of this violence are often ICE employees and contractors. ICE has been accused of doing little to monitor or prevent sexual assault against transgender detainees, and that its investigations tend to be cursory.[1358]

Other forms of abuse can be life threatening. ICE has denied HIV medication to transgender inmates. It has also subjected them to long periods of solitary confinement as punishment or to (ostensibly) keep them away from the rest of the population for their own safety. Transgender inmates have reportedly been threatened by law enforcement officials or their attorneys with solitary confinement, violence, or rape if they report sexual violence against them.[1359]

The fact that these individuals are undocumented and/or asylum seekers does not, and must not, create a legal or moral justification to fundamentally violate an individual's human rights or subject them to abuse. Unfortunately, these individuals lie at the nexus of anti-immigrant and anti-transgender rhetoric. As a result, they are treated in a way unbecoming of a nation which claims to value human rights.

12. Prisoners

Transgender prisoners face many of the same issues as transgender immigrants detained by ICE. Rape, solitary confinement, and lack of access to medications are all endemic.[1360] The level of indifference shown to transgender prisoners by prison guards is often astounding; one prisoner who was being raped tried to attract the attention of guards and was told to "sit down and shut up."[1361] In one of the worst cases, a transgender man who was being raped killed his attacker, was put in prison, raped again, and contracted HIV as a result.[1362] Tolerance of rape in prison results in additional HIV exposure, creating a new long-term medical need for inmates.

Beyond prison authority's indifference to violence and sexual assault of transgender inmates, there is the transgender community's feelings about inmates who receive transgender-related medical care during incarceration. The courts have long held that denying medically necessary care to prisoners is a form of cruel and unusual punishment prohibited by the 8th Amendment. Increasingly, denying hormones to transgender prisoners is (rightly) seen by these same courts as a denial of medically necessary care.

Chelsea Manning would be an example of how it can be difficult to discuss issues surrounding transgender prisoners. There are many within the transgender community who did not support the fact that she deliberately and indiscriminately leaked over 700,000 classified documents, and believe her sentence was appropriate. There are others who adamantly support her actions. It is possible to support her right to medical care and to not be placed in solitary confinement without cause as a matter of constitutional human rights without supporting her actions. However, this can be a difficult nuance to explain in a heated discussion.

"Why should she get medical care for committing a crime when I can't get it despite never having done anything criminal?" some ask. Equally difficult is the concept that if hormone replacement therapy is not medically necessary for prisoners who have a constitutional right to necessary medical care, it isn't medically necessary for anyone else in a legal sense.

At the end of the day, the US has a problem with the way it treats its prisoners, particularly transgender ones. Regardless of their immigration status or crime, transgender inmates deserve basic human rights protections. The movement and the transgender community need to be discussing this, because it reflects on how we, as a nation, treat "the least of my brothers."

Expected future trends

Some of what the future holds for the transgender community in the United States can be extrapolated from the observance of current trends.

Acceptance of transgender people will continue to grow

Polling data shows, nearly universally, that younger people are more accepting of LGBT people than their elders. This trend holds true even when considering younger voters who belong to the groups most hostile to transgender people, including white evangelicals and Republicans.[1363] Most Americans do not believe small business owners should be allowed to discriminate against LGBT people based on their religious beliefs,[1364] and the majority of small business owners also oppose discrimination against LGBT people.[1365]

Religious conservatives will continue to wield political power out of proportion with their size

While white evangelicals are only 16 percent of the population (and falling), the Republican Party is dependent on them as a voting bloc, both in the primaries and in the general election. Without their support, many Republican candidates are unlikely to make it out of the primaries. At the same time, voter ID laws tend to favor older whites as voters. Gerrymandering tends to promote campaigns that appeal to primary voters (who skew right) more than the mainstream. Gerrymandering also generally favors Republicans in many states, ensuring they will stay in power even when a wide majority of the public voted for Democrats.[1366]

Thus, the white evangelicals will continue to exert an influence on governance far out of proportion with their actual size and public support for their social positions.

Religious conservatives will continue to lose cultural influence

As Robert P. Jones of the Public Religion Research Institute lays out in his book *The End of White Christian America*, white evangelicals are inevitably losing both members and cultural influence.[1367] This is a result of both the "browning" of America, and of Millennials leaving organized religion (due, in great part, to their denomination's stance on LGBT people misaligning with their personal beliefs and values).

The Roman Catholic Church's stance on birth control and same-sex marriage is not reflected in the actual attitudes of its membership, and it thus seems implausible that American audiences will join the crusade against transgender people. The efforts by conservative religious organizations to re-brand their 1990s-vintage talking points on gays as a hip new defense against transgender people also seems unlikely to succeed in convincing the American public that transgender people are a threat to life, the universe, and everything.

In the end, the current wave of anti-transgender propaganda all too often veers into hyperbole, lies, and smear tactics; because of this, it will likely backfire in the long run. The evangelical brand is suffering from being radically out of step with a secular, pluralistic society. Its moral authority was further damaged in 2017 by rallying around conservative candidate Roy Moore in Alabama, and Donald Trump, despite his peccadillos. Americans can guess where the future of this lies by considering what has happened in Canada; a 2017 poll of Canadian voters showed that Canadians would be more likely to vote for a transgender person than an evangelical.[1368]

The courts are poised to make transgender lives much worse for a long time

A hard-line conservative Supreme Court appears to be a near certainty in the next few years. This court is likely to make decisions on the constitutionality of transgender protections under the Civil Rights Act, transgender rights under the Equal Protections Clause, a religious right to ignore legal protections for LGBT people on religious grounds, and the constitutionality of laws that specifically enshrine a religious right to discriminate against LGBT people on the basis of their religious beliefs on marriage and gender. The Supreme Court will also likely decide how much authority the executive branch has under the rubric of "National Security" to enact policy targeting transgender people via the transgender military ban.

Given the projected composition of the Supreme Court's members over the next five to ten years, there are almost certain to be devastating rulings that undermine current civil rights laws, while granting a broad religious right for individuals and companies to discriminate against LGBT people. SCOTUS may also find a right to demand broad accommodations based on a desire to discriminate. These rulings are likely to endure for decades due to *stare decisis*.

As religious right organizations have demanded that their adherents exercise their right to discriminate, this is likely to result in a perverse situation in which transgender people will experience *more* acts of blatant and deliberate discrimination, despite greater cultural acceptance overall.

At the same time, laws and executive orders deliberately targeting transgender people (such as bathroom or military service bans) are much more likely to be ruled constitutional if/when a hard-right Supreme Court decides what is, or is not, constitutional. States are much more likely to file anti-transgender bills once one of them has been found constitutional, and thus it would not be unexpected to see even more anti-transgender bills enacted into law going forward.

Final takeaways

For all the progress that has been made, transgender people in the US still have a long way to go before they are fully integrated into our culture. This book was an attempt to provide an intellectual framework with which to understand the challenges and nuances behind them. In conclusion, if you remember nothing else from this book, here are the things you should know about transgender people and their issues.

Transgender people are a natural part of human diversity, and are not new. Archaeological and anthropological evidence clearly shows that gender-variant people have existed throughout human history across cultures.[1369]

Transgender people often face high levels of stigma and discrimination in the US. Studies show that transgender people experience discrimination in employment, housing, education, access to medical care, and other areas of life. This results in high rates of unemployment, poverty, homelessness, and the mental health consequences of minority stress.[1370]

Quality of life for transgender people varies greatly depending where they live. The cultural and legal landscape for transgender people in the US is polarized, and growing more so. Transgender people in areas where they are culturally accepted and legally protected have a substantially better quality of life.

Transgender people are, by definition, not mentally ill. Transgender people are entirely capable of being happy, healthy, functional, and productive while living in their identified gender without further treatment.[1371]

Every major professional medical and mental health organization in the US supports access to affirming care as a medical necessity. This includes the American Medical Association, the American Psychological Association, the American Psychiatric Association, the American Academy of Child and Adolescent Psychiatry, and the American Academy of Family Physicians. They reached these positions after careful consideration of the peer-reviewed evidence.[1372]

Gender identity has biological origins. There is a substantial body of evidence indicating sexual orientation and gender identity have biological origins, and are "hard-wired."[1373]

Gender has both biological and cultural components. Pink and blue do not naturally have a gender, that is, a cultural attribution. At the same time, there are biological components to both gendered behaviors and gender identity.[1374]

Efforts to change a person's gender identity are both ineffective and harmful.[1375] Psychiatrists have known this for over 50 years.[1376] No one has demonstrated the effectiveness of any treatment to change people's gender identity. Those claiming such treatments exist are the same religiously motivated people who promoted similar (and equally ineffective) "ex-gay" treatments.

People very rarely regret transitioning. Regret rates are only about 1–2 percent, which is much lower than most other medical procedures.[1377] Many of the small number of people who regret transition do so because they were subjected to abuse, discrimination, and stigma after they came out. Access to medical care improves quality of life.[1378] Thus, preventing everyone from transitioning out of exaggerated caution against regret will harm far more people than it helps.

Poor mental health outcomes for transgender people are primarily due to minority stress. Transgender people are subjected to stigma, discrimination, isolation, and abuse that affects their mental health. Reducing exposure to these environmental factors produces healthier, happier people.

Accepting and supporting a transgender youth in their gender identity is the best thing you can do for them. Numerous recent peer-reviewed studies show that transgender youth who are supported in their gender identity by parents, schools, and their peers have significantly better mental health outcomes than those whose identities are rejected or stigmatized.[1379] [1380] [1381] Rejection includes efforts to change their gender identity, coercing them into suppressing it, or rejecting it altogether.

It's important to be a skeptical consumer of information on transgender people. Right-wing organizations, such as the Family Research Council, Heritage Foundation, and Alliance Defending Freedom, are spending a great deal of time and effort generating misinformation about transgender people using questionable sources, misinterpreted data, and omission of critical information. Always be aware of who is generating information, and look into it if it contradicts the positions of mainstream organizations such as the American Medical Association or the American Psychological Association.

Transgender people have made tremendous legal gains over the past decade, but those could disappear quickly. At the district and circuit court level there is near unanimous opinion that discrimination against transgender people is a form of sex discrimination, which is impermissible under the Equal Protection Clause of the Constitution, the Civil Rights Act, and Title IX of the Education Amendments of 1972. However, the Supreme Court has not yet ruled on this, nor on whether religious freedom laws allow religious-based discrimination to override these decisions and laws specifically protecting transgender people. Such cases are almost certain to be heard in the next decade. Given the expected composition of the court going forward, transgender civil rights are likely to be undermined for decades to come.

Transgender people will continue to be a political dog whistle for the foreseeable future. The people who care most about transgender issues, aside from transgender people themselves, are white evangelicals.[1382] This group is the political base of the Republican Party, and will continue to be for some time.[1383] As such, transgender issues will continue to be pushed to the forefront as part of what they see as an issue central to a culture war.

The Bible has very little to say about transgender people. This wasn't one of the hot-button issues in either the Old Testament or the New. Most arguments about transgender people revolve around using the single phrase "God made man and woman" as proof of a binary, which then requires logical contortions to retroactively acknowledge the reality of intersex people.

Acceptance of transgender people will continue to increase, despite opposition by evangelicals and the Catholic Church. White evangelicals are declining as a percentage of the US population, as are Catholics.[1384] Most Catholics disagree with the Church anyway on social issues such as birth control, same-sex marriage, and transgender people. The "Nones" are the fastest-growing religious demographic in the US, and are socially progressive on transgender issues.[1385]

There is no valid reason to ban transgender people from the military. The Pentagon spent years developing a policy, and then another six months re-examining it. The RAND Corporation looked at transgender people in the military as well.[1386] All of them found that the costs and effects on readiness were insignificant. Secretary of Defense Mattis supported the inclusive policy, and the DOD was not consulted on the matter prior to President Trump's tweets. The attempt to institute a ban was based on efforts by the Family Research Council, a religious-based anti-LGBT hate group, and not on any sort of actual policy analysis.[1387]

Transgender people need better representation in the media. While positive and accurate portrayals of transgender people have increased in recent years, they were most often portrayed as sex workers, serial killers, drug addicts, or as human wreckage for comedic purposes. The idea of having a transgender person as a romantic partner is treated as disgusting. Frequently the actors playing transgender people are cisgender, and their characters fall into the "pathetic-trans" stereotype. These portrayals contribute to the stigma and discrimination actual transgender people face in their daily lives.

Transgender issues are feminist issues. Some of the greatest issues facing transgender people are ones that are central to feminism in general: bodily autonomy, access to health care, and pushing back against gendered stereotypes for how people should behave and express themselves based on their sex. Transgender people are pushing back against the same patriarchal power structures that cisgender women are.

The path for transgender people over the next few decades is likely to be an arduous one in the face of a hostile legal and political climate. The most important thing you can do as a transgender person, or as an ally, is to arm yourself with knowledge and a commitment to make a difference. Hopefully, this book has contributed to both.

AFTERWORD

Kryss Shane

In the time between when I began to work with Brynn on this book and when I sat to write this afterword, I have spent significant time debating whether I was the right person to contribute my thoughts on a book about transgender people, written by a transgender person. As a white cisgender heterosexual woman, is there room for my voice in this conversation? Should there be?

Now that transgender people are on magazine covers and appear on television shows, it can be easy for majority people to saunter in and try to take over the narrative about what "transgender" means. As is often the case, it can be convenient for someone in the majority to show up when the work is almost done and to then claim the victory as their own. I didn't want to be that person and I certainly didn't want to tell you to be that person either.

But we're not there yet. We're not at the point where anyone can claim victory regarding transgender acceptance or equality. Instead, we are at a watershed moment. More people than ever before have heard the word "transgender" or know someone who is transgender. For some, this means an increased acceptance into mainstream. Other instead see acceptance of transgender people as the literal end of the world. It is overwhelming to think that no one person can fight such ignorance.

The good news, however, is that no one must fight alone. As you've probably realized as you read this book and seen within the footnotes

Brynn, and so many others, wear transgender superhero capes every day. In fact, most transgender people are fighting the good fight.

Every day.

Every.

Single.

Day.

Now, more than ever, is the time when those born into the privilege of being a member of a majority group need to show up. Because this isn't a "transgender issue." It isn't a "well they're only a small percentage of the population issue." It is a human rights issue. It is an all of us issue.

If you're like me, you've finished reading this book and all you want to do now is gather *en masse* and take to the streets. Instead, we must be careful and intentional. As majority members, our voices, our faces, and our names may be what gets shown in the media. This isn't because there aren't great activists who are transgender, but because the discrimination against transgender people continues even when talking about who should be heard.

We must be mindful of the bias when discussing the ways in which the transgender need us. We need to learn to be one of the crowd rather than one with a megaphone. We need to step back when the news crews arrive to center transgender leaders. We also need to step up. Whether it is an ignorant politician or a transphobic conversation in a restaurant, we may be the only ones in a position to speak up effectively.

It can be a difficult line to find between knowing when to step back and when to step up. If you're not sure what to do, ask. Ask the transgender leaders in your community how you can help... and then listen to them. Too often, well-meaning "saviors" get excited and try to do something other than what is asked of them, which further marginalizes transgender voices on their own issues.

If you were new to the needs of transgender people when you read this book, I have little doubt that you feel the fire in your belly to do something. If this isn't your first rodeo, but have learned new things or refreshed your knowledge, I have no doubt that you want to do even more. Let me to validate your feelings by sharing with you that it was tough for Brynn and me to work on this book. Every sentence, every source read and used, and every completed chapter tried to call us away from the screen and into yet another fight for transgender people.

The reality though is that this is not one battle for transgender acknowledgement, affirmation, and acceptance. It is a war, full of daily battles. Some people have been on the front lines of this war for decades, and it is exhausting. Spewing ignorance and hate requires little effort, writing and research like this book are hard, which is why it is so easy to find the former and so hard to find the latter. Activists like Brynn juggle careers, volunteer work, families, friends and even hobbies that pull them away from the work of trudging through the endless bog of transphobia. Our only path to victory is to support ourselves and each other. Therefore, self-care is vital.

Years ago, when I was in my high school choir, one of the songs had an incredibly long note. At first, we all tried to hold that note, but we soon realized that were producing a sound that started loudly and trailed off from lack of breath. Then, our instructor taught us about staggered breathing. The idea is that a few people take a breath at a time while the others sing to keep the sound full. In the same way, we must learn to stagger our activism too. We cannot risk starting loud and ending in a whimper because no one wanted to stop and breathe.

For all the reasons that Brynn felt compelled to write this book and I felt compelled to work on it, we know that the road before us is long. We also know that sleeping enough, eating healthy foods, exercising, and finding time to reflect, to relax, and to enjoy ourselves is vital for any person to heal and to grow stronger. To reach the finish line, we all need to make the time to do these things for ourselves, as well as encouraging others to engage in the same self-care. We need to recognize that when one person steps back for a bit, another will step forward.

At the end of the day, we are each just one person. But so was Gandhi.

So was Harvey Milk. So is Jazz Jennings. so are the 1.4 million transgender people fighting to build a more survivable world. We may feel as if we are in the battle alone because sometimes we are the only one who speaks up against transphobic rhetoric at the next table in a restaurant or at the water cooler at work. Focusing on being "just one" while there are noisy, nasty, and very vocal opposition groups can entice us to quit. However, they represent a smaller and smaller portion of society.

I know it is hard to imagine being one tiny little you taking on hordes of enraged people with tiki torches, demanding to turn our world back to a time when transgender people were hidden away, too fearful to ever come out, let alone to come out and be proud of who they were. So, I will make you this offer; if you ever want to march, to speak, to write, or to otherwise stand on your transgender inclusion soapbox, you'll have me. And Brynn. And the parents of transgender kids. And everyone else fighting for transgender people. And in turn, you will be there for them.

I look forward to continuing to open minds and hearts alongside you, and I am happy to keep singing whenever any of you need to take a breath.

~ Kryss Shane

BS Human Development, MS Education,

MSW, LSW, LMSW

ENDNOTES

1 Transgender Law Center. (2013). *Model Transgender Employment Policy: Negotiating for Inclusive Workplaces*. Retrieved from http://transgenderlawcenter.org/wp-content/uploads/2013/12/model-workplace-employment-policy-Updated.pdf

2 Saraswat, A., Weinand, J., & Safer, J. (2015). Evidence supporting the biologic nature of gender identity. *Endocrine Practice*, 21(2), 199–204. doi:10.4158/ep14351.ra

3 Todd, B. K., Fischer, R. A., Costa, S. D., Roestorf, A., *et al.* (2017). Sex differences in children's toy preferences: A systematic review, meta-regression, and meta-analysis. *Infant and Child Development*. doi:10.1002/icd.2064

4 Via Department of Labor guidelines

5 GLAAD Media Reference Guide—Transgender. (2017, April 19). Retrieved January 13, 2018, from www.glaad.org/reference/transgender

6 Retrieved September 12, 2018, from https://www.psychiatry.org/File%20Library/Psychiatrists/Practice/DSM/APA_DSM-5-Gender-Dysphoria.pdf

7 American Psychiatric Association. (2013). *Gender Dysphoria Fact Sheet: DSM-5*. Arlington, VA: Author. Retrieved July 6, 2018, from www.dsm5.org/Documents/Gender%20Dysphoria%20Fact%20Sheet.pdf

8 Bakker, J. (2014). Sex differentiation: Organizing effects of sex hormones, gender dysphoria and disorders of sex development. *Focus on Sexuality Research*, 3–23

9 Winneke, G., Ranft, U., Wittsiepe, J., Kasper-Sonnenberg, M., *et al.* (2013). Behavioral sexual dimorphism in school-age children and early developmental exposure to dioxins and PCBs: A follow-up study of the Duisburg Cohort. *Environmental Health Perspectives*, 122(3), 292–298

10 Chung, W. C. & Auger, A. P. (2013). Gender differences in neurodevelopment and epigenetics. *Pflugers Archiv*, 465(5), 573–584

11 Via Department of Labor guidelines

12 Genderqueer and gender non-binary refer to a person who does not subscribe to conventional gender distinctions but identifies with neither, both, or a combination of male and female genders. Gender fluid refers to a person who does not identify themselves as having a fixed gender. Agender can be literally translated as "without gender." It can be seen either as a non-binary gender identity or as a statement of not having a gender identity

13 Walker, B. (1988). *The Woman's Dictionary of Symbols and Sacred Objects*. San Francisco, CA: HarperCollins, p173

14 Gifford, E. S. (1958). *The Evil Eye*. New York, NY: Macmillan, p42

15 Crawley, E. (1960). *The Mystic Rose, vol. I*. New York, NY: Meridian Books, p319

16 Gaster, T. (1969). *Myth, Legend and Custom in the Old Testament*. New York, NY: Harper & Row, p317

17 Frazer, Sir J. G. (1922). *The Golden Bough*. New York, NY: Macmillan, pp403–409

18 Briffault, R. (1927). *The Mothers, vol. 3*. New York, NY: Macmillan, p372

19 Matthew 19:12. "For there are some eunuchs who were so born from their mother's womb, and there are some eunuchs who were made eunuchs by men, and there are eunuchs who have made themselves eunuchs for the Kingdom of Heaven's sake. He that is able to receive it, let him receive it"

20 Schmidt, A. (2016). Being "Like a woman": Fa'afāfine and Samoan masculinity. *The Asia Pacific Journal of Anthropology*. https://doi.org/10.1080/14442213.2016.1182208

21 Dallas Voice. (2011, April 8). Trans history unearthed in Prague, but existence of LGBTs in early cultures should be no surprise. Retrieved March 17, 2018, from www.dallasvoice.com/trans-history-unearthed-prague-existence-transgenders-early-cultures-surprise-1071599.html

22 Flores, A. R., Herman, J. L., Gates, G. J., & Brown, T. N. (2016). *How Many Adults Identify as Transgender in the United States?* [Scholarly project]. The Williams Institute at UCLA Law School. Retrieved December 18, 2017, from http://williamsinstitute.law.ucla.edu/wp-content/uploads/How-Many-Adults-Identify-as-Transgender-in-the-United-States.pdf

23 Human Rights Campaign. (2016, January 28). Cities and counties with non-discrimination ordinances that include gender identity. Retrieved July 6, 2018, from www.hrc.org/resources/cities-and-counties-with-non-discrimination-ordinances-that-include-gender

24 Grant, J. M., Mottet, L. A., Tanis, J., Harrison, J., Herman, J. L., & Keisling, M. (2011). *Injustice at Every Turn: A Report of the National Transgender Discrimination Survey*. Washington, DC: National Center for Transgender Equality & National Gay and Lesbian Task Force. Retrieved July 6, 2018, from http://endtransdiscrimination.org/PDFs/NTDS_Report.pdf

25 James, S. E., Herman, J. L., Rankin, S., Keisling, M., Mottet, L., & Anafi, M. (2016). *The Report of the 2015 U.S. Transgender Survey*. Washington, DC: National Center for Transgender Equality

26 National Center for Transgender Equality. (2015). ID Documents Center. Retrieved July 6, 2018, from www.transequality.org/documents

27 *Lusardi v. McHugh*. EEOC Appeal No. 0120133395 (April 1, 2015)

28 Grant, J. M., Mottet, L. A., Tanis, J., Harrison, J., Herman, J. L., & Keisling, M. (2011). *Injustice at Every Turn: A Report of the National Transgender Discrimination Survey*. Washington, DC: National Center for Transgender Equality & National Gay and Lesbian Task Force. Retrieved July 6, 2018, from http://endtransdiscrimination.org/PDFs/NTDS_Report.pdf

29 Tannehill, B. (2012, August 15). An interesting hypothesis. Retrieved July 6, 2018, from http://queermentalhealth.org/article/an-interesting-hypothesis

30 Think Progress. (2013, February 26). Family Research Council: Transgender people need therapy, not nondiscrimination protections. Retrieved July 6, 2018, from https://thinkprogress.org/family-research-council-transgender-people-need-therapy-not-nondiscrimination-protections-e9cb0e4c5dc1#.eg985933r

31 Gallagher, M. (2009, May 27). Redefining religious liberty. Retrieved July 6, 2018, from https://web.archive.org/web/20100809220727/http://article.nationalreview.com/395223/redefining-religious-liberty/maggie-gallagher

32 Card, O. S., (2004, February 15). Homosexual "marriage" and civilization. Retrieved July 6, 2018, from www.ornery.org/essays/warwatch/2004-02-15-1.html

33 Coleman, E., Bockting, W., Botzer, M., Cohen-Kettenis, P., *et al.* (2011). Standards of care for the health of transsexual, transgender, and gender nonconforming people, 7th version. *International Journal of Transgenderism*, 13, 165–232

34 Professional organization statements supporting transgender people in health care. (2016, May 25). Compiled by Lambda Legal. Retrieved July 6, 2018, from www.lambdalegal.org/sites/default/files/publications/downloads/ll_trans_professional_statements.rtf_.pdf

35 Vries, A. L., Steensma, T. D., Doreleijers, T. A., & Cohen-Kettenis, P. T. (2011). Puberty suppression in adolescents with gender identity disorder: A prospective follow-up study. *The Journal of Sexual Medicine*, 8(8), 2276–2283. doi:10.1111/j.1743-6109.2010.01943.x

36 Tannehill, B. (2015). *Six Reasons for Pessimism in the LGBT Movement*. Bilerico Report/LGBTQ Nation. Retrieved July 6, 2018, from http://bilerico.lgbtqnation.com/2015/01/six_reasons_for_pessimism_in_the_lgbt_movement.php

37 Tannehill, B. (2015). *Six Reasons for Pessimism in the LGBT Movement*. Bilerico Report/LGBTQ Nation. Retrieved July 6, 2018, from http://bilerico.lgbtqnation.com/2015/01/six_reasons_for_pessimism_in_the_lgbt_movement.php

38 Nearly one-third of Trump's judicial nominees have anti-LGBT records, Lambda Legal reveals in new analysis documenting record speed with which Trump is reshaping the courts. (2017, December 20). Retrieved March 18, 2018, from www.lambdalegal.org/news/dc_20171220_nearly-one-third-of-judicial-noms

39 Signorile, M. (2016). Trump's Cabinet: A who's who of homophobia. The Boston Globe. BostonGlobe.com. Retrieved July 6, 2018, from www.bostonglobe.com/opinion/2016/12/15/trump-cabinet-who-who-homophobia/9UDr8MnXIQAxjO369qzT0J/story.html

40 Lopez, G. (2017). Trump judicial nominee: I discriminate against gay people, and trans kids are part of "Satan's plan." Vox. Retrieved July 6, 2018, from www.vox.com/identities/2017/10/19/16504104/trump-jeff-mateer-lgbtq

41 Johnson, C. (2017). Senate Dems blast HHS appointee's anti-LGBT "bigoted statements." Washington Blade: Gay News, Politics, LGBT Rights. Retrieved July 6, 2018, from www.washingtonblade.com/2017/04/10/senate-dems-decry-anti-lgbt-bigoted-statements-hhs-appointee

42 Somashekhar, S., Brown, E., & Balingit, M. (2017). Trump administration rolls back protections for transgender students. Washington Post. Retrieved July 6, 2018, from www.washingtonpost.com/local/education/trump-administration-rolls-back-protections-for-transgender-students/2017/02/22/550a83b4-f913-11e6-bf01-d47f8cf9b643_story.html?utm_term=.e658b36e0d32

43 Feuer, A. (2017). Justice Department says rights law doesn't protect gays. Retrieved July 6, 2018, from www.nytimes.com/2017/07/27/nyregion/justice-department-gays-workplace.html

44 Savage, C. (2017). In shift, Justice Dept. says law doesn't bar transgender discrimination. Retrieved July 6, 2018, from www.nytimes.com/2017/10/05/us/politics/transgender-civil-rights-act-justice-department-sessions.html?_r=0

45 Barnes, R. (2017). In major Supreme Court case, Justice Dept. sides with baker who refused to make wedding cake for gay couple. Washington Post. Retrieved July 6, 2018, from www.washingtonpost.com/politics/courts_law/in-major-supreme-court-case-justice-dept-sides-with-baker-who-refused-to-make-wedding-cake-for-gay-couple/2017/09/07/fb84f116-93f0-11e7-89fa-bb822a46da5b_story.html?utm_term=.92de6fa52fde

46 Philipps, D. (2017). Judge blocks Trump's ban on transgender troops in military. Retrieved July 6, 2018, from www.nytimes.com/2017/10/30/us/military-transgender-ban.html

47 Margolin, E. (2015). Arkansas clears a new kind of anti-LGBT law. MSNBC. Retrieved July 6, 2018, from www.msnbc.com/msnbc/arkansas-clears-new-kind-anti-lgbt-law

48 Badash, D. (2015). Georgia Senate overwhelmingly passes anti-gay "Religious Freedom" Bill. The New Civil Rights Movement. Retrieved July 6, 2018, from www.thenewcivilrightsmovement.com/davidbadash/georgia_senate_overwhelmingly_passes_anti_gay_religious_freedom_bill

49 Johnson, C. (2017). Mississippi anti-LGBT "religious freedom" law takes effect. Washington Blade: Gay News, Politics, LGBT Rights. Retrieved July 6, 2018, from www.washingtonblade.com/2017/10/10/mississippi-anti-lgbt-religious-freedom-law-takes-effect

50 Texas Legislature Online—84(R) History for HB 2801. (2015). Legis.state.tx.us. Retrieved July 6, 2018, from www.legis.state.tx.us/BillLookup/History.aspx?LegSess=84R&Bill=HB2801

51 Death certificates would reflect gender identity under California bill. (2014, August 27). Retrieved March 18, 2018, from www.reuters.com/article/us-usa-california-transgender/death-certificates-would-reflect-gender-identity-under-california-bill-idUSKBN0GR24720140827

52 R29 Editors. (2015). How does your state rank on "the civil rights issue of our time"? Refinery29.com. Retrieved July 6, 2018, from www.refinery29.com/2015/03/83531/transgender-rights-by-state

53 Ipsos. (2018, January 29). Global attitudes toward transgender people. Retrieved March 12, 2018, from www.ipsos.com/en-us/news-polls/global-attitudes-toward-transgender-people

54 Mapping transgender equality in the United States. (February 2017). The Movement Advancement Project. Retrieved March 12, 2018, from www.lgbtmap.org/file/mapping-trans-equality.pdf

55 Wang, S. (2012). Gerrymanders, Part 1: Busting the both-sides-do-it myth. Election.princeton.edu. Retrieved July 6, 2018, from http://election.princeton.edu/2012/12/30/gerrymanders-part-1-busting-the-both-sides-do-it-myth

56 McBride, S., Durso, L., Gruberg, S., & Hussey, H. (2015). Fact Sheets: Comprehensive Nondiscrimination Protections—Center for American Progress. Retrieved July 6, 2018, from www.americanprogress.org/issues/lgbt/news/2015/03/10/108227/fact-sheets-comprehensive-nondiscrimination-protections

57 Right Wing Watch. (2017). Gordon Klingenschmitt. Right Wing Watch. Retrieved July 6, 2018, from www.rightwingwatch.org/people/gordon-klingenschmitt

58 Hill, N. (2015). Kelly Clarkson opens up about massive LGBT fan base: "I just live in this world where people are accepted." Contactmusic.com. Retrieved July 6, 2018, from www.contactmusic.com/kelly-clarkson/news/kelly-clarkson-opens-up-about-massive-lgbt-fan-base-i-just-live-in-this-world-where-people-are-accepted_4617009

59 Shore, J. (2014). The Southern Baptist Convention throws transgender people under the bus. John Shore. Retrieved July 6, 2018, from www.patheos.com/blogs/johnshore/2014/06/the-southern-baptist-convention-throws-transgender-people-under-the-bus

60 Anderson, R. T. (2018). *When Harry Became Sally: Responding to the Transgender Moment*. New York, NY: Encounter Books

61 Duffy, N. (2015). Pope compares transgender people to nuclear weapons. PinkNews. Retrieved July 6, 2018, from www.pinknews.co.uk/2015/02/21/pope-transgender-people-are-like-nuclear-weapons

62 Morabito, S. (2014). Trouble in Transtopia: Murmurs of sex change regret. The Federalist. Retrieved July 6, 2018, from http://thefederalist.com/2014/11/11/trouble-in-transtopia-murmurs-of-sex-change-regret

63 Ford, Z. (2014). Virginia's new policy allowing transgender student athletes bans transgender student athletes. Thinkprogress.org. Retrieved July 6, 2018, from https://thinkprogress.org/virginias-new-policy-allowing-transgender-student-athletes-bans-transgender-student-athletes-1ad493403b40

64 Williams, S. (2012). Rights denied: Tennessee kills gender change bill. Care2 Causes. Care2.com. Retrieved July 6, 2018, from www.care2.com/causes/rights-denied-tennessee-kills-gender-change-bill.html

65 Lurie, J. & Brodey, S. (2015). Get ready for the conservative assault on where transgender Americans pee. Mother Jones. Retrieved July 6, 2018, from www.motherjones.com/politics/2015/03/transgender-bathroom-discrimination-bills

66 Peled, S. (2016). Massachusetts transgender rights bill signed into law. CNN. Retrieved July 6, 2018, from www.cnn.com/2016/07/09/us/massachusetts-governor-transgender-rights/index.html

67 Concern troll: a person who disingenuously expresses concern about an issue with the intention of undermining or derailing genuine discussion

68 Reed, A. N. (2012, November 26). 13 myths and misconceptions about trans women. Retrieved January 13, 2018, from https://everydayfeminism.com/2012/11/13-myths-and-misconceptions-about-trans-women

69 Grant, J. M., Mottet, L. A., Tanis, J., Harrison, J., Herman, J. L., & Keisling, M. (2011). *Injustice at Every Turn: A Report of the National Transgender Discrimination Survey*. Washington, DC: National Center for Transgender Equality and National Gay and Lesbian Task Force. Retrieved July 6, 2018, from www.thetaskforce.org/static_html/downloads/reports/reports/ntds_full.pdf

70 Lambda Legal. (2017). Lambda Legal and OutServe-SLDN sue President Trump to reverse transgender military service ban. Lambda Legal. Retrieved November 13, 2017, from www.lambdalegal.org/blog/20170828_lambda-legal-outserve-sldn-sue-trump-over-trans-military-ban

71 Reed, A. N. (2016, January 22). 13 myths and misconceptions about trans women. Retrieved January 13, 2018, from https://everydayfeminism.com/2012/11/13-myths-and-misconceptions-about-trans-women

72 Doran, W. (2016). Equality NC director: No public safety risks in cities with transgender anti-discrimination rules. @politifact. Retrieved December 15, 2017, from www.politifact.com/north-carolina/statements/2016/apr/01/chris-sgro/equality-nc-director-no-public-safety-risks-cities

73 Stone, M. (2015, August 5). Iowa man tries to marry lawnmower, and fails. Retrieved January 13, 2018, from www.patheos.com/blogs/progressivesecularhumanist/2015/08/iowa-man-tries-to-marry-lawnmower-and-fails

74 Center for Gender Wholeness. (n.d.). Retrieved July 6, 2018, from http://genderwholeness.com/main-cgw-page/gender-wholeness

75 Rivera, C. (2006, June 2). *Ex-Gay Therapist on CNN* [Video file]. Retrieved July 6, 2018, from www.youtube.com/watch?v=jJXWFZz0Qjo&app=desktop

76 Dean, A. (2013, August 19). America Now with Andy Dean. Podcast. Retrieved July 6, 2018, from http://americanowradio.iheart.com/media/podcast-audio-audio/081913-hour-2-23604562

77 Moore, R. D. (2013, August 15). Conservative Christianity and the transgender question. Retrieved September 13, 2018, from https://www.russellmoore.com/2013/08/12/conservative-christianity-and-the-transgender-question

78 American Psychiatric Association. (2013). *Gender Dysphoria Fact Sheet: DSM-5*. Arlington, VA: Author. Retrieved July 6, 2018, from www.dsm5.org/Documents/Gender%20Dysphoria%20Fact%20Sheet.pdf

79 What is gender disruption? (n.d.). Center for Gender Wholeness. Retrieved July 6, 2018, from http://genderwholeness.com/main-cgw-page/gender-wholeness/what-is-gender-disruption

80 *Lusardi v. McHugh*. EEOC Appeal No. 0120133395 (April 1, 2015)

81 Teresa, R. & Imse, E. (2015). *Qualified and Transgender: A Report on Results of Resume Testing for Employment Discrimination Based on Gender Identity*. DC Office of Human Rights. Retrieved July 6, 2018, from http://ohr.dc.gov/sites/default/files/dc/sites/ohr/publication/attachments/QualifiedAndTransgender_FullReport_1.pdf

82 Schilt, K. & Wiswall, M. (2008). Before and after: Gender transitions, human capital, and workplace experiences. *The B.E. Journal of Economic Analysis & Policy*. Volume 8, Issue 1, ISSN (Online) 1935–1682. doi: 10.2202/1935-1682.1862, September 2008

83 Takizawa, R., Maughan, B., & Arseneault, L. (2014). Adult health outcomes of childhood bullying victimization: Evidence from a five-decade longitudinal British birth cohort. *American Journal of Psychiatry*, 171(7), 777–784. doi: 10.1176/appi.ajp.2014.13101401

84 GLAAD. (2015, September 17). Number of Americans who report knowing a transgender person doubles in seven years, according to new GLAAD survey. Retrieved July 6, 2018, from www.glaad.org/releases/number-americans-who-report-knowing-transgender-person-doubles-seven-years-according-new

85 National Coalition of Anti-Violence Programs (NCAVP). (2016). *Lesbian, Gay, Bisexual, Transgender, Queer, and HIV-Affected Hate Violence in 2016*. Retrieved July 6, 2018, from http://avp.org/wp-content/uploads/2017/06/NCAVP_2016HateViolence_REPORT.pdf

86 Ennis, D. (2016, June 2). Queer singles survey reveals divisions on dating, marriage, and kids. Retrieved October 18, 2017, from www.lgbtqnation.com/2016/06/queer-singles-survey-reveals-divisions-dating-marriage-kids

87 O'Neill, N. (2015, October 29). The new way queer people hook up in the American heartland. Retrieved October 18, 2017, from http://gizmodo.com/the-new-way-queer-people-hook-up-in-the-american-heartl-1739240606

88 Edison, A. (2014, December 12). I'm trans and on Tinder, but I am not a fetish for your sexual bucket list. Avery Edison. Retrieved October 18, 2017, from www.theguardian.com/commentisfree/2014/dec/12/trans-tinder-sexual-bucket-list

89 Trans men on Grindr. (n.d.). Retrieved October 18, 2017, from http://transmenongrindr.tumblr.com

90 Adamandeve.com asks: Would you be open to dating someone transgendered? (2016, August 4) Retrieved October 18, 2017, from www.prnewswire.com/news-releases/adamandevecom-asks-would-you-be-open-to-dating-someone-transgendered-300309316.html

91 Mock, J. (2013, September 12). How society shames men dating trans women & how this affects our lives. Retrieved October 18, 2017, from https://janetmock.com/2013/09/12/men-who-date-attracted-to-trans-women-stigma

92 Tannehill, B. (2014, July 3). To those who laughed. Retrieved October 18, 2017, from www.huffingtonpost.com/brynn-tannehill/to-those-who-laughed_b_5555954.html

93 Willis, R. (2015, October 7). The transgender dating dilemma. Retrieved October 18, 2017, from www.buzzfeed.com/raquelwillis/the-transgender-dating-dilemma?utm_term=.wkm8Jpx09#.kxqMAQjpl

94 Daley, E. (2015, December 18). College football player sentenced to life for killing Texas transgender woman. Retrieved October 18, 2017, from www.advocate.com/crime/2015/12/18/college-football-player-sentenced-life-killing-texas-transgender-woman

95 Short, J. M. (2017, August 1). LGBT-transgender disclosure and rape by fraud. Retrieved October 18, 2017, from https://rapebyfraud.com/2016/04/04/19871

96 Morgan, J. (2013, March 7). Man "guilty" of fraud for not telling girlfriend he was trans. Retrieved October 18, 2017, from www.gaystarnews.com/article/man-%E2%80%98guilty%E2%80%99-fraud-not-telling-girlfriend-he-was-trans070313/#gs.avPvPXg

97 Marshall, C. (2005, September 13). Two guilty of murder in death of a transgender teenager. Retrieved October 18, 2017, from www.nytimes.com/2005/09/13/us/two-guilty-of-murder-in-death-of-a-transgender-teenager.html?_r=0

98 Talusan, M. (2015, August 25). The failed logic of "trans panic" criminal defenses. Retrieved October 18, 2017, from www.buzzfeed.com/meredithtalusan/trans-panic-criminal-defense?utm_term=.cg40VjgDa#.ur89zA08X

99 AOL Originals. (2014, October 13). *Not Alone* [Video]. Retrieved July 6, 2018, from www.youtube.com/watch?v=pEikrnjYD6E

100 Herman, J., Haas, A., & Rodgers, P. (2014). Suicide attempts among transgender and gender non-conforming adults. The Williams Institute, UCLA. Retrieved July 6, 2018, from https://escholarship.org/uc/item/8xg8061f

101 Fagerberg, M. (2013, October 27). *Maury Povich—Man? Woman?* Swimsuit segment [Video]. Retrieved July 6, 2018, from www.youtube.com/watch?v=TvqLzYFD2kQ

102 Nichols, J. (2014, January 7). Laverne Cox and Carmen Carrera discuss transgender issues on Katie Couric Show. Retrieved July 6, 2018, from www.huffingtonpost.com/2014/01/07/laverne-cox-carmen-carrera-katie-couric_n_4555080.html

103 CyclopsCyrus. (2009, September 4). Ace Ventura—Einhorn is a man?!? [Video]. Retrieved July 6, 2018, from www.youtube.com/watch?v=alPQgx7SGms&list=PL8924506BF2564B7E

104 Molloy, P. M. (2014, January 3). Anti-LGBT activist links trans people to Satan, calls Robin Roberts "tragic." Retrieved July 6, 2018, from www.advocate.com/politics/media/2014/01/03/anti-lgbt-activist-links-trans-people-satan-calls-robin-roberts-tragic

105 Think Progress. (2011, May 18). Following criticism, FOX News removes transphobic commentary on Chaz Bono's transition. Retrieved July 6, 2018, from https://thinkprogress.org/following-criticism-fox-news-removes-transphobic-commentary-on-chaz-bonos-transition-3c0880b53388#.al6858gx8

106 Garcia, M. (2013, October 17). Former GOP official: Trans people should be "put in a camp." Retrieved July 6, 2018, from www.advocate.com/politics/2013/10/17/former-gop-official-trans-people-should-be-put-camp

107 Bailey, J. M. (2003). *The Man Who Would Be Queen: The Science of Gender-Bending and Transsexualism.* Washington, DC: Joseph Henry Press

108 Dean, A. (2013, August 19). *America Now with Andy Dean.* [Audio]. Retrieved July 6, 2018, from http://americanowradio.iheart.com/media/podcast-audio-audio/081913-hour-2-23604562

109 Morgan, J. (2013, October 17). GOP politician calls trans people "disgusting freaks," should be put in "camps." Retrieved July 6, 2018, from www.gaystarnews.com/article/gop-politician-calls-trans-people-disgusting-freaks-should-be-put-camps171013/#gs.CWAH040

110 Kapp-Klote, H. & Peoples, A. (2016, May 18). Loretta Lynch and the criminalization of trans people. Retrieved July 6, 2018, from www.truth-out.org/opinion/item/36078-loretta-lynch-and-the-criminalization-of-trans-people

111 Akfamilyaction. (2012, March 23). *Steve's Gym* [Video]. Retrieved July 6, 2018, from www.youtube.com/watch?v=o8yoAaVgJVo&list=PLokPP6TxYvVmt-8HbToA-yMGyHVNKF8kT

112 Akfamilyaction. (2012, March 23). DaycareHD.mp4 [Video]. Retrieved July 6, 2018, from www.youtube.com/watch?v=QxqYqY7vwt4&list=PLokPP6TxYvVmt-8HbToA-yMGyHVNKF8kT&index=4

113 Robinson, A. (2014, January 27). Justin Bieber's drag race. Retrieved July 6, 2018, from www.out.com/news-opinion/2014/01/27/justin-biebers-drag-race-troubled-pop-star-looks-girl-funny-right

114 Molloy, P. M. (2014, January 14). CeCe McDonald released from prison, greeted by Laverne Cox. Retrieved July 6, 2018, from www.advocate.com/politics/transgender/2014/01/14/cece-mcdonald-released-prison-greeted-laverne-cox

115 Fishbein, R. (2013, December 6). Lawyer: Murdering a transgender prostitute not such a big deal. Retrieved July 6, 2018, from http://gothamist.com/2013/12/06/lawyer_argues_transgender_murder_vi.php

116 Molloy, P. M. (2014, January 31). Calif. Bill promotes proper identification on trans death certificates. Retrieved July 6, 2018, from www.advocate.com/politics/transgender/2014/01/31/calif-bill-promotes-proper-identification-trans-death-certificates

117 Think Progress. (2014, January 31). Laverne Cox: "Loving trans people is a revolutionary act." Retrieved July 6, 2018, from https://thinkprogress.org/laverne-cox-loving-trans-people-is-a-revolutionary-act-2b79c142ae69#.7p38q5si3

118 *Littleton v. Prange*, 9 S.W.3d 223 (1999)

119 Bergler, E. (1956). *Homosexuality: Disease or Way of Life?* New York, NY: Hill & Wang

120 Spitzer, R. L. (1981). The diagnostic status of homosexuality in DSM-III: A reformulation of the issues. *American Journal of Psychiatry*, 138, 210–215

121 Drescher, J. (2015). Out of DSM: Depathologizing homosexuality. *Behav Sci (Basel)*, 5(4), 565–575

122 Love, S. (2016, July 28). The WHO says being transgender is a mental illness. But that's about to change. Retrieved March 12, 2018, from www.washingtonpost.com/news/morning-mix/wp/2016/07/28/the-w-h-o-says-being-transgender-is-a-mental-illness-but-thats-about-to-change/?utm_term=.e0ff6f9d86d1

123 DSM-IV-TR diagnostic criteria for gender identity disorder. (2003, July 18). Retrieved March 12, 2018, from https://psychnews.psychiatryonline.org/doi/10.1176/pn.38.14.0032

124 Ehrensaft, D., Giammattei, S. V., Storck, K., Tishelman, A. C., & Keo-Meier, C. (2018). Prepubertal social gender transitions: What we know; what we can learn—A view from a gender affirmative lens. *International Journal of Transgenderism*, 1–18. doi:10.1080/15532739.2017.1414649

125 Robles, R., Fresan, A., Vega-Ramírez, H., Cruz-Islas, J. *et al.* (2016). Removing transgender identity from the classification of mental disorders: A Mexican field study for ICD-11. *Lancet Psychiatry*. http://dx.doi.org/10.1016/S2215-0366(16)30165-1.

126 Love, S. (2016, July 28). The WHO says being transgender is a mental illness. But that's about to change. Retrieved March 12, 2018, from www.washingtonpost.com/news/morning-mix/wp/2016/07/28/the-w-h-o-says-being-transgender-is-a-mental-illness-but-thats-about-to-change/?utm_term=.e0ff6f9d86d1

127 Coleman, E., Bockting, W., Botzer, M., & Cohen-Kettenis, P. *et al.* (2011). Standards of care for the health of transsexual, transgender, and gender nonconforming people, 7th version. *International Journal of Transgenderism*, 13, 165–232

128 Coleman, E., *et al.* (2011), Standards of care for the health of transsexual, transgender, and gender nonconforming people, 7th version. *International Journal of Transgenderism*, 13, 165–232

129 Professional organization statements supporting transgender people in health care. (2016, May 25) Compiled by Lambda Legal. Retrieved July 6, 2018, from www.lambdalegal.org/sites/default/files/publications/downloads/ll_trans_professional_statements.rtf_.pdf

130 Murad, M. H., Elamin, M. B., Garcia, M. Z., Mullan, R. J., *et al.* (2010). Hormonal therapy and sex reassignment: A systemic review and meta-analysis of quality of life and psychosocial outcomes. *Clinical Endocrinology*, 72, 214–231, http://dx.doi.org/10.1111/j.1365-2265.2009.03625.x

131 De Cuypere, G., Elaut, E., Heylens, G., Van Maele, G., *et al.* (2006). Long-term follow-up: Psychosocial outcomes of Belgian transsexuals after sex reassignment surgery. *Sexologies*, 15, 126–133. http://dx.doi.org/10.1016/j.sexol.2006.04.002

132 Kuiper, B. & Cohen-Kettenis, P. (1988). Sex reassignment surgery: A study of 141 Dutch transsexuals. *Archives of Sexual Behavior*, 17(5), 439–457. doi:10.1007/bf01542484

133 Gorton, R. N. (2011). The costs and benefits of access to treatment for transgender people. Prepared for the San Francisco Department of Public Health, San Francisco

134 Clements-Nolle, K., Marx, R., & Katz, M. (2006). Attempted suicide among transgender persons: The influence of gender-based discrimination and victimization. *Journal of Homosexuality*, 51, 53–69. http://dx.doi.org/10.1300/J082v51n03_04

135 Grant, J. M., Mottet, L. A., Tanis, J., Harrison, J., Herman, J. L., & Keisling, M. (2011). *Injustice at Every Turn: A Report of the National Transgender Discrimination Survey*. Washington, DC: National Center for Transgender Equality & National Gay and Lesbian Task Force. Retrieved July 6, 2018, from http://endtransdiscrimination.org/PDFs/NTDS_Report.pdf

136 Professional organization statements supporting transgender people in health care. (2016, May 25). Compiled by Lambda Legal. Retrieved July 6, 2018, from www.lambdalegal.org/sites/default/files/publications/downloads/ll_trans_professional_statements.rtf_.pdf

137 Benjamin, H. (1966). *The Transsexual Phenomenon.* New York, NY: Warner Books, p. 54

138 Nichols, J. M. (2016, November 17). A survivor of gay conversion therapy shares his chilling story. Retrieved November 6, 2017, from www.huffingtonpost.com/entry/realities-of-conversion-therapy_us_582b6cf2e4b01d8a014aea66

139 Scot, J. (2013, June 28). Shock the gay away: Secrets of early gay aversion therapy revealed (Photos). Retrieved November 6, 2017, from www.huffingtonpost.com/jamie-scot/shock-the-gay-away-secrets-of-early-gay-aversion-therapy-revealed_b_3497435.html

140 Human Rights Campaign, Policy and Position Statements on Conversion Therapy. Retrieved November 6, 2017, from www.hrc.org/resources/policy-and-position-statements-on-conversion-therapy

141 Benjamin, H. (1966). *The Transsexual Phenomenon.* New York, NY: Warner Books, p. 52

142 Schulson, M., Geer, L., & Maio, H. A. (2017, August 17). Of politics, science, and gender identity: A review of Paul McHugh. Retrieved March 19, 2018, from https://undark.org/article/gender-lgbtq-paul-mchugh-science

143 Professional organization statements supporting transgender people in health care. (2016, May 25). Compiled by Lambda Legal. Retrieved July 6, 2018, from www.lambdalegal.org/sites/default/files/publications/downloads/ll_trans_professional_statements.rtf_.pdf

144 Vincent, N. (2007). *Self-Made Man: One Woman's Year Disguised as a Man.* London: Penguin Group

145 Ramachandran, V. & McGeoch, P. D. (2007). Occurrence of phantom genitalia after gender reassignment surgery. *Medical Hypotheses*, 69(5), 1001–1003. doi:10.1016/j.mehy.2007.02.024

146 Herman, J. L. (2013). Costs and benefits of providing transition-related health care coverage in employee health benefits plans: Findings from a survey of employers. Los Angeles: The Williams Institute. Retrieved September 19, 2016, from https://escholarship.org/uc/item/5z38157s

147 Kime, P. (2017, August 8). DoD spends $84M a year on Viagra, similar meds. Retrieved December 20, 2017, from www.militarytimes.com/pay-benefits/military-benefits/health-care/2015/02/13/dod-spends-84m-a-year-on-viagra-similar-meds

148 Ettner, R., Monstrey, S., & Eyler, A. E. (2007). *Principles of Transgender Medicine and Surgery.* New York, NY: Haworth Press (listing the three categories of reassignment surgeries: genital surgery, breast surgery, and non-genital, non-breast surgeries)

149 WPATH Clarification on Medical Necessity of Treatment, Sex Reassignment, and Insurance Coverage in the USA. (2016, December 21). Retrieved July 6, 2018, from www.wpath.org/media/cms/Documents/Web%20Transfer/Policies/WPATH-Position-on-Medical-Necessity-12-21-2016.pdf

150 See AMA Resolution 122 ("An established body of medical research demonstrates the effectiveness and medical necessity of mental health care, hormone therapy and sex reassignment surgery as forms of therapeutic treatment for many people diagnosed with GID... Health experts in GID, including WPATH, have rejected the myth that such treatments are 'cosmetic' or 'experimental' and have recognized that these treatments can provide safe and effective treatment for a serious health condition")

151 Best, L. & Stein, K. (1998). *Surgical Gender Reassignment for Male to Female Transsexual People.* Development and Evaluation Committee Report No 88. Wessex Institute for Health Research & Development, Southampton

152 *J. D. v. Lackner*, 80 Cal. App. 3d at 95 (requiring coverage for GRS under state Medicaid program)

153 *G. B. v. Lackner*, 80 Cal. App. 3d 64, 71 (Cal. 1st Dist. 1978) (requiring coverage for GRS under state Medicaid program)

154 *Davidson v. Aetna Life & Casualty Insurance Company*, 420 N.Y.S. 2d 450, 452 (N.Y. Sup. Ct. 1979)

155 Id. at 453

156 Grant, J. M., Mottet, L. A., Tanis, J., Harrison, J., Herman, J. L., & Keisling, M. (2011). *Injustice at Every Turn: A Report of the National Transgender Discrimination Survey.* Washington, DC: National Center for Transgender Equality & National Gay and Lesbian Task Force. Retrieved July 6, 2018, from http://endtransdiscrimination.org/PDFs/NTDS_Report.pdf

157 For a nearly comprehensive list of studies on the benefits of medical care for transgender people, see the web page "What Helps?" which describes over 100 peer reviewed studies on the benefits of HRT, social transition, and surgery at www.cakeworld.info/transsexualism/what-helps. Also see "Quality of Life in Treated Transsexuals," an online meta-database of recent studies on outcomes of medical treatment at http://transascity.org/quality-of-life-in-treated-transsexuals

158 Kellaway, M. (2014, March 5). "But how do you know you're a man?": On trans people, narrative and trust. Retrieved July 6, 2018, from www.huffingtonpost.com/mitch-kellaway/but-how-do-you-know-youre-a-man_b_4895756.html

159 FTM top surgery procedures. (n.d.). Retrieved September 20, 2016, from www.topsurgery.net/procedures

160 Djordjevic, M. L., Stanojevic, D., Bizic, M., Kojovic, V., *et al.* (2009). Original research–intersex and gender identity disorders: Metoidioplasty as a single stage sex reassignment surgery in female transsexuals: Belgrade Experience. *The Journal of Sexual Medicine*, 6(5), 1306–1313. doi:10.1111/j.1743-6109.2008.01065.x

161 Gabouev, A., Schultheiss, D., Stief, C., & Jonas, U. (2003). Nikolaj A. Bogoraz (1877–1952): Pioneer of phalloplasty and penile implant surgery. *European Urology Supplements*, 2(1), 125. doi:10.1016/s1569-9056(03)80495-5

162 Por, Y., Tan, B., Hong, S., Chia, S., *et al.* (2003). Use of the scrotal remnant as a tissue-expanding musculocutaneous flap for scrotal reconstruction in Paget's disease. *Annals of Plastic Surgery*, 51(2), 155–160. doi:10.1097/01.sap.0000058501.64655.31

163 Rashid, M. & Tamimy, M. (2013). Phalloplasty: The dream and the reality. *Indian Journal of Plastic Surgery*, 46(2), 283. doi:10.4103/0970-0358.118606

164 Kellaway, M. (2013, June 17). Transgender health insurance coverage (part 1): Ready for reforms. Retrieved July 6, 2018, from www.huffingtonpost.com/mitch-kellaway/transgender-health-insura_b_3447762.html

165 Cotten, T. T. (2012). *Hung Jury: Testimonies of Genital Surgery by Transsexual Men*. Oakland, CA: Transgress Press, p.v

166 FTM genital reconstruction surgery (GRS). (n.d.). Retrieved July 6, 2018, from www.ftmguide.org/grs.html

167 Susan's Place: Misconceptions about phalloplasty. (2012, April 10). Retrieved September 20, 2016, from www.susans.org/forums/index.php?topic=118571.0

168 Cotten, T. T. (2012). *Hung Jury: Testimonies of Genital Surgery by Transsexual Men*. Oakland, CA: Transgress Press, p.6

169 Identity documents & privacy. (n.d.). Retrieved September 19, 2016, from www.transequality.org/issues/identity-documents-privacy

170 Victory! Social Security Administration updates Gender Change Policy. (2013, June 14). Retrieved September 19, 2016, from http://transgenderlawcenter.org/archives/8339

171 Ryan Anderson interview by Tucker Carlson on *Fox News*, March 2, 2018. Retrieved March 19, 2018, from www.youtube.com/watch?v=ejHyceik0dg

172 Rivera, C. (2006, June 2). *Ex-Gay Therapist on CNN* [Video]. Retrieved July 6, 2018, from www.youtube.com/watch?v=jJXWFZz0Qjo&app=desktop

173 Duke, S. (2014, November 11). The transgender con? Many "transgender" people regret switch. Retrieved July 6, 2018, from www.thenewamerican.com/culture/item/19507-the-transgender-con-many-transgender-people-regret-switch

174 Ford, Z. (2018, February 7). "I was enraged to see my story distorted and used": Detransitioners object to anti-transgender book. Retrieved March 19, 2018, from https://thinkprogress.org/detransitioner-ryan-anderson-transgender-25fad9803c2e

175 Morabito, S. (2014, October 29). Why singles rights and same-sex marriage will abolish all marriage. Retrieved July 6, 2018, from http://thefederalist.com/2014/10/29/why-singles-rights-and-same-sex-marriage-will-abolish-all-marriage

176 Cohen-Kettenis, P. T. & Pfäfflin, F. (2003). *Transgenderism and Intersexuality in Childhood and Adolescence: Making Choices*. Thousand Oaks, CA: Sage Publications

177 Kuiper, A. J. and Cohen-Kettenis, P. T. (1998). Gender role reversal among postoperative transsexuals. *International Journal of Transgenderism*, 2, 3. Retrieved July 6, 2018, from www.researchgate.net/publication/270273121_Gender_Role_Reversal_among_Postoperative_Transsexuals

178 Pfafflin, F. & Junge, A. (1998). Sex reassignment: Thirty years of international follow-up studies. A comprehensive review, 1961–1991. *International Journal of Transgenderism*. Retrieved July 6, 2018, from www.researchgate.net/profile/Friedemann_Pfaefflin/publication/299412537_Sex_Reassignment_Thirty_Years_of_International_Follow-up_Studies_after_Sex_Reassignment_Surgery_A_Comprehensive_Review_1961-1991/links/56f527ef08ae81582bf1ed50/Sex-Reassignment-Thirty-Years-of-International-Follow-up-Studies-after-Sex-Reassignment-Surgery-A-Comprehensive-Review-1961-1991

179 Smith, Y. L., Goozen, S. H., Kuiper, A. J., & Cohen-Kettenis, P. T. (2005). Sex reassignment: Outcomes and predictors of treatment for adolescent and adult transsexuals. *Psychological Medicine*, 35(1), 89–99. doi:10.1017/s0033291704002776

180 Dhejne, C., Öberg, K., Arver, S., & Landén, M. (2014). An analysis of all applications for sex reassignment surgery in Sweden, 1960–2010: Prevalence, incidence, and regrets. *Archives of Sexual Behavior*, 43(8), 1535–1545. doi:10.1007/s10508-014-0300-8

181 Krege, S., Bex, A., Lümmen, G., & Rübben, H. (2001). Male-to-female transsexualism: A technique, results and long-term follow-up in 66 patients. *BJU International*, 88(4), 396–402. doi:10.1046/j.1464-410x.2001.02323.x

182 De Cuypere, G., Elaut, E., Heylens, G., Van Maele, G., *et al.* (2006). Long-term follow-up: Psychosocial outcomes of Belgian transsexuals after sex reassignment surgery. *Sexologies*, 15, 126–133. http://dx.doi.org/10.1016/j.sexol.2006.04.002

183 Proceedings of the 17th Annual Congress of the European Society for Sexual Medicine, Copenhagen, Denmark, February 5–7, 2015. *Journal of Sexual Medicine*, 12 Suppl 3, 188–271

184 Dhejne, C., Öberg, K., Arver, S., & Landén, M. (2014). An analysis of all applications for sex reassignment surgery in Sweden, 1960–2010: Prevalence, incidence, and regrets. *Archives of Sexual Behavior*, 43(8), 1535–1545. doi:10.1007/s10508-014-0300-8

185 Dhejne, C., Lichtenstein, P., Boman, M., Johansson, A. L., Långström, N., & Landén, M. (2011). Long-term follow-up of transsexual persons undergoing sex reassignment surgery: Cohort study in Sweden. *PLoS ONE*, 6(2). doi:10.1371/journal.pone.0016885

186 Reddit "Ask Me Anything" interview with Dr. Cecilia Dhejne. Retrieved March 12, 2018, from www.reddit.com/r/science/comments/6q3e8v/science_ama_series_im_cecilia_dhejne_a_fellow_of/#bottom-comments

187 Johansson, A., Sundbom, E., Höjerback, T., & Bodlund, O. (2009). A five-year follow-up study of Swedish adults with gender identity disorder. *Archives of Sexual Behavior*, 39(6), 1429–1437. doi:10.1007/s10508-009-9551-1

188 Dhejne, C., Lichtenstein, P., Boman, M., Johansson, A. L., Långström, N., & Landén, M. (2011). Long-term follow-up of transsexual persons undergoing sex reassignment surgery: Cohort study in Sweden. *PLoS ONE*, 6(2). doi:10.1371/journal.pone.0016885

189 Murad, M. H., Elamin, M. B., Garcia, M. Z., Mullan, R. J., *et al.* (2010). Hormonal therapy and sex reassignment: A systematic review and meta-analysis of quality of life and psychosocial outcomes. *Clinical Endocrinology*, 72(2), 214–231. doi:10.1111/j.1365-2265.2009.03625.x

190 Ainsworth, T. A. & Spiegel, J. H. (2010). Quality of life of individuals with and without facial feminization surgery or gender reassignment surgery. *Quality of Life Research*, 19(7), 1019–1024. doi:10.1007/s11136-010-9668-7

191 Batty, D. (2004, July 30). Sex changes are not effective, say researchers. The Guardian. Retrieved July 6, 2018, from www.theguardian.com/society/2004/jul/30/health.mentalhealth

192 References 9: Sex reassignment surgery helps. Retrieved September 16, 2016, from www.cakeworld.info/transsexualism/what-helps/srs

193 Dhejne, C., Öberg, K., Arver, S., & Landén, M. (2014). An analysis of all applications for sex reassignment surgery in Sweden, 1960–2010: Prevalence, incidence, and regrets. *Archives of Sexual Behavior*, 43(8), 1535–1545. doi:10.1007/s10508-014-0300-8

194 Guller, U., Klein, L. V., & Hagen, J. A. (2009). Safety and effectiveness of bariatric surgery: Roux-en-Y gastric bypass is superior to gastric banding in the management of morbidly obese patients. *Patient Safety in Surgery*, 3(1), 10. doi:10.1186/1754-9493-3-10

195 McNeil, J., Bailey, L., Ellis, S., Morton, J., & Regan, M. (2012). Trans mental health study 2012. Retrieved September 13, 2018, from https://www.gires.org.uk/wp-content/uploads/2014/08/trans_mh_study.pdf

196 Russell, S. (2014, May 27). Bungled boob jobs, crooked noses and painfully botched lipo: Why two thirds of Britons (and Katie Price) say they REGRET having cosmetic surgery. Daily Mail. Retrieved July 6, 2018, from www.dailymail.co.uk/femail/article-2640543/Two-thirds-Britons-REGRET-having-cosmetic-surgery.html

197 Cohen-Kettenis, P. T. & Pfäfflin, F. (2003). *Transgenderism and Intersexuality in Childhood and Adolescence: Making Choices*. Thousand Oaks, CA: Sage Publications

198 Lawrence, A. A. (2003). Factors associated with satisfaction or regret following male-to-female sex reassignment surgery. *Archives of Sexual Behavior*, 32, 299. doi:10.1023/A:1024086814364

199 Landén, M., Wålinder, J., Hambert, G., & Lundström, B. (1998). Factors predictive of regret in sex reassignment. *Acta Psychiatrica Scandinavica*, 97(4), 284–289. doi:10.1111/j.1600-0447.1998.tb10001.x

200 Smith, Y. L., Goozen, S. H., Kuiper, A. J., & Cohen-Kettenis, P. T. (2005). Sex reassignment: Outcomes and predictors of treatment for adolescent and adult transsexuals. *Psychological Medicine*, 35(1), 89–99. doi:10.1017/s0033291704002776

201 Lawrence, A. A. (2003). Factors associated with satisfaction or regret following male-to-female sex reassignment surgery. *Archives of Sexual Behavior*, 32, 299. doi:10.1023/A:1024086814364

202 Perovic, S. V., Stanojevic, D. S., & Djordjevic, M. L. (2005). Vaginoplasty in male to female transsexuals using penile skin and urethral flap. *International Journal of Transgenderism*, 8(1), 43–64. doi:10.1300/j485v08n01_05

203 Jarolím, L., Šedý, J., Schmidt, M., Naňka, O., Foltán, R., & Kawaciuk, I. (2009). Original research—intersex and gender identity disorders: Gender reassignment surgery in male-to-female transsexualism: A retrospective 3-month follow-up study with anatomical remarks. *The Journal of Sexual Medicine*, 6(6), 1635–1644. doi:10.1111/j.1743-6109.2009.01245.x

204 Wu, J., Li, B., Li, W., Jiang, Y., Liang, J., & Zhong, C. (2009). Laparoscopic vaginal reconstruction using an ileal segment. *International Journal of Gynecology & Obstetrics*, 107(3), 258–261. doi:10.1016/j.ijgo.2009.07.009

205 Professional organization statements supporting transgender people in health care. (2016, May 25). Compiled by Lambda Legal. Retrieved July 6, 2018, from www.lambdalegal.org/sites/default/files/publications/downloads/ll_trans_professional_statements.rtf_.pdf

206 Coleman, E., Bockting, W., Botzer, M., Cohen-Kettenis, P., *et al.* (2011). Standards of care for the health of transsexual, transgender, and gender nonconforming people, 7th version. *International Journal of Transgenderism*, 13, 165–232

207 Martin, C. & Ruble, D. (2004). Children's search for gender cues: Cognitive perspectives on gender development. *Current Directions in Psychological Science*, 13(2), 67–70

208 Chung, W. C. & Auger, A. P. (2013). Gender differences in neurodevelopment and epigenetics. *Pflügers Archiv: European Journal of Physiology*, 465(5), 573–584. doi:10.1007/s00424-013-1258-4

209 Karaismailoglu, S. & Erdem, A. (2013). The effects of prenatal sex steroid hormones on sexual differentiation of the brain. *Journal of the Turkish German Gynecological Association*, 14(3), 163–167. doi:10.5152/jtgga.2013.86836

210 Kerlin, S. (2005). Prenatal exposure to diethylsilbestrol (DES) in males and gender disorders: Results from a 5-year study. Paper prepared for International Behavioral Development Symposium 2005

211 Maines, W. (2016, July 20). Father of trans teen: I left the GOP for my daughter's sake. Retrieved February 8, 2018, from http://time.com/4415598/republican-father-lgbt-rights

212 Bao, A. & Swaab, D. F. (2010). Sex differences in the brain, behavior, and neuropsychiatric disorders. *The Neuroscientist*, 16(5), 550–565. doi:10.1177/1073858410377005

213 Bronstein, S. (2011, June 10). Therapy to change "feminine" boy created a troubled man, family says. Retrieved February 8, 2018, from www.cnn.com/2011/US/06/07/sissy.boy.experiment/index.html

214 Burroway, J. (2011, June 7). What are little boys made of? Box Turtle Bulletin. Retrieved July 6, 2018, from www.boxturtlebulletin.com/what-are-little-boys-made-of-main

215 David Reimer. (2017). En.wikipedia.org. Retrieved November 13, 2017, from https://en.wikipedia.org/wiki/David_Reimer

216 David Reimer. (2017). En.wikipedia.org. Retrieved November 13, 2017, from https://en.wikipedia.org/wiki/David_Reimer

217 Herman, J., Haas, A., & Rodgers, P. (2014). Suicide attempts among transgender and gender non-conforming adults. The Williams Institute, UCLA. Retrieved July 6, 2018, from https://escholarship.org/uc/item/8xg8061f

218 Food and Drug Administration (FDA). (July 2009). Lupron Depot-Ped (leuprolide acetate for depot suspension) injection, powder, lyophilized, for suspension. Retrieved September 20, 2016, from www.accessdata.fda.gov/drugsatfda_docs/label/2010/020263s035lbl.pdf

219 National Library of Medicine—Medical Subject Headings. (1999, January 1). Puberty, Precocious. Retrieved September 20, 2016, from www.nlm.nih.gov/cgi/mesh/2011/MB_cgi?mode=&term=precocious+puberty. "Development of SEXUAL MATURATION in boys and girls at a chronological age that is 2.5 standard deviations below the mean age at onset of PUBERTY in the population. This early maturation of the hypothalamic-pituitary-gonadal axis results in sexual precocity, elevated serum levels of GONADOTROPINS and GONADAL STEROID HORMONES such as ESTRADIOL and TESTOSTERONE"

220 Food and Drug Administration (FDA). (August 2011). Lupron Depot-Ped (leuprolide acetate) injection label. Retrieved September 20, 2016, from www.accessdata.fda.gov/drugsatfda_docs/label/2011/020263s036lbl.pdf

221 Wylie, C., Hembree, P., Cohen-Kettenis, T., Gooren, L., *et al.* (2017). Endocrine treatment of gender-dysphoric/gender-incongruent persons: An Endocrine Society clinical practice guideline. *The Journal of Clinical Endocrinology & Metabolism*, 102(11), November 1, 2017, 3869–3903. https://doi.org/10.1210/jc.2017-01658

222 Wylie, C., Hembree, P., Cohen-Kettenis, T., Gooren, L., *et al.* (2017). Endocrine treatment of gender-dysphoric/gender-incongruent persons: An Endocrine Society clinical practice guideline. *The Journal of Clinical Endocrinology & Metabolism*, 102(11), November 1, 2017, 3869–3903. https://doi.org/10.1210/jc.2017-01658

223 Wylie, C., Hembree, P., Cohen-Kettenis, T., Gooren, L., *et al.* (2017). Endocrine treatment of gender-dysphoric/gender-incongruent persons: An Endocrine Society Clinical Practice guideline. *The Journal of Clinical Endocrinology & Metabolism*, 102(11), November 1, 2017, 3869–3903. https://doi.org/10.1210/jc.2017-01658

224 Olson, K. R., Durwood, L., Demeules, M., & McLaughlin, K. A. (2016). Mental health of transgender children who are supported in their identities. *Pediatrics*, 137(3). doi:10.1542/peds.2015-3223

225 Spack, N. (April 2014). How I help transgender teens become who they want to be [Transcript]. Retrieved September 20, 2016, from www.ted.com/talks/norman_spack_how_i_help_transgender_teens_become_who_they_want_to_be/transcript

226 Zinck, S. & Pignatiello, A. (2015). External review of the Gender Identity Clinic of the Child, Youth, and Family Services in the Underserved Populations Program at the Centre for Addiction and Mental Health. Prepared for the Underserved Populations Program at CAMH, Ontario, November 26, 2015

227 Vries, A. L., Steensma, T. D., Doreleijers, T. A., & Cohen-Kettenis, P. T. (2011). Puberty suppression in adolescents with gender identity disorder: A prospective follow-up study. *The Journal of Sexual Medicine*, 8(8), 2276–2283. doi:10.1111/j.1743-6109.2010.01943.x

228 Vries, A. L., Steensma, T. D., Doreleijers, T. A., & Cohen-Kettenis, P. T. (2011). Puberty suppression in adolescents with gender identity disorder: A prospective follow-up study. *The Journal of Sexual Medicine*, 8(8), 2276–2283. doi:10.1111/j.1743-6109.2010.01943.x

229 Ehrensaft, D., Giammattei, S. V., Storck, K., Tishelman, A. C., & Keo-Meier, C. (2018). Prepubertal social gender transitions: What we know; what we can learn—a view from a gender affirmative lens. *International Journal of Transgenderism*, 1–18. doi:10.1080/15532739.2017.1414649

230 Vries, A. L., McGuire, J. K., Steensma, T. D., Wagenaar, E. C., Doreleijers, T. A., & Cohen-Kettenis, P. T. (2014). Young adult psychological outcome after puberty suppression and gender reassignment. *Pediatrics*, 134(4), 696–704. doi:10.1542/peds.2013-2958

231 Olson-Kennedy, J., Warus, J., Okonta, V., Belzer, M., & Clark, L. F. (March 2018). Chest reconstruction and chest dysphoria in transmasculine minors and young adults. *JAMA Pediatrics*. doi:10.1001/jamapediatrics.2017.5440

232 Communications via email correspondence with Dr. Keo-Meier. Available on request

233 Dreger, A. (2015, June 4). The big problem with outlawing gender conversion therapies. Retrieved September 20, 2016, from www.wired.com/2015/06/big-problem-outlawing-gender-conversion-therapies

234 O'Leary, D. & Sprigg, P. (2015). Understanding and responding to the transgender movement. Retrieved September 20, 2016, from http://downloads.frc.org/EF/EF15F45.pdf

235 Mayer, L. & McHugh, P. (2016). Sexuality and gender: Findings from the biological, psychological, and social sciences. *The New Atlantis*, Number 50, Fall 2016, 4–6

236 Steensma, T. D., Biemond, R., Boer, F. D., & Cohen-Kettenis, P. T. (2011). Desisting and persisting gender dysphoria after childhood: A qualitative follow-up study. *Clinical Child Psychology and Psychiatry*, 16(4), 499–516. doi:10.1177/1359104510378303

237 Wallien, M. S. C. & Cohen-Kettenis, P. T. (2008). Psychosexual outcome of gender-dysphoric children. *Journal of the American Academy of Child and Adolescent Psychiatry*, 47, 1413–1423

238 Winters, K. (2014, February 14). Methodological questions in childhood gender identity "desistence" research. Presented at the 23rd World Professional Association for Transgender Health Biennial Symposium. Retrieved September 20, 2016, from https://gidreform.wordpress.com/2014/02/25/methodological-questions-in-childhood-gender-identity-desistence-research

239 Ehrensaft, D., Giammattei, S. V., Storck, K., Tishelman, A. C., & Keo-Meier, C. (2018). Prepubertal social gender transitions: What we know; what we can learn—a view from a gender affirmative lens. *International Journal of Transgenderism*, 1–18. doi:10.1080/15532739.2017.1414649

240 Steensma, T. D., McGuire, J. K., Kreukels, B. P., Beekman, A. J., & Cohen-Kettenis, P. T. (2013). Factors associated with desistence and persistence of childhood gender dysphoria: A quantitative follow-up study. *Journal of the American Academy of Child & Adolescent Psychiatry*, 52(6), 582–590. doi:10.1016/j.jaac.2013.03.016

241 Olson, K. R., Key, A. C., & Eaton, N. R. (2015). Gender cognition in transgender children. *Psychological Science*, 26(4), 467–474. doi:10.1177/0956797614568156

242 Summary of the External Review of the CAMH Gender Identity Clinic of the Child, Youth & Family Services. (January 2016). Retrieved September 21, 2016, from www.camh.ca/en/hospital/about_camh/newsroom/news_releases_media_advisories_and_backgrounders/current_year/Documents/GIC-Review-26Nov2015.pdf

243 Dreger, A. (2015, December 19). Gender mad. Retrieved September 21, 2016, from http://alicedreger.com/gendermad (confirming by a friend of Dr. Zucker that he was fired, rather than resigned or retired)

244 CAMH to "wind down" gender identity clinic after review of services. (2015, December 15). Retrieved September 21, 2016, from www.cbc.ca/news/canada/toronto/camh-gender-identity-1.3366424

245 Ibid.

246 Zucker, K. J., Bradley, S. J., Sullivan, C. B. L., Kuksis, M., Birkenfeld-Adams, A., & Mitchell, J. N. (1993). A gender identity interview for children. *Journal of Personality Assessment*, 61, 443–456

247 Family Court of Australia Re: Kelvin (2017) FamCAFC 258. Retrieved March 12, 2018, from www.humanrights.gov.au/sites/default/files/Re%2BKelvin%2B30%2BNovember%2B2017.pdf

248 Lowder, B. (2014, December 31). Listen to Leelah Alcorn's final words. Retrieved September 22, 2016, from www.slate.com/blogs/outward/2014/12/31/leelah_alcorn_transgender_teen_from_ohio_should_be_honored_in_death.html

249 Tannehill, B. (2014, November 4). A come to Jesus talk on transgender youth. Retrieved September 22, 2016, from www.huffingtonpost.com/brynn-tannehill/a-come-to-jesus-talk-with_b_6100028.html

250 Bauer, G. R., Scheim, A. I., Pyne, J., Travers, R., & Hammond, R. (2015). Intervenable factors associated with suicide risk in transgender persons: A respondent driven sampling study in Ontario, Canada. *BMC Public Health*, 15. doi:10.1186/s12889-015-1867-2

251 Yadegarfard, M., Meinhold-Bergmann, M. E., & Ho, R. (2014). Family rejection, social isolation, and loneliness as predictors of negative health outcomes (depression, suicidal ideation, and sexual risk behavior) among Thai male-to-female transgender adolescents. *Journal of LGBT Youth*, 11(4), 347–363. doi:10.1080/19361653.2014.910483

252 Bauer, G. R., Scheim, A. I., Pyne, J., Travers, R., & Hammond, R. (2015). Intervenable factors associated with suicide risk in transgender persons: A respondent driven sampling study in Ontario, Canada. *BMC Public Health*, 15(1). doi:10.1186/s12889-015-1867-2

253 Simons, L., Schrager, S. M., Clark, L. F., Belzer, M., & Olson, J. (2013). Parental support and mental health among transgender adolescents. *Journal of Adolescent Health*, 53(6), 791–793. doi:10.1016/j.jadohealth.2013.07.019

254 Olson, K., Durwood, L., DeMeules, M., & McLaughlin, K. (2016). Mental health of transgender children who are supported in their identities. *Pediatrics*, 137(3), e20153223

255 Bauer, G. R., Scheim, A. I., Pyne, J., Travers, R., & Hammond, R. (2015). Intervenable factors associated with suicide risk in transgender persons: A respondent driven sampling study in Ontario, Canada. *BMC Public Health*, 15(1). doi:10.1186/s12889-015-1867-2

256 Russell, S. T., Pollitt, A. M., Li, G., & Grossman, A. H. (2018). Chosen name use is linked to reduced depressive symptoms, suicidal ideation, and suicidal behavior among transgender youth. *Journal of Adolescent Health*. doi:10.1016/j.jadohealth.2018.02.003

257 Clements-Nolle, K., Marx, R., & Katz, M. (2006). Attempted suicide among transgender persons. *Journal of Homosexuality*, 51(3), 53–69. doi:10.1300/j082v51n03_04

258 Grant, J. M., Mottet, L. A., Tanis, J., Harrison, J., Herman, J. L., & Keisling, M. (2011). *Injustice at Every Turn: A Report of the National Transgender Discrimination Survey*. Washington, DC: National Center for Transgender Equality & National Gay and Lesbian Task Force. Retrieved July 6, 2018, from http://endtransdiscrimination.org/PDFs/NTDS_Report.pdf

259 Teresa, R. & Imse, E. (2015). *Qualified and Transgender: A Report on Results of Resume Testing for Employment Discrimination Based on Gender Identity*. DC Office of Human Rights. Retrieved July 6, 2018, from http://ohr.dc.gov/sites/default/files/dc/sites/ohr/publication/attachments/QualifiedAndTransgender_FullReport_1.pdf

260 Nuttbrock, L., Hwahng, S., Bockting, W., Rosenblum, A., *et al.* (2010). Psychiatric impact of gender-related abuse across the life course of male-to-female transgender persons. *Journal of Sex Research*, 47(1), 12–23. doi:10.1080/00224490903062258

261 Barboza, G. E., Dominguez, S., & Chance, E. (2016). Physical victimization, gender identity and suicide risk among transgender men and women. *Preventive Medicine Reports*, 4, 385–390. doi:10.1016/j.pmedr.2016.08.003

262 National Coalition of Anti-Violence Programs (NCAVP). (2016). *Lesbian, Gay, Bisexual, Transgender, Queer, and HIV-Affected Hate Violence in 2016*. Retrieved July 6, 2018, from http://avp.org/wp-content/uploads/2017/06/NCAVP_2016HateViolence_REPORT.pdf

263 Herman, J., Haas, A., & Rodgers, P. (2014). Suicide attempts among transgender and gender non-conforming adults. The Williams Institute, UCLA. Retrieved July 6, 2018, from https://escholarship.org/uc/item/8xg8061f

264 Ainsworth, T. A. & Spiegel, J. H. (2010). Quality of life of individuals with and without facial feminization surgery or gender reassignment surgery. *Quality of Life Research*, 19(7), 1019–1024. doi:10.1007/s11136-010-9668-7

265 Capehart, K. (2015, October 19). A perverted campaign against LGBT rights in Houston. The Washington Post. Retrieved September 21, 2016, from www.washingtonpost.com/blogs/post-partisan/wp/2015/10/19/a-perverted-campaign-against-lgbt-rights-in-houston/?utm_term=.ccba74038428

266 Perez-Brumer, A., Hatzenbuehler, M. L., Oldenburg, C. E., & Bockting, W. (2015). Individual- and structural-level risk factors for suicide attempts among transgender adults. *Behavioral Medicine*, 41(3), 164–171. doi:10.1080/08964289.2015.1028322

267 Herman, J., Haas, A., & Rodgers, P. (2014). Suicide attempts among transgender and gender non-conforming adults. The Williams Institute, UCLA. Retrieved July 6, 2018, from https://escholarship.org/uc/item/8xg8061f

268 Perez-Brumer, A., Hatzenbuehler, M. L., Oldenburg, C. E., & Bockting, W. (2015). Individual- and structural-level risk factors for suicide attempts among transgender adults. *Behavioral Medicine*, 41(3), 164–171. doi:10.1080/08964289.2015.1028322

269 *2012 National Strategy for Suicide Prevention: Goals and Objectives for Action: A Report of the U.S. Surgeon General and of the National Action Alliance for Suicide Prevention*. (2012). Washington, DC: US Department of Health and Human Services, Office of the Surgeon General, National Action Alliance for Suicide Prevention

270 Williams, C. (2015). Fact check: Study shows transition makes trans people suicidal. The Transadvocate. Retrieved September 21, 2016, from http://transadvocate.com/fact-check-study-shows-transition-makes-trans-people-suicidal_n_15483.htm

271 Tannehill, B. (2015, December 15). The scary science at Johns Hopkins University. The Advocate. Retrieved September 21, 2016, from www.advocate.com/commentary/2015/12/15/scary-science-johns-hopkins-university

272 Meyer, I. H., Teylan, M., & Schwartz, S. (2014). The role of help-seeking in preventing suicide attempts among lesbians, gay men, and bisexuals. *Suicide and Life-Threatening Behavior*, 45(1), 25–36. doi:10.1111/sltb.12104

273 Hill, D. B., Menvielle, E., Sica, K. M., & Johnson, A. (2010). An affirmative intervention for families with gender variant children: Parental ratings of child mental health and gender. *Journal of Sex & Marital Therapy*, 36(1), 6–23. doi:10.1080/00926230903375560

274 Kuvalanka, K. A., Weiner, J. L., & Mahan, D. (2014). Child, family, and community transformations: Findings from interviews with mothers of transgender girls. *Journal of GLBT Family Studies*, 10(4), 354–379. doi:10.1080/1550428X.2013.834529

275 Ryan, C., Huebner, D., Diaz, R. M., & Sanches, J. (2009). Family rejection as a predictor of negative health outcomes in White and Latino lesbian, gay, and bisexual young adults. *Pediatrics*, 123, 346–352.

276 Travers, R., Bauer, G., Pyne, J., Bradley, K., Gale, L., & Papadimitriou, M. (2012). Impacts of strong parental support for trans youth: A report prepared for Children's Aid Society of Toronto and Delisle Youth Services. Retrieved July 6, 2018, from: http://transpulseproject.ca/wp-content/uploads/2012/10/Impacts-of-Strong-Parental-Support-for-Trans-Youth-vFINAL.pdf

277 Transgender Human Rights Institute. (2015). Enact Leelah's Law to ban transgender conversion therapy. Change.org. Retrieved September 22, 2016, from www.change.org/p/president-of-the-united-states-enact-leelah-s-law-to-ban-transgender-conversion-therapy

278 The lies and dangers of efforts to change sexual orientation or gender identity. (n.d.). Retrieved September 22, 2016, from www.hrc.org/resources/the-lies-and-dangers-of-reparative-therapy

279 Hurley, L. (2016, May 4). US Supreme Court upholds ban on gay conversion therapy. Christian Science Monitor. Retrieved September 22, 2016, from www.csmonitor.com/USA/2015/0504/US-Supreme-Court-upholds-ban-on-gay-conversion-therapy

280 Johnson, C. (2016, March 1). Supreme Court rejects another challenge to "ex-gay" therapy bans. Washington Blade. Retrieved September 22, 2016, from www.washingtonblade.com/2016/03/01/supreme-court-rejects-another-challenge-to-n-j-ex-gay-therapy-ban

281 Brydum, S. (2016, February 24). Groundbreaking complaint asks FTC to ban conversion therapy. The Advocate. Retrieved September 22, 2016, from www.advocate.com/politics/2016/2/24/groundbreaking-federal-complaint-asks-ftc-ban-conversion-therapy

282 Conversion therapy and LGBT youth: Executive summary. Williams Institute at UCLA School of Law. Retrieved March 12, 2018, from https://williamsinstitute.law.ucla.edu/wp-content/uploads/Conversion-Therapy-LGBT-Youth-Jan-2018.pdf

283 Bauer, G. R., Scheim, A. I., Pyne, J., Travers, R., & Hammond, R. (2015). Intervenable factors associated with suicide risk in transgender persons: A respondent driven sampling study in Ontario, Canada. *BMC Public Health*, 15. doi:10.1186/s12889-015-1867-2

284 Ryan, C., Huebner, D., Diaz, R. M., & Sanchez, J. (2009). Family rejection as a predictor of negative health outcomes in White and Latino lesbian, gay, and bisexual young adults. *Pediatrics*, 123(1), 346–352. doi:10.1542/peds.2007-3524

285 Herman, J., Haas, A., & Rodgers, P. (2014). Suicide attempts among transgender and gender non-conforming adults. The Williams Institute, UCLA. Retrieved July 6, 2018, from https://escholarship.org/uc/item/8xg8061f

286 Drescher, J. & Pula, J. (2014). Ethical issues raised by the treatment of gender-variant prepubescent children. *Hastings Center Report*, 44(S4). doi:10.1002/hast.365

287 Family Court of Australia Re: Kelvin (2017) FamCAFC 258. Retrieved March 12, 2018, from www.humanrights.gov.au/sites/default/files/Re%2BKelvin%2B30%2BNovember%2B2017.pdf

288 Swaab, D. & Bao, A. (2013). Sexual differentiation of the human brain in relation to gender-identity, sexual orientation, and neuropsychiatric disorders. *Neuroscience in the 21st Century*, 2973–2998. doi:10.1007/978-1-4614-1997-6_115

289 Email correspondence with author. Available on request

290 Meyer, I. H., Teylan, M., & Schwartz, S. (2014). The role of help-seeking in preventing suicide attempts among lesbians, gay men, and bisexuals. *Suicide and Life-Threatening Behavior*, 45(1), 25–36. doi:10.1111/sltb.12104

291 Meier, C., Mougianis, E., & Mizock, L. (n.d.). Fact Sheet: Gender Diversity and Transgender Identity in Adolescents. APA Division-44. Retrieved September 22, 2016, from www.apadivisions.org/division-44/resources/advocacy/transgender-adolescents.pdf

292 Gelder, M. G. & Marks, I. M. (1969). "Aversion Treatment in Transvestism and Transsexualism." In R. Green & J. Money (eds) *Transsexualism and Sex Reassignment* (pp383–413). Baltimore, MD: Johns Hopkins Press

293 Greenson, R. R. (1964). On homosexuality and gender identity. *International Journal of Psycho-Analysis*, 45, 217–219

294 Cohen-Kettenis, P. T. & Kuiper, A. J. (1984). Transseksualiteit en psychothérapie. *Tijdschrift Voor Psychotherapie*, 10, 153–166

295 Pauly, I. B. (1965). Male psychosexual inversion: Transsexualism: A review of 100 cases. *Archives of General Psychiatry*, 13(2), 172–181

296 Coleman, E., Bockting, W., Botzer, M., Cohen-Kettenis, P., *et al.* (2011). Standards of care for the health of transsexual, transgender, and gender nonconforming people, 7th version. *International Journal of Transgenderism*, 13, 165–232

297 Murad, M. H., Elamin, M. B., Garcia, M. Z., Mullan, R. J., *et al.* (2010). Hormonal therapy and sex reassignment: A systematic review and meta-analysis of quality of life and psychosocial outcomes. *Clinical Endocrinology*, 72(2), 214–231. doi:10.1111/j.1365-2265.2009.03625.x

298 Ainsworth, T. A. & Spiegel, J. H. (2010). Quality of life of individuals with and without facial feminization surgery or gender reassignment surgery. *Quality of Life Research*, 19(7), 1019–1024. doi:10.1007/s11136-010-9668-7

299 Dhejne, C., Lichtenstein, P., Boman, M., Johansson, A. L., Långström, N., & Landén, M. (2011). Long-term follow-up of transsexual persons undergoing sex reassignment surgery: Cohort study in Sweden. *PLoS ONE*, 6(2). doi:10.1371/journal.pone.0016885

300 What causes transsexualism? Retrieved September 16, 2016, from www.cakeworld.info/transsexualism/what-causes

301 Spizzirri, G., Duran, F. L., Chaim-Avancini, T. M., Serpa, M. H., *et al.* (2018). Grey and white matter volumes either in treatment-naïve or hormone-treated transgender women: A voxel-based morphometry study. *Scientific Reports*, 8(1). doi:10.1038/s41598-017-17563-z

302 Moody, O. (2018, March 19). Science pinpoints DNA behind gender identity. The Times. Retrieved March 20, 2018, from www.thetimes.co.uk/edition/news/science-pinpoints-dna-behind-gender-identity-3vmrgrdnv

303 Fernández, R., Esteva, I., Gómez-Gil, E., Rumbo, T., *et al.* (2014). Association study of ERβ, AR, and CYP19A1 genes and MtF transsexualism. *The Journal of Sexual Medicine*, 11(12), 2986–2994. doi:10.1111/jsm.12673

304 Lombardo, F., Toselli, L., Grassetti, D., Paoli, D., *et al.* (2013). Hormone and genetic study in male to female transsexual patients. *Journal of Endocrinological Investigation*, 36, 550–557

305 Cohen-Kettenis, P. T. & Pfäfflin, F. (2003). *Transgenderism and Intersexuality in Childhood and Adolescence: Making Choices*. Thousand Oaks, CA: Sage Publications

306 Kuiper, A. J. & Cohen-Kettenis, P. T. (1998). Gender role reversal among postoperative transsexuals. *International Journal of Transgenderism*, 2(3). Retrieved July 6, 2018, from www.researchgate.net/publication/270273121_Gender_Role_Reversal_among_Postoperative_Transsexuals

307 Pfäfflin, F. & Junge, A. (1998). Sex reassignment: Thirty years of international follow-up studies. A comprehensive review, 1961–1991. *International Journal of Transgenderism*. Retrieved July 6, 2018, from www.researchgate.net/profile/Friedemann_Pfaefflin/publication/299412537_Sex_Reassignment_Thirty_Years_of_International_Follow-up_Studies_after_Sex_Reassignment_Surgery_A_Comprehensive_Review_1961-1991/links/56f527ef08ae81582bf1ed50/Sex-Reassignment-Thirty-Years-of-International-Follow-up-Studies-after-Sex-Reassignment-Surgery-A-Comprehensive-Review-1961-1991

308 Smith, Y. L., Van Goozen, S. H., Kuiper, A. J., & Cohen-Kettenis, P. T. (2005). Sex reassignment: Outcomes and predictors of treatment for adolescent and adult transsexuals. *Psychological Medicine*, 35(1), 89–99

309 Dhejne, C., Öberg, K., Arver, S., & Landén, M. (2014). An analysis of all applications for sex reassignment surgery in Sweden, 1960–2010: Prevalence, incidence, and regrets. *Archives of Sexual Behavior*, 43(8), 1535–1545

310 Krege, S., Bex, A., Lümmen, G., & Rübben, H. (2001). Male-to-female transsexualism: A technique, results and long-term follow-up in 66 patients. *BJU International*, 88(4), 396–402

311 De Cuypere, G., Elaut, E., Heylens, G., Van Maele, G., *et al.* (2006). Long-term follow-up: Psychosocial outcomes of Belgian transsexuals after sex reassignment surgery. *Sexologies*, 15, 126–133. http://dx.doi.org/10.1016/j.sexol.2006.04.002

312 Russell, S. (2014, May 27). Bungled boob jobs, crooked noses and painfully botched lipo: Why two thirds of Britons (and Katie Price) say they REGRET having cosmetic surgery. Daily Mail. Retrieved July 6, 2018, from www.dailymail.co.uk/femail/article-2640543/Two-thirds-Britons-REGRET-having-cosmetic-surgery.html

313 Coleman, E., Bockting, W., Botzer, M., Cohen-Kettenis, P., *et al.* (2011). Standards of care for the health of transsexual, transgender, and gender nonconforming people, 7th version. *International Journal of Transgenderism*, 13, 165–232

314 NJ Rev Stat § 45:1–55 (2014)

315 CA Bus & Prof Code § 865 (2014)

316 Zeigler, C. (2013, October 16). Fallon Fox's loss brings out the worst in the MMA world. Retrieved September 22, 2016, from www.outsports.com/2013/10/16/4845066/fallon-foxs-loss-brings-out-the-worst-in-the-mma-world

317 Park, M. (2014, March 7). Transgender athlete sues CrossFit for banning her from competing as female. Retrieved September 22, 2016, from www.cnn.com/2014/03/07/us/transgender-lawsuit-crossfit

318 Transgender is an adjective. Adding "ed" to the word is grammatically incorrect

319 Zeigler, C. (2011, September 12). Moment #22: International Olympic Committee allows transgender athletes to compete. Retrieved September 22, 2016, from www.outsports.com/2011/9/12/4051806/moment-22-international-olympic-committee-allows-transgender-athletes

320 Zeigler, C. (2016, January 21). Exclusive: Read the Olympics' new transgender guidelines that will not mandate surgery. OutSports.com. Retrieved September 16, 2016, from www.outsports.com/2016/1/21/10812404/transgender-ioc-policy-new-olympics

321 Engber, D. (2016, August 5). Should Caster Semenya be allowed to compete against women? Retrieved September 22, 2016, from www.slate.com/articles/sports/fivering_circus/2016/08/should_caster_semenya_be_allowed_to_compete_against_women.html

322 Ludovise, B. (1988, September 18). Hegg contends Olympic ouster is unfair: Disqualified for using stimulant before a race, cyclist disputes validity of test. Los Angeles Times. Retrieved September 22, 2016, from http://articles.latimes.com/1988-09-18/sports/sp-3449_1_drug-test

323 Soda loading (bicarbonate loading, buffer boosting) for high intensity anaerobic endurance. (2012, May 7). Retrieved September 22, 2016, from www.gustrength.com/physiology:soda-loading-or-bicarbonate-loading ("It is certainly in violation of the USOC/IOC doping law which prohibits the 'administration or use by a competing athlete of any foreign substance to the body or of any physiological substance taken in abnormal quantity or taken by an abnormal route of entry into the body with the sole intention of increasing in an artificial and unfair manner his/her performance in competition.' ... although it isn't explicitly banned by the Olympic committees, it is illegal, but is just not tested for")

324 Mohney, G. (2016, August 4). Common meds Olympic athletes must forgo to avoid testing positive for doping. ABC News. Retrieved September 22, 2016, from http://abcnews.go.com/Health/common-meds-olympic-athletes-forego-avoid-testing-positive/story?id=41003449

325 Griffin, P. & Carrol, H. (August 2011). *NCAA Inclusion of Transgender Student-Athletes.* NCAA Office of Inclusion. Retrieved September 22, 2016, from www.ncaapublications.com/productdownloads/11INCL.pdf

326 Griffin, P. & Carrol, H. (August 2011). *NCAA Inclusion of Transgender Student-Athletes.* NCAA Office of Inclusion. Retrieved September 22, 2016, from www.ncaapublications.com/productdownloads/11INCL.pdf

327 Haynes, S. (2013, March 8). Leading sex reassignment physicians weigh in on Fallon Fox. Retrieved September 22, 2016, from www.bloodyelbow.com/2013/3/8/4075434/leading-sex-reassignment-physicians-weigh-in-on-fallon-fox

328 Harper, J. (2015). Race times for transgender athletes. *Journal of Sporting Cultures and Identities*, 6(1), 1–9

329 Adashi, E. Y. (1994). The climacteric ovary as a functional gonadotropin-driven androgen-producing gland. *Fertility and Sterility*, 62(1), 20–27. doi:10.1016/s0015-0282(16)56810-1

330 MMAWeekly.com Staff. (2013, May 20). Transgender fighter Fallon Fox says she is actually at a disadvantage to her opponents. Retrieved September 22, 2016, from www.mmaweekly.com/transgender-fighter-fallon-fox-says-she-is-actually-at-a-disadvantage-to-her-opponents

331 MMA Fighting Newswire. (2013, October 12). CFA 12 Results: Ashlee Evans-Smith upsets Fallon Fox. Retrieved September 22, 2016, from www.mmafighting.com/2013/10/12/4832904/cfa-12-results-ashlee-evans-smith-upsets-fallon-fox

332 Ashlee Evans-Smith MMA Cage fighter who beat Fallon Fox says she shouldn't fight woman. (2013, November 23). Retrieved September 22, 2016, from http://planetransgender.blogspot.com/2013/11/ashlee-evans-smith-mma-cage-fighter-who.html

333 McQuade, A. (2013, March 12). Dr. Johnny Benjamin's irrelevant argument against inclusion of trans fighter Fallon Fox. Retrieved September 22, 2016, from www.glaad.org/blog/dr-johnny-benjamins-irrelevant-argument-against-inclusion-trans-fighter-fallon-fox

334 *United States v. State of North Carolina* (2016, August 17). Defendants' and intervenor-defendants' brief in opposition to the United States' motion for preliminary injunction. Case no. 1:16-CV-00425-TDS-JEP. Exhibit K: declaration of Lawrence S. Mayer, MD, MS, PhD. Retrieved September 28, 2016, from http://files.eqcf.org/wp-content/uploads/2016/08/149-State-Ds_Berger_Moore-Oppn-to-PI.pdf

335 McHugh, P. (2014, June 2). Transgender surgery isn't the solution. The Wall Street Journal. Retrieved September 28, 2016, from www.wsj.com/articles/paul-mchugh-transgender-surgery-isnt-the-solution-1402615120

336 Ablow, K. (2014, January 14). All wrong—in California, girls can use urinals in the boys' restroom. Fox News. Retrieved September 28, 2016, from www.foxnews.com/opinion/2014/01/14/all-wrong-in-california-girls-can-use-urinals-in-boys-restroom.html

337 Bakker, J. (2014). "Sex Differentiation: Organizing Effects of Sex Hormones." In B. Kreukels, T. Steensma, & A. de Vries (eds) *Gender Dysphoria and Disorders of Sex Development. Focus on Sexuality Research.* Boston, MA: Springer

338 Winneke, G., Ranft, U., Wittsiepe, J., Kasper-Sonnenberg, M., *et al.* (2013). Behavioral sexual dimorphism in school-age children and early developmental exposure to dioxins and PCBs: A follow-up study of the Duisburg cohort. *Environmental Health Perspectives.* doi:10.1289/ehp.1306533

339 Chung, W. C. & Auger, A. P. (2013). Gender differences in neurodevelopment and epigenetics. *Pflügers Archiv: European Journal of Physiology*, 465(5), 573–584. doi:10.1007/s00424-013-1258-4

340 Swaab, D. & Bao, A. (2013). Sexual differentiation of the human brain in relation to gender-identity, sexual orientation, and neuropsychiatric disorders. *Neuroscience in the 21st Century*, 2973–2998. http://dx.doi.org/10.1007/978-1-4614-1997-6_115

341 Karaismailoğlu, S. & Erdem, A. (2013). The effects of prenatal sex steroid hormones on sexual differentiation of the brain. *Journal of the Turkish-German Gynecological Association*, 14(3), 163–167. doi:10.5152/jtgga.2013.86836

342 Lombardo, M., Ashwin, E., Auyeung, B., Chakrabarti, B., *et al.* (2012). Fetal testosterone influences sexually dimorphic gray matter in the human brain. *The Journal of Neuroscience*, 32(2), 674–680. http://dx.doi.org/10.1523/jneurosci.4389-11.2012

343 Lamminmäki, A., Hines, M., Kuiri-Hänninen, T., Kilpeläinen, L., Dunkel, L., & Sankilampi, U. (2012). Testosterone measured in infancy predicts subsequent sex-typed behavior in boys and in girls. *Hormones and Behavior*, 61(4), 611–616. http://dx.doi.org/10.1016/j.yhbeh.2012.02.013

344 Hisasue, S., Sasaki, S., Tsukamoto, T., & Horie, S. (2012). The relationship between second-to-fourth digit ratio and female gender identity. *The Journal of Sexual Medicine*, 9(11), 2903–2910. http://dx.doi.org/10.1111/j.1743-6109.2012.02815.x

345 Hines, M. (2011). Gender development and the human brain. *Annual Review of Neuroscience*, 34(1), 69–88. http://dx.doi.org/10.1146/annurev-neuro-061010-113654

346 Jürgensen, M., Kleinemeier, E., Lux, A., & Steensma (2010). Psychosexual development in children with disorder of sex development (DSD)—results from the German Clinical Evaluation Study. *Journal of Pediatric Endocrinology and Metabolism*, 23(6), 565–578. doi:10.1515/jpem.2010.095

347 Worrell, L. A. (2010). Sexual differentiation of the brain related to gender identity: Beyond hormones. Faculty of Medicine Theses, Netherlands Institute for Neuroscience. Retrieved July 6, 2018, from https://dspace.library.uu.nl/bitstream/handle/1874/182733/Thesis.pdf?sequence=1&isAllowed=y

348 Kerlin, Scott. (2005). PRENATAL EXPOSURE TO DIETHYLSTILBESTROL (DES) IN MALES AND GENDER-RELATED DISORDERS: RESULTS FROM A 5-YEAR STUDY. Presented at International Behavioral Development Symposium. Retrieved Aug 2, 2018 from https://www.researchgate.net/publication/268256137_PRENATAL_EXPOSURE_TO_DIETHYLSTILBESTROL_DES_IN_MALES_AND_GENDER-RELATED_DISORDERS_RESULTS_FROM_A_5-YEAR_STUDY

349 Cohen-Bendahan, C., Buitelaar, J., van Goozen, S., & Cohen-Kettenis, P. (2004). Prenatal exposure to testosterone and functional cerebral lateralization: A study in same-sex and opposite-sex twin girls. *Psychoneuroendocrinology*, 29(7), 911–916. http://dx.doi.org/10.1016/j.psyneuen.2003.07.001

350 Kruijver, F. P. M. (2004). Sex in the brain. Gender differences in the human hypothalamus and adjacent areas. Relationship to transsexualism, sexual orientation, sex hormone receptors and endocrine status. Dissertation. Faculty of Medicine, University of Amsterdam

351 Landén, M. (1999). Transsexualism. Epidemiology, phenomenology, regret after surgery, aetiology, and public attitudes. Doctoral thesis. University of Gothenburg

352 Saraswat, A., Weinand, J., & Safer, J. (2015). Evidence supporting the biologic nature of gender identity. *Endocrine Practice*, 21(2), 199–204. doi:10.4158/ep14351.ra

353 Saraswat, A., Weinand, J., & Safer, J. (2015). Evidence supporting the biologic nature of gender identity. *Endocrine Practice*, 21(2), 199–204. doi:10.4158/ep14351.ra

354 What causes transsexualism? Retrieved July 4, 2015, from www.cakeworld.info/transsexualism/what-causes

355 Dörner, G., Poppe, I., Stahl, F., Kölzsch, J., & Uebelhack, R. (1991). Gene- and environment-dependent neuroendocrine etiogenesis of homosexuality and transsexualism. *Experimental and Clinical Endocrinology*. Retrieved July 4, 2015, from http://europepmc.org/abstract/MED/1778227. "Sexual brain organization is dependent on sex hormone and neurotransmitter levels occurring during critical developmental periods. The higher the androgen levels during brain organization, caused by genetic and/or environmental factors, the higher is the biological predisposition to bi- and homosexuality or even transsexualism in females and the lower it is in males"

356 Moody, O. (2018, March 19). Science pinpoints DNA behind gender identity. The Times. Retrieved March 20, 2018, from www.thetimes.co.uk/edition/news/science-pinpoints-dna-behind-gender-identity-3vmrgrdnv

357 Spizzirri, G., Duran, F. L., Chaim-Avancini, T. M., Serpa, M. H., *et al.* (2018). Grey and white matter volumes either in treatment-naïve or hormone-treated transgender women: A voxel-based morphometry study. *Scientific Reports*, 8(1). doi:10.1038/s41598-017-17563-z

358 Turban, J. L. & Schalkwyk, G. I. (2018). "Gender dysphoria" and autism spectrum disorder: Is the link real? *Journal of the American Academy of Child & Adolescent Psychiatry*, 57(1). doi:10.1016/j.jaac.2017.08.017

359 Diamond, M. & Sigmundson, H. K. (March 1997). Sex reassignment at birth: Long-term review and clinical implications. *Archives of Pediatric and Adolescent Medicine*, 151(3), 298–304. doi:10.1001/archpedi.1997.02170400084015. PMID 9080940. Retrieved May 15, 2013.

360 Fernández, R., Esteva, I., Gómez-Gil, E., Rumbo, T., *et al.* (2014). Association study of ERβ, AR, and CYP19A1 genes and MtF transsexualism. *Journal of Sexual Medicine*, 11, 2986–2994. doi:10.1111/jsm.12673. "The study suggests that the analysis of karyotype provides limited information in these subjects. Variable regions analyzed from ERβ, AR, and CYP19A1 are not associated with MtF transsexualism. Nevertheless, this does not exclude other polymorphic regions not analyzed"

361 Ujike, H., Otani, K., Nakatsuka, M., & Ishii, K., *et al.* (2009). Association study of gender identity disorder and sex hormone-related genes. *Progress in Neuro-Psychopharmacology and Biological Psychiatry*, 33(7), 1241–1244. doi:10.1016/j.pnpbp.2009.07.008. Epub 2009, July 13. "The distributions of CAG repeat numbers in exon 1 of AR, TA repeat numbers in the promoter region of ERalpha, CA repeat numbers in intron 5 of ERbeta, TTTA repeat numbers in intron 4 of CYP19, and six polymorphisms (rs2008112, rs508653, V660L, H770H, rs572698 and PROGINS) of PGR were analyzed"

362 Lombardo, F., Toselli, L., Grassetti, D., Paoli, D., *et al.* (2013). Hormone and genetic study in male to female transsexual patients. *Journal of Endocrinological Investigation*, 36(8), 550–557. doi:10.3275/8813. Epub 2013, Jan 14. "There were no polymorphisms in the amplified gene region for SOX9, and a single nucleotide synonymous polymorphism for DAX1. No statistically significant differences were seen in the mean of CAG repeats between controls and transsexual subjects. SRY gene was present in all subjects. Qualitative analysis of the AZFa, AZFb, and AZFc regions did not reveal any microdeletions in any subject"

363 Moody, O. (2018, March 19). Science pinpoints DNA behind gender identity. The Times. Retrieved March 20, 2018, from www.thetimes.co.uk/edition/news/science-pinpoints-dna-behind-gender-identity-3vmrgrdnv

364 Rice, W. R., Friberg, U., & Gavrilets, S. (2012). Homosexuality as a consequence of epigenetically canalized sexual development. *The Quarterly Review of Biology*, 87(4), (December 2012), 343–368. "Our model predicts that homosexuality is part of a wider phenomenon in which recently evolved androgen-influenced traits commonly display gonad-trait discordances at substantial frequency, and that the molecular feature underlying most homosexuality is not DNA polymorphism(s), but epi-marks that evolved to canalize sexual dimorphic development that sometimes carryover across generations and contribute to gonad-trait discordances in opposite-sex descendants"

365 #Stand4Truth Conference Program Schedule. (2015, October 14). Retrieved September 28, 2016, from https://web.archive.org/web/20170426072527/http://libertylineup.com/stand4truth-conference-program-schedule

366 Active hate groups in the United States. (2016, January 16). Southern Poverty Law Center. Retrieved September 28, 2016, from www.splcenter.org/fighting-hate/intelligence-report/2016/active-hate-groups-united-states-2015#general

367 Paul McHugh. (n.d.). Retrieved September 22, 2016, from www.glaad.org/cap/paul-mchugh

368 Ibid.

369 Ibid.

370 McHugh, P. R. (1992). Psychiatric Misadventures. *The American Scholar*, 61, 497–510

371 McHugh, P. (November 2004). Surgical sex. First Things. Retrieved September 28, 2016, from www.firstthings.com/article/2004/11/surgical-sex

372 McHugh, P. (2015, June 17). Johns Hopkins psychiatrist: It is starkly, nakedly false that sex change is possible. Retrieved September 28, 2016, from http://cnsnews.com/commentary/paul-mchugh/johns-hopkins-psychiatrist-it-starkly-nakedly-false-sex-change-possible

373 McHugh, P. (November 2004). Surgical sex. First Things. Retrieved September 28, 2016, from www.firstthings.com/article/2004/11/surgical-sex

374 Ford, Z. (2015, June 10). Meet the doctor social conservatives depend on to justify anti-transgender hate. ThinkProgress. Retrieved September 16, 2016, from https://thinkprogress.org/meet-the-doctor-social-conservatives-depend-on-to-justify-anti-transgender-hate-fe764009b93#.vhy78bwq9

375 Gender ideology harms children. (2016, August 17). American College of Pediatrics. Retrieved October 4, 2016, from www.acpeds.org/the-college-speaks/position-statements/gender-ideology-harms-children

376 Along with NARTH, a deceptively named pediatricians' group is a second primary source used to vilify gay people. (2012, March 1). Southern Poverty Law Center. Retrieved October 4, 2016, from www.splcenter.org/fighting-hate/intelligence-report/2012/american-college-pediatricians-defames-gays-and-lesbians-name-protecting-children

377 Ford, Z. (2016, March 22). Hate group masquerading as pediatricians attacks transgender youth. Think Progress. Retrieved October 4, 2016, from https://thinkprogress.org/hate-group-masquerading-as-pediatricians-attacks-transgender-youth-544e755c6a20#.py065j04t

378 Abstinence education. (October 2010). American College of Pediatricians. Retrieved October 4, 2010, from www.acpeds.org/the-college-speaks/position-statements/sexuality-issues/abstinence-education

379 Tannehill, B. (2016, March 20). Johns Hopkins professor endangers the lives of transgender youth. Retrieved March 20, 2018, from www.huffingtonpost.com/brynn-tannehill/johns-hopkins-professor-e_b_9510808.html

380 Diversity and inclusion at Johns Hopkins. (January 2016). Retrieved September 28, 2016, from www.hopkinsmedicine.org/diversity/letters/index.html

381 Gass, N., Shafer, J., Karni, A., Wolfsthal, J. B., & Blau, M. (2015, November 6). Ben Carson's 15 most controversial quotes. Politico. Retrieved May 25, 2018, from www.politico.com/story/2015/10/ben-carson-controversial-quotes-214614

382 Ben Carson: Compares same-sex marriage to bestiality. (n.d.). Human Rights Campaign. Retrieved September 28, 2016, from www.hrc.org/2016RepublicanFacts/ben-carson

383 A message from the Dean/CEO in response to recent comments. (2015, April 3). Retrieved September 28, 2016, from www.hopkinsmedicine.org/news/stories/rothman_carson.html

384 Coleman, E., Bockting, W., Botzer, M., Cohen-Kettenis, P., *et al.* (2011). Standards of care for the health of transsexual, transgender, and gender nonconforming people, 7th version. *International Journal of Transgenderism*, 13, 165–232

385 Drescher, J. & Haller, E. (2012). Position statement on access to care for transgender and gender variant individuals. Washington, DC: American Psychiatric Association (APA Official Actions)

386 McHugh, P. (2014, June 2). Transgender surgery isn't the solution. The Wall Street Journal. Retrieved September 28, 2016, from www.wsj.com/articles/paul-mchugh-transgender-surgery-isnt-the-solution-1402615120

387 Karasic, D. (2014, July 2). Wall Street Journal Editorial critiques transgender health (July 2, 2014). Retrieved September 28, 2016, from https://web.archive.org/web/20170414233042/www.wpath.org/site_page.cfm?pk_association_webpage_menu=1635&pk_association_webpage=4905

388 Williams, C. (October 2015). Fact check: Study shows transition makes trans people suicidal. The TransAdvocate. Retrieved September 28, 2016, from http://transadvocate.com/fact-check-study-shows-transition-makes-trans-people-suicidal_n_15483.htm. "At the same time, I know of instances where *ethical researchers* and clinicians have used this study to expand and improve access to trans health care and impact systems of anti-trans oppression"

389 Beyrer, C., Blum, R. W., & Poteat, T. C. (2016, September 28). Hopkins faculty disavow "troubling" report on gender and sexuality. Retrieved March 12, 2018, from www.baltimoresun.com/news/opinion/oped/bs-ed-lgbtq-hopkins-20160928-story.html

390 www.vumc.org/lgbti/files/lgbti/publication_files/ExpertLGBTIConcensusLetter.pdf

391 Beyrer, C., Blum, R. W., & Poteat, T. C. (2016, September 28). Hopkins faculty disavow "troubling" report on gender and sexuality. Retrieved March 12, 2018, from www.baltimoresun.com/news/opinion/oped/bs-ed-lgbtq-hopkins-20160928-story.html

392 Roberts, M. (2010, September 22). Why the trans community hates Dr. Paul McHugh. Retrieved September 28, 2016, from http://transgriot.blogspot.com/2010/09/why-trans-community-hates-dr-paul.html

393 Barstow, D. (2009, July 25). An abortion battle, fought to the death. The New York Times. Retrieved September 22, 2009, from www.nytimes.com/2009/07/26/us/26tiller.html?_r=1

394 Ford, Z. (2014, December 16). First circuit reverses, denies medically necessary surgery to transgender inmate. ThinkProgress. Retrieved September 28, 2016, from https://thinkprogress.org/first-circuit-reverses-denies-medically-necessary-surgery-to-transgender-inmate-a5908cc0195b#.pc0efse3n

395 Casazza, J. L. (2014). Sex reassignment surgery: Required for transgendered prisoners but forbidden for Medicaid, Medicare, and CHAMPUS beneficiaries. *William & Mary Journal of Women and the Law*, 625. Retrieved July 6, 2018, from http://scholarship.law.wm.edu/wmjowl/vol20/iss3/4

396 *Kosilek v. Spencer*, 889 F.Supp.2d 190 (D.Mass.2012)

397 Makkai, E. (2003, November 1). The sex change charade. World Net Daily. Retrieved September 28, 2016, from www.wnd.com/2003/01/16683

398 *Kosilek v. Spencer*, 889 F.Supp.2d 190 (D.Mass.2012)

399 *Schroer v. Billington*. (2017). Casetext.com. Retrieved November 12, 2017, from https://casetext.com/case/schroer-v-billington-3

400 Debunking Dr. McHugh. (2009, February 10). Retrieved October 4, 2016, from https://crystalgaze2.blogspot.com/2009/02/debunking-dr-paul-mchugh.html

401 Wise, T. N. (1979). Psychotherapy of an aging transvestite. *Journal of Sex & Marital Therapy*, 5(4), 368–373. doi:10.1080/00926237908407081

402 Johns Hopkins University. (n.d.). Trans Road Map. Retrieved October 4, 2016, from www.tsroadmap.com/info/johns-hopkins.html

403 Transgender health and the law: Identifying and fighting health care discrimination. (July 2004). Transgender Law Center. Retrieved October 4, 2016, from http://transgenderlawcenter.org/resources/health/transgender-health-and-the-law-identifying-and-fighting-health-care-discrimination

404 Professional organization statements supporting transgender people in health care. (2016, May 25). Compiled by Lambda Legal. Retrieved July 6, 2018, from www.lambdalegal.org/sites/default/files/publications/downloads/ll_trans_professional_statements.rtf_.pdf

405 What happens when therapy is banned? (n.d.). Retrieved February 18, 2018, from www.therapyequality.org/wp-content/uploads/2018/01/FactSheet.pdf. The National Task Force for Therapy Equality (formerly known as the National Association for Research and Therapy of Homosexuality, an anti-LGBT hate group dedicated to promoting reparative therapy)

406 Littman, L. L. (2017). Rapid onset of gender dysphoria in adolescents and young adults: A descriptive study. *Journal of Adolescent Health*, 60(2). doi:10.1016/j.jadohealth.2016.10.369

407 Jones, Z. (2017, July 1). Fresh trans myths of 2017: "Rapid onset gender dysphoria." Retrieved February 19, 2018, from https://genderanalysis.net/2017/07/fresh-trans-myths-of-2017-rapid-onset-gender-dysphoria

408 Amend, A. (2017, December 6). Family Research Council's anti-SPLC campaign is promoting an anti-Semitic publication. Retrieved February 19, 2018, from www.splcenter.org/hatewatch/2017/12/06/family-research-councils-anti-splc-campaign-promoting-anti-semitic-publication ("According to Baldwin, 'homosexuality is moral perversion and deserves no special consideration under the law'")

409 Jones, Z. (2017, July 1). Fresh trans myths of 2017: "Rapid onset gender dysphoria." Retrieved February 19, 2018, from https://genderanalysis.net/2017/07/fresh-trans-myths-of-2017-rapid-onset-gender-dysphoria

410 Zane, Z. (2018, February 14). A third of Americans think transgender people are committing a sin. Retrieved February 19, 2018, from www.newnownext.com/a-third-of-americans-think-transgender-people-are-committing-a-sin/02/2018

411 Jones, Z. (2018, February 1). "Rapid onset gender dysphoria": What a hoax diagnosis looks like. Retrieved February 19, 2018, from https://genderanalysis.net/2018/02/rapid-onset-gender-dysphoria-what-a-hoax-diagnosis-looks-like

412 Payne, E. (2013). Group apologizes to gay community, then shuts down "cure" ministry. CNN. Retrieved July 6, 2018, from www.cnn.com/2013/06/20/us/exodus-international-shutdown/index.html

413 Ferguson, D. (2013). D.C. ex-gay rally draws fewer than 10 attendees. Rawstory.com. Retrieved July 6, 2018, from www.rawstory.com/2013/08/d-c-ex-gay-rally-draws-fewer-than-10-attendees

414 Wente, M. (2014). Transgender kids: Have we gone too far? The Globe and Mail. Retrieved July 6, 2018, from https://beta.theglobeandmail.com/globe-debate/transgender-kids-have-we-gone-too-far/article16897043

415 Ellis-Petersen, H. (2017, January 11). BBC film on child transgender issues worries activists. The Guardian. Retrieved December 23, 2017, from www.theguardian.com/society/2017/jan/11/bbc-film-on-child-transgender-issues-worries-activists

416 American Psychological Association. (2017). En.wikipedia.org. Retrieved November 12, 2017, from https://en.wikipedia.org/wiki/American_Psychological_Association

417 American Psychiatric Association. (2017). En.wikipedia.org. Retrieved November 12, 2017, from https://en.wikipedia.org/wiki/American_Psychiatric_Association

418 Transgenderism: Blurring the Lines. (2015, February 02). Retrieved November 13, 2017, from https://www.focusonthefamily.com/socialissues/citizen-magazine/transgenderism-blurring-the-lines/transgenderism-blurring-the-lines

419 NARTH has changed its name and become the Alliance for Therapeutic Freedom. https://web.archive.org/web/20110803212431/http://narth.com/2010/04/treatment-of-gender-disturbed-children-clinical-issues

420 Retrieved Aug 2, 2018 from https://web.archive.org/web/20110803221708/http:/\couragerc.net/Transsexual_Issues/Sex_Reassignment.pdf

421 Retrieved Aug 2, 2018 from https://web.archive.org/web/20090107135840/http://www.alliancealert.org/2008/05/08/two-families-two-approaches-to-gender-preferences

422 Andersen, K., EXCLUSIVE: APA still considers transgenderism a mental disorder, just changed the name. (December 7, 2012). Retrieved November 13, 2017, from https://www.lifesitenews.com/news/apa-still-considers-transgenderism-a-mental-disorder-just-changed-the-name

423 http://afaofpa.org/wp-content/uploads/2011/10/December-7-2012.pdf

424 http://www.lc.org/media/9980/attachments/pr_ca_change_therapy_rebuttal_declarations_111612.pdf

425 https://americansfortruth.com/2006/12/05/letting-your-son-wear-a-dress-nyt-helps-mainstream-gender-confusion-in-children

426 http://www.pfox.org/transgender-gender-identity

427 Paul McHugh filed an amicus brief in Grimm v. Gloucester County School Board and cited Zucker glowingly ("Dr. Kenneth Zucker, long acknowledged as one of the foremost authorities on gender dysphoria in children, spent years helping his patients align their subjective gender identity with their objective biological sex"), www.scotusblog.com/wp-content/uploads/2017/01/16-273-amicuspetitioner-mchugh.pdf, as did the Liberty Counsel (an anti-LGBT hate group) in the case of Perry v. Schwarzenegger: http://cdn.ca9.uscourts.gov/datastore/general/2010/10/25/amicus7.pdf ("The girls had difficulty in forming an emotional connection to their mothers. In some instances, it seemed to us that either a girl failed to identify with her mother, or disidentified from her mother because she perceived her mother as weak, incompetent or helpless. In fact, many of the mothers devalued their own efficacy and regarded the female gender role with disdain"))

428 York, F. (2004, September 23). How should clinicians deal with GID in children? Psychologist Kenneth J. Zucker explains the current research on children and adolescents who develop a gender identity disorder. Retrieved November 13, 2017, from https://web.archive.org/web/20121018111530/http://www.narth.com/docs/gid.html ("He [Zucker] notes that the 'most acute ethical issue may concern the relation between GID and a later homosexual sexual orientation. Follow-up studies of boys who have GID that largely is untreated, indicated that homosexuality is the most common long-term psychosexual outcome...' Zucker says that clinicians have an ethical obligation to inform parents of the relationship between GID and homosexuality")

429 Muskus, J. (2010). George Rekers, anti-gay activist, caught with male escort "rentboy." HuffPost UK. Retrieved July 6, 2018, from www.huffingtonpost.com/2010/05/05/george-rekers-anti-gay-ac_n_565142.html

430 Spiegel, A. (2008). Two families grapple with sons' gender identity. NPR.org. Retrieved July 6, 2018, from www.npr.org/2008/05/07/90247842/two-families-grapple-with-sons-gender-preferences?sc=emaf

431 Bronstein, S. & Joseph, J. (2011). Therapy to change "feminine" boy created a troubled man, family says. Cnn.com. Retrieved July 6, 2018, from www.cnn.com/2011/US/06/07/sissy.boy.experiment/index.html

432 Wilkinson, S. (2001, Fall). Drop the Barbie! If you bend gender far enough, does it break? Brainchild. Retrieved May 25, 2018 from https://web.archive.org/web/20060212133812/http://www.brainchildmag.com/essays/fall2001_wilkinson.htm

433 Grant, J. (2009). Dr. Kenneth Zucker's war on transgenders. Queerty.com. Retrieved July 6, 2018, from www.queerty.com/dr-kenneth-zuckers-war-on-transgenders-20090206#ixzz2f9pCTnso

434 Becker, J. (2017). John M Becker. Retrieved July 6, 2018, from www.johnmbecker.com

435 Blanchard's transsexualism typology. (2017). En.wikipedia.org. Retrieved July 6, 2018, from https://en.wikipedia.org/wiki/Blanchard's_transsexualism_typology

436 Schwartzapfel, B. (2013). Born this way? The American Prospect. Retrieved July 6, 2018, from http://prospect.org/article/born-way

437 David Reimer. (2017). En.wikipedia.org. Retrieved July 6, 2018, from https://en.wikipedia.org/wiki/David_Reimer

438 Schwartzapfel, B. (2013). Born this way? The American Prospect. Retrieved July 6, 2018, from http://prospect.org/article/born-way

439 Bradley, S. J. & Zucker, K. J. (1990). Gender identity disorder and psychosexual problems in children and adolescents. *Canadian Journal of Psychiatry*, 35(6), 477–486

440 Zucker, K. J. & Bradley, S. J. (1995). *Gender Identity Disorder and Psychosexual Problems in Children and Adolescents*. New York, NY: Guilford Press

441 Becker, J. (2017). John M Becker. Retrieved July 6, 2018, from www.johnmbecker.com

442 Carey, B. (2012). Psychiatry giant sorry for backing gay "cure." Nytimes.com. Retrieved July 6, 2018, from www.nytimes.com/2012/05/19/health/dr-robert-l-spitzer-noted-psychiatrist-apologizes-for-study-on-gay-cure.html?pagewanted=all&_r=0

443 Spitzer, Zucker, and reparative therapy: Ex and pre-gay. (2017). Retrieved July 6, 2018, from http://ipgcounseling.com/queer-mind/spitzer-zucker-and-reparative-therapy-ex-and-pre-gay

444 York, F. (2004, September 23). How should clinicians deal with GID in children? Psychologist Kenneth J. Zucker explains the current research on children and adolescents who develop a gender identity disorder. Retrieved November 13, 2017, from https://web.archive.org/web/20121018111530/http://www.narth.com/docs/gid.html

445 Morton, G. (2001, January 10). Drop the doll! Retrieved November 13, 2017, from www.dailyxtra.com/drop-the-doll-46535

446 Zinck, S. & Pignatiello, A. (2015). External review of the Gender Identity Clinic of the Child, Youth, and Family Services in the Underserved Populations Program at the Centre for Addiction and Mental Health. Prepared for the Underserved Populations Program at CAMH, Ontario, November 26, 2015

447 Dreger, A. (2015, December 19). Gender mad. Retrieved September 21, 2016, from http://alicedreger.com/gendermad

448 How the psychiatrist who co-wrote the manual on sex talks about sex. (2013, April 11). Motherboard. Retrieved February 8, 2018, from https://web.archive.org/web/20130527233428/http://motherboard.vice.com:80/blog/heres-how-the-guy-who-wrote-the-manual-on-sex-talks-about-sex

449 Williams, C. (2013). The shame of Sheila Jeffreys' hate. TransAdvocate. Retrieved October 4, 2016, from http://transadvocate.com/the-shame-of-sheila-jeffreys-hate_n_12766.htm

450 What many transgender activists don't want you to know: And why you should know it anyway (2012, November 12). GenderTrender. Retrieved October 4, 2016, from https://gendertrender.wordpress.com/2012/11/21/what-many-transgender-activists-dont-want-you-to-know-and-why-you-should-know-it-anyway

451 Fitzgibbons, R., Sutton, P. M., & O'Leary, D. (2009). The psychopathology of "sex reassignment" surgery: Assessing its medical, psychological, and ethical appropriateness. *National Catholic Bioethics Quarterly*, 9(1), 109–137.

452 O'Leary, D. & Sprigg, P. (2015). Understanding and responding to the transgender movement. Retrieved September 20, 2016, from http://downloads.frc.org/EF/EF15F45.pdf

453 Subsequent to the publication of this article, the American Family Association removed the link

454 Fitzgibbons, R., Sutton, P. M., & O'Leary, D. (2009). The psychopathology of "sex reassignment" surgery: Assessing its medical, psychological, and ethical appropriateness. *National Catholic Bioethics Quarterly*, 9(1), 109–137

455 American Psychiatric Association. (June 2000). *Diagnostic and Statistical Manual of Mental Disorders-IV (Text Revision)*. Arlington, VA: American Psychiatric Publishing, Inc., 566–576. doi:10.1176/appi.books.9780890423349. ISBN 978-0-89042-024-9

456 How the psychiatrist who co-wrote the manual on sex talks about sex. (2013, April 11). Motherboard. Retrieved February 8, 2018, from https://web.archive.org/web/20130527233428/http://motherboard.vice.com:80/blog/heres-how-the-guy-who-wrote-the-manual-on-sex-talks-about-sex

457 Bailey, J. M. (2003). *The Man Who Would Be Queen: The Science of Gender-Bending and Transsexualism*. Washington, DC: Joseph Henry Press

458 Blanchard, R. (2005). Early history of the concept of autogynephilia. *Archives of Sexual Behavior*, 34(4), August 2005, 439–446 (C 2005). doi:10.1007/s10508-005-4343-8

459 Blanchard, R. (1985). Typology of male-to-female transsexualism. *Archives of Sexual Behavior*, 14, 247–261; Blanchard, R. (1988). Nonhomosexual gender dysphoria. *Journal of Sex Research*, 24, 188–193; Blanchard, R. (1989a). The classification and labeling of nonhomosexual gender dysphorias. *Archives of Sexual Behavior*, 18, 315–334; Blanchard, R. (1989b). The concept of autogynephilia and the typology of male gender dysphoria. *Journal of Nervous and Mental Disease*, 177, 616–623

460 Bailey, J. M. (2003). *The Man Who Would Be Queen: The Science of Gender-Bending and Transsexualism*. Washington, DC: Joseph Henry Press

461 Bailey, J. M. & Triea, K. (2007). What many transgender activists don't want you to know: And why you should know it anyway. *Perspectives in Biology and Medicine*, 50, 521–534

462 Blanchard, R. (1985). Typology of male-to-female transsexualism. *Archives of Sexual Behavior*, 14, 247–261

463 Blanchard, R., Clemmensen, L., & Steiner, B. W. (1987). Heterosexual and homosexual gender dysphoria. *Archives of Sexual Behavior*, 16, 139–152

464 Blanchard, R. (2005). Early history of the concept of Autogynephilia. *Archives of Sexual Behavior*, 34(4), August 2005, 439–446 (C 2005). doi:10.1007/s10508-005-4343-8

465 How the psychiatrist who co-wrote the manual on sex talks about sex. (2013, April 11). Motherboard. Retrieved February 8, 2018, from https://web.archive.org/web/20130527233428/http://motherboard.vice.com:80/blog/heres-how-the-guy-who-wrote-the-manual-on-sex-talks-about-sex

466 O'Leary, D. & Sprigg, P. (2015). Understanding and responding to the transgender movement. Retrieved September 20, 2016, from http://downloads.frc.org/EF/EF15F45.pdf

467 Bailey, J. M. (2003). *The Man Who Would Be Queen: The Science of Gender-Bending and Transsexualism*. Washington, DC: Joseph Henry Press

468 Hendershott, A. (2013, August 27). The transgender culture wars. The Catholic World Report. Retrieved October 4, 2016, from www.catholicworldreport.com/Item/2527/the_transgender_culture_wars.aspx

469 How the psychiatrist who co-wrote the manual on sex talks about sex. (2013, April 11). Motherboard. Retrieved February 8, 2018, from https://web.archive.org/web/20130527233428/http://motherboard.vice.com:80/blog/heres-how-the-guy-who-wrote-the-manual-on-sex-talks-about-sex

470 Bailey, J. M. & Blanchard, R. (2017, October 13). Suicide or transition: The only options for gender dysphoric kids? Retrieved February 1, 2018, from https://4thwavenow.com/2017/09/08/suicide-or-transition-the-only-options-for-gender-dysphoric-kids

471 How the psychiatrist who co-wrote the manual on sex talks about sex. (2013, April 11). Motherboard. Retrieved February 8, 2018, from https://web.archive.org/web/20130527233428/http://motherboard.vice.com:80/blog/heres-how-the-guy-who-wrote-the-manual-on-sex-talks-about-sex

472 Eckholm, E. (2014, March 21). Federal judge strikes down Michigan's ban on same-sex marriage. Retrieved November 6, 2017, from www.nytimes.com/2014/03/22/us/michigan-ban-on-same-sex-marriage-is-struck-down.html?_r=0. "Lawyers for the plaintiffs described the scholars who appeared for the state as religiously motivated and part of a 'desperate fringe,' and subjected them to withering cross-examination. Judge Friedman agreed with the criticism, describing the state's witnesses as 'unbelievable' and calling their studies deeply flawed... He wrote with particular animus about the best-known—and most widely discredited—of the researchers, Mark Regnerus, a sociologist at the University of Texas"

473 Dhejne, C., Lichtenstein, P., Boman, M., Johansson, A., Långström, N., & Landén, M. (2011). Long-term follow-up of transsexual persons undergoing sex reassignment surgery: Cohort study in Sweden. *Plos ONE*, 6(2), e16885. http://dx.doi.org/10.1371/journal.pone.0016885

474 Williams, C. (2015). Fact check: Study shows transition makes trans people suicidal. The TransAdvocate. Retrieved November 13, 2017, from http://transadvocate.com/fact-check-study-shows-transition-makes-trans-people-suicidal_n_15483.htm

475 Tannehill, B. (2017). The desistance narrative is junk science. HuffPost. Retrieved November 13, 2017, from www.huffingtonpost.com/brynn-tannehill/the-end-of-the-desistance_b_8903690.html

476 Zucker, K., Wood, H., Singh, D., & Bradley, S. (2012). A developmental, biopsychosocial model for the treatment of children with gender identity disorder. *Journal of Homosexuality*, 59(3), 369–397. http://dx.doi.org/10.1080/00918369.2012.653309

477 Schwartzapfel, B. (2013). Born this way? The American Prospect. Retrieved July 6, 2018, from http://prospect.org/article/born-way

478 WPATH. (2017). *Standards of Care*. Wpath.org. Retrieved November 13, 2017, from www.wpath.org/media/cms/Documents/Web%20Transfer/SOC/Standards%20of%20Care%20V7%20-%202011%20WPATH.pdf

479 Groups. (2017). Southern Poverty Law Center. Retrieved November 13, 2017, from www.splcenter.org/fighting-hate/extremist-files/groups

480 Ford, Z. (2016). Fake medical organization publishes lie-ridden manifesto attacking transgender kids. Thinkprogress.org. Retrieved November 13, 2017, from https://thinkprogress.org/american-college-pediatricians-transgender-kids-falsehoods-384716df13c5

481 Tannehill, B. (2015). The scary science at Johns Hopkins University. Advocate.com. Retrieved November 13, 2017, from www.advocate.com/commentary/2015/12/15/scary-science-johns-hopkins-university

482 Professional organization statements supporting transgender people in health care. (2016, May 25). Compiled by Lambda Legal. Retrieved July 6, 2018, from www.lambdalegal.org/sites/default/files/publications/downloads/ll_trans_professional_statements.rtf_.pdf

483 Tannehill, B. (2014). Myths about transition regrets. HuffPost. Retrieved November 13, 2017, from www.huffingtonpost.com/brynn-tannehill/myths-about-transition-regrets_b_6160626.html

484 Jones, Z. (2015). Walt Heyer and "sex change regret" (Gender Analysis 09). Gender Analysis. Retrieved November 13, 2017, from https://genderanalysis.net/2015/07/walt-heyer-and-sex-change-regret-gender-analysis-09

485 Policy and position statements on conversion therapy. Human Rights Campaign. Retrieved November 13, 2017, from www.hrc.org/resources/policy-and-position-statements-on-conversion-therapy

486 Coleman, E., Bockting, W., Botzer, M., Cohen-Kettenis, P., *et al.* (2011). Standards of care for the health of transsexual, transgender, and gender nonconforming people, 7th version. *International Journal of Transgenderism*, 13, 165–232

487 Flier from "Christian Manhood Men's Retreat" by Courage Catholic. Retrieved November 13, 2017, from https://web.archive.org/web/20180129065627/http://couragerc.org/wp-content/uploads/2017_Retreat_Register-Now.pdf

488 Tannehill, B. (2015). The truth about transgender suicide. HuffPost. Retrieved November 13, 2017, from www.huffingtonpost.com/brynn-tannehill/the-truth-about-transgend_b_8564834.html

489 Fogarty, T. (2017). What two former trans men want you to know about all the lies. The Federalist. Retrieved November 13, 2017, from http://thefederalist.com/2017/10/11/what-two-former-trans-men-want-you-to-know-about-all-the-lies

490 Anderson, R. T. (2018). *When Harry Became Sally: Responding to the Transgender Moment*. New York, NY: Encounter Books

491 Carey, B. (2006). Long-awaited medical study questions the power of prayer. Nytimes.com. Retrieved November 13, 2017, from www.nytimes.com/2006/03/31/health/31pray.html

492 Gibbs, J. & Goldbach, J. (2015). Religious conflict, sexual identity, and suicidal behaviors among LGBT young adults. *Archives of Suicide Research*, 19(4), 472–488. http://dx.doi.org/10.1080/13811118.2015.1004476

493 Much of this section is adapted from course handouts on the US legal system provided by Jillian Weiss, Professor of Law at Ramapo College and former Executive Director of the Transgender Legal Defense and Education Fund. These were provided and used with her permission

494 While gender and sex are different, in recent years, courts have treated sex stereotyping almost synonymously with the concept of gender

495 United States Equal Opportunity Commission, Unabridged Text of the Civil Rights Act of 1964. Retrieved August 2, 2018 from https://www.eeoc.gov/eeoc/history/35th/thelaw/civil_rights_act.html

496 The inclusion of "sex" in the 1964 Civil Rights Act was actually added as a legislative "poison pill" in an attempt to prevent it from passing. This attempt did not succeed

497 Strasser, R. (2008, July 21). Strict scrutiny. Cornell Law School Legal Information Institute. Retrieved November 2, 2017, from www.law.cornell.edu/wex/strict_scrutiny

498 The intermediate scrutiny test was created by the Supreme Court in 1976 (*Craig v. Boren*), which involved a statute that involved gender discrimination. Thus, all US courts treat sex and gender as a classification protected by the intermediate scrutiny test. It has expanded somewhat over time to include other classes and rights (Hashmall, J. Intermediate scrutiny. Cornell Law School Legal Information Institute. Retrieved November 2, 2017, from www.law.cornell.edu/wex/intermediate_scrutiny)

499 Hashmall, J. (2009, September 17). Rational basis. Cornell Law School Legal Information Institute. Retrieved November 2, 2017, from www.law.cornell.edu/wex/rational_basis

500 In *Lawrence v. Texas*, the Supreme Court decided that laws against consensual sodomy were unconstitutional

501 Wintemute, R. (2002). *Sexual Orientation and Human Rights: The United States Constitution, The European Convention, and The Canadian Charter*. Oxford: Oxford University Press

502 *Jai Lok Ling v. U.S. Attorney General*, No. 10-10724 (11th Cir. 2010)

503 *United States v. Carolene Products Co.*, 304 U.S. 144 (1938)

504 *Frontiero v. Richardson*, 411 U.S. 677, 686 (1973)

505 Additionally, this case cited *Holloway v. Arthur Andersen*'s conclusion that "The total lack of legislative history supporting the sex amendment coupled with the circumstances of the amendment's adoption clearly indicates that Congress never considered nor intended that this 1964 legislation apply to anything other than the traditional concept of sex"

506 *Romer v. Evans*, 517 U.S. 620 (1996)

507 Diane Schroer was represented by Sharon McGowan of the American Civil Liberties Union's LGBT Rights Project at trial (www.windycitymediagroup.com/lgbt/Transgender-Veteran-Gets-Maximum-Compensation-in-case-Against-Library-of-Congress/21019.html)

508 *Glenn v. Brumby*, 663 F.3d 1312 (2011)

509 The EEOC is responsible for enforcing federal laws that make it illegal to discriminate against a job applicant or an employee because of the person's race, color, religion, sex (including pregnancy, gender identity, and sexual orientation), national origin, age (40 or older), disability, or genetic information. EEOC decisions are effectively binding on federal agencies. Retrieved December 28, 2017, from www.eeoc.gov/eeoc

510 *Tudor v. Southeastern Oklahoma State University*, 2015 WL 4606079 (W.D. Okla. 2015)

511 Barnes, R. (2017, March 7). Justices send transgender case back to lower court. The Washington Post. Retrieved December 28, 2017, from www.highbeam.com/doc/1P2-40521457.html?refid=easy_hf

512 Discrimination News. (2017). LGBTQ Nation. Retrieved November 13, 2017, from www.lgbtqnation.com/tag/discrimination

513 Marriage Equality News. (2017). LGBTQ Nation. Retrieved November 13, 2017, from www.lgbtqnation.com/tag/gay-marriage

514 Transgender News. (2017). LGBTQ Nation. Retrieved November 13, 2017, from www.lgbtqnation.com/tag/transgender

515 Schwartz, J. (2013). Between the lines of the defense of Marriage Act opinion. Nytimes.com. Retrieved November 13, 2017, from www.nytimes.com/interactive/2013/06/26/us/annotated-supreme-court-decision-on-doma.html

516 Alliance Defending Freedom. (2017). Southern Poverty Law Center. Retrieved November 13, 2017, from www.splcenter.org/fighting-hate/extremist-files/group/alliance-defending-freedom

517 Impact litigation is the "planning, preparing, and filing or defending law suits focused on changing or advancing or retaining laws or on the rights of specific groups of people. Impact litigation is brought or defended typically when the case affects more than one individual even if there is one individual involved. Many impact litigation organizations are also deeply involved in policy work," per the Harvard Law School website. Retrieved January 1, 2018, from http://hls.harvard.edu/dept/opia/what-is-public-interest-law/public-interest-work-types/impact-litigation

518 Stanley, P. (2011). Tenn. governor voids anti-discrimination law. Christianpost.com. Retrieved November 13, 2017, from www.christianpost.com/news/tenn-governor-voids-anti-discrimination-law-50470

519 In the 2014 case of *Lisa Howe, et al. v. Bill Haslam*, the Tennessee Court of Appeals dismissed the claims of the plaintiffs Wesley Roberts and the Gay/Straight Alliance of Hume-Fogg Academic Magnet High School for lack of standing. Retrieved July 6, 2018, from www.tncourts.gov/sites/default/files/howelisaopn_0.pdf

520 Arkansas Supreme Court strikes city's LGBT protections. (2017). Cbsnews.com. Retrieved November 13, 2017, from www.cbsnews.com/news/arkansas-supreme-court-strikes-lgbt-protections-fayetteville

521 Stern, M. (2017). The HB2 "Repeal" Bill is an unmitigated disaster for LGBTQ rights and North Carolina. *Slate Magazine*. Retrieved November 13, 2017, from www.slate.com/blogs/outward/2017/03/30/hb2_repeal_bill_is_a_disaster_for_north_carolina_and_lgbtq_rights.html

522 *Burwell v. Hobby Lobby Stores*. (2014, June 30). Retrieved November 13, 2017, from www.oyez.org/cases/2013/13-354

523 *Zubik v. Burwell*. (2017). En.wikipedia.org. Retrieved November 13, 2017, from https://en.wikipedia.org/wiki/Zubik_v._Burwell

524 *Citizens United v. Federal Election Commission*. (2010, January 21). Retrieved November 13, 2017, from www.bloomberglaw.com/public/desktop/document/Citizens_United_v_Federal_Election_Commission_130_S_Ct_876_175_L_

525 Wiessner, D. (2016). U.S. judge says funeral home had religious right to fire transgender worker. Retrieved November 13, 2017, from www.reuters.com/article/us-michigan-lgbt-lawsuit/u-s-judge-says-funeral-home-had-religious-right-to-fire-transgender-worker-idUSKCN10T2EI

526 *EEOC and Stephens v. Harris Funeral Homes*. (2018, 6th No. 16-2424). Retrieved March 12, 2018, from www.opn.ca6.uscourts.gov/opinions.pdf/18a0045p-06.pdf

527 Barnes, R. (2014). Retrieved November 13, 2017, from Wiessner, D. (2016). U.S. judge says funeral home had religious right to fire transgender worker. www.reuters.com/article/us-michigan-lgbt-lawsuit/u-s-judge-says-funeral-home-had-religious-right-to-fire-transgender-worker-idUSKCN10T2EI

528 New Mexico News. (2017). LGBTQ Nation. Retrieved November 13, 2017, from www.lgbtqnation.com/tag/new-mexico

529 *Masterpiece Cakeshop, Ltd. v. Colorado Civil Rights Commission*. (2016). SCOTUSblog. Retrieved November 13, 2017, from www.scotusblog.com/case-files/cases/masterpiece-cakeshop-ltd-v-colorado-civil-rights-commn

530 Barnes, R. (2017). Key decisions from Supreme Court nominee Neil Gorsuch. The Washington Post. Retrieved November 13, 2017, from www.washingtonpost.com/politics/courts_law/key-decisions-from-supreme-court-nominee-neil-gorsuch/2017/01/31/47c36836-e736-11e6-b82f-687d6e6a3e7c_story.html?utm_term=.2e540d97e6d0

531 Religion News. (2017). LGBTQ Nation. Retrieved November 13, 2017, from www.lgbtqnation.com/tag/religion

532 *Burwell v. Hobby Lobby Stores, Inc.* (2017). En.wikipedia.org. Retrieved November 13, 2017, from https://en.wikipedia.org/wiki/Burwell_v._Hobby_Lobby_Stores,_Inc

533 Department of Justice's gay rights brief slammed by advocates as "license to discriminate." (2017, September 11). Retrieved December 28, 2017, from www.nbcnews.com/feature/nbc-out/department-justice-s-gay-rights-brief-slammed-advocates-license-discriminate-n800316

534 Attorney General Sessions issues guidance on Federal Law Protections for Religious Liberty. (2017). Justice.gov. Retrieved November 13, 2017, from www.justice.gov/opa/pr/attorney-general-sessions-issues-guidance-federal-law-protections-religious-liberty

535 Department of Justice Memorandum "Federal Law Protections for Religious Liberty." (2017, October 6). Retrieved November 13, 2017, from www.justice.gov/opa/press-release/file/1001891/download

536 Department of Justice Memorandum "Implementation of Memorandum on Federal Law Protections for Religious Liberty." (2017, October 6). Retrieved November 13, 2017, from www.justice.gov/opa/press-release/file/1001886/download

537 First Amendment and religious beliefs. (2017). Fsis.usda.gov. Retrieved November 13, 2017, from www.fsis.usda.gov/wps/portal/informational/aboutfsis/civil-rights/policy-statements/first-amendment-q-and-a/first-amendment-and-religious-beliefs

538 Bowden, J. (2017). Mattis appalled by Trump tweets announcing transgender ban: Report. TheHill. Retrieved November 13, 2017, from http://thehill.com/policy/defense/344290-mattis-appalled-by-trump-tweets-announcing-transgender-military-ban-report

539 Starr, B., Cohen, Z., & Sciutto, J. (2017). Trump transgender ban blindsides Joint Chiefs. CNN. Retrieved November 13, 2017, from www.cnn.com/2017/07/27/politics/trump-military-transgender-ban-joint-chiefs/index.html

540 Linehan, A. (2017). Mattis tried to kill plan to bar transgender surgery for troops. Task & Purpose. Retrieved November 13, 2017, from http://taskandpurpose.com/mattis-tried-to-kill-plan-to-bar-transgender-surgery-for-troops

541 ACLU files lawsuit challenging Trump's transgender service member ban. (2017). American Civil Liberties Union. Retrieved November 13, 2017, from www.aclu.org/news/aclu-files-lawsuit-challenging-trumps-transgender-service-member-ban

542 NCLR and GLAD File lawsuit challenging Trump's transgender military ban. (2017). National Center for Lesbian Rights. Retrieved November 13, 2017, from www.nclrights.org/press-room/press-release/nclr-and-glad-file-lawsuit-challenging-trumps-transgender-military-ban

543 Lambda Legal. (2017). Lambda Legal and OutServe-SLDN sue President Trump to reverse transgender military service ban. Retrieved November 13, 2017, from www.lambdalegal.org/blog/20170828_lambda-legal-outserve-sldn-sue-trump-over-trans-military-ban

544 TLDEF: TLDEF files brief in support of transgender servicemembers challenging Trump Administration's military ban. (2017). Transgenderlegal.org. Retrieved November 13, 2017, from http://transgenderlegal.org/headline_show.php?id=899

545 The reliance doctrine, also known as promissory estoppel, prevents one party from withdrawing a promise made to a second party if the latter has reasonably relied on that promise. While a promise made without consideration is generally not enforceable, the military policy on transgender troops was enacted after years of study and thousands of man-hours spent on developing it

546 According to the Cornell Law School website, "A per curiam decision is a court opinion issued in the name of the Court rather than specific judges. Most decisions on the merits by the courts take the form of one or more opinions written and signed by individual justices. Often, other judges/justices will join these opinions. Even when these signed opinions are unanimous, they are not per curiam, as the judges'/justices' names still appear." Retrieved January 1, 2018, from www.law.cornell.edu/wex/per_curiam. *Per curiam* decisions are given that label by the court issuing the opinion, and these opinions tend to be short. The opinions will typically deal with issues which the issuing court views as relatively non-controversial

547 *Pavan v. Smith*. (2017). SCOTUSblog. Retrieved November 13, 2017, from www.scotusblog.com/case-files/cases/pavan-v-smith

548 Arkansas News. (2017). LGBTQ Nation. Retrieved November 13, 2017, from www.lgbtqnation.com/tag/arkansas

549 *Obergefell v. Hodges*. News. (2017). LGBTQ Nation. Retrieved November 13, 2017, from www.lgbtqnation.com/tag/obergefell-v-wymyslo

550 Stern, M. (2017). Texas Supreme Court defies Obergefell, refuses to extend spousal benefits to same-sex couples. *Slate Magazine*. Retrieved November 13, 2017, from www.slate.com/articles/news_and_politics/jurisprudence/2017/06/texas_supreme_court_refuses_to_extend_spousal_benefits_to_same_sex_couples.html

551 Houston TX News. (2017). LGBTQ Nation. Retrieved November 13, 2017, from www.lgbtqnation.com/tag/houston

552 Texas News. (2017). LGBTQ Nation. Retrieved November 13, 2017, from www.lgbtqnation.com/tag/texas

553 Gordon, M., Price, M., & Peralta, K. (2016). Understanding HB2: North Carolina's newest law solidifies state's role in defining discrimination. charlotteobserver. Retrieved November 13, 2017, from www.charlotteobserver.com/news/politics-government/article68401147.html

554 Domonoske, C. (2017). North Carolina repeals portions of controversial "Bathroom Bill." NPR.org. Retrieved November 13, 2017, from www.npr.org/sections/thetwo-way/2017/03/30/522009335/north-carolina-lawmakers-governor-announce-compromise-to-repeal-bathroom-bill

555 Higgins, T. (2016). Why I hate the TSA. HuffPost. Retrieved November 13, 2017, from www.huffingtonpost.com/tristan-higgins/why-i-hate-the-tsa_b_2762692.html

556 Polycystic ovary syndrome. (2017). En.wikipedia.org. Retrieved November 13, 2017, from https://en.wikipedia.org/wiki/Polycystic_ovary_syndrome

557 Acromegaly. (2017). En.wikipedia.org. Retrieved November 13, 2017, from https://en.wikipedia.org/wiki/Acromegaly

558 Trayvon Martin Case News. 911 Call, "Stand Your Ground" Law—HuffPost Black Voices. (2017). Huffingtonpost.com. Retrieved November 13, 2017, from www.huffingtonpost.com/topic/trayvon-martin

559 Callan, P. (2017, March 21). Judge Gorsuch and the frozen truck driver. Retrieved March 21, 2018, from www.cnn.com/2017/03/21/opinions/judge-gorsuch-the-frozen-truck-driver-opinion-callan/index.html

560 The "vagueness doctrine" requires criminal laws to state explicitly and definitively what conduct is punishable. Vagueness doctrine rests on the due process clauses of the 5th and 14th Amendments of the US Constitution. A statute is also void for vagueness if a legislature's delegation of authority to judges and/or administrators is so extensive that it would lead to arbitrary prosecutions. HB2 did not stipulate what punishments should be meted out for using a bathroom, and relied on "birth certificates" to determine what sexual organs a person possesses. Given the patchwork of laws on how to amend a birth certificate in the US, and how few people carry a birth certificate with them to the bathroom, it would have been impossible to apply the law uniformly, unless police were willing to strip search people. Because of the broad latitude given to judges on how to punish transgender people, and the impossibility of enforcing the law uniformly, HB2 would likely have been difficult to uphold as constitutional, so long as a plaintiff with standing could be found

561 Yes. Trillions

562 *Reductio ad absurdam* is a form of argument which attempts either to disprove a statement by showing it inevitably leads to a ridiculous, absurd, or impractical conclusion, or to prove one by showing that if it were not true, the result would be absurd or impossible

563 Posner, S. (2018, January 22). How a local religious-right faction launched anti-trans bathroom debate. Retrieved January 23, 2018, from www.rollingstone.com/politics/how-houstons-religious-right-launched-the-anti-lgbtq-bathroom-movement-w515477

564 Drabold, W. (2016, July 18). Republican platform on same-sex marriage, guns and Wall Street. Retrieved March 12, 2018, from http://time.com/4411842/republican-platform-same-sex-marriage-abortion-guns-wall-street

565 Beaumont, T. (2018, February 2). RNC sides with Trump ban of transgender people in military. Retrieved March 12, 2018, from www.chicagotribune.com/news/nationworld/politics/ct-rnc-transgender-military-20180202-story.html

566 Savransky, R. (2018, February 18). Kansas GOP approves resolution opposing efforts "to validate transgender identity": Report. Retrieved March 12, 2018, from http://thehill.com/homenews/state-watch/374464-kansas-gop-approves-resolution-opposing-efforts-to-validate-transgender

567 While conservatives may point out a single poll showing less acceptance of LGBT people in 2017 than in 2016, this could just as easily be statistical noise, or a by-product of people feeling they can say more socially unacceptable things now that Donald Trump is President rather than an actual dip in support. GLAAD unveils study with the Harris Poll showing alarming erosion of LGBTQ acceptance at World Economic Forum in Davos, Switzerland and calls for change as President Trump prepares to address forum. (2018, January 25). Retrieved March 12, 2018, from www.glaad.org/releases/glaad-unveils-study-harris-poll-showing-alarming-erosion-lgbtq-acceptance-world-economic

568 Browning, B. (2014). Laverne Cox & trans* rights featured in *Time Magazine*. Bilerico Report/LGBTQ Nation. Retrieved December 14, 2017, from http://bilerico.lgbtqnation.com/2014/05/laverne_cox_trans_rights_featured_in_time_magazine.php

569 Erbentraut, J. (2014, June 3). Chicago Sun-Times pulls "disgusting and transphobic" op-ed on Laverne Cox. The Huffington Post. Retrieved January 1, 2018, from www.huffingtonpost.com/2014/06/03/chicago-sun-times-laverne-cox-op-ed_n_5439513.html

570 Becker, J. (2014). Houston passes Equal Rights Ordinance. Bilerico Report/LGBTQ Nation. Retrieved December 14, 2017, from http://bilerico.lgbtqnation.com/2014/05/houston_passes_equal_rights_ordinance.php

571 YouTube. (2014). Houston religious cray cray HERO. Retrieved July 6, 2018, from www.youtube.com/watch?v=2ipSU2logPY

572 Shadwick, L. (2014). Ordinance allowing transgendered men in women's restrooms spurs protest. Breitbart. Retrieved December 14, 2017, from www.breitbart.com/Texas/2014/05/20/Ordinance-Allowing-Transgendered-Men-in-Womens-Restrooms-Spurs-Protest

573 Ablow, K. (2011). Do not let your kids watch Chaz Bono on "Dancing With the Stars." Fox News. Retrieved December 14, 2017, from www.foxnews.com/opinion/2011/09/02/dont-let-your-kids-watch-chaz-bono-on-dancing-with-stars.html

574 Ablow, K. (2011). Do not let your kids watch Chaz Bono on "Dancing With the Stars." Fox News. Retrieved December 14, 2017, from www.foxnews.com/opinion/2011/09/02/dont-let-your-kids-watch-chaz-bono-on-dancing-with-stars.html

575 Badash, D. (2016). Liberty Counsel President warns her glock "identifies" as her bodyguard in restrooms. The New Civil Rights Movement. Retrieved December 15, 2017, from www.thenewcivilrightsmovement.com/davidbadash/head_of_law_firm_that_has_drafted_anti_lgbt_bills_in_20_states_says_she_carries_a_45_into_restrooms

576 Molloy, P. (2016). Todd Kincannon, Former Executive Director of South Carolina GOP, believes transgender people should be "put in a camp." HuffPost. Retrieved December 14, 2017, from www.huffingtonpost.com/parker-marie-molloy/todd-kincannon-transgender-camps_b_4100777.html

577 Browning, B. (2013). Jindal: We are the stupid party. Bilerico Report/LGBTQ Nation. Retrieved December 14, 2017, from http://bilerico.lgbtqnation.com/2013/01/jindal_we_are_the_stupid_party.php

578 *DSM-5*. (2017). Psychiatry.org. Retrieved December 14, 2017, from www.psychiatry.org/psychiatrists/practice/dsm

579 Becker, J. (2013). Fox plays "Dude (Looks Like a Lady)" in Manning teaser. Bilerico Report/LGBTQ Nation. Retrieved December 14, 2017, from http://bilerico.lgbtqnation.com/2013/08/fox_plays_dude_looks_like_a_lady_in_manning_teaser.php

580 Professional organization statements supporting transgender people in health care. (2017). Lambda Legal. Retrieved December 14, 2017, from www.lambdalegal.org/publications/fs_professional-org-statements-supporting-trans-health

581 *Doe v. Minnesota Department of Public Welfare and Hennepin County Welfare Board*, 257 N.W. 2d 816, 819 (Minn. 1977); *Pinneke v. Preisser*, 623 F.2d 546, 549 (8th Cir. 1980); *Fields v. Smith*, 653 F.3d 550 (2011); *Kossilek v. Spencer*, 889 F.Supp.2d 190 (2012). See also: *Battista v. Clark*, 645 F.3d 449, 455 (1st Cir. 2011); *Soneeya v. Spencer*, 851 F.Supp.2d 228 (D. Mass. 2012); *De'Lonta v. Angelone*, 330 F.3d 630, 634 (4th Cir. 2003); *Phillips v. Michigan Department of Corrections*, 731 F.Supp. 792, 800 (W.D. Mich. 1990) decision affirmed 932 F.2d 969 (6th Cir. 1991); *Meriwether v. Faulkner*, 821 F.2d 408, 411–13 (7th Cir. 1987); *White v. Farrier*, 849 F.2d 322, 325–27 (8th Cir. 1988); *Allard v. Gomez*, 9 Fed. Appx. 793, 794 (9th Cir. 2001); *Brown v. Zavaras*, 63 F.3d 967, 970 (10th Cir. 1995)

582 Walshe, S. (2013). RNC completes "Autopsy" on 2012 loss, calls for inclusion not policy change. ABC News. Retrieved December 14, 2017, from http://abcnews.go.com/Politics/OTUS/rnc-completes-autopsy-2012-loss-calls-inclusion-policy/story?id=18755809

583 Ollstein, A. M. & Lerner, K. (2016, November 15). Republicans were wildly successful at suppressing voters in 2016. Retrieved December 25, 2017, from https://thinkprogress.org/2016-a-case-study-in-voter-suppression-258b5f90ddcd

584 Peters, J. W. Emerging Republican platform goes far to the right. The New York Times, July 12, 2016, www.nytimes.com/2016/07/13/us/politics/republican-convention-issues.html?_r=0

585 When someone in power over you forces something upon you, and you in turn force something on someone under you, like when parents punish you, then you turn around and beat on your little brother. Kick the Dog. TV Tropes. (2017). Retrieved December 14, 2017, from http://tvtropes.org/pmwiki/pmwiki.php/Main/KickTheDog

586 Anderson, R. T. (2018). *When Harry Became Sally: Responding to the Transgender Moment*. New York, NY: Encounter Books

587 Walker, A. T. & Mohler, R. A. (2017). *God and the Transgender Debate: What Does the Bible Actually Say About Gender Identity?* Centralia, WA: The Good Book Co.

588 Ford, Z. (2016, April 22). It takes a village to bully a transgender kindergartner. Retrieved December 27, 2017, from https://thinkprogress.org/it-takes-a-village-to-bully-a-transgender-kindergartner-67d6ec2195e1

589 Tannehill, B. (2015, September 14). The classmates of trans teen Lila Perry should be ashamed. Retrieved February 14, 2018, from www.advocate.com/commentary/2015/9/14/classmates-trans-teen-lila-perry-should-be-ashamed

590 Badash, D. (2016). Liberty Counsel President warns her glock "identifies" as her bodyguard in restrooms. The New Civil Rights Movement. Retrieved December 15, 2017, from www.thenewcivilrightsmovement.com/davidbadash/head_of_law_firm_that_has_drafted_anti_lgbt_bills_in_20_states_says_she_carries_a_45_into_restrooms

591 Dobson, J. (2016). Protect your kids from tyrant Obama. WND. Retrieved November 19, 2017, from www.wnd.com/2016/05/protect-your-kids-from-tyrant-obama

592 Posner, S. (2017, December 11). The Christian legal army behind "Masterpiece Cakeshop." The Nation. Retrieved March 11, 2018, from www.thenation.com/article/the-christian-legal-army-behind-masterpiece-cakeshop

593 GLAAD. (2015, September 17). Number of Americans who report knowing a transgender person doubles in seven years, according to new GLAAD survey. Retrieved July 6, 2018, from www.glaad.org/releases/number-americans-who-report-knowing-transgender-person-doubles-seven-years-according-new

594 YouTube. (2013). All this and rabbit stew [Remastered HD]. Retrieved July 6, 2018, from www.youtube.com/watch?v=1jmQ7MpYjJI

595 Bill Dana as Jose Jimenez. (2010). Retrieved July 6, 2018, from www.youtube.com/watch?v=x1MOLzFpqrU

596 YouTube. (2007). Disney's Peter Pan: What makes the red man red? Retrieved July 6, 2018, from www.youtube.com/watch?v=Y_at9dOElQk

597 WWII anti-Japanese propaganda. (2012). Retrieved July 6, 2018, from www.youtube.com/watch?v=jxtlcrIkIbI

598 Men on TV. (2008). Retrieved July 6, 2018, from www.youtube.com/watch?v=OMLvWX9DtGs

599 Tannehill, B. (2016). The choice that isn't. HuffPost. Retrieved December 14, 2017, from www.huffingtonpost.com/brynn-tannehill/the-choice-that-isnt_b_3574277.html

600 Tannehill, B. (2016). Do your homework, Dr. Ablow. HuffPost. Retrieved December 14, 2017, from www.huffingtonpost.com/brynn-tannehill/how-much-evidence-does-it_b_4616722.html

601 Tannehill, B. (2013, September 16). We're not astroturf: Why open trans military service is a worthy fight. The Huffington Post. Retrieved January 1, 2018, from www.huffingtonpost.com/brynn-tannehill/were-not-astroturf_b_3903502.html

602 Tannehill, B. (2016). How not to sound like a creationist to a trans person. The Huffington Post. Retrieved December 14, 2017, from www.huffingtonpost.com/brynn-tannehill/how-not-to-sound-like-a-c_b_4987906.html

603 National Coalition of Anti-Violence Programs (NCAVP). (2016). *Lesbian, Gay, Bisexual, Transgender, Queer, and HIV-Affected Hate Violence in 2016*. Retrieved July 6, 2018, from http://avp.org/wp-content/uploads/2017/06/NCAVP_2016HateViolence_REPORT.pdf

604 Dry, J. (2018, March 13). Ricky Gervais new Netflix special opens with smugly transphobic Caitlyn Jenner jokes. Retrieved March 21, 2018, from www.indiewire.com/2018/03/ricky-gervais-netflix-transphobic-jenner-1201938675

605 Ford, Z. (2012). Tennessee bathroom bill sponsor: "I would stomp a mudhole" in a transgender person. Thinkprogress.org. Retrieved December 14, 2017, from https://thinkprogress.org/tennessee-bathroom-bill-sponsor-i-would-stomp-a-mudhole-in-a-transgender-person-3e4f7b8c4866

606 Molloy, P. (2013). Former GOP Executive Director says transgender people belong "in a camp." Thought Catalog. Retrieved December 14, 2017, from https://thoughtcatalog.com/parker-marie-molloy/2013/10/former-gop-executive-director-says-transgender-people-belong-in-a-camp

607 Boothroyd III, H. (2013). Cathy Brennan the Phyllis Schlafly of our time. Daily Kos. Retrieved December 14, 2017, from www.dailykos.com/stories/2013/07/11/1222933/-Cathy-Brennan-the-Phyllis-Schlafly-of-our-time

608 rserven. (2013). Conservative "reporter" poses as pervert in order to demean transwomen. Daily Kos. Retrieved December 14, 2017, from www.dailykos.com/stories/2013/08/19/1232276/-Conservative-reporter-poses-as-pervert-in-order-to-demean-transwomen

609 *DeBoer v. Snyder*, 772 F.3d 388, 2014 WL 5748990 (6th Cir. 2014). Retrieved July 6, 2018, from www.opn.ca6.uscourts.gov/opinions.pdf/14a0275p-06.pdf

610 Groups. (2017). Southern Poverty Law Center. Retrieved December 14, 2017, from www.splcenter.org/fighting-hate/extremist-files/groups

611 Anti-LGBT. (2017). Southern Poverty Law Center. Retrieved February 13, 2018, from www.splcenter.org/fighting-hate/extremist-files/ideology/anti-lgbt

612 Posner, S. (2018, January 22). How a local religious-right faction launched anti-trans bathroom debate. Retrieved January 23, 2018, from www.rollingstone.com/politics/how-houstons-religious-right-launched-the-anti-lgbtq-bathroom-movement-w515477

613 Pullmann, J. (2014). Discrimination is healthy and normal—sex confusion is not. The Federalist. Retrieved December 14, 2017, from http://thefederalist.com/2014/06/19/discrimination-is-healthy-and-normal-sex-confusion-is-not

614 Anderson, R. T. (2018). *When Harry Became Sally: Responding to the Transgender Moment*. New York, NY: Encounter Books, p211

615 Wong, C. (2014). Laura Jane Klug, teacher suspended for being transgender, returns to position outside the classroom. HuffPost UK. Retrieved December 15, 2017, from www.huffingtonpost.com/2014/04/25/laura-jane-klug-returns_n_5214503.html

616 Briggs Initiative. (2017). En.wikipedia.org. Retrieved September 13, 2018, from https://web.archive.org/web/20170127101927/http://nounequalrights.com/information

617 No Unequal Rights. (2017). Nounequalrights.com. Retrieved September 13, 2018, from https://web.archive.org/web/20170127101927/http://nounequalrights.com/information

618 McEwen, A. (2013). How they see us; unmasking the religious right war on gay America. Retrieved February 13, 2018, from https://howtheyseeus.files.wordpress.com/2013/12/howthey-see-us-with-index2.pdf

619 Maza, C. & Brinker, L. (2014). 15 experts debunk right-wing transgender bathroom myth. Media Matters for America. Retrieved December 15, 2017, from www.mediamatters.org/research/2014/03/20/15-experts-debunk-right-wing-transgender-bathro/198533

620 Marsh, J. (1993). No good basis for military ban on gays. tribunedigital-chicagotribune. Retrieved December 15, 2017, from http://articles.chicagotribune.com/1993-01-18/news/9303163202_1_gay-ban-robert-maginnis-homosexuality

621 Martel, F. (2011). Jon Stewart celebrates end of DADT (with Jason Jones in Daisy Dukes). Mediaite.com. Retrieved December 15, 2017, from www.mediaite.com/tv/jon-stewart-celebrates-end-of-dadt-with-jason-jones-in-daisy-dukes

622 Millhiser, I. (2016, November 6). How the religious right learned to use bathrooms as a weapon against justice. ThinkProgress. Retrieved July 6, 2018, from https://thinkprogress.org/how-the-religious-right-learned-to-use-bathrooms-as-a-weapon-against-justice-fa8db0e7e949

623 Brinker, L. (2014). Fox's Ablow: There's no such thing as being transgender. Media Matters for America. Retrieved December 15, 2017, from www.mediamatters.org/blog/2014/01/15/foxs-ablow-theres-no-such-thing-as-being-transg/197604

624 Tannehill, B. (2014). Do your homework, Dr. Ablow. HuffPost. Retrieved December 15, 2017, from www.huffingtonpost.com/brynn-tannehill/how-much-evidence-does-it_b_4616722.html

625 LDS/Center for Gender Wholeness. (2017). Genderwholeness.com. Retrieved December 15, 2017, from http://genderwholeness.com/lds

626 Ex-gay therapist on CNN. (2006). Retrieved July 6, 2018, from www.youtube.com/watch?v=jJXWFZzoQjo

627 Donegan, M. (2017, March 13). The abominable legacy of gay-conversion therapy. Retrieved February 14, 2018, from https://newrepublic.com/article/141294/abominable-legacy-gay-conversion-therapy

628 No Unequal Rights. (2017). Nounequalrights.com. Retrieved September 13, 2018, from https://web.archive.org/web/20170127101927/http://nounequalrights.com/information

629 Oritz, F. (2015, November 4). Failure to woo minority voters helps tank Houston's bathroom ordinance. Retrieved February 14, 2018, from www.reuters.com/article/us-usa-election-houston/failure-to-woo-minority-voters-helps-tank-houstons-bathroom-ordinance-idUSKCN0ST2U720151104

630 Tashman, B. (2014). Linda Harvey thinks Satan is behind Laverne Cox's transgender rights advocacy. Right Wing Watch. Retrieved December 15, 2017, from www.rightwingwatch.org/post/linda-harvey-thinks-satan-is-behind-laverne-coxs-transgender-rights-advocacy

631 Ford, Z. (2013). Bill O'Reilly: Supporting transgender equality in schools is "truly madness." Thinkprogress.org. Retrieved December 15, 2017, from https://thinkprogress.org/bill-oreilly-supporting-transgender-equality-in-schools-is-truly-madness-6846e668b803

632 Morabito, S. (2014). How the trans-agenda seeks to redefine everyone. The Federalist. Retrieved December 15, 2017, from http://thefederalist.com/2014/06/23/how-the-trans-agenda-seeks-to-redefine-everyone

633 O'Leary, D. & Sprigg, P. (2017). Understanding and responding to the transgender movement. FRC. Retrieved December 14, 2017, from www.frc.org/transgender

634 Pomerantz, A. (2015). *Qualified and Transgender: A Report on Results of Resume Testing for Employment Discrimination Based on Gender Identity*. Office of Human Rights, District of Columbia.

635 Woman gets five years in savage beating of transgender woman in McDonald's. (2011). Mail Online. Retrieved December 14, 2017, from www.dailymail.co.uk/news/article-2037058/Teonna-Brown-gets-years-savage-beating-transgender-woman-Chrissy-Polis-Maryland-McDonalds.html

636 Rubin Erdely, S. (2014). The transgender crucible. Rolling Stone. Retrieved December 14, 2017, from www.rollingstone.com/culture/news/the-transgender-crucible-20140730

637 Ennis, D. (2015). Black trans woman Ashley Diamond released from prison after 3 years. Advocate.com. Retrieved December 14, 2017, from www.advocate.com/transgender/2015/08/31/black-trans-woman-ashley-diamond-released-prison-after-3-years

638 Grant, J. M., Mottet, L. A., Tanis, J., Harrison, J., Herman, J. L., & Keisling, M. (2011). *Injustice at Every Turn: A Report of the National Transgender Discrimination Survey*. Washington DC: National Center for Transgender Equality and National Gay and Lesbian Task Force

639 Peters, J. W. (2017, August 2). Trump keeps his conservative movement allies closest. Retrieved December 27, 2017, from www.nytimes.com/2017/08/02/us/politics/trump-conservative-republicans.html?_r=0

640 Cesca, B. (2015, March 31). Indiana Gov. Mike Pence continues to dodge the discrimination question. Retrieved March 21, 2018, from www.huffingtonpost.com/bob-cesca/mike-pence-discrimination-question_b_6978848.html

641 The Southern Baptist Convention passed a resolution in 2014 effectively decreeing that anyone who treats a transgender person based on their gender identity is committing an unforgivable sin. Retrieved July 6, 2018, from www.sbc.net/resolutions/2250/on-transgender-identity

642 Jarrett, L. (2017, July 13). AG Sessions under fire for closed-door speech. Retrieved December 27, 2017, from www.cnn.com/2017/07/12/politics/jeff-sessions-alliance-defending-freedom-summit/index.html

643 "We believe all forms of sexual immorality (including adultery, fornication, homosexual behavior, polygamy, polyandry, bestiality, incest, pornography, and acting upon any disagreement with one's biological sex) are sinful and offensive to God." Retrieved July 6, 2018, from www.adflegal.org/about-us/careers/statement-of-faith

644 Madden, P. (2017, October 6). Jeff Sessions consulted Christian right legal group on religious freedom memo. Retrieved December 27, 2017, from http://abcnews.go.com/Politics/jeff-sessions-consulted-christian-legal-group-religious-freedom/story?id=50336322

645 Posner, S. (2018, January 22). How a local religious-right faction launched anti-trans bathroom debate. Retrieved January 23, 2018, from www.rollingstone.com/politics/how-houstons-religious-right-launched-the-anti-lgbtq-bathroom-movement-w515477

646 Busey, K. (2009, January 10). Gainesville FL: Misleading anti transgender ad exposed. Retrieved February 14, 2018, from http://planettransgender.com/gainesville-fl-misleading-anti-transgender-ad-exposed

647 Yardley, W. (2012, April 4). Anchorage voters reject extension of rights protections to gay residents. Retrieved February 14, 2018, from www.nytimes.com/2012/04/05/us/proposition-5-gay-rights-anchorage-alaska.html

648 Oakley, C. (2016, November 15). State report: anti-transgender legislation spreads. Retrieved December 27, 2017, from www.hrc.org/blog/2016-state-legislative-report-anti-transgender-legislation-spread-nationwid

649 Based on the National Center for Transgender Equality bill tracking web page. Retrieved December 27, 2017, from https://transequality.org/action-center

650 Indiana General Assembly. (2016). Senate Bill 35: Single sex facilities. Retrieved December 15, 2017, from https://iga.in.gov/legislative/2016/bills/senate/35

651 Illinois General Assembly: Bill Status for HB4474. (2017). Ilga.gov. Retrieved December 15, 2017, from www.ilga.gov/legislation/BillStatus.asp?DocNum=4474&GAID=13&DocTypeID=HB&SessionID=88&GA=99

652 South Dakota Legislative Research Council. (2017). 2016 House Bill 1008. Sdlegislature.gov. Retrieved December 15, 2017, from http://sdlegislature.gov/legislative_session/bills/Bill.aspx?Bill=1008&Session=2016

653 LIS > Bill Tracking > HB781 > 2016 session. (2017). Lis.virginia.gov. Retrieved December 15, 2017, from http://lis.virginia.gov/cgi-bin/legp604.exe?161+sum+HB781

654 Wisconsin Legislature: AB469: Bill Text. (2015). Docs.legis.wisconsin.gov. Retrieved December 15, 2017, from http://docs.legis.wisconsin.gov/2015/related/proposals/ab469

655 Molloy, P. (2014). U.S. Department of Education extends protections to trans students. Advocate.com. Retrieved December 15, 2017, from www.advocate.com/politics/transgender/2014/04/29/us-department-education-extends-protections-trans-students

656 Boren, C. (2018, February 25). Transgender wrestler Mack Beggs wins second Texas girls' state championship. Retrieved March 21, 2018, from www.chicagotribune.com/sports/breaking/ct-mack-beggs-transgender-wrestler-texas-20180225-story.html

657 Abeni, C. (2016). No one is happy with Nebraska's transphobic student policy. Advocate.com. Retrieved December 15, 2017, from www.advocate.com/transgender/2016/1/16/no-one-happy-nebraskas-transphobic-student-policy

658 Kellaway, M. (2015). Subjected to "constant" bullying, California trans teen dies by suicide. Advocate.com. Retrieved December 15, 2017, from www.advocate.com/politics/transgender/2015/04/09/subjected-constant-bullying-california-trans-teen-dies-suicide

659 Kosciw, J. G., Greytak, E. A., Giga, N. M., Villenas, C., & Danischewski, D. J. (2016). *The 2015 National School Climate Survey: The Experiences of Lesbian, Gay, Bisexual, Transgender, and Queer Youth in Our Nation's Schools*. New York, NY: GLSEN

660 Indiana General Assembly. (2016). Senate Bill 35: Single sex facilities. Retrieved December 15, 2017, from https://iga.in.gov/legislative/2016/bills/senate/35

661 Massachusetts H1320/2015–2016/189th General Court. (2015). LegiScan. Retrieved December 15, 2017, from https://legiscan.com/MA/bill/H1320/2015

662 Ford, Z. (2016). Washington state lawmakers: Transgender people's bodies are "security concerns." Thinkprogress.org. Retrieved December 15, 2017, from https://thinkprogress.org/washington-state-lawmakers-transgender-peoples-bodies-are-security-concerns-7b0adc493fdb

663 Broverman, N. (2015). Houston repeals LGBT-inclusive HERO. Advocate.com. Retrieved December 15, 2017, from www.advocate.com/election/2015/11/03/houston-repeals-lgbt-inclusive-hero

664 Nichols, J. (2016). Poll shows way more education needed to understand lives and rights of trans people. HuffPost UK. Retrieved December 15, 2017, from www.huffingtonpost.com/2014/06/13/transgender-bathroom-rights_n_5492286.html

665 Posner, S. (2018, January 22). How a local religious-right faction launched anti-trans bathroom debate. Retrieved January 23, 2018, from www.rollingstone.com/politics/how-houstons-religious-right-launched-the-anti-lgbtq-bathroom-movement-w515477

666 Doran, W. (2016). Equality NC director: No public safety risks in cities with transgender anti-discrimination rules. @politifact. Retrieved December 15, 2017, from www.politifact.com/north-carolina/statements/2016/apr/01/chris-sgro/equality-nc-director-no-public-safety-risks-cities

667 2015–2016 Bill 108: Department of Corrections: South Carolina Legislature Online. (2016). Scstatehouse.gov. Retrieved December 15, 2017, from www.scstatehouse.gov/sess121_2015-2016/bills/108.htm

668 Kellaway, M. (2015). DOJ tells state prisons: Denying trans inmates hormone therapy is unconstitutional. Advocate.com. Retrieved December 15, 2017, from www.advocate.com/politics/transgender/2015/04/08/doj-tells-state-prisons-denying-trans-inmates-hormone-therapy-uncons

669 Kellaway, M. (2015). Federal judge: California must provide trans inmate with access to gender-affirming surgery. Advocate.com. Retrieved December 15, 2017, from www.advocate.com/politics/transgender/2015/04/06/federal-judge-california-must-provide-trans-inmate-access-gender-aff

670 LIS > Bill Tracking > HB431 > 2016 session. (2016). Lis.virginia.gov. Retrieved December 15, 2017, from http://lis.virginia.gov/cgi-bin/legp604.exe?161+sum+HB431

671 Lavers, M. (2016). Va. bill seeks to limit gender changes on birth certificates. Washington Blade: Gay News, Politics, LGBT Rights. Retrieved December 15, 2017, from www.washingtonblade.com/2016/01/09/va-bill-seeks-to-limit-gender-changes-on-birth-certificates

672 Kornet, T. (2015). Gender cannot be changed on birth certificates in TN. Wsmv.com. Retrieved December 15, 2017, from www.wsmv.com/story/29249433/gender-cannot-be-changed-on-birth-certificates-in-tn

673 Associated Press. (2016, May 13). Kansas to toughen rules on transgender birth certificates. Retrieved December 27, 2017, from www.kansascity.com/news/state/kansas/article77388952.html

674 ID Documents Center. (2017). National Center for Transgender Equality. Retrieved December 15, 2017, from https://transequality.org/documents

675 Chibbaro Jr., L. (2015). Sting reveals anti-trans job bias. Washington Blade: Gay News, Politics, LGBT Rights. Retrieved December 15, 2017, from www.washingtonblade.com/2015/11/04/sting-reveals-anti-trans-job-bias

676 Bill Information. (2017). Oklegislature.gov. Retrieved December 15, 2017, from www.oklegislature.gov/BillInfo.aspx?Bill=hb2215

677 HB 77: Sex or gender discrimination; applicable federal law. (2017). Retrieved December 15, 2017, from https://lis.virginia.gov/cgi-bin/legp604.exe?161+sum+HB77

678 H.R.2796—Civil Rights Uniformity Act of 2017. (2017). Retrieved February 13, 2018, from www.congress.gov/bill/115th-congress/house-bill/2796/text

679 FRC. Pro Marriage & Pro Life Organization in Washington DC. (2017). Frc.org. Retrieved December 15, 2017, from www.frc.org

680 Liberty Counsel. (2017). Lc.org. Retrieved December 15, 2017, from www.lc.org

681 Alliance Defending Freedom: For Faith. For Justice. (2017). Adflegal.org. Retrieved December 15, 2017, from www.adflegal.org

682 Mindock, C. (2017, July 3). Texas Republican says he blocked a transgender bathroom bill because he didn't want a single suicide on his hands. Retrieved February 13, 2018, from www.independent.co.uk/news/world-0/us-politics/texas-transgender-bathroom-bill-law-blocked-name-suicide-a7821921.html

683 Botelho, G. & Drash, W. (2016, March 2). South Dakota Governor vetoes transgender bathroom bill. Retrieved February 13, 2018, from www.cnn.com/2016/03/01/us/south-dakota-transgender-bathroom-bill/index.html

684 Kendell, K. E. (2017). Homepage. National Center for Lesbian Rights. Retrieved December 15, 2017, from www.nclrights.org

685 Even the new law, HB142, was challenged and led to a consent decree

686 Eason, B. (2016). Official: RFRA cost Indy up to 12 conventions and $60M. Indianapolis Star. Retrieved December 15, 2017, from www.indystar.com/story/news/politics/2016/01/25/official-rfra-cost-indy-up-12-conventions-and-60m/79328422

687 Ellis, E. G. (2017, June 3). Guess how much that anti-LGBTQ law is costing North Carolina. Retrieved December 27, 2017, from www.wired.com/2016/09/guess-much-anti-lgbtq-law-costing-north-carolina

688 Batheja, A. (2017, November 9). How a chaotic night in the Texas House paved the way for Speaker Straus. Retrieved December 27, 2017, from www.texastribune.org/2017/11/09/how-rough-night-tom-craddick-paved-way-joe-straus

689 Doran, W. (2016). N.C. Lt. Gov. Dan Forest says new state law HB2 prevented a bathroom free-for-all in Charlotte. @politifact. Retrieved December 15, 2017, from www.politifact.com/north-carolina/statements/2016/apr/08/dan-forest/nc-lt-gov-dan-forest-says-new-state-law-hb2-preven

690 James, S. E., Herman, J. L., Rankin, S., Keisling, M., Mottet, L., & Anafi, M. (2016). *The Report of the 2015 U.S. Transgender Survey*. Washington, DC: National Center for Transgender Equality

691 Johnson, C. (2017, April 19). DOJ withdraws lawsuit against N.C. anti-trans bathroom law. Retrieved December 27, 2017, from www.washingtonblade.com/2017/04/14/breaking-doj-withdraws-lawsuit-n-c-anti-trans-bathroom-law

692 Botelho, G. & Drash, W. (2016, March 2). South Dakota Governor vetoes transgender bathroom bill. Retrieved December 27, 2017, from www.cnn.com/2016/03/01/us/south-dakota-transgender-bathroom-bill/index.html

693 Miller, S. (2017, April 11). Beyond the bathroom: Report shows laws' harm for transgender students. Retrieved March 21, 2018, from www.usatoday.com/story/news/nation/2017/04/11/beyond-bathroom-report-shows-laws-harm-transgender-students/100265266

694 *Whitaker v. Kenosha Unified School District* complaint, Civ. Action No. 2:16-cv-00943. Retrieved July 6, 2018, from www.relmanlaw.com/docs/AWvKUSDcomplaint.pdf

695 Lang, N. (2017, January 19). Separate is never equal: What "Hidden Figures" says about America's trans bathroom debate. Retrieved December 27, 2017, from www.salon.com/2017/01/18/separate-is-never-equal-what-hidden-figures-says-about-americas-trans-bathroom-debate

696 Joyce, K. (2017, March 26). She was an ultraconservative Texas Christian. Then Kai was born and everything changed. Retrieved March 21, 2018, from https://splinternews.com/she-was-an-ultraconservative-texas-christian-then-kai-1793859323

697 South Dakota State Senator Brock Greenfield said during debate of the bill that the bill banning transgender students was a good thing since people "stop being transgender with great frequency." Retrieved December 27, 2017, from www.facebook.com/kelley.winters/videos/10208513178685494

698 Tannehill, B. (2017). The end of the desistance myth. HuffPost. Retrieved December 14, 2017, from www.huffingtonpost.com/brynn-tannehill/the-end-of-the-desistance_b_8903690.html

699 Tannehill, B. (2017). Not one more. HuffPost. Retrieved December 14, 2017, from www.huffingtonpost.com/brynn-tannehill/not-one-more_b_6400854.html

700 Rose, R. (2015). Transgender teen Jazz Jennings shares the horrifying comments and threats she gets. Cosmopolitan. Retrieved December 14, 2017, from www.cosmopolitan.com/entertainment/news/a44787/transgender-teen-jazz-jennings-shares-the-horrifying-death-threats-she-gets

701 Ford, Z. (2016, April 22). It takes a village to bully a transgender kindergartner. Retrieved December 27, 2017, from https://thinkprogress.org/it-takes-a-village-to-bully-a-transgender-kindergartner-67d6ec2195e1

702 Badash, D. (2017). North Carolina at The New Civil Rights Movement. The New Civil Rights Movement. Retrieved December 15, 2017, from www.thenewcivilrightsmovement.com/tags/North_Carolina

703 Badash, D. (2017). HB2 at The New Civil Rights Movement. The New Civil Rights Movement. Retrieved December 15, 2017, from www.thenewcivilrightsmovement.com/tags/HB2

704 Doran, W. (2016). N.C. Lt. Gov. Dan Forest says new state law HB2 prevented a bathroom free-for-all in Charlotte. @politifact. Retrieved December 15, 2017, from www.politifact.com/north-carolina/statements/2016/apr/08/dan-forest/nc-lt-gov-dan-forest-says-new-state-law-hb2-preven

705 Public Accommodations. (2017). National Center for Transgender Equality. Retrieved December 15, 2017, from https://transequality.org/know-your-rights/public-accommodations

706 Maza, C. & Brinker, L. (2014). 15 experts debunk right-wing transgender bathroom myth. Media Matters for America. Retrieved December 15, 2017, from www.mediamatters.org/research/2014/03/20/15-experts-debunk-right-wing-transgender-bathro/198533

707 Percelay, R. (2016). Florida experts debunk the transgender "bathroom predator" myth. Media Matters for America. Retrieved December 15, 2017, from www.mediamatters.org/research/2016/01/12/florida-experts-debunk-the-transgender-bathroom/207916

708 Percelay, R. (2016). Florida experts debunk the transgender "bathroom predator" myth. Media Matters for America. Retrieved December 15, 2017, from www.mediamatters.org/research/2016/01/12/florida-experts-debunk-the-transgender-bathroom/207916

709 Borrello, S. (2016, April 22). Sexual assault and domestic violence organizations debunk "bathroom predator myth." ABC News. Retrieved December 27, 2017, from http://abcnews.go.com/US/sexual-assault-domestic-violence-organizations-debunk-bathroom-predator/story?id=38604019

710 Haver-Triller, K. (2015, December 9). A rape survivor speaks out about transgender bathrooms. Retrieved February 13, 2018, from http://thefederalist.com/2015/11/23/a-rape-survivor-speaks-out-about-transgender-bathrooms

711 Human Rights Campaign. (2017). *Corporate Equality Index 2018: Rating American Workplaces on Gay, Lesbian, Bisexual, and Transgender Equality*. Washington, DC: Author. Retrieved July 6, 2018, from https://assets2.hrc.org/files/assets/resources/CEI-2018-FullReport.pdf?_ga=2.114385991.1103353226.1513791816-2124830380.1513791816

712 Golgowski, N. (2016). Anti-queer Christians invading Target stores to preach are wreaking havoc. HuffPost UK. Retrieved December 15, 2017, from www.huffingtonpost.com/entry/protesters-invade-target-stores-to-preach_us_5728acf7e4b0bc9cb044862e?utm_hp_ref=mostpopular

713 Allen, S. (2016). All the things you can no longer buy if you're really boycotting trans-friendly businesses. The Daily Beast. Retrieved December 15, 2017, from www.thedailybeast.com/all-the-things-you-can-no-longer-buy-if-youre-really-boycotting-trans-friendly-businesses

714 Ford, Z. (2011, October 19). Non-discrimination protections are good for businesses of all sizes. Retrieved February 14, 2018, from https://thinkprogress.org/non-discrimination-protections-are-good-for-businesses-of-all-sizes-890a88ae3476

715 Ford, Z. (2011, June 21). STUDY: Employees who can come out at work "flourish," closeted workers "languish or leave." Retrieved February 14, 2018, from https://thinkprogress.org/study-employees-who-can-come-out-at-work-flourish-closeted-workers-languish-or-leave-633c31f0a408

716 Ford, Z. (2011, August 25). STUDY: Openly gay employees improve their coworkers productivity. Retrieved February 14, 2018, from https://thinkprogress.org/study-openly-gay-employees-improve-their-coworkers-productivity-bf84ae9d05ba

717 Maza, C. & Brinker, L. (2014). 15 experts debunk right-wing transgender bathroom myth. Media Matters for America. Retrieved December 15, 2017, from www.mediamatters.org/research/2014/03/20/15-experts-debunk-right-wing-transgender-bathro/198533

718 Percelay, R. (2016). Florida experts debunk the transgender "bathroom predator" myth. Media Matters for America. Retrieved December 15, 2017, from www.mediamatters.org/research/2016/01/12/florida-experts-debunk-the-transgender-bathroom/207916

719 Maza, C. & Percelay, R. (2015). Texas experts debunk the transgender "bathroom predator" myth ahead of HERO referendum. Media Matters for America. Retrieved December 15, 2017, from www.mediamatters.org/research/2015/10/15/texas-experts-debunk-the-transgender-bathroom-p/206178

720 Percelay, R. (2016). Florida experts debunk the transgender "bathroom predator" myth. Media Matters for America. Retrieved December 15, 2017, from www.mediamatters.org/research/2016/01/12/florida-experts-debunk-the-transgender-bathroom/207916

721 Maza, C. & Percelay, R. (2015). Texas experts debunk the transgender "bathroom predator" myth ahead of HERO referendum. Media Matters for America. Retrieved December 15, 2017, from www.mediamatters.org/research/2015/10/15/texas-experts-debunk-the-transgender-bathroom-p/206178

722 Doran, W. (2016). N.C. Lt. Gov. Dan Forest says new state law HB2 prevented a bathroom free-for-all in Charlotte. @politifact. Retrieved December 15, 2017, from www.politifact.com/north-carolina/statements/2016/apr/08/dan-forest/nc-lt-gov-dan-forest-says-new-state-law-hb2-preven

723 Doran, W. (2016). Equality NC director: No public safety risks in cities with transgender anti-discrimination rules. @politifact. Retrieved December 15, 2017, from www.politifact.com/north-carolina/statements/2016/apr/01/chris-sgro/equality-nc-director-no-public-safety-risks-cities

724 FRC. Pro Marriage & Pro Life Organization in Washington DC. (2017). Frc.org. Retrieved December 15, 2017, from www.frc.org

725 Kim Davis' lawyers offer to defend HB2. (2016). ABC11 Raleigh-Durham. Retrieved December 15, 2017, from http://abc11.com/politics/kim-davis-lawyers-offer-to-defend-hb2-/1270836

726 Badash, D. (2016). Liberty Counsel President warns her glock "identifies" as her bodyguard in restrooms. The New Civil Rights Movement. Retrieved December 15, 2017, from www.thenewcivilrightsmovement.com/davidbadash/head_of_law_firm_that_has_drafted_anti_lgbt_bills_in_20_states_says_she_carries_a_45_into_restrooms

727 Michaels, S. (2016). We tracked down the lawyers behind the recent wave of anti-trans bathroom bills. Mother Jones. Retrieved December 15, 2017, from www.motherjones.com/politics/2016/04/alliance-defending-freedom-lobbies-anti-lgbt-bathroom-bills

728 Michaels, S. (2016). We tracked down the lawyers behind the recent wave of anti-trans bathroom bills. Mother Jones. Retrieved December 15, 2017, from www.motherjones.com/politics/2016/04/alliance-defending-freedom-lobbies-anti-lgbt-bathroom-bills

729 Badash, D. (2016). Liberty Counsel President warns her glock "identifies" as her bodyguard in restrooms. The New Civil Rights Movement. Retrieved December 15, 2017, from www.thenewcivilrightsmovement.com/davidbadash/head_of_law_firm_that_has_drafted_anti_lgbt_bills_in_20_states_says_she_carries_a_45_into_restrooms

730 Dobson, J. (2016). Protect your kids from tyrant Obama. WND. Retrieved November 19, 2017, from www.wnd.com/2016/05/protect-your-kids-from-tyrant-obama

731 Ennis, D. (2016). She is Cait, and I am not: Face to face with Jenner. Advocate.com. Retrieved December 15, 2017, from www.advocate.com/caitlyn-jenner/2016/3/02/she-cait-and-i-am-not-face-face-jenner

732 Tannehill, B. (2016). Ted Cruz scares me the most. HuffPost. Retrieved December 15, 2017, from www.huffingtonpost.com/brynn-tannehill/ted-cruz-scares-the-me-th_b_9138720.html

733 Signorile, M. (2015, November 12). Why is the media ignoring Ted Cruz's embrace of "kill the gays" pastor? Retrieved December 27, 2017, from www.huffingtonpost.com/michelangelo-signorile/post_10496_b_8544540.html

734 Ring, T. (2016). WATCH: Hate group leader Tony Perkins endorses Ted Cruz. Advocate.com. Retrieved December 15, 2017, from www.advocate.com/election/2016/1/27/watch-hate-group-leader-tony-perkins-endorses-ted-cruz

735 Ring, T. (2016). WATCH: Hate group leader Tony Perkins endorses Ted Cruz. Advocate.com. Retrieved December 15, 2017, from www.advocate.com/election/2016/1/27/watch-hate-group-leader-tony-perkins-endorses-ted-cruz

736 Jenkins, J. (2016). The story behind Ted Cruz's religious beliefs. Thinkprogress.org. Retrieved December 15, 2017, from https://thinkprogress.org/the-story-behind-ted-cruzs-religious-beliefs-b21ada9ca2c9

737 Ford, Z. (2014). How the Southern Baptists are still completely failing transgender people. Thinkprogress.org. Retrieved December 15, 2017, from https://thinkprogress.org/how-the-southern-baptists-are-still-completely-failing-transgender-people-173dac9fcf11

738 Southern Baptist Convention. On Transgender Identity. (2017). Sbc.net. Retrieved December 15, 2017, from www.sbc.net/resolutions/2250/on-transgender-identity

739 HRC. (2016). Mark Kirk becomes first Senate Republican to co-sponsor the Equality Act. Human Rights Campaign. Retrieved December 15, 2017, from www.hrc.org/blog/mark-kirk-becomes-first-senate-republican-to-co-sponsor-the-equality-act

740 Rothaus, S. (2015). Rep. Ileana Ros-Lehtinen's transgender son, Rodrigo, to be honored at SAVE reception in Miami. miamiherald. Retrieved December 15, 2017, from www.miamiherald.com/news/local/community/gay-south-florida/article20432967.html

741 Cillizza, C. (2015). The remarkable Republican takeover of state legislatures, in 1 chart. The Washington Post. Retrieved December 15, 2017, from www.washingtonpost.com/news/the-fix/wp/2015/03/04/the-remarkable-republican-takeover-of-state-legislatures-in-1-chart/?utm_term=.b5706c9cc9e7

742 Ferguson, D. (2016). Gov: Transgender meeting "helped me see things through their eyes." Argus Leader. Retrieved December 15, 2017, from www.argusleader.com/story/news/politics/2016/02/23/governor-daugaard-meets-transgender-students/80792620

743 Wagner, L. & Chappell, B. (2016). South Dakota Governor vetoes bill stipulating transgender students' bathroom use. NPR.org. Retrieved December 15, 2017, from www.npr.org/sections/thetwo-way/2016/03/01/468732723/south-dakota-s-transgender-bathroom-bill-hits-deadline-for-governor

744 Hiscott, R. (2014). Homophobia is hurting the economy. HuffPost UK. Retrieved December 15, 2017, from www.huffingtonpost.com/2014/06/13/homophobia-economy-india_n_5488662.html

745 Table A-15. Alternative measures of labor underutilization. (2017). Bls.gov. Retrieved December 15, 2017, from www.bls.gov/news.release/empsit.t15.htm

746 Carney, J. (2016). Senate Dems slam "disrespectful" GOP for ignoring Obama budget. TheHill. Retrieved December 15, 2017, from http://thehill.com/blogs/floor-action/senate/268744-sanders-dems-slam-gop-over-obama-budget

747 Transgender Equality Map, The Transgender Law Center. Retrieved February 13, 2018, from https://transgenderlawcenter.org/equalitymap

748 James, S. E., Herman, J. L., Rankin, S., Keisling, M., Mottet, L., & Anafi, M. (2016). *The Report of the 2015 U.S. Transgender Survey*. Washington, DC: National Center for Transgender Equality

749 Senzee, T. (2015). 7 reasons to be hopeful in 2015. Advocate.com. Retrieved November 20, 2017, from www.advocate.com/commentary/2015/01/04/7-reasons-be-hopeful-2015

750 Silver, N. (2017, November 8). The fundamentals favor Democrats in 2018. Retrieved December 27, 2017, from https://fivethirtyeight.com/features/the-fundamentals-favor-democrats-in-2018

751 Becker, J. (2014). Indiana will consider "Right to Discriminate" Bill. Bilerico Report/LGBTQ Nation. Retrieved November 20, 2017, from http://bilerico.lgbtqnation.com/2014/12/indiana_will_consider_right_to_discriminate_bill.php

752 Ocamb, K. (2013). Trans legal eagle Masen Davis on Arizona's "Bathroom" Bill. Bilerico Report/LGBTQ Nation. Retrieved November 20, 2017, from http://bilerico.lgbtqnation.com/2013/04/trans_legal_eagle_masen_davis_on_arizonas_bathroom.php

753 Ford, Z. (2015). One lawmaker's sneaky attempt to keep marriage equality out of Texas. Thinkprogress.org. Retrieved November 20, 2017, from https://thinkprogress.org/one-lawmakers-sneaky-attempt-to-keep-marriage-equality-out-of-texas-340df2c55e7f

754 Resnick, E. (2011). Kasich lets LGBT job bias rule expire. Gaypeopleschronicle.com. Retrieved November 20, 2017, from www.gaypeopleschronicle.com/stories11/january/0114111.htm

755 LGBTQ Nation (2011). More Tennessee hate: Senate OK's bill to repeal Nashville gay protections law. Retrieved November 20, 2017, from www.lgbtqnation.com/2011/05/more-tennessee-hate-senate-oks-bill-to-repeal-nashville-gay-protections-law

756 Becker, J. (2014). Texas GOP officially endorses "ex-gay" quackery. Bilerico Report/LGBTQ Nation. Retrieved November 20, 2017, from http://bilerico.lgbtqnation.com/2014/06/texas_gop_officially_endorses_ex-gay_quackery.php

757 IRS Form 990 for the National Center for Transgender Equality in CY 2016. Retrieved March 11, 2018, from www.transequality.org/sites/default/files/docs/NCTE%202016%20Form%20990%20-%20Public%20Diclosure%20Copy.PDF

758 Hasenbush, A., Flores, A. R., Kastanis, A., Sears, B., & Gates, G. J. (December 2014). *The LGBT Divide: A Data Portrait of LGBT People in the Midwestern, Mountain, & Southern States*. The Williams Institute at UCLA. Retrieved December 27, 2017, from http://williamsinstitute.law.ucla.edu/wp-content/uploads/LGBT-divide-Dec-2014.pdf

759 Callan, P. (2017, March 21). Judge Gorsuch and the frozen truck driver. Retrieved December 27, 2017, from www.cnn.com/2017/03/21/opinions/judge-gorsuch-the-frozen-truck-driver-opinion-callan/index.html

760 Somin, I. (2014, October 20). Does Justice Thomas support the Supreme Court's notorious Korematsu decision? Retrieved December 27, 2017, from www.washingtonpost.com/news/volokh-conspiracy/wp/2014/10/20/does-justice-thomas-endorse-the-supreme-courts-notorious-decision-inkorematsu-v-united-states/?utm_term=.8735c56ecc6a

761 Liptak, A. & Blinder, A. (2018, January 18). Supreme Court temporarily blocks North Carolina gerrymandering ruling. Retrieved March 11, 2018, from www.nytimes.com/2018/01/18/us/politics/supreme-court-north-carolina-gerrymandering.html

762 Millhiser, I. (2017, December 5). LGBTQ rights just had a horrible day in the Supreme Court. Retrieved March 11, 2018, from https://thinkprogress.org/lgbtq-rights-horrible-day-scotus-e189ca49c6c3

763 Becker, J. (2014). Klingenschmitt to Pakman: I won't legislate gay exorcisms. Bilerico Report/LGBTQ Nation. Retrieved November 20, 2017, from http://bilerico.lgbtqnation.com/2014/11/klingenschmitt_to_pakman_i_wont_legislate_gay_exor.php

764 Mantyla, K. (2011). As Navy chaplain, Klingenschmitt performed gay exorcism on rape victim. Right Wing Watch. Retrieved November 20, 2017, from www.rightwingwatch.org/post/as-navy-chaplain-klingenschmitt-performed-gay-exorcism-on-rape-victim-2

765 Mantyla, K. (2013). Klingenschmitt: "American law needs to reflect God's law." Right Wing Watch. Retrieved November 20, 2017, from www.rightwingwatch.org/post/klingenschmitt-american-law-needs-to-reflect-gods-law

766 Mantyla, K. (2014). Klingenschmitt: America must base foreign policy on the Bible or face God's judgment. Right Wing Watch. Retrieved November 20, 2017, from www.rightwingwatch.org/post/klingenschmitt-america-must-base-foreign-policy-on-the-bible-or-face-gods-judgment

767 Mantyla, K. (2014). Klingenschmitt: Gay activists "want your soul." Right Wing Watch. Retrieved December 14, 2017, from www.rightwingwatch.org/post/klingenschmitt-gay-activists-want-your-soul

768 Mantyla, K. (2013). Klingenschmitt: Photo of gay couple with a baby "looks to me a little bit like lust." Right Wing Watch. Retrieved December 14, 2017, from www.rightwingwatch.org/post/klingenschmitt-photo-of-gay-couple-with-a-baby-looks-to-me-a-little-bit-like-lust

769 Mantyla, K. (2013). Klingenschmitt: If you are gay, "then you should be discriminated against." Right Wing Watch. Retrieved December 14, 2017, from www.rightwingwatch.org/post/klingenschmitt-if-you-are-gay-then-you-should-be-discriminated-against

770 Mantyla, K. (2013). Klingenschmitt: People not going to heaven do not deserve equal treatment by the government. Right Wing Watch. Retrieved December 14, 2017, from www.rightwingwatch.org/post/klingenschmitt-people-not-going-to-heaven-do-not-deserve-equal-treatment-by-the-government

771 Mantyla, K. (2014). Gay soldiers undermine the military because they have to take breaks in the middle of combat to change their diapers. Right Wing Watch. Retrieved December 14, 2017, from www.rightwingwatch.org/post/gay-soldiers-undermine-the-military-because-they-have-to-take-breaks-in-the-middle-of-combat-to-change-their-diapers

772 Mantyla, K. (2014). Gordon Klingenschmitt says those who can't enter church should not be able to use public restrooms. Right Wing Watch. Retrieved December 14, 2017, from www.rightwingwatch.org/post/gordon-klingenschmitt-says-those-who-cant-enter-church-shouldnt-be-able-to-use-public-restrooms

773 Mantyla, K. (2013). Klingenschmitt: "Obamacare causes cancer." Right Wing Watch. Retrieved December 14, 2017, from www.rightwingwatch.org/post/klingenschmitt-obamacare-causes-cancer

774 Mantyla, K. (2014). Klingenschmitt: The Bible says "all the citizens ought to be armed so they can defend themselves against left wing crazies." Right Wing Watch. Retrieved December 14, 2017, from www.rightwingwatch.org/post/klingenschmitt-the-bible-says-all-the-citizens-ought-to-be-armed-so-they-can-defend-themselves-against-left-wing-crazies

775 Mantyla, K. (2014). Klingenschmitt: ISIS is "a sign of the End Times." Right Wing Watch. Retrieved December 14, 2017, from www.rightwingwatch.org/post/klingenschmitt-isis-is-a-sign-of-the-end-times

776 Mantyla, K. (2013). Klingenschmitt: The FCC is letting demonic spirits "molest and visually rape your children." Right Wing Watch. Retrieved December 14, 2017, from www.rightwingwatch.org/post/klingenschmitt-the-fcc-is-letting-demonic-spirits-molest-and-visually-rape-your-children

777 Tashman, B. (2014). Gordon Klingenschmitt's book reveals Obama is ruled by gay demons, "worthy of death." Right Wing Watch. Retrieved November 20, 2017, from www.rightwingwatch.org/post/gordon-klingenschmitts-book-reveals-obama-is-ruled-by-gay-demons-worthy-of-death

778 Mantyla, K. (2013). Klingenschmitt: A demonic spirit of tyranny is using Obama to oppress us. Right Wing Watch. Retrieved November 20, 2017, from www.rightwingwatch.org/post/klingenschmitt-a-demonic-spirit-of-tyranny-is-using-obama-to-oppress-us

779 Rustin, B., Carbado, D. W., & Weise, D. (2015). *Time on Two Crosses: The Collected Writings of Bayard Rustin*. New York, NY: Cleis Press

780 Ipsos. (2018, January 29). Global attitudes toward transgender people. Retrieved March 12, 2018, from www.ipsos.com/en-us/news-polls/global-attitudes-toward-transgender-people

781 Jadin Bell, gay Oregon teen, taken off life support after hanging himself. (2016). HuffPost. Retrieved November 14, 2017, from www.huffingtonpost.com/2013/01/29/jadin-bell-gay-oregon-teen-hanging-suicide-life-support-_n_2576404.html?utm_hp_ref=gay-voices

782 Mantyla, K. (2010). Fischer: "If we want to see fewer students commit suicide, we want fewer homosexual students." Right Wing Watch. Retrieved November 14, 2017, from www.rightwingwatch.org/post/fischer-if-we-want-to-see-fewer-students-commit-suicide-we-want-fewer-homosexual-students

783 Allen, M. (2013). NARTH-affiliated doc: Trans individuals deluded, psychotic. Bilerico Report/LGBTQ Nation. Retrieved November 14, 2017, from http://bilerico.lgbtqnation.com/2013/01/narth-affiliated_doc_trans_deluded_psychotic.php

784 Often, surveys of the LGBT community do not include enough transgender people to have a statistically significant number of transgender people represented. Thus, these surveys only meaningfully represent the LGB community. Additionally, in the past there was far less money to study transgender issues than LGB ones

785 Mosbergen, D. (2012, December 14). Pope says gay marriage poses a threat to "justice and peace" in World Day of Peace 2013 Address. Retrieved December 18, 2017, from www.huffingtonpost.com/2012/12/14/pope-gay-marriage-threat-justice-peace-world-day-of-peace-2013_n_2303534.html

786 Broverman, N. (2013). Bryan Fischer claims flaming gays will sue Christian businesses after ENDA. Advocate.com. Retrieved November 14, 2017, from www.advocate.com/politics/religion/2013/01/06/bryan-fischer-claims-flaming-gays-will-sue-christian-businesses-after

787 Levesque, B. (2012). MD police official: Transgender rights bill did not lead to rapes, assaults in public restrooms. LGBTQ Nation. Retrieved November 14, 2017, from www.lgbtqnation.com/2012/01/maryland-police-official-says-claims-of-rapes-by-transgender-persons-false

788 Kohler, W. (2012). Abramoff linked tradition values coalition leads attack on ENDA spreading lies and trans-panic. Back2Stonewall. Retrieved November 14, 2017, from www.back2stonewall.com/2012/06/abramoff-linked-tradition-values-coalition-leads-attack-enda-spreading-lies-trans-panic.html

789 McEwen, A. (2013). How they see us. Scribd. Retrieved November 14, 2017, from www.scribd.com/document/119413856/How-They-See-Us

790 WATCH: Pastor says put gays and lesbians in electrified pen to kill them off. (2016). HuffPost. Retrieved November 14, 2017, from www.huffingtonpost.com/2012/05/21/north-carolina-pastor-gay-rant-starvation_n_1533463.html

791 Brammer, J. P. (2018, January 3). None of America's 100 largest churches are LGBTQ-affirming, new report says. Retrieved March 23, 2018, from www.nbcnews.com/feature/nbc-out/none-america-s-100-largest-churches-are-lgbtq-affirming-new-n834266

792 Badash, D. (2013). Democratic senators have now been filibustering an anti-gay bill for a full day. The New Civil Rights Movement. Retrieved November 14, 2017, from www.thenewcivilrightsmovement.com/1-vast-majority-of-evangelical-christians-say-gays-trying-to-remove-christian-values-from-u-s/politics/2013/01/24/59077

793 Chellew-Hodge, C. (2009). New poll shows gays and lesbians believe in God. Religion Dispatches. Retrieved November 14, 2017, from http://religiondispatches.org/new-poll-shows-gays-and-lesbians-believe-in-god

794 Badash, D. (2013). Democratic senators have now been filibustering an anti-gay bill for a full day. The New Civil Rights Movement. Retrieved November 14, 2017, from www.thenewcivilrightsmovement.com/1-vast-majority-of-evangelical-christians-say-gays-trying-to-remove-christian-values-from-u-s/politics/2013/01/24/59077

795 Open and affirming in the UCC. (n.d.). United Church of Christ. Retrieved December 18, 2017, from www.ucc.org/lgbt_ona

796 Baldock, K. (2017). Welcome to Canyonwalker Connections. Canyonwalker Connections—LGBTQ Advocacy. Retrieved November 14, 2017, from http://canyonwalkerconnections.com

797 Gates, S. (2016). POLL: Majority of Americans support gay marriage. HuffPost UK. Retrieved November 17, 2017, from www.huffingtonpost.com/2012/11/14/gay-marriage-support-majority-americans-poll_n_2130371.html

798 HRC. (2011). New HRC poll finds vast majority of voters support employment anti-discrimination laws. Human Rights Campaign. Retrieved November 17, 2017, from www.hrc.org/press/new-hrc-poll-finds-vast-majority-of-voters-support-employment-anti-discrimi

799 Wong, C. M. (2013, January 11). Americans who believe homosexuality is a sin decrease significantly: LifeWay Research Poll. Retrieved December 18, 2017, from www.huffingtonpost.com/2013/01/11/americans-homosexuality-sin-lifeway-research-poll-_n_2456326.html

800 The Nashville Statement is a declaration by leading evangelicals holding that marriage can only be between a man and a woman, and that sex and gender cannot be different. It is effectively a prohibition on acceptance of LGBT people. https://cbmw.org/nashville-statement

801 Nolan, B. (2011). Evangelicals divided on gay marriage. HuffPost. Retrieved November 17, 2017, from www.huffingtonpost.com/2011/09/07/gay-marriage-evangelicals_n_952888.html

802 Why the Westboro Baptist Church is a scam. (2006). Kanewj.com. Retrieved November 17, 2017, from http://kanewj.com/wbc

803 Brown, S. (2012). The 10 most dangerous religious right organizations. Alternet. Retrieved November 17, 2017, from www.alternet.org/belief/10-most-dangerous-religious-right-organizations

804 Dawson, K. (2012). How Cable News made me lose my religion and my mother. HuffPost. Retrieved November 17, 2017, from www.huffingtonpost.com/kathryn-dawson/losing-my-religion-and-my_b_1098081.html

805 Murray, R. (2012). Where are the pro-LGBT religious voices in mainstream media? HuffPost. Retrieved November 17, 2017, from www.huffingtonpost.com/ross-murray/pro-lgbt-christian-voices_b_1418604.html

806 Liu, J. (2012, October 8). "Nones" on the rise. Retrieved December 18, 2017, from www.pewforum.org/2012/10/09/nones-on-the-rise

807 Ford, Z. (2012). STUDY: 40 percent of homeless youth are LGBT, family rejection is leading cause. Thinkprogress.org. Retrieved November 17, 2017, from https://thinkprogress.org/study-40-percent-of-homeless-youth-are-lgbt-family-rejection-is-leading-cause-a2aaa72c414a

808 Welsh, J. (2011). Homosexual teen suicide rates raised in bad environments. Live Science. Retrieved November 17, 2017, from www.livescience.com/13755-homosexual-lgb-teen-suicide-rates-environments.html

809 Cincinnati Children's Hospital Medical Center. (2016, August 31). High rates of suicide and self-harm among transgender youth. ScienceDaily. Retrieved December 18, 2017, from www.sciencedaily.com/releases/2016/08/160831110833.htm

810 Wood, D. (2012). Beyond the battlefield: Wounded veterans struggle with genital injuries. HuffPost UK. Retrieved November 18, 2017, from www.huffingtonpost.com/2012/03/21/beyond-the-battlefield-afghanistan-genital-injuries_n_1335356.html

811 Eiesland, N. L. & Saliers, D. E. (1998). *Human Disability and the Service of God: Reassessing Religious Practice*. Nashville: Abingdon Press

812 Complete androgen insensitivity syndrome. (2017). En.wikipedia.org. Retrieved November 18, 2017, from https://en.wikipedia.org/wiki/Complete_androgen_insensitivity_syndrome

813 Stern, M. J. (2016, February 8). The tragic results of the Mormon Church's new policy against gay members. Retrieved December 31, 2017, from www.slate.com/blogs/outward/2016/02/08/mama_dragons_respond_to_gay_mormon_youth_suicide.html

814 Jones, R. P. (2017). *The End of White Christian America*. New York, NY: Simon & Schuster Paperbacks

815 Gervais, W. M. & Najle, M. B. (2017). How many atheists are there? *Social Psychological and Personality Science*, 9(1), 3–10. doi:10.1177/1948550617707015

816 Woodruff, B. (2012). The "Nones" and the GOP. National Review. Retrieved November 17, 2017, from www.nationalreview.com/article/335763/nones-and-gop-betsy-woodruff

817 Newport, F. (2012). Half of Americans support legal gay marriage. Gallup.com. Retrieved November 17, 2017, from http://news.gallup.com/poll/154529/Half-Americans-Support-Legal-Gay-Marriage.aspx

818 Cox, PhD, D., Navarro-Rivera, J., & Jones, PhD, R. (2014). *A Shifting Landscape: A Decade of Change in American Attitudes about Same-Sex Marriage and LGBT Issues*. PRRI. Retrieved November 17, 2017, from www.prri.org/research/2014-lgbt-survey/#.VV5lUZ3D-M8

819 Badash, D. (2015). Breaking: "I acted inexcusably"—Josh Duggar apologizes, resigns from Family Research Council. The New Civil Rights Movement. Retrieved November 17, 2017, from www.thenewcivilrightsmovement.com/davidbadash/breaking_i_acted_inexcusably_josh_duggar_apologizes_resigns_from_family_research_council

820 Badash, D. (2015). Breaking: "I acted inexcusably"—Josh Duggar apologizes, resigns from Family Research Council. The New Civil Rights Movement. Retrieved November 17, 2017, from www.thenewcivilrightsmovement.com/davidbadash/breaking_i_acted_inexcusably_josh_duggar_apologizes_resigns_from_family_research_council

821 Ennis, D. (2015). WATCH: Josh Duggar plays the victim card. Advocate.com. Retrieved November 17, 2017, from www.advocate.com/politics/media/2015/04/29/watch-josh-duggar-plays-victim-card

822 Larson, L. (2015). The Duggar family just deserted Rick Santorum for Mike Huckabee. Business Insider. Retrieved November 17, 2017, from www.businessinsider.com/duggar-family-deserts-rick-santorum-for-mike-huckabee-2015-5

823 Malloy, P. (2014). LISTEN: *19 Kids and Counting* star records transphobic robocall. Advocate.com. Retrieved November 17, 2017, from www.advocate.com/politics/transgender/2014/08/19/listen-19-kids-and-counting-star-records-transphobic-robocall

824 Burleigh, N. (2014). The Duggars seem so nice until you meet their terrifying political agenda. Observer. Retrieved November 17, 2017, from http://observer.com/2014/12/the-duggars-politics

825 Gettys, T. (2015). Jessa Duggar lashes out at liberal Christians: You're going to hell, but I'm not. Alternet. Retrieved November 17, 2017, from www.alternet.org/belief/jessa-duggar-lashes-out-liberal-christians-youre-going-hell-im-not

826 Pew Research Center. (2015). America's changing religious landscape. Pew Research Center's Religion & Public Life Project. Retrieved November 17, 2017, from www.pewforum.org/2015/05/12/americas-changing-religious-landscape

827 Evans, R. (2015). Want millennials back in the pews? Stop trying to make church "cool." Washington Post. Retrieved November 17, 2017, from www.washingtonpost.com/opinions/jesus-doesnt-tweet/2015/04/30/fb07ef1a-ed01-11e4-8666-a1d756d0218e_story.html?utm_term=.2e40233d0e69

828 Lipka, M. (2015). A closer look at America's rapidly growing religious "nones." Pew Research Center. Retrieved November 17, 2017, from www.pewresearch.org/fact-tank/2015/05/13/a-closer-look-at-americas-rapidly-growing-religious-nones

829 Kinnaman, D. & Hawkins, A. (2016). *You Lost Me: Why Young Christians are Leaving Church... And Rethinking Faith*. Grand Rapids, MI: Baker Books

830 A conversation with Kenda Creasy Dean. Retrieved February 26, 2018, from www.resourcingchristianity.org/sites/default/files/transcripts/interview/KendaCreasyDean_on_Young_Peoples_Faith_Interview.pdf

831 Stastna, K. (2013). Do countries lose religion as they gain wealth? CBC News. Retrieved November 17, 2017, from www.cbc.ca/news/world/do-countries-lose-religion-as-they-gain-wealth-1.1310451

832 Cooper, B. (2015). The right's made-up God: How bigots invented a white supremacist Jesus. Salon. Retrieved November 17, 2017, from www.salon.com/2015/04/01/the_rights_made_up_god_how_bigots_invented_a_white_supremacist_jesus

833 Ford, Z. (2014). Inside the Southern Baptists' new, media-savvy approach to homosexuality. Thinkprogress.org. Retrieved November 18, 2017, from https://thinkprogress.org/inside-the-southern-baptists-new-media-savvy-approach-to-homosexuality-a44d7eb3e143

834 Fitzgerald, M. (2014). Southern Baptist leader denounces "ex-gay" therapy [Video]. Towleroad. Retrieved November 18, 2017, from www.towleroad.com/2014/10/southern-baptist-leader-denounces-ex-gay-therapy-video

835 Tashman, B. (2014). Richard Land "exposes" the "dirty little secret" of the gay community. Right Wing Watch. Retrieved November 18, 2017, from www.rightwingwatch.org/post/richard-land-exposes-the-dirty-little-secret-of-the-gay-community

836 Romano, A. (2014). Homophobic Southern Baptist conference sparks massive online backlash. The Daily Dot. Retrieved November 18, 2017, from www.dailydot.com/irl/glbtq-twitter-reacts-to-baptist-erlc-conference

837 Southern Baptist Convention and homosexuality. (2012). Religioustolerance.org. Retrieved November 18, 2017, from www.religioustolerance.org/hom_sbc5.htm

838 Lupfer, J. (2014). Southern Baptists change their tone but not their substance on homosexuality (Commentary). Religion News Service. Retrieved November 18, 2017, from http://religionnews.com/2014/10/30/southern-baptists-change-tone-substance-homosexuality-commentary

839 Southern Baptist Convention claims to harbor no ill will toward LGBT people, but its actions suggest otherwise. (2016, March 25). Southern Poverty Law Center. Retrieved December 31, 2017, from www.splcenter.org/hatewatch/2016/03/25/southern-baptist-convention-claims-harbor-no-ill-will-toward-lgbt-people-its-actions

840 Ford, Z. (2014). Southern Baptist Convention compromises improving tone by promoting anti-gay discrimination. Thinkprogress.org. Retrieved November 18, 2017, from https://thinkprogress.org/southern-baptist-convention-compromises-improving-tone-by-promoting-anti-gay-discrimination-87c6c10759af

841 Badash, D. (2014). 16 year old girl stabbed at Jerusalem Gay Pride parade dies. The New Civil Rights Movement. Retrieved November 18, 2017, from www.thenewcivilrightsmovement.com/gays-are-gay-because-they-were-sexually-molested-when-they-were-children-says-top-baptist/discrimination/2014/04/16/85903

842 Carpenter, T. (2013). How can Southern Baptist military chaplains continue to serve "God and country"? HuffPost. Retrieved November 18, 2017, from www.huffingtonpost.com/tom-carpenter/military-chaplains-lgbt_b_3870436.html

843 https://erlc.com/resource-library/event-messages/a-gospel-centered-assessment-of-gender-identity-transgender-and-polygamy-denny-burk

844 Lupfer, J. (2014). Southern Baptists change their tone but not their substance on homosexuality (Commentary). Religion News Service. Retrieved November 18, 2017, from http://religionnews.com/2014/10/30/southern-baptists-change-tone-substance-homosexuality-commentary

845 Tannehill, B. (2014). The "ex-gay" movement's dangerous new myths. Bilerico Report/LGBTQ Nation. Retrieved November 18, 2017, from http://bilerico.lgbtqnation.com/2014/08/the_ex-gay_movements_dangerous_new_myths.php

846 Shore, J. (2014). The Southern Baptist Convention throws transgender people under the bus. Retrieved November 18, 2017, from www.patheos.com/blogs/johnshore/2014/06/the-southern-baptist-convention-throws-transgender-people-under-the-bus

847 The difference between reparative therapy with religious underpinnings, and the "pray away the trans" option offered by the ERLC, is that reparative therapy is supposedly based on psychology, while the ERLC option insists that being transgender is a result of original sin, and that the only thing that can redeem original sin is Jesus

848 Ford, Z. (2014). How the Southern Baptists are still completely failing transgender people. Thinkprogress.org. Retrieved November 18, 2017, from https://thinkprogress.org/how-the-southern-baptists-are-still-completely-failing-transgender-people-173dac9fcf11

849 Southern Baptist Convention > On Transgender Identity. (2014). Sbc.net. Retrieved November 18, 2017, from www.sbc.net/resolutions/2250/on-transgender-identity

850 "Our love for the gospel and urgency for the Great Commission must include declaring what God's word teaches about God's design for us as male and female persons created in His image and for His glory"

851 Allen, B. (2014). AWAB asks SBC to recant transgender resolution. Baptist News Global. Retrieved November 18, 2017, from https://baptistnews.com/article/awab-asks-sbc-to-recant-transgender-resolution/#.Wg97slIi7m4

852 Burk, D. (2014). Transgender: When psychological identity trumps bodily identity. Denny Burk. Retrieved November 18, 2017, from www.dennyburk.com/transgender-when-psychological-identity-trumps-bodily-identity

853 Anderson, D. (2014). Why conservative Christians fear the affirmation of transgender identity. Rewire. Retrieved November 18, 2017, from https://rewire.news/article/2014/09/09/conservative-christians-fear-transgender-identity

854 Cox, D. (2018, January 24). Are white evangelicals sacrificing the future in search of the past? Retrieved March 12, 2018, from https://fivethirtyeight.com/features/are-white-evangelicals-sacrificing-the-future-in-search-of-the-past/?ex_cid=538twitter

855 Bailey, S. P. (2016, November 9). White evangelicals voted overwhelmingly for Donald Trump, exit polls show. The Washington Post. Retrieved December 31, 2017, from www.washingtonpost.com/news/acts-of-faith/wp/2016/11/09/exit-polls-show-white-evangelicals-voted-overwhelmingly-for-donald-trump/?utm_term=.2496d9aaf9d9

856 Grindley, L. (2013). The Advocate's Person of the Year: Pope Francis. Advocate.com. Retrieved November 18, 2017, from www.advocate.com/year-review/2013/12/16/advocates-person-year-pope-francis

857 Garcia, M. (2014). Pope Francis looks to U.S. leaders on marriage, demotes antigay cardinal. Advocate.com. Retrieved November 18, 2017, from www.advocate.com/politics/religion/2014/11/09/pope-francis-looks-us-leaders-marriage-demotes-antigay-cardinal

858 St. John, S. (2015). Pope calls same-sex marriage a "threat" to the family. Advocate.com. Retrieved November 18, 2017, from www.advocate.com/politics/religion/2015/01/16/pope-calls-same-sex-marriage-threat-family

859 Lopez, G. (2015). Pope Francis compared the arguments for transgender rights to nuclear weapons. Vox. Retrieved November 18, 2017, from www.vox.com/2015/2/20/8078979/pope-francis-trans-rights

860 Associated Press. (2016). Pope Francis denounces transgender people as "annihilation of man." LGBTQ Nation. Retrieved November 18, 2017, from www.lgbtqnation.com/2016/08/pope-francis-denounces-transgender-people-annihilation-man

861 Lind, D. "Junipero Serra was a brutal colonialist. So why did Pope Francis just make him a saint?" Vox, Sept. 24, 2015, www.vox.com/2015/9/24/9391995/junipero-serra-saint-pope-francis

862 Pope Francis compares transgender people to nuclear weapons in new book. (2015). Sanfrancisco.cbslocal.com. Retrieved November 18, 2017, from http://sanfrancisco.cbslocal.com/2015/02/20/pope-francis-compares-transgender-people-to-nuclear-weapons-in-new-book

863 Pope Francis compares transgender people to nuclear weapons in new book. (2015). Sanfrancisco.cbslocal.com. Retrieved November 18, 2017, from http://sanfrancisco.cbslocal.com/2015/02/20/pope-francis-compares-transgender-people-to-nuclear-weapons-in-new-book

864 Chretien, C. (2016). Cardinal Burke: Gender theory is "madness," transgender bathrooms "inhuman." LifeSiteNews. Retrieved November 18, 2017, from www.lifesitenews.com/news/cardinal-burke-gender-theory-is-madness-men-going-in-womens-bathrooms-is-in

865 Duffy, N. (2016). Senior Vatican Cardinal warns "demonic" transgender rights are causing the "death of God." PinkNews. Retrieved November 18, 2017, from www.pinknews.co.uk/2016/05/18/senior-vatican-cardinal-warns-demonic-trans gender-rights-are-causing-the-death-of-god

866 Clarke, K. (2014). Church in dramatic revision of nuclear weapons stance. America Magazine. Retrieved November 18, 2017, from www.americamagazine.org/content/dispatches/church-dramatic-revision-nuclear-weapons-stance

867 Stone, M. (2014). Catholic Bishop praises genocide of LGBT in Uganda. Progressive Secular Humanist. Retrieved November 18, 2017, from www.patheos.com/blogs/progressivesecularhumanist/2014/04/catholic-bishop-praises-genocide-of-lgbt-in-uganda

868 Buckley, B. (2014). Ugandan Catholic bishop preaches genocide. Wisecatholic.blogspot.com. Retrieved November 18, 2017, from http://wisecatholic.blogspot.com/2014/04/donald-molosi-rehearsal-star-of-david_6771.html

869 McGreal, C. (2014). The Catholic Church must apologise for its role in Rwanda's genocide. The Guardian. Retrieved November 18, 2017, from www.theguardian.com/commentisfree/2014/apr/08/catholic-church-apologise-failure-rwanda-genocide-vatican

870 Castrato. (2017). En.wikipedia.org. Retrieved November 18, 2017, from https://en.wikipedia.org/wiki/Castrato

871 Waterfield, B. (2012). Dutch Roman Catholic Church "castrated at least 10 boys." Telegraph.co.uk. Retrieved November 18, 2017, from www.telegraph.co.uk/news/worldnews/europe/netherlands/9153676/Dutch-Roman-Catholic-Church-castrated-at-least-10-boys.html

872 Stone, M. (2015). Catholic bishop blames victims of child molesting priests. Progressive Secular Humanist. Retrieved November 18, 2017, from www.patheos.com/blogs/progressivesecularhumanist/2015/09/catholic-bishop-blames-victims-of-child-molesting-priests

873 United States Conference of Catholic Bishops. (2017, December 15). Created male and female: An open letter from religious leaders. Retrieved December 18, 2017, from www.usccb.org/issues-and-action/marriage-and-family/marriage/promotion-and-defense-of-marriage/created-male-and-female.cfm

874 Changing attitudes on gay marriage. (2017). Pew Research Center's Religion & Public Life Project. Retrieved November 18, 2017, from www.pewforum.org/fact-sheet/changing-attitudes-on-gay-marriage

875 Piacenza, J. & Jones, R. P. (2017, February 3). Most American religious groups support same-sex marriage, oppose religiously based service refusals. Retrieved March 13, 2018, from www.prri.org/spotlight/religious-americans-same-sex-marriage-service-refusals

876 Culp-Ressler, T. (2015). Birth control goes against Catholicism's teachings, but most Catholics use it anyway. Thinkprogress.org. Retrieved November 18, 2017, from https://thinkprogress.org/birth-control-goes-against-catholicisms-teachings-but-most-catholics-use-it-anyway-d22f2da560a1/#.ybjs1wq9a

877 Lipka, M. (2015). Most U.S. Catholics hope for change in church rule on divorce, Communion. Pew Research Center. Retrieved November 18, 2017, from www.pewresearch.org/fact-tank/2015/10/26/most-u-s-catholics-hope-for-change-in-church-rule-on-divorce-communion

878 Smith, G. A. (2017, November 27). Views of transgender issues divide along religious lines. Retrieved January 12, 2018, from www.pewresearch.org/fact-tank/2017/11/27/views-of-transgender-issues-divide-along-religious-lines

879 Jones, R. P., Cox, D., Cooper, B., & Lienesch, R. (2017) Majority of Americans oppose transgender bathroom restrictions. PRRI. Retrieved July 6, 2018, from www.prri.org/research/lgbt-transgender-bathroom-discrimination-religious-liberty

880 Piacenza, J. & Jones, R. P. (2017, February 3). Most American religious groups support same-sex marriage, oppose religiously based service refusals. Retrieved March 13, 2018, from www.prri.org/spotlight/religious-americans-same-sex-marriage-service-refusals

881 Jenkins, J. (2015). The surprising religious breakdown of same-sex marriage support. Thinkprogress.org. Retrieved November 18, 2017, from https://thinkprogress.org/the-surprising-religious-breakdown-of-same-sex-marriage-support-3721651534ea

882 Wiering, M. (2015). Cavins' reaction to new Pew survey: Sound the alarm. TheCatholicSpirit.com. Retrieved November 18, 2017, from http://thecatholicspirit.com/featured/cavins-reaction-to-new-pew-survey-sound-the-alarm/?utm_source=feedburner&utm_medium=feed&utm_campaign=Feed%3A+thecatholicspiritcom+%28Latest+Content+from+TheCatholicSpirit.com%29

883 McSwain, S. (2015). "NONES!" are now "DONES." Is the Church dying? HuffPost. Retrieved November 18, 2017, from www.huffingtonpost.com/steve-mcswain/nones-and-now-the-dones-t_b_6164112.html

884 Hendershott, A. (2015). Digging deeper into the Pew data about nones, millennials, and Christians. Catholic World Report. Catholicworldreport.com. Retrieved November 18, 2017, from www.catholicworldreport.com/2015/05/25/digging-deeper-into-the-pew-data-about-nones-millennials-and-christians

885 Hendershott, A. (2015). Digging deeper into the Pew data about nones, millennials, and Christians. Catholic World Report. Catholicworldreport.com. Retrieved November 18, 2017, from www.catholicworldreport.com/2015/05/25/digging-deeper-into-the-pew-data-about-nones-millennials-and-christians

886 Jones, R. P., Cox, D., Cooper, B., & Lienesch, R. (2016). Exodus: Why Americans are leaving religion—and why they're unlikely to come back. PRRI. Retrieved July 6, 2018, from www.prri.org/research/prri-rns-poll-nones-atheist-leaving-religion

887 Jones, R. P. & Cox, D. (2017). America's changing religious identity. PRRI. Retrieved July 6, 2018, from www.prri.org/research/american-religious-landscape-christian-religiously-unaffiliated

888 Stances of faiths on LGBTQ issues: Episcopal Church. Human Rights Campaign. Retrieved February 26, 2018, from www.hrc.org/resources/stances-of-faiths-on-lgbt-issues-episcopal-church

889 Sandstrom, A. (2015, December 2). Religious groups' policies on transgender members vary widely. Pew Research Center. Retrieved July 6, 2018, from www.pewresearch.org/fact-tank/2015/12/02/religious-groups-policies-on-transgender-members-vary-widely

890 Zauzmer, J. (2017, June 7). The United Methodist Church has appointed a transgender deacon. The Washington Post. Retrieved July 6, 2018, from www.washingtonpost.com/news/acts-of-faith/wp/2017/06/07/the-united-methodist-church-just-appointed-a-transgender-deacon/?utm_term=.77a1c39548dd

891 Stances of faiths on LGBTQ issues: Episcopal Church. Human Rights Campaign. Retrieved February 26, 2018, from www.hrc.org/resources/stances-of-faiths-on-lgbt-issues-episcopal-church

892 Cox, D. (2018, January 24). Are white evangelicals sacrificing the future in search of the past? Retrieved March 12, 2018, from https://fivethirtyeight.com/features/are-white-evangelicals-sacrificing-the-future-in-search-of-the-past/?ex_cid=538twitter

893 Piacenza, J. & Jones, R. P. (2017, February 3). Most American religious groups support same-sex marriage, oppose religiously based service refusals. Retrieved March 13, 2018, from www.prri.org/spotlight/religious-americans-same-sex-marriage-service-refusals

894 LoGiurato, B. (2012, March 27). Read the leaked anti-gay marriage memo whose authors wanted to "drive a wedge between gays and blacks." Retrieved March 13, 2018, from www.businessinsider.com/nom-gay-marriage-memos-drive-a-wedge-between-gays-and-blacks-2012-3

895 Maniam, S. (2016, September 13). 2. Party affiliation among voters: 1992–2016. Pew Research Center. Retrieved March 13, 2018, from www.people-press.org/2016/09/13/2-party-affiliation-among-voters-1992-2016

896 Robertson, C. (2018, March 9). A quiet exodus: Why black worshipers are leaving white evangelical churches. Retrieved March 23, 2018, from www.nytimes.com/2018/03/09/us/blacks-evangelical-churches.html

897 Piacenza, J. & Jones, R. P. (2017, February 3). Most American religious groups support same-sex marriage, oppose religiously based service refusals. Retrieved March 13, 2018, from www.prri.org/spotlight/religious-americans-same-sex-marriage-service-refusals

898 Perkins, T. (2017, January 6). TODAY: Black pastors to hold Capitol Hill News Conference in support of Sen. Jeff Sessions. Retrieved March 13, 2018, from www.frc.org/newsroom/black-pastors-to-hold-capitol-hill-news-conference-in-support-of-sen-jeff-sessions

899 Smith, G. A. (2017, November 27). Views of transgender issues divide along religious lines. Retrieved January 12, 2018, from www.pewresearch.org/fact-tank/2017/11/27/views-of-transgender-issues-divide-along-religious-lines

900 Pew Research Center. (2015). America's changing religious landscape. Pew Research Center's Religion & Public Life Project. Retrieved November 17, 2017, from www.pewforum.org/2015/05/12/americas-changing-religious-landscape

901 Hendershott, A. (2015). Digging deeper into the Pew data about nones, millennials, and Christians. Catholic World Report. Catholicworldreport.com. Retrieved November 18, 2017, from www.catholicworldreport.com/2015/05/25/digging-deeper-into-the-pew-data-about-nones-millennials-and-christians

902 Denominational decline related to birthrates, societal changes. (2017). Insights into Religion. Retrieved November 18, 2017, from http://religioninsights.org/denominational-decline-related-birthrates-societal-changes

903 Wright, R. (2010). Book review—*American Grace* by Robert D. Putnam and David E. Campbell. Nytimes.com. Retrieved November 18, 2017, from www.nytimes.com/2010/10/10/books/review/Wright-t.html?pagewanted=all&_r=0&mtrref=undefined&gwh=0FBF9B4F500E63416C252FB1E84E4A7B&gwt=pay

904 Knoll, B. (2016). Theological liberalization is not to blame for decline in Mainline Protestantism. HuffPost. Retrieved November 18, 2017, from www.huffingtonpost.com/benjamin-knoll/theological-liberalizatio_b_7279822.html

905 Stone, M. (2015, February 24). Poll: GOP majority wants Christianity as national religion. Retrieved December 18, 2017, from www.patheos.com/blogs/progressivesecularhumanist/2015/02/poll-gop-majority-wants-christianity-as-national-religion

906 *Trinity Lutheran v. Comer*. US Supreme Court. Retrieved December 18, 2017, from www.supremecourt.gov/opinions/16pdf/15-577_khlp.pdf

907 Bailey, S. P. (2017, July 14). Trump promised to destroy the Johnson amendment. Congress is targeting it now. Retrieved December 18, 2017, from www.washingtonpost.com/news/acts-of-faith/wp/2017/06/30/trump-promised-to-destroy-the-johnson-amendment-congress-is-targeting-it-now/?utm_term=.63ec21ba0bea

908 Burns, A. & Martin, J. (2017, December 12). Once a long shot, Democrat Doug Jones wins Alabama Senate race. Retrieved December 18, 2017, from www.nytimes.com/2017/12/12/us/politics/alabama-senate-race-winner.html

909 Goodstein, L. (2011). Mormon ad campaign seeks to improve perceptions. Nytimes.com. Retrieved November 17, 2017, from www.nytimes.com/2011/11/18/us/mormon-ad-campaign-seeks-to-improve-perceptions.html?_r=0

910 Ryan, C. & Rees, R. A. (2012). *Supportive Families, Healthy Children: Helping Latter-Day Saint Families with Lesbian, Gay, Bisexual & Transgender Children*. San Francisco, CA: Family Acceptance Project, Marian Wright Edelman Institute, San Francisco State University. Retrieved December 31, 2017, from https://familyproject.sfsu.edu/sites/default/files/FAP%20LDS%20Booklet%20pst.pdf

911 Knoll, B. (2016, March 7). Youth suicide rates and Mormon religious context: An additional empirical analysis. Retrieved December 31, 2017, from https://rationalfaiths.com/mormon-religious-context-and-lgbt-youth-suicides-an-additional-empirical-analysis

912 Davidson, L. (2015). The truest GOP believers? Mormons. Religion News Service. Retrieved November 17, 2017, from http://religionnews.com/2015/04/08/truest-gop-believers-mormons

913 Burke, D. (2015). Mormon Church backs LGBT rights—with one condition. CNN. Retrieved November 17, 2017, from www.cnn.com/2015/01/27/us/mormon-church-lgbt-laws

914 Mormon and Gay. (2017). LDS.org. Retrieved November 17, 2017, from https://mormonandgay.lds.org

915 Transcript of News Conference on Religious Freedom and Nondiscrimination. (2015). Mormonnewsroom.org. Retrieved November 17, 2017, from www.mormonnewsroom.org/article/publicstatement-on-religious-freedom-and-nondiscrimination

916 DelVecchio, P. (2015). As Utah goes...no other state can follow. Advocate.com. Retrieved November 17, 2017, from www.advocate.com/politics/2015/05/12/utah-goes-no-other-state-can-follow

917 Halloran, L. (2015). HRC to LDS leadership: True protections shouldn't leave anyone behind. Human Rights Campaign. Retrieved November 17, 2017, from www.hrc.org/blog/hrc-to-lds-leadership-true-protections-shouldnt-leave-anyone-behind

918 Dehlin, J. (2013). Josh and Lolly Weed on their love story, mixed-orientation marriages and LBS/LGBT issues. Mormonstories.org. Retrieved November 17, 2017, from www.mormonstories.org/josh-and-lolly-weed-on-their-love-story-mixed-orientation-marriages-and-ldslgbt-issues

919 Ring, T. (2015). STUDY: Mixed-orientation Mormon marriages likely to fail. Advocate.com. Retrieved November 17, 2017, from www.advocate.com/politics/religion/2015/01/13/study-mixed-orientation-mormon-marriages-likely-fail

920 Opsahl, K. (2015). USU study: LDS mixed-orientation marriages often fail. The Herald Journal. Retrieved November 17, 2017, from https://news.hjnews.com/allaccess/usu-study-lds-mixed-orientation-marriages-often-fail/article_09646f90-9b89-11e4-8e70-87249c047437.html

921 Frequently Asked Questions. (2017). Northstarlds.org. Retrieved November 17, 2017, from http://northstarlds.org/faq

922 Weed, J. & Weed, L. (2018, January 28). Turning a unicorn into a bat: The post in which we announce the end of our marriage. Retrieved March 23, 2018, from http://joshweed.com/2018/01/turning-unicorn-bat-post-announce-end-marriage

923 Walch, T. (2015). Mormon families are America's largest, new study finds. DeseretNews.com. Retrieved November 17, 2017, from www.deseretnews.com/article/865628480/Mormon-families-are-Americas-largest-new-study-finds.html?pg=all

924 Goble, C. (2016, April 15). Converts per missionary. Retrieved December 18, 2017, from www.timesandseasons.org/index.php/2016/04/converts-per-missionary

925 Peggy Fletcher Stack. Religion News Service. (2014, January 13). New almanac offers look at the world of Mormon membership. Retrieved December 18, 2017, from www.washingtonpost.com/national/religion/new-almanac-offers-look-at-the-world-of-mormon-membership/2014/01/13/7beb7888-7c86-11e3-97d3-b9925ce2c57b_story.html?utm_term=.6355459d465d

926 Henderson, P. & Cooke, K. (2012). Special report—Mormonism besieged by the modern age. Retrieved November 17, 2017, from https://uk.reuters.com/article/uk-mormonchurch/special-report-mormonism-besieged-by-the-modern-age-idUKTRE80T1CP20120130

927 Utah Republicans defend Romney after Bannon's "Mormon" jab. Reuters. Retrieved July 6, 2018, from www.reuters.com/article/us-usa-politics-romney/utah-republicans-defend-romney-after-bannons-mormon-jab-idUSKBN1E02R1

928 Piacenza, J. & Jones, R. P. (2017, February 3). Most American religious groups support same-sex marriage, oppose religiously based service refusals. Retrieved March 13, 2018, from www.prri.org/spotlight/religious-americans-same-sex-marriage-service-refusals

929 Murphy, C. (2016, November 4). The most and least educated U.S. religious groups. Retrieved March 13, 2018, from www.pewresearch.org/fact-tank/2016/11/04/the-most-and-least-educated-u-s-religious-groups

930 Fingerhut, H. (2016, May 12). Support steady for same-sex marriage and acceptance of homosexuality. Retrieved March 13, 2018, from www.pewresearch.org/fact-tank/2016/05/12/support-steady-for-same-sex-marriage-and-acceptance-of-homosexuality

931 Piacenza, J. & Jones, R. P. (2017, February 3). Most American religious groups support same-sex marriage, oppose religiously based service refusals. Retrieved March 13, 2018, from www.prri.org/spotlight/religious-americans-same-sex-marriage-service-refusals

932 Andersson, J. (2018, January 23). Hindus have a long and surprising history of supporting transgender people. Retrieved March 13, 2018, from www.pinknews.co.uk/2018/01/23/hindus-have-a-long-and-surprising-history-of-supporting-transgender-people-says-expert-on-thought-of-the-day

933 Resolution on the rights of transgender and gender non-conforming people. (2016, January 19). Retrieved March 13, 2018, from https://urj.org/what-we-believe/resolutions/resolution-rights-transgender-and-gender-non-conforming-people

934 www.washingtonpost.com/news/acts-of-faith/wp/2016/06/01/the-rabbis-of-conservative-judaism-pass-a-resolution-supporting-transgender-rights/?utm_term=.5a9f27f57433

935 Heilman, U. (2016, April 8). Orthodox rabbis wrestle with Jewish law and transgender issues. Retrieved March 13, 2018, from www.timesofisrael.com/orthodox-rabbis-wrestle-with-jewish-law-and-transgender-issues

936 Stances of faiths on LGBTQ issues: Buddhism. (n.d.). Retrieved March 13, 2018, from www.hrc.org/resources/stances-of-faiths-on-lgbt-issues-buddhism

937 Wormald, B. (2015, May 11). Religious Landscape Study. Retrieved March 13, 2018, from www.pewforum.org/religious-landscape-study/party-affiliation

938 Sprigg, P. (n.d.). Sexual Orientation and Gender Identity (SOGI) laws: A threat to free markets and freedom of conscience and religion. Retrieved March 13, 2018, from www.frc.org/issuebrief/sexual-orientation-and-gender-identity-sogi-laws-a-threat-to-free-markets-and-freedom-of-conscience-and-religion

939 Piacenza, J. & Jones, R. P. (2017, February 3). Most American religious groups support same-sex marriage, oppose religiously based service refusals. Retrieved March 13, 2018, from www.prri.org/spotlight/religious-americans-same-sex-marriage-service-refusals

940 Newport, F. (2014). LGBT population in U.S. significantly less religious. Gallup.com. Retrieved November 18, 2017, from http://news.gallup.com/poll/174788/lgbt-population-significantly-less-religious.aspx

941 The Institute for Welcoming Resources. (2017). Multi-faith LGBT organizations. Welcomingresources.org. Retrieved November 18, 2017, from www.welcomingresources.org/multifaithlinks.htm

942 Human Rights Campaign. (2017). Explore: Religion & faith. Retrieved November 18, 2017, from www.hrc.org/explore/topic/religion-faith

943 Underwood, M. (2014, May 14). Why is the Human Rights Campaign launching $8.5 million gay rights effort in Alabama today? HRC's Chad Griffin explains. Retrieved May 25, 2018, from http://blog.al.com/wire/2014/05/why_is_the_human_rights_campai.html

944 Voelkel, R. (2009). *A Time to Build Up: Analysis of the No on Proposition 8 Campaign and Its Implications for Future Pro-LGBTQQIA Religious Organizing* [Scholarly project]. National LGBTQ Task Force. Retrieved December 18, 2017, from www.thetaskforce.org/static_html/downloads/reports/reports/time_to_build_up_rev.pdf

945 Homepage. (2017). Right Wing Watch. Retrieved November 18, 2017, from www.rightwingwatch.org

946 Issues. (2017). Thinkprogress.org. Retrieved November 18, 2017, from https://thinkprogress.org/issues-a98f1c6c495c

947 MIT Technology Review. (2014, September 19). How the internet is taking away America's religion. Retrieved May 25, 2018, from www.technologyreview.com/s/526111/how-the-internet-is-taking-away-americas-religion

948 Sandlin, M. (2015). Why the fundie freakout about LGBT equality is a GOOD thing. The God article with Mark Sandlin. Retrieved November 18, 2017, from www.patheos.com/blogs/thegodarticle/2015/03/why-the-fundie-freakout-about-lgbt-equality-is-a-good-thing

949 Zuckerman, P. (2014). We're putting an end to religion: Richard Dawkins, Bill Maher and the exploding new American secularism. Retrieved November 18, 2017, from www.salon.com/2014/12/20/were_putting_an_end_to_religion_richard_dawkins_bill_maher_and_the_exploding_new_american_secularism

950 Chellew-Hodge, C. (2015). Pew confirms LGBT rejection of religion: Why that's a good thing. Religion Dispatches. Retrieved November 18, 2017, from http://religiondispatches.org/pew-confirms-lgbt-rejection-of-religion-why-thats-a-good-thing

951 In U.S., 87% approve of black-white marriage, vs. 4% in 1958. (2013, July 25). Retrieved December 31, 2017, from http://news.gallup.com/poll/163697/approve-marriage-blacks-whites.aspx

952 Griswold, A. (2014). How to shrink your church in one easy step. The Federalist. Retrieved November 18, 2017, from http://thefederalist.com/2014/08/21/how-to-shrink-your-church-in-one-easy-step

953 Cox, D. (2018, January 24). Are white evangelicals sacrificing the future in search of the past? Retrieved March 12, 2018, from https://fivethirtyeight.com/features/are-white-evangelicals-sacrificing-the-future-in-search-of-the-past/?ex_cid=538twitter

954 Mehta, H. (2013). Why are millennials leaving church? Try atheism. Religion.blogs.cnn.com. Retrieved November 18, 2017, from http://religion.blogs.cnn.com/2013/07/30/why-are-millennials-leaving-church-try-atheism

955 Goodstein, L. (2017, December 14). Has support for Moore stained evangelicals? Some are worried. Retrieved December 28, 2017, from www.nytimes.com/2017/12/14/us/alabama-evangelical-christians-moore.html?_r=0

956 McCarthy, J. (2014). Same-sex marriage support reaches new high at 55%. Gallup.com. Retrieved November 18, 2017, from http://news.gallup.com/poll/169640/sex-marriage-support-reaches-new-high.aspx

957 Kinnaman, D. & Lyons, G. (2008). *UnChristian: What a New Generation Really Thinks About Christianity... And Why It Matters*. Grand Rapids, MI: Baker Books

958 Jones, R. P., Cox, D., & Bancoff, T. (2012, April 19). *A Generation in Transition. Religion, Values, and Politics Among College Age Millennials: Findings from the 2012 Millennial Values Survey*. Public Religion Research Institute. Retrieved December 31, 2017, from https://prri.org/wp-content/uploads/2012/04/Millennials-Survey-Report.pdf

959 Public Religion Research Institute. (2014, February 26). *A Shifting Landscape: A Decade of Change in American Attitudes about Same-Sex Marriage and LGBT Issues*. Retrieved November 13, 2017, from www.prri.org/wp-content/uploads/2014/02/2014.LGBT_REPORT.pdf

960 Smith, Sr., J. (2015). "First-ever" evangelical conference on transgender issues set for Oct. 5 in Louisville. News—Southern Baptist Theological Seminary. Retrieved November 18, 2017, from http://news.sbts.edu/2015/09/14/first-ever-evangelical-conference-on-transgender-issues-set-for-oct-5-in-louisville

961 Walker, A. T. & Mohler, R. A. (2017). *God and the Transgender Debate: What Does the Bible Actually Say About Gender Identity?* Centralia, WA: The Good Book Co.

962 Allen, B. (2015, October 5). Conference confronts transgender "confusion." Baptist News Global. Retrieved December 31, 2017, from https://baptistnews.com/article/conference-confronts-transgender-confusion/#.Wkkoud-nGUk

963 Lopez, G. (2017, March 10). Survey: White evangelicals think Christians face more discrimination than Muslims. Vox. Retrieved December 31, 2017, from www.vox.com/identities/2017/3/10/14881446/prri-survey-muslims-christians-discrimination

964 Christensen, J. (2018, February 13). Parents want custody to stop transgender teen having hormone treatment. Retrieved March 12, 2018, from https://edition.cnn.com/2018/02/13/health/transgender-teen-medical-custody-fight/index.html

965 Baldock, K. V. (2017, August 20). *God and the Transgender Debate* by Andrew T. Walker—A book Review. Retrieved January 12, 2018, from http://canyonwalkerconnections.com/9913-2

966 Walker, A. T. & Mohler, R. A. (2017). *God and the Transgender Debate: What Does the Bible Actually Say About Gender Identity?* Centralia, WA: The Good Book Co.

967 Barrington Wolff, T. (2012). Civil rights reform and the body. *Harvard Law & Policy Review* 6(1), p201, U of Penn Law School, Public Law Research Paper 12–27. Retrieved July 6, 2018, from https://ssrn.com/abstract=2019632

968 Ford, Z. (2015). Southern Baptist Conference: "Struggling" LGBT people can change through Christ. Thinkprogress.org. Retrieved November 18, 2017, from https://thinkprogress.org/southern-baptist-conference-struggling-lgbt-people-can-change-through-christ-7085b94dcd0e

969 Egan Morrissey, T. (2012). Mormon Church officially states that being gay is not a choice. Jezebel.com. Retrieved November 18, 2017, from https://jezebel.com/5966688/mormon-church-officially-states-that-being-gay-is-not-a-choice

970 Lopez, G. (2017). Myth #8: Transgender people are mentally ill. Vox. Retrieved November 18, 2017, from www.vox.com/cards/transgender-myths-fiction-facts/transgender-people-mentally-ill-myth

971 Maza, C. (2015). What the media should know about Walt Heyer and "transition regrets." Media Matters for America. Retrieved November 18, 2017, from www.mediamatters.org/blog/2015/06/02/what-the-media-should-know-about-walt-heyer-and/203855

972 Heyer, W. (2015). I was a transgender woman. Public Discourse. Retrieved November 18, 2017, from www.thepublicdiscourse.com/2015/04/14688

973 Tannehill, B. (2015). The scary science at Johns Hopkins University. Advocate.com. Retrieved November 18, 2017, from www.advocate.com/commentary/2015/12/15/scary-science-johns-hopkins-university

974 #Stand4Truth Conference—Program. (2015). Massresistance.org. Retrieved November 18, 2017, from www.massresistance.org/docs/gen2/15d/Stand4Truth-conference/program.html

975 Anti-LGBT hate group releases anti-trans position statement. (2016). Southern Poverty Law Center. Retrieved November 18, 2017, from www.splcenter.org/hatewatch/2016/04/07/anti-lgbt-hate-group-releases-anti-trans-position-statement

976 Tannehill, B. (2016). The truth about transgender suicide. HuffPost. Retrieved November 19, 2017, from www.huffingtonpost.com/brynn-tannehill/the-truth-about-transgend_b_8564834.html

977 Restored Hope Network. (2017). Restoredhopenetwork.com. Retrieved November 19, 2017, from www.restoredhopenetwork.com/index.php/component/search/?searchword=transgender&searchphrase=all&Itemid=101

978 Institute for Marital Healing: Strengthening marriages and families. (2017). Maritalhealing.com. Retrieved November 19, 2017, from www.maritalhealing.com

979 Help4Families. (2017). Retrieved November 19, 2017, from www.help4families.com/upcoming-events

980 Gender Identity Disorder. (2017). Maritalhealing.com. Retrieved November 19, 2017, from http://maritalhealing.com/conflicts/genderidentitydisorder.php

981 Coleman, E., Bockting, W., Botzer, M., Cohen-Kettenis, P., *et al.* (2011). Standards of care for the health of transsexual, transgender, and gender nonconforming people, 7th version. *International Journal of Transgenderism*, 13, 165–232

982 Tannehill, B. (2017). The desistance narrative is junk science. HuffPost. Retrieved November 19, 2017, from www.huffingtonpost.com/brynn-tannehill/the-end-of-the-desistance_b_8903690.html

983 Colero, E. (2016). Controversial CAMH gender identity clinic winds down. The Varsity. Retrieved November 19, 2017, from https://thevarsity.ca/2016/01/11/controversial-camh-gender-identity-clinic-winds-down

984 Tannehill, B. (2015). Meet the last "respectable" reparative therapist. Bilerico Report/LGBTQ Nation. Retrieved November 19, 2017, from http://bilerico.lgbtqnation.com/2015/01/meet_the_last_respectable_reparative_therapist.php

985 Tannehill, B. (2016). The 5th column in trans health care. HuffPost. Retrieved November 19, 2017, from www.huffingtonpost.com/entry/the-5th-column-in-trans-health-care_us_5771a6b8e4b0fa01a1407c52?ir=Healthy%20Living&section=us_healthy-living&utm_hp_ref=healthy-living

986 Fitzgibbons, R., Sutton, P. M., & O'Leary, D. (2009). The psychopathology of "sex reassignment" surgery: Assessing its medical, psychological, and ethical appropriateness. *National Catholic Bioethics Quarterly*, 9(1), 109–137. Retrieved July 6, 2018, from www.massresistance.org/docs/gen/10b/transgender_health/srs_final.pdf

987 O'Leary, D. & Sprigg, P. (2015). Understanding and responding to the transgender movement. Retrieved September 20, 2016, from http://downloads.frc.org/EF/EF15F45.pdf

988 Olson, K. R. (2016). Prepubescent transgender children: What we do and do not know. *Journal of the American Academy of Child & Adolescent Psychiatry*, 55(3). doi:10.1016/j.jaac.2015.11.015

989 Summary of the External Review of the CAMH Gender Identity Clinic of the Child, Youth & Family Services. (January 2016). Retrieved September 21, 2016, from https://web.archive.org/web/20160304033148/www.camh.ca/en/hospital/about_camh/newsroom/news_releases_media_advisories_and_backgrounders/current_year/Documents/GIC-Review-26Nov2015.pdf

990 Olson, K., Durwood, L., DeMeules, M., & McLaughlin, K. (2016). Mental health of transgender children who are supported in their identities. *Pediatrics*, 137(3), e20153223. http://dx.doi.org/10.1542/peds.2015-3223

991 Mozes, A. (2014). Transgender teens become happy, healthy young adults. Cbsnews.com. Retrieved November 19, 2017, from www.cbsnews.com/news/transgender-teens-become-happy-healthy-young-adults

992 The Endocrine Society. (2015). San Diego clinic finds high need for treatment of transgender youth. EurekAlert! Retrieved November 19, 2017, from www.eurekalert.org/pub_releases/2015-03/tes-sdc030615.php

993 Keo-Meier, C., Mizok, L., & Mougianis, E. (n.d.). APA fact sheet: Gender diversity and transgender identity in adolescents [Scholarly project]. Retrieved December 18, 2017, from www.apadivisions.org/division-44/resources/advocacy/transgender-adolescents.pdf

994 Brydum, S. (2016). Groundbreaking federal complaint asks FTC to ban conversion therapy. Advocate.com. Retrieved November 19, 2017, from www.advocate.com/politics/2016/2/24/groundbreaking-federal-complaint-asks-ftc-ban-conversion-therapy

995 Michaelson, J. (2014). Iran's new gay executions. The Daily Beast. Retrieved November 19, 2017, from www.thedailybeast.com/irans-new-gay-executions

996 Duffy, N. (2016). Saudi Arabia: Push for gays to be executed because social media is "making too many homosexuals." PinkNews. Retrieved November 19, 2017, from www.pinknews.co.uk/2016/03/31/saudi-arabia-push-for-gays-to-be-executed-because-social-media-is-making-too-many-homosexuals

997 O'Leary, D. & Sprigg, P. (2017). Understanding and responding to the transgender movement. FRC. Retrieved September 20, 2016, from http://downloads.frc.org/EF/EF15F45.pdf

998 Shore, J. (2014). The Southern Baptist Convention throws transgender people under the bus. John Shore. Retrieved November 18, 2017, from www.patheos.com/blogs/johnshore/2014/06/the-southern-baptist-convention-throws-transgender-people-under-the-bus

999 Savransky, R. (2018, February 18). Kansas GOP approves resolution opposing efforts "to validate transgender identity": Report. Retrieved March 12, 2018, from http://thehill.com/homenews/state-watch/374464-kansas-gop-approves-resolution-opposing-efforts-to-validate-transgender

1000 O'Leary, D. & Sprigg, P. (2015). Understanding and responding to the transgender movement. Retrieved September 20, 2016, from http://downloads.frc.org/EF/EF15F45.pdf

1001 Shackford, S. (2015). What the heck is the First Amendment Defense Act, and should we be worried? Reason.com. Retrieved November 19, 2017, from http://reason.com/blog/2015/12/22/what-the-heck-is-the-first-amendment-def

1002 Green, E. (2016). Why Mississippi's law on religious rights and LGBT discrimination got blocked. The Atlantic. Retrieved November 19, 2017, from www.theatlantic.com/politics/archive/2016/07/why-mississippis-law-on-religious-rights-and-lgbt-got-blocked/489731

1003 United States Department of Justice Office of the Attorney General. (2017, October 6). Memorandum for all Executive Departments and Agencies: Federal Protections for Religious Liberty. Retrieved December 18, 2017, from www.justice.gov/opa/press-release/file/1001891/download

1004 Tannehill, B. (2016). And then they came for transgender people. HuffPost. Retrieved November 19, 2017, from www.huffingtonpost.com/brynn-tannehill/and-then-they-came-for-tr_b_9258678.html

1005 Tannehill, B. (2016). And then they came for transgender people. HuffPost. Retrieved November 19, 2017, from www.huffingtonpost.com/brynn-tannehill/and-then-they-came-for-tr_b_9258678.html

1006 Tannehill, B. & Gill, A. (2016). A user's guide to this year's transphobic legislation. Advocate.com. Retrieved November 19, 2017, from www.advocate.com/transgender/2016/2/02/users-guide-years-transphobic-legislation

1007 Past anti-LGBT religious exemption legislation across the country. (2017). American Civil Liberties Union. Retrieved November 19, 2017, from www.aclu.org/other/past-anti-lgbt-religious-exemption-legislation-across-country?redirect=anti-lgbt-religious-refusals-legislation-across-country#rfra16

1008 Past anti-LGBT religious exemption legislation across the country. (2017). American Civil Liberties Union. Retrieved November 19, 2017, from www.aclu.org/other/past-anti-lgbt-religious-exemption-legislation-across-country?redirect=anti-lgbt-religious-refusals-legislation-across-country#rfra16

1009 Past anti-LGBT religious exemption legislation across the country. (2017). American Civil Liberties Union. Retrieved November 19, 2017, from www.aclu.org/other/past-anti-lgbt-religious-exemption-legislation-across-country?redirect=anti-lgbt-religious-refusals-legislation-across-country#rfra16

1010 Gordon, M., Price, M., & Peralta, K. (2016). Understanding HB2: North Carolina's newest law solidifies state's role in defining discrimination. charlotteobserver. Retrieved November 19, 2017, from www.charlotteobserver.com/news/politics-government/article68401147.html

1011 Skinner-Thompson, S. (2016). North Carolina's Bathroom Bill puts transgender people in an impossible catch-22. Slate Magazine. Retrieved November 19, 2017, from www.slate.com/blogs/outward/2016/05/16/north_carolina_s_hb2_puts_transgender_people_in_an_impossible_catch_22.html

1012 Tucker, N. (2016). U.S. district judge strikes down Mississippi's "religious freedom" law. The Washington Post. Retrieved November 19, 2017, from www.washingtonpost.com/lifestyle/style/us-district-judge-strikes-down-mississippis-religious-freedom-law/2016/07/01/f98dc2ca-3ec9-11e6-a66f-aa6c1883b6b1_story.html?utm_term=.9514e4269893

1013 Stern, M. J. (2016, March 24). North Carolina's new anti-LGBTQ law is vicious, shameful, and unconstitutional. Retrieved December 18, 2017, from www.slate.com/blogs/outward/2016/03/24/north_carolina_s_anti_lgbtq_law_is_unconstitutional.html

1014 Riley, J. (2016). Trans student Gavin Grimm wins injunction, school must let him use boys' restroom. Metro Weekly. Retrieved November 19, 2017, from www.metroweekly.com/2016/06/court-gloucester-county-allow-transgender-student-use-boys-restroom

1015 Stern, M. J. (2016, March 24). North Carolina's new anti-LGBTQ law is vicious, shameful, and unconstitutional. Retrieved December 18, 2017, from www.slate.com/blogs/outward/2016/03/24/north_carolina_s_anti_lgbtq_law_is_unconstitutional.html

1016 *Romer v. Evans*. (1995). Oyez. Retrieved November 19, 2017, from www.oyez.org/cases/1995/94-1039

1017 *Village of Arlington Heights v. Metropolitan*. (1977). LII/Legal Information Institute. Retrieved November 19, 2017, from www.law.cornell.edu/supremecourt/text/429/252

1018 *Reitman v. Mulkey*, 387 U.S. 369. (1967). Justia Law. Retrieved November 19, 2017, from https://supreme.justia.com/cases/federal/us/387/369

1019 *Brown v. Board of Education*. (2017). En.wikipedia.org. Retrieved November 19, 2017, from https://en.wikipedia.org/wiki/Brown_v._Board_of_Education

1020 Ryan White was a hemophiliac teen who died in 1990 of AIDS related complications after receiving a tainted blood transfusion in the 1980s. It wasn't until Ryan White that the public began to see the disease as something affecting "normal" people

1021 Mantyla, K. (2012). Barton suggests we can't cure AIDS because it is punishment for sin. Right Wing Watch. Retrieved November 19, 2017, from www.rightwingwatch.org/post/barton-suggests-we-cant-cure-aids-because-it-is-punishment-for-sin

1022 Marcus, A. (2001). Do some people "deserve" AIDS? TheBody.com. Retrieved November 19, 2017, from www.thebody.com/content/art377.html

1023 Swier, D. (2014). The 2% solution: How homosexuals are fundamentally transforming America. Drrichswier.com. Retrieved November 19, 2017, from http:/drrichswier.com/2014/07/18/2-solution-homosexuals-fundamentally-transforming-america

1024 Blumberg, A. (2014). Shocking number of Americans believe AIDS could be punishment from God. HuffPost UK. Retrieved November 19, 2017, from www.huffingtonpost.com/2014/02/28/aids-hiv-gods-punishment_n_4876381.html

1025 Badash, D. (2015). "I kill them!": HBO's VICE goes to Uganda to see what American anti-gay Christians have created. The New Civil Rights Movement. Retrieved November 19, 2017, from www.thenewcivilrightsmovement.com/davidbadash/_i_kill_them_hbo_s_vice_goes_to_uganda_to_see_what_american_anti_gay_christians_have_created

1026 Mai, T. (2014). Pastor calls for killing gays to end AIDS. USA Today. Retrieved November 19, 2017, from www.usatoday.com/story/news/nation/2014/12/04/pastor-calls-for-killing-gays-to-end-aids/19929973

1027 Mantyla, K. (2010). FRC's Sprigg wants to see homosexuality criminalized. Right Wing Watch. Retrieved November 19, 2017, from www.rightwingwatch.org/post/frcs-sprigg-wants-to-see-homosexuality-criminalized

1028 Grant, J. M., Mottet, L. A., Tanis, J., Harrison, J., Herman, J. L., & Keisling, M. (2011). *Injustice at Every Turn: A Report of the National Transgender Discrimination Survey*. Washington, DC: National Center for Transgender Equality and National Gay and Lesbian Task Force. Retrieved July 6, 2018, from www.thetaskforce.org/static_html/downloads/reports/reports/ntds_full.pdf

1029 Khazan, O. (2016). The true harm of bathroom bills. The Atlantic. Retrieved November 19, 2017, from www.theatlantic.com/health/archive/2016/05/transgender-bathrooms-suicide/483351

1030 Swartz, M. (2015, October 27). The equal rights fight over Houston's bathrooms. Retrieved December 31, 2017, from www.nytimes.com/2015/10/28/opinion/the-equal-rights-fight-over-houstons-bathrooms.html?_r=0

1031 Badash, D. (2016). Liberty Counsel President warns her glock "identifies" as her bodyguard in restrooms. The New Civil Rights Movement. Retrieved November 19, 2017, from www.thenewcivilrightsmovement.com/davidbadash/head_of_law_firm_that_has_drafted_anti_lgbt_bills_in_20_states_says_she_carries_a_45_into_restrooms

1032 Dobson, J. (2016). Protect your kids from tyrant Obama. WND. Retrieved November 19, 2017, from www.wnd.com/2016/05/protect-your-kids-from-tyrant-obama

1033 Blair, L. (2016). Dr. James Dobson: Christian parents will violate scripture if daughters use trans-inclusive bathrooms. Christianpost.com. Retrieved November 19, 2017, from www.christianpost.com/news/dr-james-dobson-christian-parents-will-violate-scripture-if-daughters-use-trans-inclusive-bathrooms-165063

1034 Walsh, M. (2016). No, gays and "transgenders" are not being bullied. They are the bullies. TheBlaze. Retrieved November 19, 2017, from www.theblaze.com/contributions/no-gays-and-transgenders-are-not-being-bullied-they-are-the-bullies

1035 *Brandenburg v. Ohio*, 395 U.S. 444 (1969), was a landmark 1st Amendment case heard by the Supreme Court. The Court held that government cannot punish inflammatory speech unless that speech is "directed to inciting or producing imminent lawless action and is likely to incite or produce such action"

1036 These are the trans people killed in 2016. (2016). Advocate.com. Retrieved November 19, 2017, from www.advocate.com/transgender/2016/10/14/these-are-trans-people-killed-2016

1037 Nicholson, E. (2016). Self-appointed bathroom cop catches Dallas woman using women's restroom. Dallas Observer. Retrieved November 19, 2017, from www.dallasobserver.com/news/self-appointed-bathroom-cop-catches-dallas-woman-using-womens-restroom-8259104

1038 Cisgender woman mistaken for trans, told to get out of Walmart women's restroom. (2016). Instinct. Retrieved November 19, 2017, from http://instinctmagazine.com/post/cisgender-woman-mistaken-trans-told-get-out-walmart-womens-restroom

1039 Kellaway, M. (2015). Detroit woman kicked out of restaurant bathroom for looking "like a man" sues. Advocate.com. Retrieved November 19, 2017, from www.advocate.com/business/2015/06/17/detroit-woman-kicked-out-restaurant-bathroom-looking-man-sues

1040 Compton, J. (2015). Op-ed: I'm a lesbian targeted by the bathroom police. Advocate.com. Retrieved November 19, 2017, from www.advocate.com/commentary/2015/07/07/op-ed-im-lesbian-targeted-bathroom-police

1041 Mandell, S. (2016). Viral video of lesbian kicked out of women's room for not showing I.D. exposes dangers of bathroom policing. Towleroad. Retrieved November 19, 2017, from www.towleroad.com/2016/04/police-force-lesbian-to-leave-bathroom-for-failing-to-show-id-prove-shes-a-woman-watch

1042 Flores, A. R., Herman, J. L., Gates, G. J., & Brown, T. N. (2016). *How Many Adults Identify as Transgender in the United States?* [Scholarly project]. The Williams Institute at UCLA Law School. Retrieved December 18, 2017, from http://williamsinstitute.law.ucla.edu/wp-content/uploads/How-Many-Adults-Identify-as-Transgender-in-the-United-States.pdf

1043 Cohen, R. (2017). Christian "therapist" shows how to beat the gay out! Retrieved July 6, 2018, from www.youtube.com/watch?v=4jU65-3l588

1044 Lambda Legal. (2017, November 2). The Senate is falling over itself to fill courts with Donald Trump's extremist anti-LGBT judges. Retrieved December 18, 2017, from www.lambdalegal.org/blog/20171102_republicans-stack-federal-courts-with-toxic-judges

1045 Klain, R. A. (2017, November 21). Conservatives have a breathtaking plan for Trump to pack the courts. Retrieved December 18, 2017, from www.washingtonpost.com/opinions/conservatives-have-a-breathtaking-plan-for-trump-to-pack-the-courts/2017/11/21/b7ce90d4-ce43-11e7-9d3a-bcbe2af58c3a_story.html?utm_term=.6db7e0d77e78

1046 "SPARTA is a group of LGBT people who currently serve or have served in the military and our families as well as veteran and uniformed allies. We are a membership organization, built by, for and with members from all parts of the LGBT military community." Retrieved December 20, 2017, from https://spartapride.org

1047 In the case of *Goldman v. Weinberger*, 475 US 503—1986, the Supreme Court ruled that the military has broad leeway to impinge on the fundamental rights of service members. In this case, an observant Jewish officer was forbidden from wearing a yarmulke, even though it infringed on his ability to exercise his religion, and wearing it had no effect on his ability to do his job. Thus, we concluded that a lawsuit based on transgender identity was very unlikely to succeed. Retrieved December 20, 2017, from www.oyez.org/cases/1985/84-1097

1048 Baird, J. (2014, February 21). The courage of transgender soldiers. The New York Times. Retrieved December 20, 2017, from www.nytimes.com/2014/02/22/opinion/sunday/baird-the-courage-of-trans-soldiers.html?_r=0

1049 Londono, E. (2014, April 28). For transgender service members, honesty can end career. The Washington Post. Retrieved December 20, 2017, from www.highbeam.com/doc/1P2-35986420.html?refid=easy_hf

1050 Dunham, W. (2014, May 11). Hagel backs review of U.S. military ban on transgender troops. Retrieved December 20, 2017, from www.reuters.com/article/us-usa-military-transgender/hagel-backs-review-of-u-s-military-ban-on-transgender-troops-idUSBREA4A09A20140511

1051 http://archive.palmcenter.org/publications/recent. Retrieved December 20, 2017

1052 Tannehill, B., Fulton, B. S., & Robinson, A. D. (2015, March 22). *Transgender Military Service: A Guide to Implementation* [Scholarly project]. SPARTA. Retrieved December 20, 2017, from https://github.com/Arkwin/SPARTA-DOCS/raw/master/SPARTA_Transgender_Policy_Implementation_Guide_3.22.15.pdf

1053 US Department of Defense. (2015, July 13). Working group to study implications of transgender service. Retrieved December 20, 2017, from www.defense.gov/News/Article/Article/612640

1054 US Department of Defense. (2016, June 30). Secretary of Defense Ash Carter announces policy for transgender service members. Press Release No: NR-246-16. Retrieved December 20, 2016, from www.defense.gov/News/News-Releases/News-Release-View/Article/821675/secretary-of-defense-ash-carter-announces-policy-for-transgender-service-members

1055 DOD Instruction 1300.28: In-service transition for transgender service members (2016, October 1). Retrieved December 20, 2017, from www.defense.gov/Portals/1/features/2016/0616_policy/DoD-Instruction-1300.28.pdf

1056 Protess, B., Ivory, D., & Eder, S. (2017, September 10). Where Trump's hands-off approach to governing does not apply. Retrieved December 20, 2017, from www.nytimes.com/2017/09/10/business/trump-regulations-religious-conservatives.html

1057 Epps, G. (2017, November 1). Trump's tweets take down his military ban on trans people. Retrieved December 20, 2017, from www.theatlantic.com/politics/archive/2017/11/pricking-of-his-thumbs/544547

1058 Images, W. M. (2017, July 27). Chairman of Joint Chiefs wants direct orders, not tweets, before starting transgender ban. Retrieved December 20, 2017, from http://nymag.com/daily/intelligencer/2017/07/chairman-of-joint-chiefs-tweets-not-enough-to-start-ban.html

1059 Bowden, J. (2017, July 28). Mattis appalled by Trump tweets announcing transgender ban: Report. Retrieved December 20, 2017, from http://thehill.com/policy/defense/344290-mattis-appalled-by-trump-tweets-announcing-transgender-military-ban-report

1060 Starr, B., Cohen, Z., & Sciutto, J. (2017, July 27). Trump transgender ban blindsides Joint Chiefs. Retrieved December 20, 2017, from www.cnn.com/2017/07/27/politics/trump-military-transgender-ban-joint-chiefs/index.html

1061 Beauchamp, Z. (2017, July 27). Trump: I consulted the military about the transgender ban. Military: No, you didn't. Retrieved December 20, 2017, from www.vox.com/world/2017/7/27/16051892/trump-transgender-ban-army-chief-staff

1062 Schaefer, A. G., Iyengar, R., Kadiyala, S., Kavanagh, J., *et al.* (2016). Assessing the implications of allowing transgender personnel to serve openly. RAND Corporation, RR-1530-OSD, 2016. Retrieved December 20, 2017, from www.rand.org/pubs/research_reports/RR1530.html

1063 Presidential Memorandum for the Secretary of Defense and the Secretary of Homeland Security. (2017, August 25). Retrieved December 20, 2017, from www.whitehouse.gov/presidential-actions/presidential-memorandum-secretary-defense-secretary-homeland-security

1064 Stern, M. J. (2017, August 28). Trump's trans troops ban may be on a fast track to the Supreme Court. Retrieved December 20, 2017, from www.slate.com/blogs/outward/2017/08/28/trump_s_transgender_troops_ban_may_be_heading_to_the_supreme_court.html

1065 Jouvenal, J. (2017, October 30). Federal judge in D.C. blocks part of Trump's transgender military ban. Retrieved May 25, 2018, from www.washingtonpost.com/local/public-safety/federal-judge-in-dc-blocks-part-of-trumps-transgender-military-ban/2017/10/30/41d41526-bd94-11e7-959c-fe2b598d8c00_story.html?utm_term=.739dd663a0be

1066 Marimow, A. E. (2017, November 21). Federal judge says Trump administration can't stop funding sex-reassignment surgeries for military members. Retrieved December 20, 2017, from www.washingtonpost.com/local/public-safety/a-second-judge-blocks-trump-administrations-proposed-transgender-military-ban/2017/11/21/d91f65e4-cee1-11e7-81bc-c55a220c8cbe_story.html?utm_term=.89b3d7443bd4

1067 *Karnoski v. Trump*, CASE NO. C17-1297-MJP. Retrieved December 20, 2017, from www.lambdalegal.org/sites/default/files/legal-docs/downloads/karnoski_pi_order.pdf

1068 https://media.defense.gov/2018/Mar/23/2001894037/-1/-1/0/MILITARY-SERVICE-BY-TRANSGENDER-INDIVIDUALS.PDF

1069 Ford, Z. (2018, March 25). Pence secretly drafted Trump's latest transgender military ban. Retrieved August 2, 2018, from https://thinkprogress.org/pence-responsible-for-trump-transgender-military-ban-f4d3b67bde47

1070 Ford, Z. (2018, May 2). New documents suggest Trump administration rigged military panel on transgender ban. Retrieved August 2, 2018, from https://thinkprogress.org/documents-from-military-panel-contradict-transgender-ban-13941471093d

1071 American Medical Association Letter to Secretary of Defense Mattis dated April 3, 2018. https://www.politico.com/f/?id=00000162-927c-d2e5-ade3-d37e69760000

1072 APA Reiterates Its Strong Opposition to Ban of Transgender Americans from Serving in U.S. Military, March 24, 2018. https://www.psychiatry.org/newsroom/news-releases/apa-reiterates-its-strong-opposition-to-ban-of-transgender-americans-from-serving-in-u-s-military

1073 Statement Regarding Transgender Individuals Serving in Military (March 26, 2018). Accessed http://www.apa.org/news/press/releases/2018/03/transgender-military.aspx

1074 American Medical Association Letter to Secretary of Defense Mattis dated April 3, 2018. https://www.politico.com/f/?id=00000162-927c-d2e5-ade3-d37e69760000

1075 Tannehill, B., Fulton, B. S., & Robinson, A. D. (2015, March 22). *Transgender Military Service: A Guide to Implementation* [Scholarly project]. SPARTA. Retrieved December 20, 2017, from https://github.com/Arkwin/SPARTA-DOCS/raw/master/SPARTA_Transgender_Policy_Implementation_Guide_3.22.15.pdf

1076 Flores, A. R., Herman, J. L., Gates, G. J., & Brown, T. N. (2016). *How Many Adults Identify as Transgender in the United States?* [Scholarly project]. The Williams Institute at UCLA Law School. Retrieved December 18, 2017, from http://williamsinstitute.law.ucla.edu/wp-content/uploads/How-Many-Adults-Identify-as-Transgender-in-the-United-States.pdf

1077 Harrison-Quintana, J. & Herman, J. L. (2013). Still serving in silence: Transgender service members and veterans in the National Transgender Discrimination Survey. *Harvard Kennedy School LGBTQ Policy Journal*, 3. Retrieved July 6, 2018, from www.thetaskforce.org/downloads/reports/reports/still_serving_in_silence.pdf

1078 Gates, G. J. & Herman, J. L. (2014). *Transgender Military Service in the United States*. Los Angeles, CA: Williams Institute Press. Retrieved July 6, 2018, from http://williamsinstitute.law.ucla.edu/wp-content/uploads/Transgender-Military-Service-May-2014.pdf

1079 Schaefer, A. G., Iyengar, R., Kadiyala, S., Kavanagh, J., *et al.* (2016). Assessing the implications of allowing transgender personnel to serve openly. RAND Corporation, RR-1530-OSD, 2016. Retrieved December 20, 2017, from www.rand.org/pubs/research_reports/RR1530.html

1080 American Psychiatric Association. (2013). Gender Dysphoria Fact Sheet: *DSM-5*. Arlington, VA: Author. Retrieved July 6, 2018, from www.dsm5.org/Documents/Gender%20Dysphoria%20Fact %20Sheet.pdf

1081 Coleman, E., Bockting, W., Botzer, M., Cohen-Kettenis, P., *et al.* (2011). Standards of care for the health of transsexual, transgender, and gender nonconforming people, 7th version. *International Journal of Transgenderism*, 13, 165–232

1082 Bockting, W. O. & Goldberg, J. M. (2006). Guidelines for transgender care (special issue). *International Journal of Transgenderism*, 9(3/4); Bolin, A. (1994). Transcending and Transgendering: Male-to-Female Transsexuals, Dichotomy and Diversity. In G. Herdt (ed.) *Third Sex, Third Gender: Beyond Sexual Dimorphism in Culture and History* (pp447–486). New York, NY: Zone Books; Rachlin, K. (1999). Factors which influence individuals' decisions when considering female-to-male genital reconstructive surgery. *International Journal of Transgenderism*, 3(3); Rachlin, K., Green, J., & Lombardi, E. (2008). Utilization of health care among female-to-male transgender individuals in the United States. *Journal of Homosexuality*, 54(3), 243–258. doi:10.1080/00918360801982124; Rachlin, K., Hansbury, G., & Pardo, S. T. (2010). Hysterectomy and oophorectomy experiences of female-to-male transgender individuals. *International Journal of Transgenderism*, 12(3), 155–166. doi:10.1080/15532739.2010.514220

1083 Coleman, E., Bockting, W., Botzer, M., Cohen-Kettenis, P., *et al.* (2011). Standards of care for the health of transsexual, transgender, and gender nonconforming people, 7th version. *International Journal of Transgenderism*, 13, 165–232

1084 American Medical Association (AMA) House of Delegates' Resolution 122, Removing Financial Barriers to Care for Transgender Patients at 115–117 (April 18, 2008)

1085 Herman, J. L. (2013). *Costs and Benefits of Providing Transition-Related Health Care Coverage in Employee Health Benefits Plans: Findings from a Survey of Employers*. Los Angeles: Williams Institute Press. Retrieved July 6, 2018, from https://williamsinstitute.law.ucla.edu/research/transgender-issues/costs-benefits-providing-transition-related-health-care-coverage-herman-2013

1086 Schaefer, A. G., Iyengar, R., Kadiyala, S., Kavanagh, J., *et al.* (2016). Assessing the implications of allowing transgender personnel to serve openly. RAND Corporation, RR-1530-OSD, 2016. Retrieved December 20, 2017, from www.rand.org/pubs/research_reports/RR1530.html

1087 Belkin, A. (2015). Caring for our transgender troops—the negligible cost of transition-related care. *New England Journal of Medicine*, 373(12), 1089–1092. doi:10.1056/nejmp1509230

1088 Kime, P. (2017, August 8). DoD spends $84M a year on Viagra, similar meds. Retrieved December 20, 2017, from www.militarytimes.com/pay-benefits/military-benefits/health-care/2015/02/13/dod-spends-84m-a-year-on-viagra-similar-meds

1089 Philipps, D. (2016, July 1). Military is asked to march to a less expensive tune. Retrieved December 20, 2017, from www.nytimes.com/2016/07/02/us/military-bands-budget.html

1090 Londoño, E. (2014, April 26). For transgender service members, honesty can end career. The Washington Post. Retrieved July 6, 2018, from www.washingtonpost.com/world/national-security/for-transgender-service-members-concept-of-dont-ask-dont-tell-remains-a-reality/2014/04/26/c0597936-ccb6-11e3-93eb-6c0037dde2ad_story.html

1091 Department of Insurance, State of California. (2012). *Economic Impact Assessment: Gender Nondiscrimination in Health Insurance*. Sacramento: Author. Retrieved July 6, 2018, from http://transgenderlawcenter.org/wp-content/uploads/2013/04/Economic-Impact-Assessment-Gender-Nondiscrimination-In-Health-Insurance.pdf

1092 National Health Service, UK. (2013). *Interim Gender Dysphoria Protocol and Service Guideline 2013–2014*. London: Author. Retrieved July 6, 2018, from www.england.nhs.uk/wp-content/uploads/2013/10/int-gend-proto.pdf

1093 TRICARE. (n.d.). List of covered services: Hormone replacement therapy. Retrieved July 6, 2018, from www.tricare.mil/CoveredServices/IsItCovered/HormoneReplacementTherapy.aspx

1094 TRICARE. (n.d.). Out-of-network requests for TRICARE Prime beneficiaries. Retrieved July 6, 2018, from www.tricare-west.com/content/hnfs/home/tw/bene/auth/nnw-requests.html

1095 Feldman, J. (2007). Preventive Care of the Transgendered Patient. In R. Ettner, S. Monstrey, & E. Eyler (eds) *Principles of Transgender Surgery and Medicine*. Binghamton, NY: Haworth Press, pp33–72

1096 Coleman, E., Bockting, W., Botzer, M., Cohen-Kettenis, P., *et al.* (2011). Standards of care for the health of transsexual, transgender, and gender nonconforming people, 7th version. *International Journal of Transgenderism*, 13, 165–232

1097 Elders, M. J., Brown, G. R., Kolditz, T. A., & Steinman, A. M. (2014). Medical aspects of transgender military service. *Armed Forces and Society*, 1–22

1098 Tannehill, B. (2013, June 11). A life of service. Outserve Magazine. Retrieved July 6, 2018, from https://web.archive.org/web/20140417121105/http://outservemag.com/2013/06/a-life-of-service

1099 Stetson, E. A. (March 2013). Deployed, trans and OUT. Outserve Magazine. Retrieved July 6, 2018, from https://web.archive.org/web/20140413034524/http://outservemag.com/2013/03/deployed-trans-and-out

1100 Tannehill, B., (2013, April 25). Deployed while trans: The Rachel Bolyard story. Outserve Magazine. Retrieved July 6, 2018, from https://web.archive.org/web/20140417121053/http://outservemag.com:80/2013/04/deployed-while-trans-the-rachel-bolyard-story

1101 New York Times. (1992, November 4). Canadian military can't bar homosexuals, court rules. New York Times. Retrieved July 6, 2018, from www.nytimes.com/1992/11/04/world/canadian-military-can-t-bar-homosexuals-a-court-rules.html?pagewanted=1

1102 TRICARE. (n.d.). List of covered services: Hormone replacement therapy. Retrieved July 6, 2018, from www.tricare.mil/CoveredServices/IsItCovered/HormoneReplacementTherapy.aspx

1103 A. Holdom, personal communication, April 7, 2013. Available on request

1104 Non-deployable status, meaning unable to deploy for medical reasons

1105 Based on tables dated September 17, 2015, provided by Dr. William M. Kuzon, Professor of Surgery at the University of Michigan, and Chief of Surgery at the Ann Arbor VA Medical Center since 1992. He estimates that currently half his workload concerns gender-related surgeries. He notes that recovery times tend to be even faster for individuals who are healthy, young, and non-smokers. Available on request

1106 A. Holdom, personal communication, April 7, 2013. Available on request

1107 Royal Australian Air Force. (2013). *Air Force Diversity Handbook: Transitioning Gender in the Air Force*. Melbourne: Author. Retrieved July 6, 2018, from www.defglis.com.au/resources/GenderTransitionGuide.pdf

1108 Anonymous UK transgender servicemember, personal communication, April 7, 2013. Available on request

1109 R. Anderson, personal communication, August 2013. Available on request

1110 "The rules for transsexual personnel should be no different to those that apply to the gender group to which the transsexual person intends to transition and that apply to all individuals who live within SLA. The same applies to the use of ablutions" (Ministry of Defence, UK, 2009, para. 78)

1111 (Ministry of Defence, UK, 2009, para. 80). *UK Defence Instruction Notice 2009DIN01-007: Policy for the Recruitment and Management of Transsexual Personnel in the Armed Forces*. London: Author

1112 Anonymous UK transgender servicemember, personal communication, August 2013. Available on request

1113 A. Holdom, personal communication, April 7, 2013. Available on request

1114 Devries, C. D. (2008). Do transitioned athletes compete at an advantage or disadvantage as compared with physically born men and women? A review of the scientific literature. AthletesCAN. Retrieved September 13, 2018, from http://www.caaws.ca/e/wp-content/uploads/2013/02/Devries_lit_review2.pdf

1115 Griffin, P. & Carroll, H. (2011). NCAA inclusion of transgender student-athletes. NCAA Office of Inclusion. Retrieved July 6, 2018, from www.ncaa.org/sites/default/files/Transgender_Handbook_ 2011_Final.pdf

1116 "To account for physiological differences in absolute fitness standards between males and females, tests of 'general fitness' must, and do, set appropriate standards relative to the gender (and age) of those taking the test. The point at which an individual is considered to have completed gender transition may vary from individual to individual, depending on medical treatment and other factors, thus each case should be considered on an individual basis" (Ministry of Defence, UK, 2009, para 54)

1117 A. Holdom, personal communication, April 7, 2013. Available on request

1118 "It is unlawful to treat a transsexual person as though they are neither male nor female and to insist on him or her using separate facilities, such as an accessible toilet for disabled people, on a permanent basis. Each case should be individually managed in consultation between the individual, chain of command and medical officers" (Ministry of Defence, UK, 2009, para. 79)

1119 A. Holdom, personal communication, April 7, 2013. Available on request

1120 "Transition is often very challenging and transsexual people undergoing a long and difficult transition may feel isolated and distressed. For this reason recruitment into the Armed Forces and initial training may not be compatible with the supportive environment that is essential for transsexual people at this time" (Ministry of Defence, UK, 2009, para. 48)

1121 DOD Memorandum for Sector Commanders. (2017, December 8). Policy Memorandum 2–5, Transgender Applicant Processing. Retrieved December 20, 2017, from www.documentcloud.org/documents/4333346-DOD-Trans-Accession-Memo.html

1122 See, for example, Human Rights Campaign. (2009). San Francisco transgender benefit: Actual cost & utilization (2001–2006). Retrieved July 6, 2018, from www.hrc.org/resources/entry/san-francisco-transgender-benefit-actual-cost-utilization-2001-2006

1123 Human Rights Campaign. (2017). *Corporate Equality Index 2018: Rating American Workplaces on Gay, Lesbian, Bisexual, and Transgender Equality*. Washington, DC: Author. Retrieved July 6, 2018, from https://assets2.hrc.org/files/assets/resources/CEI-2018-FullReport.pdf?_ga=2.114385991.1103353226.1513791816-2124830380.1513791816

1124 Transgender soldier meets the President. (2013, May 31). Available at https://web.archive.org/web/20130701001714/http://outservemag.com/2013/06/trans-man-soldier-meets-the-president

1125 Polchar, J., Sweijs, T., Marten, P., & Galdiga, J. (2014). *LGBT Military Personnel: A Strategic Vision for Inclusion*. The Hague: The Hague Centre for Strategic Studies. Retrieved September 13, 2018, from https://hcss.nl/sites/default/files/files/reports/HCSS_LGBT_webversie.pdf

1126 Adm. Mullen testimony before the Senate Armed Services Committee. (2010, February 2). Video. Retrieved July 6, 2018, from www.youtube.com/watch?v=X83IdnqOSdk

1127 Coley, J. (2018, March 20). The 8 best films we saw at SXSW 2018. Retrieved March 22, 2018, from https://editorial.rottentomatoes.com/article/the-8-best-films-we-saw-at-sxsw-2018

1128 DeFore, J. (2018, March 10). "TransMilitary": Film review. SXSW 2018. Retrieved March 22, 2018, from www.hollywoodreporter.com/review/transmilitary-review-1093596

1129 Pew Research Center. (2016, September 28). *Where the Public Stands on Religious Liberty vs. Nondiscrimination*. Retrieved December 21, 2017, from http://assets.pewresearch.org/wp-content/uploads/sites/11/2016/09/Religious-Liberty-full-for-web.pdf

1130 Rodriguez, M. (2016). Cisgender actor Matt Bomer will play transgender sex worker in a new film. Mic.com. Retrieved July 6, 2018, from https://mic.com/articles/153059/cisgender-actor-matt-bomer-will-play-transgender-sex-worker-in-a-new-film#.Kg1iUCqtC

1131 Rodriguez, M. (2016). Actress Jen Richards just nailed the problem with casting cisgender actors in trans roles. Mic.com. Retrieved July 6, 2018, from https://mic.com/articles/153149/actress-jen-richards-just-nailed-the-problem-with-casting-cisgender-actors-in-trans-roles#.ySnvnlpJE

1132 Richards, J. (2017, June 16). Matt Bomer playing a trans woman is more than problematic—it's dangerous. Retrieved January 21, 2018, from www.newnownext.com/matt-bomer-anything-transgender/06/2017

1133 Twitter. (2016). Retrieved July 6, 2018, from https://twitter.com/MarkRuffalo/status/771100395242459137

1134 Tannehill, B. (2014). Why Jared Leto's Rayon is bad for the trans community. Bilerico Report/LGBTQ Nation. Retrieved July 6, 2018, from http://bilerico.lgbtqnation.com/2014/03/why_jared_letos_rayon_is_bad_for_the_trans_communi.php

1135 Tannehill, B. (2015). Op-ed: You can't handle the truth about trans people. Advocate.com. Retrieved July 6, 2018, from www.advocate.com/commentary/2015/05/08/op-ed-you-cant-handle-truth-about-trans-people

1136 *Her Story*. (2015). IMDb. Retrieved July 6, 2018, from www.imdb.com/title/tt4858316/?ref_=nv_sr_1

1137 *Sense8* (TV Series 2015–2018). (2018). IMDb. Retrieved July 6, 2018, from www.imdb.com/title/tt2431438/?ref_=nv_sr_1

1138 *Tangerine*. (2015). IMDb. Retrieved July 6, 2018, from www.imdb.com/title/tt3824458/?ref_=nv_sr_1

1139 *Tropic Thunder*. (2008). IMDb. Retrieved July 6, 2018, from www.imdb.com/title/tt0942385/?ref_=fn_al_tt_1

1140 Modell, J. (2014). Simple Jacks (and Janes): 17 mostly awful portrayals of people with intellectual disabilities. Tv.avclub.com. Retrieved July 6, 2018, from https://tv.avclub.com/simple-jacks-and-janes-17-mostly-awful-portrayals-of-1798269332

1141 Robert Downey Jr. (2018). IMDb. Retrieved July 6, 2018, from www.imdb.com/name/nm0000375/?ref_=tt_trv_qu

1142 *Ace Ventura* (1994 film). (2017). En.wikipedia.org. Retrieved July 6, 2018, from https://en.wikipedia.org/wiki/Ace_Ventura

1143 *The Silence of the Lambs* (1991 film). (2017). En.wikipedia.org. Retrieved July 6, 2018, from https://en.wikipedia.org/wiki/The_Silence_of_the_Lambs_%28film%29

1144 *Dressed to Kill* (1980 film). (2017). En.wikipedia.org. Retrieved July 6, 2018, from https://en.wikipedia.org/wiki/Dressed_to_Kill_%281980_film%29

1145 *Psycho* (1960 film). (2017). En.wikipedia.org. Retrieved July 6, 2018, from https://en.wikipedia.org/wiki/Psycho_%281960_film%29

1146 Aguilera, L. (2015). "Pretty Little Liars" boss explains the transgender twist: "We did not jump on the bandwagon." Entertainment Tonight. Retrieved July 6, 2018, from www.etonline.com/news/169830_pretty_little_liars_boss_marlene_king_explains_the_transgender_twist_we_did_not_jump_on_the_bandwagon

1147 CeCe McDonald. (2017). En.wikipedia.org. Retrieved July 6, 2018, from https://en.wikipedia.org/wiki/CeCe_McDonald

1148 Female hysteria. (2017). En.wikipedia.org. Retrieved July 6, 2018, from https://en.wikipedia.org/wiki/Female_hysteria

1149 Rucker, P. (2015, August 8). Trump says Fox's Megyn Kelly had "blood coming out of her wherever." Retrieved December 21, 2017, from www.washingtonpost.com/news/post-politics/wp/2015/08/07/trump-says-foxs-megyn-kelly-had-blood-coming-out-of-her-wherever

1150 Stahler, K. (2015, August 13). The Charles is transgender "Pretty Little Liars" theory is actually really problematic. Retrieved December 21, 2017, from www.bustle.com/articles/72065-the-charles-is-transgender-pretty-little-liars-theory-is-actually-really-problematic

1151 Lankston, C. (2015, August 24). "This is an abomination": Official Twitter account for hit ABC show Pretty Little Liars slammed by viewers after referring to transgender character as "he, she, it." Retrieved December 21, 2017, from www.dailymail.co.uk/femail/article-3209623/This-abomination-Official-Twitter-account-hit-ABC-Pretty-Little-Liars-slammed-viewers-referring-transgender-character-it.html

1152 Tannehill, B. (2015). Op-ed: You can't handle the truth about trans people. Advocate.com. Retrieved July 6, 2018, from www.advocate.com/commentary/2015/05/08/op-ed-you-cant-handle-truth-about-trans-people

1153 Silverman, S. (2014). Sarah Silverman closes the gap. Retrieved July 6, 2018, from www.youtube.com/watch?v=Jz3khtAdwXo

1154 Sarah Silverman and the misplaced outrage machine. (2014). Bilerico Report/LGBTQ Nation. Retrieved July 6, 2018, from http://bilerico.lgbtqnation.com/2014/10/sarah_silverman_and_the_misplaced_outrage_machine.php

1155 Coleman, E., Bockting, W., Botzer, M., Cohen-Kettenis, P., *et al.* (2011). Standards of care for the health of transsexual, transgender, and gender nonconforming people, 7th version. *International Journal of Transgenderism*, 13, 165–232

1156 Molloy, P. (2014). Why Sarah Silverman's wage equality campaign made me feel awful. HelloGiggles. Retrieved July 6, 2018, from https://hellogiggles.com/lifestyle/sarah-silverman-wage-equality

1157 Kellaway, M. (2014). 8 myths about transgender men's genital reconstructions. HuffPost. Retrieved July 6, 2018, from www.huffingtonpost.com/mitch-kellaway/8-myths-about-transgender-mens-genital-reconstructions_b_4510196.html

1158 Lambda Legal. (2017, July 12). Professional organization statements supporting transgender people in health care. Lambda Legal. Retrieved July 6, 2018, from www.lambdalegal.org/sites/default/files/publications/downloads/ll_trans_professional_statements_17.pdf

1159 Lambda Legal. (2017, July 12). Professional organization statements supporting transgender people in health care. Lambda Legal. Retrieved July 6, 2018, from www.lambdalegal.org/sites/default/files/publications/downloads/ll_trans_professional_statements_17.pdf

1160 Tannehill, B. (2013). Myths about gender confirmation surgery. HuffPost. Retrieved July 6, 2018, from www.huffingtonpost.com/brynn-tannehill/myths-gender-confirmation-surgery_b_4384701.html

1161 Barness, S. (2014). 84-year-old Ray Jessel surprises judges with a naughty original song. HuffPost UK. Retrieved July 6, 2018, from www.huffingtonpost.com/2014/07/02/ray-jessel-americas-got-talent_n_5552221.html

1162 Tannehill, B. (2014). Loving a transgender person is a revolutionary act. HuffPost. Retrieved July 6, 2018, from www.huffingtonpost.com/brynn-tannehill/loving-a-transgender-pers_b_4718307.html

1163 Grant, J. M., Mottet, L. A., Tanis, J., Harrison, J., Herman, J. L., & Keisling, M. (2011). *Injustice at Every Turn: A Report of the National Transgender Discrimination Survey*. Washington, DC: National Center for Transgender Equality and National Gay and Lesbian Task Force. Retrieved July 6, 2018, from www.thetaskforce.org/static_html/downloads/reports/reports/ntds_full.pdf

1164 Molloy, P. (2014). Laverne Cox and "transgender tipping point" cover, Time. Advocate.com. Retrieved July 6, 2018, from www.advocate.com/politics/transgender/2014/05/29/laverne-cox-and-transgender-tipping-point-cover-time

1165 Tannehill, B. (2015). The pitfalls of transgender celebrity. Bilerico Report/LGBTQ Nation. Retrieved July 6, 2018, from http://bilerico.lgbtqnation.com/2015/03/the_pitfalls_of_transgender_celebrity.php

1166 Ennis, D. (2015). Bruce Jenner: "I'm a woman." Advocate.com. Retrieved July 6, 2018, from www.advocate.com/politics/media/2015/04/24/bruce-jenner-tells-all-tonight

1167 Ennis, D. (2015). WATCH: Bruce Jenner and Kim Kardashian bond over nail polish. Advocate.com. Retrieved July 6, 2018, from www.advocate.com/politics/media/2015/05/05/watch-bruce-jenner-and-kim-kardashian-bond-over-nail-polish

1168 Boyd, H. (2009). Trans documentary drinking game. en|gender. Retrieved July 6, 2018, from www.myhusbandbetty.com/2009/07/20/trans-documentary-drinking-game

1169 Robinson, A. (2015). Why I didn't watch the Jenner interview. Medium. Retrieved July 6, 2018, from https://medium.com/@allysonrobinson/why-i-didn-t-watch-the-jenner-interview-c8cb5eb2243a

1170 In film and television production, B-roll, B roll, B-reel, or B reel is supplemental or alternative footage intercut with the main shot

1171 Kellaway, M. (2014). WATCH: Trans advocate Brynn Tannehill's powerful advice on anger, allies. Advocate.com. Retrieved July 6, 2018, from www.advocate.com/politics/transgender/2014/09/17/watch-trans-advocate-brynn-tannehills-powerful-advice-anger-allies

1172 Kellaway, M. (2015). PHOTOS: Hundreds mourn Leelah Alcorn in vigils worldwide. Advocate.com. Retrieved July 6, 2018, from www.advocate.com/youth/2015/01/05/photos-hundreds-mourn-leelah-alcorn-vigils-worldwide

1173 Kellaway, M. (2014). Trans teen girl's public suicide note stirs outcry, reflection on youth safety. Advocate.com. Retrieved July 6, 2018, from www.advocate.com/youth/2014/12/31/trans-teen-girls-public-suicide-note-stirs-outcry-reflection-youth-safety

1174 Ring, T. (2015). STUDY: Mixed-orientation Mormon marriages likely to fail. Advocate.com. Retrieved July 6, 2018, from www.advocate.com/politics/religion/2015/01/13/study-mixed-orientation-mormon-marriages-likely-fail

1175 Tannehill, B. (2015). These 10 "acceptable" trans narratives are actually holding us back. Everyday Feminism. Retrieved July 6, 2018, from https://everydayfeminism.com/2015/04/acceptable-trans-narratives

1176 Brydum, S. (2015). What happened inside the Supreme Court today. Advocate.com. Retrieved July 6, 2018, from www.advocate.com/politics/marriage-equality/2015/04/28/what-happened-inside-supreme-court-today

1177 Rodriguez-Jimenez, J. (2014). Laverne Cox joins leading trans women activists on fashion magazine cover. Advocate.com. Retrieved July 6, 2018, from www.advocate.com/politics/transgender/2014/12/18/laverne-cox-joins-leading-trans-women-activists-fashion-magazine-cov

1178 Breen, M. (2014). Laverne Cox: The making of an icon. Advocate.com. Retrieved July 6, 2018, from www.advocate.com/print-issue/current-issue/2014/07/10/laverne-cox-making-icon

1179 Pacific Justice Institute. (2017). Advocate.com. Retrieved July 6, 2018, from www.advocate.com/pacific-justice-institute

1180 Kohner, C. (2015). Trans man behind #WeJustNeedtoPee isn't selfie-centered. Advocate.com. Retrieved July 6, 2018, from www.advocate.com/politics/transgender/2015/03/17/trans-man-behind-wejustneedtopee-isnt-selfie-centered

1181 Ennis, D. (2015). WATCH: Activist talks #WeJustNeedtoPee campaign with Thomas Roberts. Advocate.com. Retrieved July 6, 2018, from www.advocate.com/politics/media/2015/03/18/watch-activist-talks-wejustneedtopee-campaign-thomas-roberts

1182 Kellaway, M. (2015). Trans folks respond to "bathroom bills" with #WeJustNeedtoPee selfies. Advocate.com. Retrieved July 6, 2018, from www.advocate.com/politics/transgender/2015/03/14/trans-folks-respond-bathroom-bills-wejustneedtopee-selfies

1183 Haywood, M. (2013). GLAAD speaks to transgender author Jennifer Finney Boylan on her new memoir, "Stuck in the Middle with You." GLAAD. Retrieved July 6, 2018, from www.glaad.org/blog/glaad-speaks-transgender-author-jennifer-finney-boylan-her-new-memoir-stuck-middle-you

1184 Seattle.cbslocal.com. (2015). Oregon bar to pay $400K for banning transgender customers. Retrieved July 6, 2018, from http://seattle.cbslocal.com/2015/09/23/oregon-bar-to-pay-400k-for-banning-transgender-customers

1185 Ennis, D. (2015). Transgender student at center of Illinois school locker room debate speaks out. Advocate.com. Retrieved July 6, 2018, from www.advocate.com/transgender/2015/12/10/transgender-student-center-illinois-school-locker-room-debate-speaks-out

1186 Molloy, P. (2014). Trans woman sues Crossfit after being told to compete in men's division. Advocate.com. Retrieved July 6, 2018, from www.advocate.com/politics/transgender/2014/03/10/trans-woman-sues-crossfit-after-being-told-compete-mens-division

1187 Norwood, C. (2016). Some colleges exclude LGBTQ students using religion, but students are fighting back. Vox. Retrieved July 6, 2018, from www.vox.com/identities/2016/2/11/10962160/title-ix-waivers

1188 Chibbaro Jr., L. (2015). Sting reveals anti-trans job bias. Washington Blade: Gay News, Politics, LGBT Rights. Retrieved July 6, 2018, from www.washingtonblade.com/2015/11/04/sting-reveals-anti-trans-job-bias

1189 Rodriguez-Jimenez, J. (2014). Local Virginia school board rejects bathroom rights for trans students. Advocate.com. Retrieved July 6, 2018, from www.advocate.com/virginia/2014/12/10/local-virginia-school-board-rejects-bathroom-rights-trans-students

1190 Michelson, N. (2015). More Americans claim to have seen a ghost than have met a trans person. HuffPost UK. Retrieved July 6, 2018, from www.huffingtonpost.com/entry/more-americans-claim-to-have-seen-a-ghost-than-have-met-a-trans-person_us_5677fee5e4b014efe0d5ed62

1191 Boyd, H. (2009). Trans documentary drinking game. en|gender. Retrieved July 6, 2018, from www.myhusbandbetty.com/2009/07/20/trans-documentary-drinking-game

1192 Tannehill, B. (2014). To those who laughed. HuffPost. Retrieved July 6, 2018, from www.huffingtonpost.com/brynn-tannehill/to-those-who-laughed_b_5555954.html

1193 Her Story. (2017). Her Story. Retrieved July 6, 2018, from www.herstoryshow.com

1194 Kovvali, S. (2015). One family's journey to accept their transgender child. Refinery29.com. Retrieved July 6, 2018, from www.refinery29.com/2015/10/96129/when-your-transgender-children-becoming-nicole

1195 The Kansas City Star. (2014). Speech from Debi Jackson, mother of a KC transgender girl, garners global attention. kansascity. Retrieved July 6, 2018, from www.kansascity.com/news/local/article749869.html

1196 Nichols, J. (2014). Poll shows way more education needed to understand lives and rights of trans people. HuffPost UK. Retrieved July 6, 2018, from www.huffingtonpost.com/2014/06/13/transgender-bathroom-rights_n_5492286.html

1197 Maza, C. & Brinker, L. (2014). 15 experts debunk right-wing transgender bathroom myth. Media Matters for America. Retrieved July 6, 2018, from www.mediamatters.org/research/2014/03/20/15-experts-debunk-right-wing-transgender-bathro/198533

1198 Fernandez, M. & Smith, M. (2015). Houston voters reject broad anti-discrimination ordinance. Nytimes.com. Retrieved July 6, 2018, from www.nytimes.com/2015/11/04/us/houston-voters-repeal-anti-bias-measure.html?_r=0

1199 Phillips, A. (2016). How impossible is it for Democrats to win back the House? This impossible. The Washington Post. Retrieved July 6, 2018, from www.washingtonpost.com/news/the-fix/wp/2016/01/28/how-impossible-is-it-for-democrats-to-win-back-the-house-this-impossible/?utm_term=.4e40ba4b2a91

1200 Tannehill, B. (2015). The Trans Movement needs a new, science based strategy. HuffPost. Retrieved July 6, 2018, from www.huffingtonpost.com/brynn-tannehill/the-trans-movement-needs_b_8468062.html

1201 Raymond, J. G. (1994). *The Transsexual Empire: The Making of the She-Male*. New York, NY: Teachers College Press

1202 TERFs prefer the term "gender critical." However, they're the only ones using this term

1203 Williams, C. (2014, March 15). TERF: What it means and where it came from. Retrieved January 13, 2018, from http://transadvocate.com/terf-what-it-means-and-where-it-came-from_n_13066.htm

1204 Baker, R. (2017, April 12). Fake "radical feminist" group a paid political front for anti-LGBT organization. Retrieved December 22, 2017, from www.lgbtqnation.com/2017/04/fake-radical-feminist-group-paid-political-front-anti-lgbt-organization

1205 Turning the "War on Women" to the "War for Women." (2014, July 16). Retrieved December 22, 2017, from www.frc.org/op-eds/turning-the-war-on-women-to-the-war-for-women

1206 Serano, J. (2007). *Whipping Girl: A Transsexual Woman on Sexism and the Scapegoating of Femininity*. Seattle, WA: Seal Press

1207 Gender non-conforming: a person whose behavior or appearance does not conform to prevailing cultural and social expectations about what is appropriate to their gender

1208 Geen, J. (2011, April 6). 5,000-year-old "transgender" skeleton discovered. Retrieved December 22, 2017, from www.pinknews.co.uk/2011/04/06/5000-year-old-transgender-skeleton-discovered

1209 For example, in California 4.6 percent of the population identifies as LGBT, and only 2.6 percent do in South Carolina. Retrieved December 22, 2017, from https://williamsinstitute.law.ucla.edu/visualization/lgbt-stats/?topic=LGBT#density

1210 Gallup International. (2017, January 11). In U.S., more adults identifying as LGBT. Retrieved December 22, 2017, from http://news.gallup.com/poll/201731/lgbt-identification-rises.aspx

1211 Gender fluid refers to a gender expression that changes over time

1212 Associated Press. (2017, April 25). GOP senator regrets saying guy in tutu "kind of asks for it." Retrieved December 22, 2017, from www.nydailynews.com/news/national/gop-senator-regrets-guy-tutu-kind-asks-article-1.3100920

1213 The extraordinary case of the guevedoces. (2015, September 20). Retrieved December 22, 2017, from www.bbc.com/news/magazine-34290981

1214 Trotta, D. (2016, December 23). U.S. parents accept children's transgender identity by age three. Retrieved January 13, 2018, from www.reuters.com/article/us-usa-lgbt-parenting/u-s-parents-accept-childrens-transgender-identity-by-age-three-idUSKBN14B1C8

1215 Todd, B. K., Fischer, R. A., Costa, S. D., Roestorf, A., *et al.* (2017). Sex differences in children's toy preferences: A systematic review, meta-regression, and meta-analysis. *Infant and Child Development*. doi:10.1002/icd.2064

1216 Mohan, M. (2017, March 16). Why transgender Africans turned against a famous feminist. Retrieved December 22, 2017, from www.bbc.com/news/blogs-trending-39271690

1217 Tannehill, B. (2013, August 13). Pondering male privilege post-transition. Retrieved December 22, 2017, from www.huffingtonpost.com/brynn-tannehill/pondering-male-privilege-post-transition_b_3744103.html

1218 Herman, J., Haas, A., & Rodgers, P. (2014). Suicide attempts among transgender and gender non-conforming adults. The Williams Institute, UCLA. Retrieved July 6, 2018, from https://escholarship.org/uc/item/8xg8061f

1219 Ring, T. (2016, June 1). James Dobson: Be a man, shoot a transgender woman in the bathroom. Retrieved December 22, 2017, from www.advocate.com/transgender/2016/6/01/james-dobson-be-man-shoot-transgender-woman-bathroom

1220 O'Neill, T. (2014). Why transphobia is a feminist issue. HuffPost. Retrieved July 6, 2018, from www.huffingtonpost.com/terry-oneill/why-transphobia-is-a-femi_b_5785820.html

1221 Steinem, G. (2013). Op-ed: On working together over time. Advocate.com. Retrieved July 6, 2018, from www.advocate.com/commentary/2013/10/02/op-ed-working-together-over-time

1222 Lavender Menace. (2017). En.wikipedia.org. Retrieved July 6, 2018, from https://en.wikipedia.org/wiki/Lavender_Menace

1223 United States Supreme Court. (1989). *Price Waterhouse v. Hopkins*. Retrieved July 6, 2018, from https://scholar.google.com/scholar_case?case=7807524183771349398&q=Price+Waterhouse+v.+Hopkins&hl=en&as_sdt=2,47&as_vis=1

1224 McHugh, P. (2016, May 13). Transgender surgery isn't the solution. Retrieved December 22, 2017, from www.wsj.com/articles/paul-mchugh-transgender-surgery-isnt-the-solution-1402615120

1225 Williamson, K. (2014). Laverne Cox is not a woman. National Review. Retrieved July 6, 2018, from www.nationalreview.com/article/379188/laverne-cox-not-woman-kevin-d-williamson

1226 Goode, E. (2002). Psychiatrist says he was surprised by furor over his role on abuse panel. Nytimes.com. Retrieved July 6, 2018, from www.nytimes.com/2002/08/05/us/psychiatrist-says-he-was-surprised-by-furor-over-his-role-on-abuse-panel.html?pagewanted=all

1227 Paul McHugh. (2017). GLAAD. Retrieved July 6, 2018, from www.glaad.org/cap/paul-mchugh

1228 Dr. McHugh has misrepresented data, rigged studies, left out significant details in his research, and is nothing more than a poorly regarded fringe element in his own field. You can read about it in greater detail here: Brighe, M. (2014). Clinging to a dangerous past: Dr Paul McHugh's selective reading of transgender medical literature. The TransAdvocate. Retrieved July 6, 2018, from http://transadvocate.com/clinging-to-a-dangerous-past-dr-paul-mchughs-selective-reading-of-transgender-medical-literature_n_13842.htm; McHugh, D. (2009). Debunking Dr. Paul McHugh. Crystalgaze2.blogspot.com. Retrieved July 6, 2018, from https://crystalgaze2.blogspot.com/2009/02/debunking-dr-paul-mchugh.html; Magdalena, A. (2014). A critique of Paul McHugh's "surgical sex." Catholic Trans*. Retrieved July 6, 2018, from https://catholictrans.wordpress.com/2014/02/09/a-critique-of-paul-mchughs-surgical-sex; Frank, N. (2014). The Wall Street Journal's ignorance on LGBTQ issues is alarming. Slate Magazine. Retrieved July 6, 2018, from www.slate.com/blogs/outward/2014/06/16/the_wall_street_journal_displays_shocking_ignorance_about_lgbtq_issues.html; Barstow, D. (2009). An abortion battle, fought to the death. Nytimes.com. Retrieved July 6, 2018, from www.nytimes.com/2009/07/26/us/26tiller.html?pagewanted=all; Brinker, L. (2014). The Wall Street Journal Op-Ed: Being transgender is just a "confusion." Media Matters for America. Retrieved July 6, 2018, from www.mediamatters.org/blog/2014/06/13/wall-street-journal-op-ed-being-transgender-is/199720

1229 Barstow, D. (2009). An abortion battle, fought to the death. Nytimes.com. Retrieved July 6, 2018, from www.nytimes.com/2009/07/26/us/26tiller.html?pagewanted=all

1230 Isquith, E. (2014). Quiz: Can you tell the difference between National Review's Kevin Williamson and a 4chan troll? Salon.com. Retrieved July 6, 2018, from www.salon.com/2014/09/29/quiz_can_you_tell_the_difference_between_national_reviews_kevin_williamson_and_a_4chan_troll

1231 Patriarchy is a social system in which males hold primary power and predominate in roles of political leadership, moral authority, social privilege, and control of property. In the domain of the family, fathers or father-figures hold authority over women and children. Kyriarchy is a social system or set of connecting social systems built around domination, oppression, and submission

1232 Men and Women of The Truman Project. (2014). An open letter to Fox News about "boobs on the ground." Talking Points Memo. Retrieved July 6, 2018, from http://talkingpointsmemo.com/cafe/an-open-letter-to-fox-news

1233 Utt, J. (2014). Slut shaming|change from within. Changefromwithin.org. Retrieved July 6, 2018, from https://changefromwithin.org/tag/slut-shaming

1234 Autogynephilia. (2017). Rationalwiki.org. Retrieved July 6, 2018, from https://rationalwiki.org/wiki/Autogynephilia

1235 Tannehill, B. (2014). Transgender: The perfect social conservative storm. Bilerico Report/LGBTQ Nation. Retrieved July 6, 2018, from http://bilerico.lgbtqnation.com/2014/06/transgender_the_perfect_social_conservative_storm.php

1236 Tannehill, B. (2014). Discarding the world's labels and embracing the gray. HuffPost. Retrieved July 6, 2018, from www.huffingtonpost.com/brynn-tannehill/post_7571_b_5310517.html

1237 Polcyn, B. & Davis, S. (2016, June 8). Transgender issues are driving a wedge in LGBT community, says activist ousted from Pride Parade. Retrieved December 28, 2017, from http://fox6now.com/2016/06/08/transgender-issues-are-driving-a-rift-in-lgbt-community-says-activist-ousted-from-milwaukee-pride-parade

1238 Bongiovanni, A. (2015). 4 ways to support queer femmes—instead of erasing us from queer communities. Everyday Feminism. Retrieved July 6, 2018, from https://everydayfeminism.com/2015/06/end-queer-femmephobia

1239 Oppression—SJWiki. (2017). Sjwiki.org. Retrieved July 6, 2018, from http://sjwiki.org/wiki/Oppression

1240 Gender presentation—SJWiki. (2017). Sjwiki.org. Retrieved July 6, 2018, from http://sjwiki.org/wiki/Gender_presentation

1241 Gender binary—SJWiki. (2017). Sjwiki.org. Retrieved July 6, 2018, from http://sjwiki.org/wiki/Gender_binary

1242 Theriault, A. (2015). We need to stop devaluing femininity. Ravishly. Retrieved July 6, 2018, from https://ravishly.com/2015/03/20/why-we-need-stop-devaluing-femininity

1243 Cooper, D. (2012). "No fats or fems." HuffPost. Retrieved July 6, 2018, from www.huffingtonpost.com/dale-cooper/grindr-discrimination_b_1948766.html

1244 Tlatenchi, F. (2012). Femmephobia is alive and well in LGBT community. The Sundial. Retrieved July 6, 2018, from https://sundial.csun.edu/2012/05/femmephobia-is-alive-and-well-in-lgbt-community

1245 Brand, N. (2017). Femmephobia—The Good Men Project. Retrieved July 6, 2018, from https://goodmenproject.com/featured-content/femmephobia

1246 femme: The "acceptable" lesbian? (2011). femme on a mission. Retrieved July 6, 2018, from https://femmeonamission.com/2011/04/21/femme-the-acceptable-lesbian

1247 Ewing, R. & Anti-Palindrome, A. (2016, February 10). 11 common assumptions about being a queer femme—debunked. Everyday Feminism. Retrieved January 13, 2018, from https://everydayfeminism.com/2016/02/queer-femme-assumptions

1248 The monosexual privilege checklist. (2011). Bi radical. Retrieved July 6, 2018, from https://radicalbi.wordpress.com/2011/07/28/the-monosexual-privilege-checklist

1249 Rampell, C. (2008). Before that sex change, think about your next paycheck. Economix Blog. Retrieved July 6, 2018, from https://economix.blogs.nytimes.com/2008/09/25/before-that-sex-change-think-about-your-next-paycheck/?_r=0

1250 Ben Barres. (2017). En.wikipedia.org. Retrieved July 6, 2018, from https://en.wikipedia.org/wiki/Ben_Barres

1251 Herman, J., Haas, A., & Rodgers, P. (2014). Suicide attempts among transgender and gender non-conforming adults. The Williams Institute, UCLA. Retrieved July 6, 2018, from https://escholarship.org/uc/item/8xg8061f

1252 Juzwiak, R. (2015). 22 trans/gender non-conforming people were found murdered in 2015: Were there more murders or better reporting? Gawker. Retrieved July 6, 2018, from http://gawker.com/22-trans-gender-non-conforming-people-were-found-murder-1749497964

1253 Judith Butler. (2017). En.wikipedia.org. Retrieved July 6, 2018, from https://en.wikipedia.org/wiki/Judith_Butler

1254 Tourjée, D. (2015, December 16). Why do men kill trans women? Gender theorist Judith Butler explains. Retrieved December 22, 2017, from https://broadly.vice.com/en_us/article/z4jd7y/why-do-men-kill-trans-women-gender-theorist-judith-butler-explains

1255 Roberts, M. (2010, November 13). Jim Fouratt's May 27, 2000 transphobic NY Times letter. Retrieved December 22, 2017, from http://transgriot.blogspot.com/2010/11/jim-fouratts-may-27-2000-transphobic-ny.html

1256 Abernathy, M. (2010). ENDA and Barney Frank's trans penis panic. The TransAdvocate. Retrieved July 6, 2018, from http://transadvocate.com/enda-and-barney-franks-trans-penis-panic_n_2441.htm

1257 Heywood, T. (2008). HRC leader stands by non-inclusive ENDA decision. Pridesource. Retrieved July 6, 2018, from www.pridesource.com/article.html?article=29930

1258 Rivas, J. (2015). After damning diversity report, Human Rights Campaign says it's proud of staff. Splinternews.com. Retrieved July 6, 2018, from https://splinternews.com/after-damning-diversity-report-human-rights-campaign-s-1793848156

1259 Costello, C. (2014). Who belongs in women's spaces, again? Women's College Edition. Trans-fusion.blogspot.com. Retrieved July 6, 2018, from http://trans-fusion.blogspot.com/2014/10/who-belongs-in-womens-spaces-again.html

1260 Anderson-Minshall, D. (2015). Op-ed: Michfest's founder chose to shut down rather than change with the times. Advocate.com. Retrieved July 6, 2018, from www.advocate.com/commentary/2015/04/24/op-ed-michfests-founder-chose-shut-down-rather-change-times

1261 Burkett, E. (2015, June 6). What makes a woman? The New York Times. Retrieved December 22, 2017, from www.nytimes.com/2015/06/07/opinion/sunday/what-makes-a-woman.html

1262 Aronson, J. & Jordan, A. (2006). Beautiful Daughters: A documentary about the first-ever all-transgender staging of Eve Ensler's "Vagina Monologues." Ai.eecs.umich.edu. Retrieved July 6, 2018, from http://ai.eecs.umich.edu/people/conway/TS/Beautiful%20Daughters/Beautiful%20Daughters.html

1263 Ensler, E. (2015). Eve: "I never defined a woman as a person with a vagina." Time. Retrieved July 6, 2018, from http://time.com/3672912/eve-ensler-vagina-monologues-mount-holyoke-college

1264 Tannehill, B. (2013). Pondering male privilege post-transition. Retrieved December 22, 2017, from www.huffingtonpost.com/brynn-tannehill/pondering-male-privilege-post-transition_b_3744103.html. Public Relations. (2015). Review article provides evidence on the biological nature of gender identity. Bu.edu. Retrieved July 6, 2018, from www.bu.edu/news/2015/02/13/review-article-provides-evidence-on-the-biological-nature-of-gender-identity

1265 Gold-star lesbian or gold-star gay refers to someone who is sexually active but has never slept with a member of the opposite sex

1266 Phyllis Schlafly was the ultra-conservative of the Eagle Forum political action committee. She was a staunch anti-feminist, religious conservative, opposed abortion and birth control under all circumstances, opposed LGBT rights, and led the campaign against the Equal Rights Amendment. She believed that women enjoyed enough social privilege that they were better off not legally being treated equally with men

1267 Kate Millett's "Feminism": A vehicle for totalitarianism. (2014). Stella Morabito. Retrieved July 6, 2018, from http://stellamorabito.net/2014/09/05/kate-milletts-feminism-a-vehicle-for-totalitarianism

1268 Morabito, S. (2012). Feminist enablers of the war against women. Washington Examiner. Retrieved July 6, 2018, from www.washingtonexaminer.com/feminist-enablers-of-the-war-against-women/article/361536

1269 Morabito, S. (2014). How the trans-agenda seeks to redefine everyone. The Federalist. Retrieved July 6, 2018, from http://thefederalist.com/2014/06/23/how-the-trans-agenda-seeks-to-redefine-everyone

1270 James, S. E., Herman, J. L., Rankin, S., Keisling, M., Mottet, L., & Anafi, M. (2016). *The Report of the 2015 U.S. Transgender Survey*. Washington, DC: National Center for Transgender Equality

1271 James, S. E., Herman, J. L., Rankin, S., Keisling, M., Mottet, L., & Anafi, M. (2016). *The Report of the 2015 U.S. Transgender Survey*. Washington, DC: National Center for Transgender Equality

1272 Napikoski, L. (2017). Lavender Menace: The phrase, the group, the controversy. ThoughtCo. Retrieved July 6, 2018, from www.thoughtco.com/lavender-menace-feminism-definition-3528970

1273 Audrey. (2015). New report finally gives crucial numbers on economic disparities hurting LGBT women. Autostraddle. Retrieved July 6, 2018, from www.autostraddle.com/new-report-finally-gives-crucial-numbers-on-economic-disparities-hurting-lgbt-women-281302

1274 MIT OpenCourseWare. (2014). Readings in Old and Middle English. Retrieved July 6, 2018, from www.youtube.com/watch?v=5NB2Z6pZBNA

1275 Tannehill, B. (2014). Discarding the world's labels and embracing the gray. HuffPost. Retrieved July 6, 2018, from www.huffingtonpost.com/brynn-tannehill/post_7571_b_5310517.html

1276 Murder of Gwen Araujo. (2017). En.wikipedia.org. Retrieved July 6, 2018, from https://en.wikipedia.org/wiki/Murder_of_Gwen_Araujo

1277 Brandon Teena. (2017). En.wikipedia.org. Retrieved July 6, 2018, from https://en.wikipedia.org/wiki/Brandon_Teena

1278 Frosch, D. (2008, August 02). Death of a Transgender Woman Is Called a Hate Crime. Retrieved August 2, 2018, from https://www.nytimes.com/2008/08/02/us/02murder.html

1279 Death of Jennifer Laude. (2017). En.wikipedia.org. Retrieved July 6, 2018, from https://en.wikipedia.org/wiki/Death_of_Jennifer_Laude

1280 McCarty, J. (2013). Jury convicts Andrey Bridges of stabbing to death Cemia "Ce Ce" Dove. cleveland.com. Retrieved July 6, 2018, from www.cleveland.com/metro/index.ssf/2013/11/jury_convicts_andrey_bridges_o.html

1281 McNamara, M. (2013). Review: "Valentine Road" offers clear-eyed view of Larry King murder. latimes. Retrieved July 6, 2018, from http://articles.latimes.com/2013/oct/06/entertainment/la-et-st-valentine-road-20131007

1282 Dobson, J. (2016, May 30). Protect your kids from tyrant Obama. Retrieved January 12, 2018, from www.wnd.com/2016/05/protect-your-kids-from-tyrant-obama

1283 Chapman, M. W. (2016, June 10). Dobson on "bathroom" bills: "Where is manhood that we don't stand up and defend our families?" Retrieved January 12, 2018, from www.cnsnews.com/blog/michael-w-chapman/dobson-bathroom-bills-where-manhood-we-dont-stand-and-defend-our-families

1284 Women CEOs of the S&P 500. (2017). Catalyst. Retrieved July 6, 2018, from www.catalyst.org/knowledge/women-ceos-sp-500

1285 Maloney, C. B. (December 2010). *Invest in Women, Invest in America: A Comprehensive Review of Women in the U.S. Economy*. A Report by the Majority Staff of the Joint Economic Committee Representative. Senate Joint Economic Council. Retrieved September 13, 2018, from https://www.in.gov/icw/files/invest_women.pdf

1286 Rosenthal, L. & Miller, K. (2013). 5 myths about military sexual assault. Center for American Progress. Americanprogress.org. Retrieved July 6, 2018, from www.americanprogress.org/issues/security/news/2013/06/06/65602/5-myths-about-military-sexual-assault

1287 Do trans men have it easier overall than trans women? Quora. Retrieved January 12, 2018, from www.quora.com/Do-trans-men-have-it-easier-overall-than-trans-women

1288 National Coalition of Anti-Violence Programs (NCAVP). (2016). *Lesbian, Gay, Bisexual, Transgender, Queer, and HIV-Affected Hate Violence in 2016*. Retrieved July 6, 2018, from http://avp.org/wp-content/uploads/2017/06/NCAVP_2016HateViolence_REPORT.pdf

1289 Tannehill, B. (2013). Why ENDA matters to the trans community. HuffPost. Retrieved July 6, 2018, from www.huffingtonpost.com/brynn-tannehill/why-enda-matters-to-the-trans-community_b_3223419.html

1290 Seriously, if you enjoy feminist humor and comics, go visit www.gynostar.com

1291 Allis, G. (2013). What does a woman's body possess that makes it a woman's body? Decolonizing Yoga. Retrieved July 6, 2018, from www.decolonizingyoga.com/what-does-a-womans-body-possess-that-makes-it-a-womans-body

1292 Ennis, D. (2015). With marriage off the table, is trans community the new target? Advocate.com. Retrieved July 6, 2018, from www.advocate.com/politics/marriage-equality/2015/05/01/marriage-table-trans-community-new-target

1293 Browning, B. (2016). South Carolina sheriff says he would "whip" trans woman in restroom. LGBTQ Nation. Retrieved July 6, 2018, from www.lgbtqnation.com/2016/04/south-carolina-sheriff-says-he-would-whip-trans-woman-in-restroom

1294 Brydum, S. (2016). Right-wingers pledge to carry guns to bathroom to fend off trans folks. Advocate.com. Retrieved July 6, 2018, from www.advocate.com/transgender/2016/4/25/right-wingers-pledge-carry-guns-bathroom-fend-trans-folks

1295 Ennis, D. (2016). ESPN fires Curt Schilling for transphobic post [Video]. Advocate.com. Retrieved July 6, 2018, from www.advocate.com/transgender/2016/4/20/espn-fires-curt-schilling-transphobic-post-video

1296 Ford, Z. (2016). Ted Cruz doesn't want any transgender people in any bathroom anywhere. Thinkprogress.org. Retrieved July 6, 2018, from https://thinkprogress.org/ted-cruz-doesnt-want-any-transgender-people-in-any-bathroom-anywhere-b6f1a0e3e72e

1297 Pat McCrory's file. (2017). @politifact. Retrieved July 6, 2018, from www.politifact.com/personalities/pat-mccrory

1298 Board, The. (2016). Opinion: Transgender bathroom hysteria, cont'd. Nytimes.com. Retrieved July 6, 2018, from www.nytimes.com/2016/04/18/opinion/transgender-bathroom-hysteria-contd.html?_r=0

1299 Burns, M. (2016). Berger says HB2 won't be repealed. WRAL.com. Retrieved July 6, 2018, from www.wral.com/berger-says-hb2-won-t-be-repealed/15653522

1300 Campbell, C. (2016). House Bill 2 repeal legislation sent to Senate committee that never meets. newsobserver. Retrieved July 6, 2018, from www.newsobserver.com/news/politics-government/politics-columns-blogs/under-the-dome/article74440742.html

1301 Lang, N. (2016). Could Texas become the next trans bathroom battleground? Advocate.com. Retrieved July 6, 2018, from www.advocate.com/transgender/2016/5/02/could-texas-become-next-trans-bathroom-battleground

1302 Wiernicki, A. (2016). Controversial "bathroom bill" could be coming to Texas. KXAN.com. Retrieved July 6, 2018, from http://kxan.com/2016/04/28/controversial-bathroom-bill-could-be-coming-to-texas

1303 Brydum, S. (2016). Alabama City's new anti-trans law is nation's most terrifying. Advocate.com. Retrieved July 6, 2018, from www.advocate.com/transgender/2016/4/27/alabama-citys-new-anti-trans-law-nations-most-terrifying

1304 Lang, N. (2016). Could Texas become the next trans bathroom battleground? Advocate.com. Retrieved July 6, 2018, from www.advocate.com/transgender/2016/5/02/could-texas-become-next-trans-bathroom-battleground

1305 Levi, J., Dulka, M., & Dieter, C. (2016). Why Gavin Grimm's case will reverberate for all trans students. Advocate.com. Retrieved July 6, 2018, from www.advocate.com/commentary/2016/5/03/why-gavin-grimms-case-will-reverberate-all-trans-students

1306 Daley, E. (2016). Transgender men, lesbian professor join lawsuit over North Carolina law. Advocate.com. Retrieved July 6, 2018, from www.advocate.com/politics/2016/3/28/transgender-men-lesbian-professor-join-lawsuit-over-north-carolina-law

1307 Badash, D. (2018, January 8). Supreme Court refuses to hear case against Mississippi's anti-gay religious "License to Discriminate" law. Retrieved January 8, 2018, from www.thenewcivilrightsmovement.com/davidbadash/supreme_court_refuses_to_hear_case_against_mississippi_s_anti_gay_license_to_discriminate_law

1308 HRC. (2015). HRC releases first corporate equality index to rate global LGBT workplace inclusion. Human Rights Campaign. Retrieved July 6, 2018, from www.hrc.org/blog/hrc-launches-first-global-lgbt-workplace-equality-rating-with-unprecedented

1309 Human Rights Campaign. (2017). *Corporate Equality Index 2018: Rating American Workplaces on Gay, Lesbian, Bisexual, and Transgender Equality*. Washington, DC: Author. Retrieved July 6, 2018, from https://assets2.hrc.org/files/assets/resources/CEI-2018-FullReport.pdf?_ga=2.114385991.1103353226.1513791816-2124830380.1513791816

1310 Heller, L. (2016). Target's perception takes a hit after transgender bathroom statement. Forbes.com. Retrieved July 6, 2018, from www.forbes.com/sites/lauraheller/2016/04/30/targets-perception-takes-a-hit-after-transgender-bathroom-statement/#e00d564bf13e

1311 Tannehill, B. (2016). Why visibility is not enough for trans equality. Advocate.com. Retrieved July 6, 2018, from www.advocate.com/commentary/2016/3/31/why-visibility-not-enough-trans-equality

1312 GLAAD. (2015). The number of Americans who report knowing a transgender person doubles in seven years, according to new GLAAD survey. Retrieved July 6, 2018, from www.glaad.org/releases/number-americans-who-report-knowing-transgender-person-doubles-seven-years-according-new

1313 Tannehill, B. (2017). And then they came for transgender people. HuffPost. Retrieved July 6, 2018, from www.huffingtonpost.com/brynn-tannehill/and-then-they-came-for-tr_b_9258678.html

1314 Ennis, D. (2015). Victory at Supreme Court on marriage equality. Advocate.com. Retrieved July 6, 2018, from www.advocate.com/politics/marriage-equality/2015/06/25/victory-supreme-court-marriage-equality

1315 Psychological operations (PSYOP) are planned operations to convey selected information and indicators to audiences to influence their emotions, motives, and objective reasoning, and ultimately the behavior of governments, organizations, groups, and individuals

1316 Anita Bryant. (2017). En.wikipedia.org. Retrieved July 6, 2018, from https://en.wikipedia.org/wiki/Anita_Bryant

1317 Save Our Children. (2017). En.wikipedia.org. Retrieved July 6, 2018, from https://en.wikipedia.org/wiki/Save_Our_Children

1318 Reilly, R. (2010). Groups opposed to DADT repeal "latching" on to shower issue. Talking Points Memo. Retrieved July 6, 2018, from http://talkingpointsmemo.com/muckraker/groups-opposed-to-dadt-repeal-latching-on-to-shower-issue

1319 On Violence. (2012). The military's gay shower fiasco...and 5 other anti-DADT predictions that never came true. Onviolence.com. Retrieved July 6, 2018, from http://onviolence.com/?e=629

1320 Doran, W. (2016). Equality NC director: No public safety risks in cities with transgender anti-discrimination rules. @politifact. Retrieved July 6, 2018, from www.politifact.com/north-carolina/statements/2016/apr/01/chris-sgro/equality-nc-director-no-public-safety-risks-cities

1321 Human Rights Campaign. (2016). 250+ sexual assault, domestic violence orgs condemn anti-trans leg. Retrieved July 6, 2018, from www.hrc.org/blog/more-than-250-sexual-assault-domestic-violence-organizations-condemn-anti-t

1322 Maza, C. & Brinker, L. (2014). 15 experts debunk right-wing transgender bathroom myth. Media Matters for America. Retrieved July 6, 2018, from www.mediamatters.org/research/2014/03/20/15-experts-debunk-right-wing-transgender-bathro/198533

1323 Wong, C. (2015). 50 percent of millennials believe gender is a spectrum, Fusion's massive millennial poll finds. HuffPost UK. Retrieved July 6, 2018, from www.huffingtonpost.com/2015/02/05/fusion-millennial-poll-gender_n_6624200.html

1324 Matthews, D. (2015). My husband, the woman: The private anguish of having a spouse in transition. Retrieved July 6, 2018, from www.salon.com/2015/03/09/my_husband_the_woman_the_private_anguish_of_having_a_spouse_in_transition

1325 Napikoski, L. (2017). Lavender Menace: The phrase, the group, the controversy. ThoughtCo. Retrieved July 6, 2018, from www.thoughtco.com/lavender-menace-feminism-definition-3528970

1326 New report finally gives crucial numbers on economic disparities hurting LGBT women. (2015). Autostraddle. Retrieved July 6, 2018, from www.autostraddle.com/new-report-finally-gives-crucial-numbers-on-economic-disparities-hurting-lgbt-women-281302

1327 Hurst, E. (2013). In sexual orientation change efforts, the converse is also true. Truth Wins Out. Truthwinsout.org. Retrieved July 6, 2018, from https://truthwinsout.org/opinion/2013/09/37193

1328 Nelson, S. (2013). Polyamory advocate: Gay marriage "blazing the marriage equality trail." US News. Retrieved July 6, 2018, from www.usnews.com/news/articles/2013/06/24/polyamorous-advocate-gay-marriage-blazing-the-marriage-equality-trail

1329 Kacere, L. (2013). More than two: Examining the myths and facts of polyamory. Everyday Feminism. Retrieved July 6, 2018, from https://everydayfeminism.com/2013/10/myths-and-facts-of-polyamory

1330 Anderson, E. (2013). Five myths about cheating. The Washington Post. Retrieved July 6, 2018, from www.washingtonpost.com/opinions/five-myths-about-cheating/2012/02/08/gIQANGdaBR_story.html?utm_term=.7a0f72cb6055

1331 Weed, J. & Weed, L. (2018, January 28). Turning a unicorn into a bat: The post in which we announce the end of our marriage. Retrieved March 23, 2018, from http://joshweed.com/2018/01/turning-unicorn-bat-post-announce-end-marriage

1332 For example, https://sillyolme.wordpress.com

1333 Kane, C. (2013). Seeing other women as allies, rather than enemies: A how-to. Everyday Feminism. Retrieved July 6, 2018, from https://everydayfeminism.com/2013/12/seeing-other-women-as-allies

1334 Roberts, M. (2010). Why the trans community hates Dr. Janice G. Raymond. Transgriot.blogspot.com. Retrieved July 6, 2018, from http://transgriot.blogspot.com/2010/09/why-trans-community-hates-dr-janice-g.html

1335 Tannehill, B. (2014). New Yorker shamefully cites anti-LGBT "researcher." Bilerico Report/LGBTQ Nation. Retrieved July 6, 2018, from http://bilerico.lgbtqnation.com/2014/07/new_yorker_shamefully_cites_anti-lgbt_researcher.php

1336 Tannehill, B. (2015). What you need to know about anti-trans bathroom bills. HuffPost. Retrieved July 6, 2018, from www.huffingtonpost.com/brynn-tannehill/last-chance-to-see-transg_b_6753712.html

1337 Maza, C. & Brinker, L. (2014). 15 experts debunk right-wing transgender bathroom myth. Media Matters for America. Retrieved July 6, 2018, from www.mediamatters.org/research/2014/03/20/15-experts-debunk-right-wing-transgender-bathro/198533

1338 Ford, Z. (2015). Gym stands up for trans woman, kicks out member who wouldn't stop complaining. Thinkprogress.org. Retrieved July 6, 2018, from https://thinkprogress.org/gym-stands-up-for-trans-woman-kicks-out-member-who-wouldnt-stop-complaining-3e587bc32460

1339 Tannehill, B. (2014). What it's really like dating as a transgender woman. Bilerico Report/LGBTQ Nation. Retrieved July 6, 2018, from http://bilerico.lgbtqnation.com/2014/12/what_its_really_like_dating_as_a_transgender_woman.php

1340 *Fifty Shades of Grey*. (2015). Rottentomatoes.com. Retrieved July 6, 2018, from www.rottentomatoes.com/m/fifty_shades_of_grey

1341 *Fifty Shades of Grey*. (2011). En.wikipedia.org. Retrieved July 6, 2018, from https://en.wikipedia.org/wiki/Fifty_Shades_of_Grey

1342 Saad, L. (2012). U.S. acceptance of gay/lesbian relations is the new normal. Gallup.com. Retrieved July 6, 2018, from http://news.gallup.com/poll/154634/acceptance-gay-lesbian-relations-new-normal.aspx

1343 Autogynephilia. (2017). RationalWiki. Retrieved July 6, 2018, from https://rationalwiki.org/wiki/Autogynephilia

1344 Grant, J. M., Mottet, L. A., Tanis, J., Harrison, J., Herman, J. L., & Keisling, M. (2011). *Injustice at Every Turn: A Report of the National Transgender Discrimination Survey*. Washington, DC: National Center for Transgender Equality and National Gay and Lesbian Task Force. Retrieved July 6, 2018, from www.thetaskforce.org/static_html/downloads/reports/reports/ntds_full.pdf

1345 Flaherty, J. (2013, October 16). Are police profiling transgender Americans? Retrieved January 15, 2018, from http://america.aljazeera.com/watch/shows/america-tonight/america-tonight-blog/2013/10/16/rise-in-transgenderharassmentviolencebypolicelinkedtoprofiling.html

1346 Tannehill, B. (2014). Myths about transition regrets. HuffPost. Retrieved July 6, 2018, from www.huffingtonpost.com/brynn-tannehill/myths-about-transition-regrets_b_6160626.html

1347 Tannehill, B. (2014). Myths about transition regrets. HuffPost. Retrieved July 6, 2018, from www.huffingtonpost.com/brynn-tannehill/myths-about-transition-regrets_b_6160626.html

1348 Walt Heyer. Transgender Christians. Transchristians.org. Retrieved July 6, 2018, from www.transchristians.org/people/walt-heyer

1349 Ford, Z. (2018, February 7). "I was enraged to see my story distorted and used": Detransitioners object to anti-transgender book. Retrieved March 19, 2018, from https://thinkprogress.org/detransitioner-ryan-anderson-transgender-25fad9803c2e

1350 Robles, R., Fresán, A., Vega-Ramírez, H., Cruz-Islas, J., *et al.* (2016). Removing transgender identity from the classification of mental disorders: A Mexican field study for ICD-11. *The Lancet Psychiatry*, 3(9), 850–859. doi:10.1016/s2215-0366(16)30165-1

1351 Tannehill, B. (2014). Papers, please. HuffPost. Retrieved July 6, 2018, from www.huffingtonpost.com/brynn-tannehill/papers-please-transgender_b_5084768.html

1352 Eugenics in the United States. (2017). En.wikipedia.org. Retrieved July 6, 2018, from https://en.wikipedia.org/wiki/Eugenics_in_the_United_States#Compulsory_sterilization

1353 Fenton, S. (2016, May 17). LGBT relationships are illegal in 74 countries, research finds. Retrieved January 9, 2018, from www.independent.co.uk/news/world/gay-lesbian-bisexual-relationships-illegal-in-74-countries-a7033666.html

1354 Lopes, M. (2017, March 23). A horrific murder has awakened Brazil's transgender community. Retrieved January 9, 2018, from www.washingtonpost.com/news/worldviews/wp/2017/03/23/a-horrific-murder-has-awakened-brazils-transgender-community/?utm_term=.e37be555532a

1355 Rivas, J. (2015, September 4). Court blasts judge who compared transgender immigrant to Pee-wee Herman. Retrieved January 9, 2018, from https://splinternews.com/court-blasts-judge-who-compared-transgender-immigrant-t-1793850542

1356 TLC wins BIA (Board of Immigration Appeal) appeal for remand for trans immigrant to apply for asylum. (2017, October 18). Retrieved January 9, 2018, from https://transgenderlawcenter.org/archives/14065

1357 Lind, D. (2015, May 14). The US knows LGBTQ immigrants are often raped in detention. It puts them there anyway. Retrieved January 9, 2018, from www.vox.com/2015/5/14/8606199/transgender-immigrant-detention

1358 Ali, S. S. (2017, April 12). Sexual assaults in immigration detention centers rarely get investigated, group charges. Retrieved January 9, 2018, from www.nbcnews.com/news/us-news/sexual-assaults-immigration-detention-centers-don-t-get-investigated-says-n745616

1359 Carcamo, C. (2016, March 23). Transgender asylum-seekers often mistreated in detention, study finds. Retrieved January 9, 2018, from www.latimes.com/local/lanow/la-me-ln-transgender-immigrants-20160323-story.html

1360 Conti, A. (2014, October 1). Does the US prison system expose transgender prisoners to rape? Retrieved January 9, 2018, from www.vice.com/en_uk/article/nnqkvk/when-will-the-us-prison-system-protect-transgender-prisoners-from-rape-101

1361 Mustian, J. & Roberts, F. (2017, June 8). Lawsuit: Deputies ignored cries of transgender woman raped in Tangipahoa Parish Prison. Retrieved January 9, 2018, from www.theadvocate.com/baton_rouge/news/courts/article_51d6aa30-4c7c-11e7-aba6-c373cc7d742a.html

1362 Brydum, S. & Kellaway, M. (2015, April 8). This black trans man is in prison for killing his rapist. Retrieved January 9, 2018, from www.advocate.com/politics/transgender/2015/04/08/black-trans-man-prison-killing-his-rapist

1363 Mitchell, T. (2017, June 26). Changing attitudes on gay marriage. Retrieved January 10, 2018, from www.pewforum.org/fact-sheet/changing-attitudes-on-gay-marriag

1364 Cox, D. & Jones, R. P. (2017, September 14). Most Americans oppose restricting rights for LGBT people. Retrieved January 10, 2018, from www.prri.org/research/poll-wedding-vendors-refusing-service-same-sex-couples-transgender-military-ban

1365 Schneider, J. & Auten, D. (2017, November 16). Small business owners say that discrimination against queer people is bad for business. Retrieved January 10, 2018, from www.forbes.com/sites/debtfreeguys/2017/11/16/small-business-owners-say-that-discrimination-against-queer-people-is-bad-for-business/#195bdc82f00d

1366 Stern, M. J. (2017, November 8). Blue wave, meet red wall. Retrieved January 10, 2018, from www.slate.com/articles/news_and_politics/politics/2017/11/gerrymandering_saved_republicans_in_virginia.html

1367 Jones, R. P. (2016). *The End of White Christian America*. New York, NY: Simon & Schuster

1368 Could our national leader be: ____? Most in Canada, U.S. say they'd vote for more diverse candidates. (2017, August 21). Retrieved January 10, 2018, from http://angusreid.org/who-could-be-prime-minister-president

1369 Feinberg, L. (1996). *Transgender Warriors: Making History from Joan of Arc to RuPaul*. Boston, MA: Beacon Press

1370 James, S. E., Herman, J. L., Rankin, S., Keisling, M., Mottet, L., & Anafi, M. (2016). *The Report of the 2015 U.S. Transgender Survey*. Washington, DC: National Center for Transgender Equality

1371 American Psychiatric Association. (2013). *Gender Dysphoria Fact Sheet: DSM-5*. Arlington, VA: Author. Retrieved July 6, 2018, from www.dsm5.org/Documents/Gender%20Dysphoria%20Fact %20Sheet.pdf

1372 Professional organization statements supporting transgender people in health care. (2016, May 25). Lambda Legal. Retrieved July 6, 2018, from www.lambdalegal.org/sites/default/files/publications/downloads/ll_trans_professional_statements.rtf_.pdf

1373 Saraswat, A., Weinand, J., & Safer, J. (2015). Evidence supporting the biologic nature of gender identity. *Endocrine Practice, 21*(2), 199–204. doi:10.4158/ep14351.ra

1374 Todd, B. K., Fischer, R. A., Costa, S. D., Roestorf, A., *et al.* (2017). Sex differences in children's toy preferences: A systematic review, meta-regression, and meta-analysis. *Infant and Child Development*. doi:10.1002/icd.2064

1375 Coleman, E., Bockting, W., Botzer, M., Cohen-Kettenis, P., *et al.* (2011). Standards of care for the health of transsexual, transgender, and gender nonconforming people, 7th version. *International Journal of Transgenderism*, 13, 165–232

1376 Benjamin, H. (1966). *The Transsexual Phenomenon*. New York, NY: Warner Books

1377 Dhejne, C., Öberg, K., Arver, S., & Landén, M. (2014). An analysis of all applications for sex reassignment surgery in Sweden, 1960–2010: Prevalence, incidence, and regrets. *Archives of Sexual Behavior*, 43(8), 1535–1545. doi:10.1007/s10508-014-0300-8

1378 Gorin-Lazard, A., Baumstarck, K., Boyer, L., Maquigneau, A., *et al.* (2013). Hormonal therapy is associated with better self-esteem, mood, and quality of life in transsexuals. *The Journal of Nervous and Mental Disease* 201(11), 996–1000

1379 Simons, L., Schrager, S. M., Clark, L. F., Belzer, M., & Olson, J. (2013). Parental support and mental health among transgender adolescents. *Journal of Adolescent Health*, 53(6), 791–793. doi:10.1016/j.jadohealth.2013.07.019

1380 Olson, K., Durwood, L., DeMeules, M., & McLaughlin, K. (2016). Mental health of transgender children who are supported in their identities. *Pediatrics*, 137(3), e20153223

1381 Bauer, G. R., Scheim, A. I., Pyne, J., Travers, R., & Hammond, R. (2015). Intervenable factors associated with suicide risk in transgender persons: A respondent driven sampling study in Ontario, Canada. *BMC Public Health*, 15. doi:10.1186/s12889-015-1867-2

1382 Smith, G. A. (2017, November 27). Views of transgender issues divide along religious lines. Retrieved January 12, 2018, from www.pewresearch.org/fact-tank/2017/11/27/views-of-transgender-issues-divide-along-religious-lines

1383 New survey: Emerging GOP divisions on President Trump loom over 2018 and 2020 elections. (2017, December 5). Retrieved March 14, 2018, from www.prri.org/press-release/new-survey-emerging-gop-divisions-president-trump-loom-2018-2020-elections

1384 Cox, D. (2018, January 24). Are white evangelicals sacrificing the future in search of the past? Retrieved March 12, 2018, from https://fivethirtyeight.com/features/are-white-evangelicals-sacrificing-the-future-in-search-of-the-past/?ex_cid=538twitter

1385 Jones, R. P., Cox, D., Cooper, B., & Lienesch, R. (2016). Exodus: Why Americans are leaving religion—and why they're unlikely to come back." PRRI. Retrieved July 6, 2018, from www.prri.org/research/prri-rns-poll-nones-atheist-leaving-religion

1386 Schaefer, A. G., Iyengar, R., Kadiyala, S., Kavanagh, J., *et al.* (2016). Assessing the implications of allowing transgender personnel to serve openly. RAND Corporation, RR-1530-OSD, 2016. Retrieved December 20, 2017, from www.rand.org/pubs/research_reports/RR1530.html

1387 Protess, B., Ivory, D., & Eder, S. (2017, September 10). Where Trump's hands-off approach to governing does not apply. Retrieved December 20, 2017, from www.nytimes.com/2017/09/10/business/trump-regulations-religious-conservatives.html

1388 Sevelius, J. M. (2013). Gender affirmation: A framework for conceptualizing risk behavior among transgender women of color. *Sex Roles*, 68(11–12), 675–689

INDEX